1989

Science Year

**The World Book Annual
Science Supplement**

A Review of Science and Technology
During the 1988 School Year

World Book, Inc.

a Scott Fetzer company

Chicago London Sydney Toronto

Staff

Publisher
William H. Nault

Editor in Chief
Robert O. Zeleny

Editorial

Executive Editor
A. Richard Harmet

Managing Editor
Wayne Wille

Associate Editor
Darlene R. Stille

Senior Editors
David L. Dreier
Jinger Hoop
Mary A. Krier
Barbara A. Mayes
Jay Myers
Rod Such

Contributing Editors
Sara Dreyfuss
Joan Stephenson

Research Editor
Irene B. Keller

Index Editor
David Pofelski

Cartographic Services
H. George Stoll, Head
Wayne K. Pichler

Editorial Assistant
Ethel Matthews

Art

Art Director
Alfred de Simone

Senior Artist, Science Year
Lucy Smith

Senior Artists
Nikki Conner
Melanie J. Lawson

Artists
Alice Dole
Deirdre Wroblewski

Photographs

Photography Director
John S. Marshall

Senior Photographs Editor
Sandra M. Ozanick

Photographs Editors
Barbara A. Bennett
Geralyn Swietek

Research Services

Director
Mary Norton

Library Services
Mary Kayaian, Head

Product Production

Executive Director
Peter Mollman

Director of Manufacturing
Henry Koval

Manufacturing, Manager
Sandra Van den Broucke

Pre-Press Services
Jerry Stack, Director
Madelyn Krzak
Randi Park
Barbara Podczerwinski

Proofreaders
Anne Dillon
Marguerite Hoye
Esther Johns
Daniel Marotta

ISBN 0-7166-0589-9

ISSN 0080-7621
Library of Congress Catalog Number: 65-21776
Printed in the United States of America.

Editorial Advisory Board

Contents

See page 164.

See page 371.

Contributors

Adelman, George, M.S.
Editorial Director and Editor,
Encyclopedia of Neuroscience.
[*Neuroscience*]

Andrews, Peter J., M.S.
Free-Lance Writer, Chemist.
[*Chemistry;* Science You Can Use:
What Makes Paint Stick]

Baldwin, Ian T., B.A.
Doctoral Candidate,
Cornell University.
[Special Report, *The Wars Between
Plants and Predators*]

Bierzychudek, Paulette, Ph.D.
Associate Professor,
Department of Biology,
Pomona College.
[*Ecology*]

Boatner, Lynn A., Ph.D.
Senior Researcher,
Oak Ridge National Laboratory.
[*Materials Science*]

Booth, Stephen A., B.A.
Electronics and Photography Editor,
Popular Mechanics magazine.
[*Electronics*]

Bower, Bruce, M.A.
Behavioral Sciences Editor,
Science News magazine.
[*Anthropology* (Close-Up)]

Brett, Carlton E., Ph.D.
Associate Professor,
Department of Geological Sciences,
University of Rochester.
[*Paleontology*]

Brodsky, Arthur R., M.S.J.
Senior Editor,
Communications Daily.
[Science You Can Use: *How Cellular
Phones Work*]

Callahan, Maureen
Nutritionist and Free-Lance Medical
Writer.
[Science You Can Use: *Defending
Yourself Against Salmonella*]

Cicerone, Ralph J., Ph.D.
Director,
Atmospheric Chemistry Division,
National Center for Atmospheric
Research.
[Special Report, *The Hole in the
Ozone Layer*]

Covault, Craig P., B.S.
Space Technology Editor,
Aviation Week magazine.
[*Space Technology*]

Done, Terence J.
Senior Research Scientist,
Australian Institute of Marine
Science.
[Special Report, *Protecting the Great
Barrier Reef*]

Dorozynski, Alexander
Free-Lance Writer.
[Special Report, *The Pasteur Institute
at 100*]

Eisner, Thomas, Ph.D.
Schurman Professor of Biology,
Cornell University.
[Special Report, *The Wars Between
Plants and Predators*]

Euler, Robert C., Ph.D.
Adjunct Professor of Anthropology,
Arizona State University.
[Special Report, *The Anasazi of the
Southwest*]

Fisher, Arthur, M.A.
Science and Engineering Editor,
Popular Science magazine.
[Special Report, *Plugging into
Superconductors*]

Goldhaber, Paul, D.D.S.
Dean and Professor of Periodontology,
Harvard School of Dental Medicine.
[*Dentistry*]

Goodman, Richard A., M.D.
Assistant Professor,
Department of Community Medicine,
Emory University.
[*Public Health*]

Halpin, James E., Ph.D.
Director at Large,
State Agricultural Experiment Station,
Southern Region.
[*Agriculture*]

Hay, William W., Ph.D.
Professor of Geology,
University of Colorado, Boulder.
[*Geology*]

Haymer, David S., Ph.D.
Assistant Professor of Genetics,
University of Hawaii.
[*Genetic Science; Genetic Science
(Close-Up)*]

Hellemans, Alexander, B.S.
Commissioning Editor,
Academic Press, London.
[*Physics, Fluids and Solids*]

Hester, Thomas R., Ph.D.
Professor of Anthropology and
Director,
Texas Archaeological Research
Laboratory,
University of Texas at Austin.
[*Archaeology, New World*]

Jones, William G., A.M.L.S.
Assistant University Librarian,
University of Illinois at Chicago.
[*Books of Science*]

Kalson, David A., M.A.
Manager, Public Information Division,
American Institute of Physics.
[Special Report, *Using Computers to
Design Drugs*]

Katz, Paul, M.D.
Associate Professor of Medicine,
Georgetown University Medical
Center.
[*Immunology*]

Kies, Constance Virginia, Ph.D.
Professor of Human Nutrition,
University of Nebraska.
[*Nutrition; Nutrition* (Close-Up)]

King, Lauriston R., Ph.D.
Deputy Director,
Sea Grant Program,
Texas A&M University.
[*Oceanography*]

Lang, Jean M., M.S.
Science Editor,
University of Wisconsin, Madison.
[Special Report, *Has Success Spoiled the Whitetail?*]

Limburg, Peter R., M.A.
Author and Free-Lance Writer.
[People in Science, *Edward O. Wilson*]

Lunine, Jonathan I., Ph.D.
Assistant Professor,
Lunar Planetary Lab,
University of Arizona.
[*Astronomy, Solar System*]

March, Robert H., Ph.D.
Professor of Physics,
University of Wisconsin.
[*Physics, Subatomic*]

Merbs, Charles F., Ph.D.
Professor of Anthropology,
Arizona State University.
[*Anthropology*]

Merz, Beverly, A.B.
Associate Editor,
Journal of the American Medical Association.
[*Medical Research; Medical Research* (Close-Up)]

Meyer, B. Robert, M.D.
Chief, Division of Clinical Pharmacology,
North Shore University Hospital.
[*Drugs*]

Murray, Stephen S., Ph.D.
Astrophysicist,
Harvard/Smithsonian Center for Astrophysics.
[*Astronomy, Extragalactic*]

Page, Don N., Ph.D.
Professor of Physics,
Pennsylvania State University.
[People in Science, *Stephen W. Hawking*]

Patrusky, Ben, B.E.E.
Free-Lance Science Writer.
[Special Report, *The Search for an AIDS Vaccine*]

Pennisi, Elizabeth J., M.S.
Free-Lance Science Writer.
[Special Report, *The Making of Biosphere II; Zoology*]

Raloff, Janet, M.S.J.
Policy/Technology Editor,
Science News magazine.
[*Environment*]

Reddy, Francis, B.A.
Free-Lance Science Writer.
[Special Report, *Finding Out How Old Things Are*]

Salisbury, Frank B., Ph.D.
Professor of Plant Physiology,
Utah State University.
[*Botany*]

Scibilia, Ronald D., M.F.A.
Senior Editor,
Consumer Electronics Monthly magazine.
[*Computer Hardware; Computer Software*]

Snow, John T., Ph.D.
Associate Professor,
Purdue University.
[*Meteorology*]

Snow, Theodore P., Ph.D.
Professor of Astrophysics,
University of Colorado, Boulder.
[*Astronomy, Galactic*]

Swanton, Donald W., Ph.D.
Chairman, Department of Finance,
Roosevelt University.
[Science You Can Use: *Sorting Out Per Cents from Percentage Points*]

Tobin, Thomas R., Ph.D.
Assistant Professor,
ARL Division of Neurobiology,
University of Arizona.
[*Zoology*]

Trotter, Robert J., B.S.
Senior Editor,
Psychology Today magazine.
[*Psychology*]

Tuchman, Janice Lyn, M.A.
Senior Editor,
Engineering News-Record magazine.
[Special Report, *Tunneling Under the Sea*]

Visich, Marian, Jr., Ph.D.
Associate Dean of Engineering,
State University of New York.
[*Energy;* Science You Can Use: *Decoding Bar Codes*]

Wallace, Joseph, B.A.
Free-Lance Writer.
[Special Report, *New Discoveries About Dinosaurs*]

Wenke, Robert J., Ph.D.
Associate Professor,
Department of Anthropology,
University of Washington.
[*Archaeology, Old World*]

White, Clark W., Ph.D.
Group Leader,
Solid State Division,
Oak Ridge National Laboratory.
[*Materials Science*]

Winter, Christine, B.A.
Business Writer,
Chicago Tribune.
[*Computer Software* (Close-Up)]

Woosley, Stan, Ph.D.
Professor of Astronomy and Astrophysics,
University of California, Santa Cruz.
[*Astronomy, Extragalactic* (Close-Up)]

Yager, Robert E., Ph.D.
Professor of Science Education,
University of Iowa.
[*Science Education*]

Special Reports

Twelve articles—plus a special two-part feature—give
in-depth treatment to major advances in science and technology.

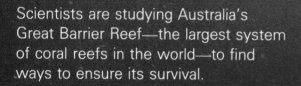

Scientists are studying Australia's Great Barrier Reef—the largest system of coral reefs in the world—to find ways to ensure its survival.

Protecting the Great Barrier Reef

BY TERENCE J. DONE

My first dive on Australia's Great Barrier Reef was an experience I'll never forget. Descending through the warm, diamond-clear water of the Coral Sea, the part of the Pacific Ocean that washes the northeast coast of Australia, my companion and I glided easily down a slope covered with multicolored formations of coral. Below us were somber green plate-shaped corals and, nearby, a pastel forest of giant staghorn corals resembling the antlers of some fantastic species of deer. At the bottom of the slope, a huge brain coral, its round furrowed surface suggesting a human brain, stood alone on the sea floor.

I approached the giant coral—large as a reclining elephant—causing teeming masses of tiny fish to part before me. Swimming gently around the coral wall, I was startled by a face-to-face encounter with a large, bug-eyed fish coming from the other direction. A flick of his tail and he was off, joining a dozen of his finny friends hovering in loose formation at the edge of my vision. I exhaled a stream of air bubbles from the mouthpiece of my scuba gear and settled under the overhanging, cavelike base of the giant brain coral. Trapped by the roof of this small cavern, the bubbles flattened and quivered like quicksilver among the many algae and other marine organisms encrusting the overhang. My flashlight revealed the colors and forms of this dense array of life: rich purples, reds, yellows, and oranges in an infinity of shades and shapes.

Suddenly, I felt the beckoning touch of my companion's hand on my arm. Side by side, we swam upward to join a pair of graceful manta rays circling the giant coral. For fully five minutes, the huge fish effortlessly maneuvered their broad, flat bodies around us in sweeping arcs. Curious about the strange-looking intruders in their world, the rays allowed us to stroke them as they passed nearby. Then they departed, as did we, making our way slowly up the slope in a state of gentle euphoria. Later in the day, as we relaxed aboard our boat, I resolved to return to the Great Barrier Reef many times in the future and to make its study my life's work.

Both those ambitions have been amply fulfilled. By 1980, 10 years after that first encounter with the reef, I had earned a doctorate in zoology and obtained a position as a research scientist at the Australian Institute of Marine Science (AIMS) in Queensland. I had also spent many hours underwater on the Great Barrier Reef, making observations, collecting coral specimens, and taking photographs. Although I had a scientific reason for each of my dives, rarely did a visit to the reefs fail to result in some joyful experience.

But on one dive, in November 1983, the sight before me was anything but joyful. The corals on a section of reefs were dead, covered with a thick, shaggy carpet of drab seaweed. The area had been devastated by the crown-of-thorns starfish, a large spiny starfish that preys on coral. The crown-of-thorns population sometimes explodes for no apparent reason. Is this phenomenon part of an unsuspected but normal cycle of coral growth and destruction, or are scientists witnessing the beginning of a long-term process of reef deteriora-

The author:
Terence J. Done is a Senior Research Scientist at the Australian Institute of Marine Science in Townsville, Queensland.

tion? If the latter, is human activity somehow responsible? And even if human beings are not causing the crown-of-thorns infestation, to what extent might they be jeopardizing the Great Barrier Reef in other ways, such as by polluting its waters? Only research will be able to answer those questions. Scientists, myself included, are striving to learn as much as possible about the Great Barrier Reef to ensure that it will be around for future generations.

That commitment is shared by the Australian government, which in 1975 created the Great Barrier Reef Marine Park. Nearly the entire complex of reefs is now under the control of a federal agency, the Great Barrier Reef Marine Park Authority. The Marine Park Authority tries to protect the reefs while at the same time allowing them to be used for many recreational and commercial purposes. Increasingly, it has had its work cut out for it. Tourism, especially, has expanded markedly in the 1980's, stimulated in part by Australia's 1988 bicentennial celebration. Each year, new resort hotels are built on the Great Barrier Reef, so the authority must be diligent in its watchdog duties.

Extending along the coast of Queensland, one of the Australian states, for a distance of about 2,000 kilometers (1,250 miles), the Great Barrier Reef consists of some 2,900 individual reefs and islands—the largest reef system in the world. The reefs range from a few hectares in area to more than 30 kilometers (18.5 miles) from end to end. Some of the reefs are more than 160 kilometers (100 miles) out at sea. Each reef is a flat-topped wall, mound, or pinnacle composed in large part of the limestone skeletons of countless generations of corals.

The Great Barrier Reef sits on the continental shelf, a submerged plain at the edge of Australia covered with sediments from the land and the ocean that built up over millions of years. The oldest parts of the reef system originated about 25 million years ago.

Most parts of the Great Barrier Reef, however, developed over the past 2 million years. During that time, sea levels varied with the coming and going of the ice ages, which in turn locked up and then released tremendous amounts of water. Over the past 2 million years, Australia's continental shelf has been covered by water only about 10 per cent of the time, and it was during those periods of higher water that reefs were able to form. Each time an ice age caused the sea level to fall, the exposed limestone reefs were eroded by wind and rain into rugged, pitted hills and ridges. The sea began its latest advance across Earth's continental shelves about 15,000 years ago, submerging the Great Barrier Reef once more. Covered with water, the reefs again teemed with life and grew. About 5,000 or 6,000 years ago, sea levels stabilized but the reefs continued to grow or to shrink in response to changing conditions in the Coral Sea region.

Not surprisingly, the many reefs have taken on marked differ-

Some of the reef area's islands are large enough to accommodate hotels, such as this resort on Green Island, *top.* One of the newest attractions is the floating Four Seasons hotel, *above,* which is moored in a shallow coral lagoon.

ences, depending on where they developed. Outer reefs, which have had to withstand the power of ocean waves, are massive and solid. In the more sheltered areas closer to land, less sturdy reefs have developed. Corals on these reefs grow into delicate fans, branches, vases, and other shapes.

The reef system consists of *barrier reefs* and *fringing reefs.* Barrier reefs, which make up the great majority of the formations, are separated from the coast by wide and deep channels of water. Fringing reefs are connected to land.

About 250 of the 2,900 reefs developed into low, sandy islands called *cays* (sometimes known as *keys*). The sand was created by the breaking down of dead corals and other limestone-containing organisms. Cays largely devoid of vegetation are found all along the Great Barrier Reef. Cays among the northern and southern reefs are covered with shrubs, trees, and other plants. Many of the cays are important nesting grounds for sea birds and turtles.

Another group of more than 500 islands, though not true limestone reefs, are counted as part of the Great Barrier Reef. These *continental islands*, clustered mainly in the central region, were once part of the mainland but became surrounded by water when the sea rose.

The abundance of life on the reefs is particularly striking underwater. There are, for starters, many hundreds of species of coral—hard corals, soft corals, lace corals, fan corals, and whip corals.

Researchers at AIMS, working with other Australian scientists, recently concluded a 10-year effort to classify all the corals of the Great Barrier Reef. Because many of the species look identical to one another, the task was not an easy one. The investigators spent thousands of hours scuba diving among the reefs to observe living corals in their natural habitat and ascertain the range of form and color for each species. In the laboratory, the researchers made microscopic examinations of the coral skeletons, comparing them with museum specimens collected by earlier scientists. Gradually, they were able to unravel the tangle, and the corals of the Great Barrier Reef are finally well understood.

Most corals live in colonies. Colonies of hard corals are responsible for most of the growth of reefs. A hard-coral colony begins its life as a single *polyp*, a hollow-bodied animal, much like a sea anemone, that is usually less than 1.2 centimeters (½ inch) in diameter. The polyp sits in a limestone cup formed by special limestone-producing cells in the base and walls of the polyp. After a few weeks or months, the polyp reproduces itself by either budding off a smaller "daughter" polyp or by dividing into "sister" polyps of equal size. The duplicated polyps, which remain attached to each other, continue to grow, add new limestone to their cups, and duplicate again and again. With the ever-increasing number of polyps, the interconnected cups become the skeleton of the colony, and the living polyps form a thin veneer of soft tissue on the surface of the skeleton. This process continues for many centuries with some kinds of coral, resulting in colonies many meters high and weighing tons. With other corals, the life expectancy of a colony is just a few years to several decades. The accumulation of skeletons from many generations of coral colonies produces a reef.

New coral colonies develop by two methods, *asexual reproduction* and *sexual reproduction*. Asexual reproduction occurs when a new colony forms from a piece of a colony that has been broken off, perhaps by a storm wave, and transplanted to an-

The World's Largest Coral Reef
Consisting of some 2,900 individual reefs and islands, the Great Barrier Reef extends for about 2,000 kilometers (1,250 miles) along Australia's northeast coast. Most of it has been named a national marine park.

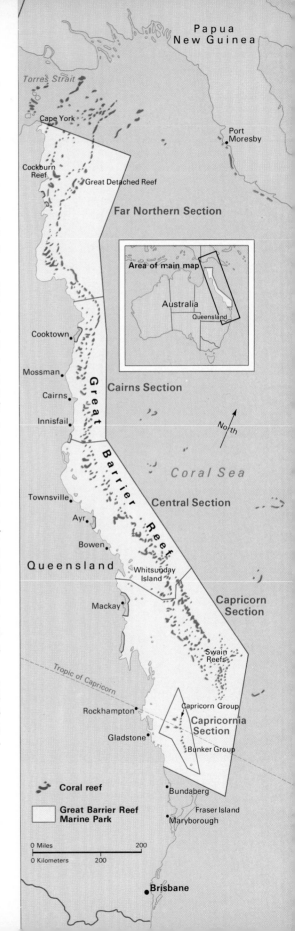

The clear waters of the Great Barrier Reef allow sunlight to penetrate and provide energy for a rich variety of multicolored coral formations.

other area. Sexual reproduction results from the union of egg and sperm cells released by male and female polyps.

Until the late 1970's, scientists had thought that all corals reproduce sexually throughout the year. But in the early 1980's, graduate students at James Cook University of North Queensland found that most of the hard corals on the Great Barrier Reef release eggs and sperm only in November or December with the approach of summer in the Southern Hemisphere. These mass spawnings, triggered by rising water temperatures and the tidal effects of the full moon, occur at night and are completed in less than a week. The eggs and sperm rise to the surface of the water, where many of them join to form embryos. The embryos develop into free-swimming larvae, most of which are eaten by fish. The surviving larvae make their way back to the sea floor and settle onto reefs, where they develop into polyps and begin to form new colonies by budding. Since the completion of the James Cook study, mass spawnings of coral have been noted in several other areas of the Pacific, including Japan and the Fiji Islands.

Besides corals, many other animals, from some species of *protozoans* (one-celled animals) to giant clams, produce limestone and contribute to the build-up of the reefs when they die. Algae also play an important role in reef construction. About 10 per cent of all species of algae manufacture limestone in their cells. Such algae grow and die in great numbers on tropical reefs, adding their limestone to that of the corals and other animals.

Scientists have learned that algae are vital to reefs in other ways as well. Varieties of algae called *turf algae* bore into the skeletons and shells of dead corals and other limestone-producing marine animals, breaking them into fragments that are frequently swept off the reefs by storms. Other kinds of algae, known as *encrusting coralline algae*, cement living coral and the disintegrating limestone bits together into sturdy, wave-resistant walls and platforms.

Algae also provide food for many reef animals. One form of algae, *zooxanthellae* (*zoe zan THELL lee*), lives within the bodies of corals, furnishing

Here are your
1989 SCIENCE YEAR
Cross-Reference Tabs

For insertion in your WORLD BOOK

Each year, SCIENCE YEAR, THE WORLD BOOK ANNUAL SCIENCE SUPPLEMENT, adds a valuable dimension to your WORLD BOOK set. The Cross-Reference Tab System is designed especially to help students and parents alike link SCIENCE YEAR's major articles to the related WORLD BOOK articles they update.

How to Use These Tabs

The top Tab on this page is AIDS. Turn to the A volume of your WORLD BOOK and find the page with the AIDS article on it. Affix the AIDS Tab to that page. If your WORLD BOOK is an older set without an AIDS article in it, put the AIDS Tab in the A volume in its proper alphabetical order.

Now do the same with the remaining Tabs, and your new SCIENCE YEAR will be linked to your WORLD BOOK set.

the animals with nutrients and enabling them to produce their limestone skeletons many times faster than would otherwise be possible.

Most corals and reef-forming algae need warm water to flourish. In addition, algae need plenty of sunlight for photosynthesis. Those requirements explain why nearly all coral reefs are found in the shallower parts of tropical and subtropical seas.

The waters of the Great Barrier Reef are home to some 2,000 species of fish. The fish find abundant food on the reefs. Some of them, such as solitary manta rays and dense schools of tiny damselfish, feed on microscopic marine organisms washed in from the open seas. Others "graze" on the reefs themselves. Swarms of colorful parrot fish, rabbitfish, and surgeonfish nip and scrape turf algae from coral rocks. Small, delicate butterfly fish pick at living coral polyps, and massive hump-headed wrasse wrench off coral pieces with their powerful teeth to get at burrowing worms. Sharks

The hundreds of varieties of corals on the Great Barrier Reef include both hard corals, such as the bright yellow formation shown *above left*, and soft corals, such as the lacy pink variety at *left.* Algae, such as the sargassum alga, *above right,* are also abundant on the reefs. Algae are an important food source for many reef animals, and some algae also help build reefs, either by producing limestone or by cementing coral skeletons into the reefs.

and other large fish form the pinnacle of the reefs' complex food chain, dining on the smaller fish that are unlucky enough to cross their path.

Biologists have studied few of the 2,000 species of fish in detail, but they are learning how the reefs are able to support such a remarkable diversity of smaller fish. The scientists have found that many kinds of fish living at the same reef outcrop eat the same foods and use the same sorts of nooks and crannies for shelter. In nature, this sort of crowding does not normally continue for long; the strongest, fastest, or smartest species soon beats out the competition and claims the habitat for itself. But on the Great Barrier Reef, coexistence rather than monopolization is the rule. Among the smaller fishes, researchers have identified several reasons why that is so, including a life span of just a few years and great variability from one year to another in the number and types of young fish arriving on a reef in the water currents. Similar factors seem to operate among the larger, longer-lived fish of the reefs, but scientists have scarcely begun to study those species' ecology.

Other animals populating the reef waters include giant clams, sea turtles, poisonous sea snakes, and a number of marine mammals—dolphins, whales, and the dugong, a type of sea cow. As with the corals and fishes, biologists are still learning about many of these creatures.

The giant clams, which are found only in the South Pacific and Indian oceans, live mainly in shallow reef areas. They measure up to 120 centimeters (50 inches) across and weigh as much as 230 kilograms (500 pounds). Scientists had long assumed that the huge mollusks depended for survival upon microscopic organisms filtered from seawater. Research in the 1980's, however, has revealed that clams deprived of that source of food continue to thrive. In a remarkable parallel to hard corals, the millions of zooxanthellae inhabiting the mantle of the clam, the fleshy area just inside the shell, apparently provide the animal with ample nutrition.

Of the six species of sea turtles that live on the reefs, the one scientists have learned the most about is the green turtle. The green turtle is endangered elsewhere in the world, owing mainly to its habit of laying all its eggs on sandy beaches where many are eaten by predators. The turtles mate in the waters adjacent to their nesting islands in spring and summer, and the female lays about 500 eggs, in *clutches* (groups) of about 100, over a period of several weeks. In late summer, the baby turtles hatch from their eggs, climb up through the sand, and make their way down the beach to the sea. Very few of the hatchlings reach adulthood; the vast majority end up as food for birds, fish, and other predators, including human beings. Despite the high mortality rate of their offspring, green turtles mate infrequently. In fact, some scientists now believe that females of the species reproduce only once in their lives, spending

Some 2,000 species of fish live on the reefs. One of the smaller ones is the clown fish, *top,* 5 centimeters (2 inches) long. Among the most colorful is the tusk fish, *left.* Blue tang surgeonfish and reticulated dascyllus, *above,* feed together on *plankton* (microscopic marine organisms), demonstrating the harmony among many of the reefs' fish populations.

decades at sea before returning to the beach where they were born to lay their eggs.

The Great Barrier Reef is one of the few places on Earth where green turtles are protected by law. The same is true of dugongs. Although hunted to near-extinction in other parts of the western Pacific and Indian oceans, these peaceful creatures—relatives of the manatees of the Southeastern United States, South America, and Africa—are fairly common in Great Barrier Reef waters. Often traveling in herds numbering as many as 600 animals, dugongs feed on sea grasses in shallow waters. Under Australian law, only Aborigines, who have hunted dugongs for thousands of years, are allowed to kill the animals—and only a limited number of them each year.

The Australian government, recognizing the immense value of the Great Barrier Reef as a national and international resource, has taken an active role in managing and protecting the reefs. The Marine Park Authority has primary control of the reefs. The agency tries to strike a balance between conserving the reefs in their natural state and allowing them to be used for recreation, tourism, shipping, commercial and sport fishing, scientific research, and other activities. The authority has divided the marine park into a number of usage zones and allows only a limited range of activities in each zone. To further protect the reefs, the authority prohibits oil exploration, mining, and the taking of certain species of fish and mollusks throughout the park.

Australian scientists work closely with the Marine Park Authority to monitor the health of the reefs. Their research makes use of some of today's most advanced technology. Oceanographers and biologists analyze satellite images to determine, among other things, how water circulates among the reefs and how the growth of algae and other reef vegetation changes in response to varying environ-

The gentle dugong, *below,* a type of sea cow, and a huge green turtle, trying to ignore the attentions of a diver, *below right,* are among the reefs' largest residents. The Great Barrier Reef is one of the few places in the world where these increasingly rare creatures are protected by law.

mental conditions. Physiologists use watertight instruments that can be left in place on the reefs to study the biochemical processes of reef organisms in their natural surroundings. Other investigators study reef and water samples in the laboratory. And scientists of all disciplines use computers to analyze the vast quantity of data they collect each year and to simulate a variety of natural processes, from ocean currents flowing around reefs to population cycles of reef predators and their prey.

Researchers are especially interested in learning which parts of reefs are growing and which are being eroded, and why. Such information is obtained with the aid of floating instrument packages that are towed across reefs. The instruments detect changes in the levels of dissolved oxygen and carbon dioxide and the *pH* (acidity or alkalinity) in a current of water as it flows over a reef. Such variations in water chemistry are due to the reef's *metabolism*, the sum of all the biochemical processes occurring on the reef, including photosynthesis and the production of limestone. Research has shown that all healthy coral reefs in the Pacific have similar rates of metabolism. Thus, a metabolism that is slower or faster than normal may indicate that a reef is in trouble.

Reefs can decline for a number of reasons. In some cases, the destruction of a reef results from *bioerosion*, or erosion caused by biological organisms. Such organisms include fish that graze on corals. They also include a variety of *borers*—algae (including turf algae), bacteria, and small marine animals—that penetrate dead coral formations and reduce them to rubble. Bioerosion is a natural part of reef ecology, and it is usually counterbalanced by the reef-building processes of corals and limestone-forming algae. On some reefs, however, the balance between growth and destruction tips in favor of the latter. When that occurs, the reef ceases to develop until the balance is reversed.

Giving the impression—despite the balmy climate—that it's bundled up against the cold, a young frigatebird sits in its nest. This relative of the pelican is just one of many sea birds living on the islands of the Great Barrier Reef.

Some of the worst reef destruction has been caused by the crown-of-thorns starfish. An adult crown of thorns, which can have up to 23 arms and measure 30 to 40 centimeters (12 to 15 inches) across, eats a patch of coral approximately equal to the area of its body each day. Although starfish have been present on the Great Barrier Reef for millions of years, their numbers are usually low enough so that corals can reestablish themselves in denuded areas. Sometimes, however, the adult starfish population increases so dramatically that some areas have thousands of starfish in each hectare (2.5 acres) of reefs. When such outbreaks occur, 90 per cent or more of the corals in infested areas are killed within a few weeks or months. When the starfish move on, they leave behind them the white skeletons of the many dead corals and the damaged but still-living remnants of others. Over the following years, the reefs slowly regenerate.

In the 1980's, the government of Australia has funded a series of scientific studies of the crown of thorns to learn the causes and long-term effects of the outbreaks. The work, coordinated jointly by AIMS and the Marine Park Authority, has involved scientists from the United States as well as Australia.

Annual surveys made by the researchers indicate that major increases in the starfish population since 1980 have occurred mostly in the middle section of the Great Barrier Reef. The outbreaks have involved several generations of starfish moving from reef to reef as larvae and possibly as adults. The first notable infestations occurred on reefs near Cairns, Queensland. From there, they spread south in a broad front for a distance of some 600 kilometers (375 miles). As the starfish moved south, corals began to recolonize the devastated reefs. Computer simulations suggest that while the populations of the slowest-growing corals will take from 10 to 100 years to replace their losses, crown-of-thorns infestations could have occurred as often as every 30 years throughout the reefs' history. The last major outbreak, however, was in the 1960's, just 15 years before the start of the current starfish problem. The computer studies suggest that a series of infestations with so little time between them would leave the reefs permanently devoid of large coral colonies.

Scientists have proposed several theories to account for these starfish outbreaks. One explanation, which is supported by the finding of extensive starfish remains deep in the sands of reef lagoons, holds that the outbreaks are a completely normal phenomenon. This natural-cycle hypothesis suggests that the number of adult starfish fluctuates in response to the amount of coral available as food in a "boom and bust" fashion. Many scientists, on the other hand, believe that sizable fluctuations in the crown-of-thorns population are unnatural occurrences caused by human activity, such as the excessive harvesting of the starfish's natural predators. These include the triton, a large and beautiful shellfish that is now protected by law from collectors.

While scientists continue to seek a solid explanation for crown-of-thorns outbreaks, the starfish are being removed from some reefs in tourist areas to protect the coral. At present, the Marine Park

The crown-of-thorns starfish, *below,* has caused great damage on the reefs. Periodically, these large, spiny predators increase dramatically in number and destroy coral on large areas of the reefs. A researcher, *below right,* measures a crown of thorns on a damaged reef. The white patches are the limestone skeletons of corals that were eaten by starfish. Scientists are trying to determine whether the starfish outbreaks are natural occurrences or have been caused—or made worse—by human activity on the reefs.

Authority cannot afford to protect all the reefs, nor is there any general agreement among scientists and government officials that such interference is advisable.

Whether or not they bear responsibility for the recurrent population explosions among the starfish, human beings have unquestionably had an impact on the reefs. Pesticides, fertilizers, and animal wastes from Queensland's agricultural regions could well be producing a variety of subtle but detrimental effects on the reefs, and toxic metal pollution from a huge gold mine in Papua New Guinea—175 kilometers (110 miles) north of Australia—may be tainting the upper stretches of the reefs. Cities and towns along the Queensland coast release treated sewage and other wastes into the sea. Commercial and recreational fishing boats haul in huge numbers of fish and shellfish. And an unprecedented boom in tourism has resulted in a proliferation of island resorts, and even a floating hotel anchored in a reef lagoon. No one knows what the combined effect of all these activities will eventually be.

Some scientists believe that degradation of the reefs on a major scale has already taken place. In 1978, Sir Charles Maurice Yonge, a British zoologist who made a pioneering study of the Great Barrier Reef in the late 1920's, revisited the reefs. At a section called Low Isles, Yonge found barren reef flats where corals had previously flourished. They were now covered with silt, which he believed came from soil runoff resulting from the clearing of forests and tin mining on the nearby mainland. Other reefs have also become smothered in silt, apparently as a result of channel dredging for some of Queensland's larger ports.

Science has told us much about the origins and functioning of the Great Barrier Reef. The greatest challenge now is to identify the most serious threats to the reefs. Because human impact on the reefs is bound to increase in years to come, the proper application of scientific knowledge will become ever more important to ensure the system's long-term vitality. Scientists must continue trying to determine which changes in the reefs are caused by human activity and which are a natural part of reef ecology.

Scientists are constantly on the alert for signs of biological trouble on the reefs. With the aid of a computer terminal, a researcher, *above left,* studies a satellite image of a reef area. Satellite pictures reveal such information as the patterns of water currents and the growth of algae in response to changing environmental conditions. Scientists also dive on the reefs to inspect them firsthand. A diver, *above,* checks a computerized instrument that provides data on how well coral and other reef organisms are functioning.

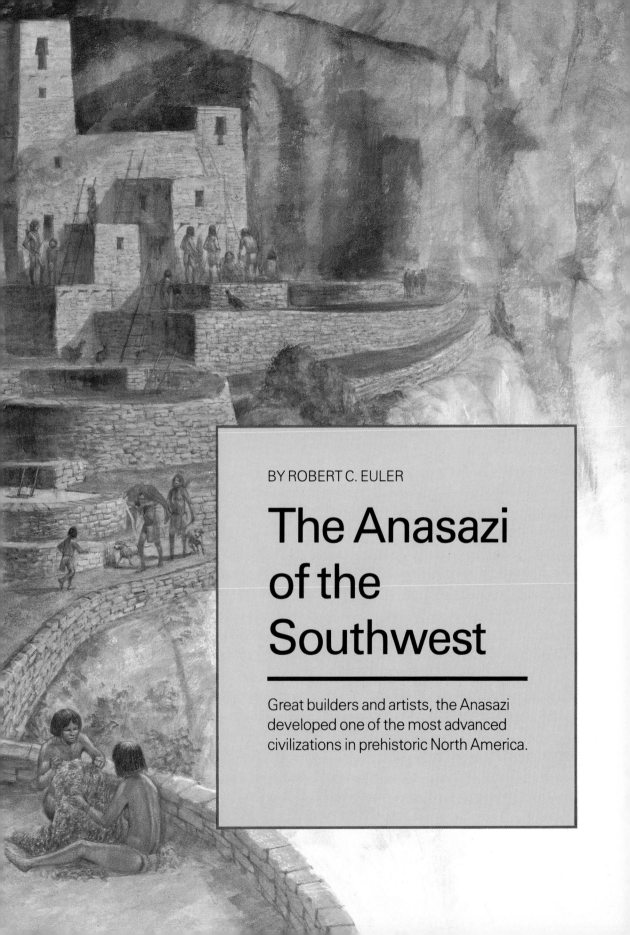

BY ROBERT C. EULER

The Anasazi of the Southwest

Great builders and artists, the Anasazi
developed one of the most advanced
civilizations in prehistoric North America.

The author:
Robert C. Euler is a con-
sulting anthropologist
specializing in the Indi-
ans of the American
Southwest, and an ad-
junct professor of an-
thropology at Arizona
State University in
Tempe.

The illustrator:
The drawings of Anasazi
life are by Richard Hook,
a free-lance artist with a
particular interest in
American Indians.
He lives in Sussex,
England.

On a hot, sunny day in August 1849, a troop of United States cavalry riding through Chaco Canyon in western New Mexico came upon an amazing sight. Rising against the rugged walls of the canyon were the ruins of immense buildings. Long abandoned, they lay open to the sun, their roofs collapsed, their jagged walls either crumbling to the desolate canyon's stony floor or nearly buried by windswept sand.

One of the troop's officers, Lieutenant James H. Simpson, was so intrigued by the ruins that he spent two days exploring the buildings. Simpson, probably unaware that Spaniards had discovered these same ruins 26 years earlier, wrote a detailed description of them that, along with sketches, has been preserved in the National Archives in Washington, D.C. In Chaco Canyon, Simpson counted seven major ruins and several smaller ones. Some of these ruins, called *pueblos* by the troop's Indian guides, stood four stories tall and sprawled over several hectares.

At the time, Simpson did not realize that he was looking at some of the most spectacular examples of prehistoric Indian architecture north of Mexico. He also would have been astounded to learn that within a few decades hundreds of ruins similar to those in Chaco Canyon would be discovered on the Colorado Plateau. This region, marked by broad, rough uplands cut by deep canyons and valleys, covers parts of what are now Colorado, Arizona, New Mexico, and Utah. Archaeological expeditions over the past 100 years have revealed that the pueblos were built and occupied by Indians now known as the Anasazi. The name comes from a Navajo word meaning *ancient people*, though they were unrelated to the Navajo.

The discovery and investigation of Anasazi settlements in the Grand Canyon has been the focus of my work as an archaeologist for more than 25 years—beginning in 1960 when I was a university teacher, and continuing after 1974 when I joined the National Park Service. By 1988, my colleagues and I had discovered more than 2,000 small Anasazi ruins throughout the Grand Canyon.

Other archaeologists have found the earliest evidences of the Anasazi dating to about 300 B.C. Originally hunters and gatherers of edible wild plants, the Anasazi had by A.D. 750 developed an advanced and flourishing civilization. But by A.D. 1300, long before any Europeans—or even Navajo Indians—arrived in the region, the Anasazi had abandoned much of their homeland. They had left their pueblos and moved farther south and east, becoming the ancestors of the Hopi, Zuni, and other modern Pueblo Indians.

After Simpson's exploration in 1849, rugged terrain and hostile Indians discouraged further exploration of Chaco Canyon until the 1870's. By the end of that decade, however, explorers and settlers moving into sparsely populated New Mexico had found many more ruins in and around Chaco Canyon.

Then in 1888, a search for lost cattle led to the discovery of more astonishing evidence of the Anasazi in southwestern Colorado. While rounding up strays in the deep canyons of Mesa Verde, an

The long-abandoned ruins of Cliff Palace, the largest cliff dwelling at Mesa Verde, stand as a silent reminder of a once-flourishing civilization. Beginning about 1200, many Anasazi, for reasons not yet known, abandoned above-ground pueblos for these uncomfortable, hard-to-reach cliff dwellings.

area of flat-topped hills with steep sides, rancher Richard Wetherill and one of his cowhands found more large pueblos. But these pueblos were perched on the sides of the vertical canyon walls, built into hollow spaces or under rock overhangs. By 1890, Wetherill and his brothers had found more than 100 of these cliff dwellings.

Their curiosity and excitement whetted by their Mesa Verde discoveries, the Wetherills fanned out into other isolated regions of northern Arizona. By 1895, they had discovered many Anasazi ruins near the trading post of Kayenta, including the largest of all Arizona cliff dwellings, Keet Seel, now part of Navajo National Monument. The Kayenta region, Mesa Verde, and Chaco Canyon were the most densely populated areas of the Anasazi homeland.

In the late 1800's, scientific archaeology in the United States was in its infancy, and the emphasis of the early explorers was on collecting pottery, baskets, and other artifacts for museums in the East. It was not until the first few decades of the 1900's that trained archaeologists began a scientific investigation of Anasazi sites. They still collected artifacts, but their studies were also aimed at understanding the Anasazi way of life and how it changed over time.

Since then, the lure of the Anasazi has continued to draw archaeologists to the Colorado Plateau. Their investigations have benefited from two natural phenomena—the Southwest's climate and the yearly growth rings in trees.

The hot dry climate of the Southwest has helped preserve not only the ruins but also many Anasazi artifacts. Over the years, archaeologists have uncovered an abundance of their tools and weapons and the beautiful baskets and pottery for which these Indians have become known. Archaeologists have also found the mummified remains of many of the Anasazi themselves. These remains have yielded valuable information about the Anasazi's appearance, dress, jewelry, health problems, and even their hairstyles.

Yearly growth rings—the basis of a dating system called *tree-ring dating*—have enabled archaeologists to compile an unusually precise timetable for Anasazi sites and cultural developments. Tree-ring dating is based on the knowledge that in some types of trees, the growth rings—each of which represents one year's growth—form an irregular pattern. This irregularity results mainly from annual variations in rainfall. In dry years, the rings are narrow; in wet years, they are wider. Luckily for archaeologists studying the Anasazi, the kinds of trees these Indians most often used as support beams for their dwellings develop these patterns.

To determine the age of a support beam by tree-ring dating, scientists compare the pattern of the rings in a cross section of the beam to a master pattern for that area compiled from cross sections from the trunks of very old living trees and from timbers cut in known years. Calculating the age of a number of support beams in a structure thus provides an accurate date for the dwelling.

Tree-ring dating has also helped archaeologists develop another dating technique, one which makes use of Anasazi pottery. The designs on Anasazi bowls, jars, and other pottery changed frequently over time. By dating the dwellings in which the pottery was found, archaeologists have been able to establish fairly precise periods for these designs. As a result, a good Southwestern archaeologist can examine the broken pottery at a site and quickly determine when the ruin was occupied. In addition, because pottery styles differed from area to area, the archaeologist can also identify the group of Anasazi that occupied the site and determine whether they traded pottery with other groups, and—if so—with whom.

Archaeologists also use a technique called *radiocarbon dating* to establish the age of Anasazi sites. This system of dating, which involves analyzing the amount of a radioactive form of carbon, has been particularly useful in dating charcoal and organic remains, such as bones and corncobs, found at Anasazi sites. Radiocarbon dating, however, provides only an approximate date—usually within a few hundred years. So, in this case, it is less useful than the more precise tree-ring dating. (In the Special Reports section, see FINDING OUT HOW OLD THINGS ARE.)

Archaeologists have also tried an indirect way of learning about the Anasazi—by studying their descendants. Modern Pueblo Indians build structures, use tools, and create baskets and pottery similar to those found at Anasazi sites. Information gathered from an-

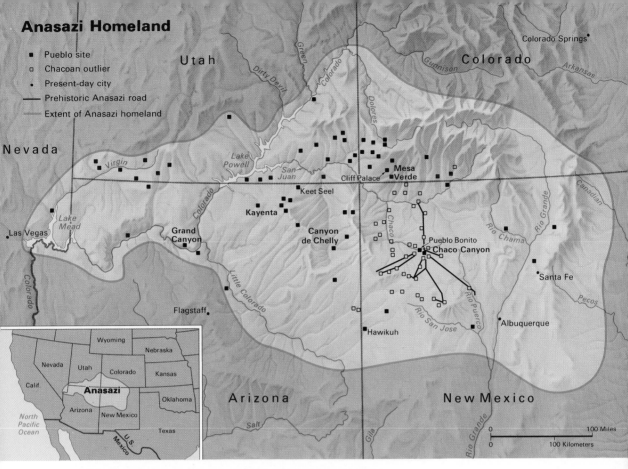

Anasazi Homeland

- ■ Pueblo site
- □ Chacoan outlier
- • Present-day city
- ── Prehistoric Anasazi road
- ── Extent of Anasazi homeland

Utah

Colorado

Nevada

Colorado Springs

Las Vegas

Lake Mead

Lake Powell

Grand Canyon

Keet Seel

Kayenta

Canyon de Chelly

Mesa Verde

Cliff Palace

Pueblo Bonito

Chaco Canyon

Santa Fe

Albuquerque

Hawikuh

Flagstaff

Arizona

New Mexico

Wyoming

Nebraska

Nevada

Utah

Colorado

Kansas

Calif.

Anasazi

Oklahoma

Arizona

New Mexico

Texas

North Pacific Ocean

U.S. Mexico

0   100 Miles
0   100 Kilometers

At the height of their civilization in the early 1100's, the Anasazi occupied a territory stretching nearly from Las Vegas, Nev., in the west to the Rio Grande Valley of New Mexico in the east, *above.* The most densely populated areas of this territory were the Kayenta region of Arizona, the Mesa Verde region of Colorado and Utah, and Chaco Canyon in New Mexico. Well-constructed roads linked the pueblos in Chaco Canyon with outlying pueblos and villages. Traces of these roads, such as those converging on the ruins of outlying Pueblo Alto, *below* (arrows), are still visible.

Developments in Anasazi History

Originally a hunting people who appeared in the Southwest about 300 B.C., the Anasazi developed one of the most advanced civilizations in prehistoric North America. By A.D. 1300, however, they had abandoned most of their homeland.

300 B.C. to A.D. 1—The Anasazi move into the Southwest and begin to grow corn, though they still live mainly by hunting and gathering.

A.D. 1—The Anasazi begin to make beautiful, well-crafted baskets.

A.D. 400—The Anasazi learn to make pottery.

A.D. 750 to 1100—The Anasazi begin to live in pueblos, build *kivas* (underground ceremonial chambers), and grow cotton. The Anasazi in Chaco Canyon develop water-control systems to divert rain water run-off flowing over the rim of the canyon into streams on the canyon floor. During rainstorms, the system's channels and dams are opened and closed to direct water to crops being grown on the canyon floor.

A.D. 550 to 750—The Anasazi become farmers and settle in villages. They begin to live in *pithouses* (houses partially underground). They also begin to grow beans and raise turkeys.

A.D. 700—The Anasazi begin to use the bow and arrow.

A.D. 900—The first Great Houses are built in Chaco Canyon. Construction reaches a peak between 1075 and 1115.

A.D. 1200—Many Anasazi at Mesa Verde and Kayenta begin to live in cliff dwellings, accessible only by steps and handholds cut into the canyon walls.

Tree-Ring Dating
Scientists can determine when many Anasazi dwellings were built by examining the pattern of yearly growth rings in the trees used as beams. This pattern reflects differences in the width of the rings caused by annual variations in rainfall. Scientists compare the pattern in a core sample from the beam, *below,* with a master pattern, *below left,* compiled from living trees and trees cut in known years.

Master pattern

A.D. 1150

A.D. 1160

Core sample

A.D. 1170

A.D. 1180

A.D. 1190

A.D. 1200

A.D. 1210

A.D. 1220

thropological studies of these modern Indians—along with accounts of Pueblo Indians written by early explorers and settlers—have helped archaeologists theorize about Anasazi behavior, ceremonies, and other activities for which there is no direct evidence. So despite the fact that the Anasazi had no written language, archaeologists have been able to develop a remarkably detailed picture of these Indians and their way of life.

The Anasazi first arrived in the Southwest about 300 B.C., probably from Nevada and western Utah. At earlier sites in those areas, archaeologists have found spearpoints and other artifacts nearly identical to those discovered at the earliest Anasazi sites, most of which are in northern Arizona and southwestern Colorado.

The first Anasazi lived by gathering edible wild plants and hunting the animals of the region—rabbits, deer, and bighorn sheep. By about 300 B.C., knowledge of agriculture, which developed in the New World in central Mexico about 7000 B.C., had spread to the Anasazi, and they began to grow corn, pumpkins, and beans. But they still relied on wild plants and hunting for most of their food.

About A.D. 1, the Anasazi began to weave the beautiful baskets for which they are renowned among archaeologists. Some baskets were smeared with pine gum or pitch to make them waterproof and were probably used chiefly for carrying water. Anasazi weavers also made tote bags, sandals, and fur and feather robes.

At Anasazi sites dating to about A.D. 400, archaeologists have found evidence of a new skill probably learned from southern neighbors—making pottery. This early pottery, crude and usually plain gray, enabled the Anasazi to expand their cooking techniques. Instead of just roasting food over an open fire or baking it in hot coals, the Anasazi could also boil or stew it.

Modern Pueblo Indians fire their pottery by covering it with cakes of sheep dung, which produces high temperatures when burned. The Anasazi, however, who never had domesticated sheep, used wood fires. Archaeologists believe the pottery was made by women because potter's tools have been found only in the graves of women.

In about the year 500, the Anasazi settled in villages. Farming became more important, though the Anasazi still hunted and gathered wild plants. In addition, they began to raise turkeys. These were probably wild turkeys that they caught and domesticated.

Anasazi villages of this period consisted of a collection of *pithouses.* Circular in shape, the pithouses were 2 to 4.5 meters (6½ to 15 feet) in diameter and were set about 2 meters into the ground. Long wooden posts placed around the lower walls and extending a few meters aboveground served as support beams for the roof and upper walls of the house. Sticks were placed among the beams to form the upper walls and roof, then the whole outer surface was covered with thick coats of clay and mud. The Anasazi probably entered by climbing down a ladder through a hole in the roof.

One reason archaeologists know so much about Anasazi architecture, tools, and crafts of this period is that many of these pithouses burned with their contents inside. Accidental blazes were probably a constant danger because the open fires used for cooking and heat were only about 3 meters (10 feet) from the roof. Some archaeologists also have suggested that when an Anasazi died, it may have been customary to burn his or her dwelling and its contents.

In about 700, important changes occurred in several aspects of Anasazi life. One of the most important was that the Anasazi began to live in aboveground houses. These houses, named *pueblos* by Spanish explorers, were usually made up of square, one-story-tall rooms connected in the form of an L or a U. Archaeologists do not know why the Anasazi abandoned their pithouses for pueblos. Perhaps the stone and mud pueblos built aboveground were simply more comfortable than the cold, damp, dark pithouses.

Even after the Anasazi began living in pueblos, however, they continued to build pithouses. But the pithouses took on a very different purpose. They became religious and ceremonial structures called *kivas*. Archaeologists believe that the development of the kiva indicates that religious ceremonies became more important at this time. Only sketchy evidence of religious practices, including some rock art and graves, has been found for the period before the development of the kiva.

Anasazi kivas are similar to those of modern Pueblo Indians, so archaeologists believe they were used in much the same way. Archaeologists suspect that the Anasazi kivas, like modern kivas, served not only a religious function, but were also used as a kind of clubhouse for men. Most kivas had a small hole in the floor that served as a symbolic entrance to the spirit world.

Also about 700, Anasazi crafts, especially pottery, began to flourish. The shapes, colors, and designs of pottery became more varied and sophisticated. Advances in design were due in large part to the discovery of a type of clay that stayed white after firing instead of turning gray. The white color provided an excellent background for intricate designs done in black with paints made from plants and minerals.

Two other advances also took place about this time. The Anasazi began growing cotton, which they wove into loose-fitting clothing, such as loincloths for men and apronlike garments for women. And the bow and arrow replaced the spear as the chief hunting weapon, enabling these already skilled hunters to capture more prey more effectively.

These developments took place against a background of environmental change. Pollen studies—studies of ancient pollen found in soil that reveal changes in the amount and type of vegetation growing at a specific time—and studies of tree-ring growth have revealed periods of drought between 700 and 900.

Anasazi Pottery: Creativity in Clay

Changes in Anasazi pottery reflect changes in the culture as it grew more advanced. An early Anasazi bowl dating from A.D. 500, *above,* is gray with little decoration. A water pitcher dating from between 800 and 900, *right,* bears black geometric designs, which became popular after 700, when the Anasazi discovered a type of clay that stayed white after firing. A water jug, *below,* dating from between 1200 and 1300, displays the elaborate designs common in Anasazi pottery of that period.

Shortly after 900, however, the climate on the plateau improved. Pollen, tree-ring, and geologic studies have shown that the amount of rainfall increased and that rain fell more regularly throughout the year. The Anasazi population grew, and they spread into many areas of the plateau. Their settlements have been found from almost as far west as Las Vegas, Nev., and east to the Rio Grande Valley of New Mexico.

Beginning about 1000, the Anasazi also began moving into the Grand Canyon in increasing numbers. The Anasazi were probably attracted by the abundant plant and animal life resulting from variations in climate within the canyon, some of whose walls rise nearly 1.6 kilometers (1 mile) from the canyon floor. The Anasazi probably ranged up and down the canyon with the seasons, farming at higher elevations, where rainfall is plentiful, in the summer, and returning to lower elevations, where temperatures are warmer, in the winter.

The small Anasazi pueblos in the Grand Canyon—only 10 to 12 rooms—were similar in size to those found nearly everywhere else on the Colorado Plateau at this time. Interestingly, archaeologists have found that most Anasazi pueblos built after 900 were probably not occupied for more than 40 or 50 years, contrary to the previously held belief that pueblos were inhabited for centuries. The Anasazi may simply have wanted a change of scenery, or perhaps the accumulation of trash finally drove them on. Garbage and refuse were simply thrown into unused rooms or out the doors of the pueblos. These mountains of trash have been a bonanza for archaeologists, because they often served as grave sites, but they must have caused serious health problems for the Anasazi.

The Anasazi may also have moved because of disagreements with neighbors. Anthropologists have documented that five modern Pueblo villages were established for that reason. Moving away may have been a peaceful solution to village disputes among people for whom there is little evidence of hostilities.

Until the early 900's, the ways of life of various Anasazi groups on the Colorado Plateau were remarkably similar. About that time, however, a great flourishing of Anasazi culture began in Chaco Canyon. Within a period of about 100 years, the art, architecture, technology, and, perhaps, the political and social organizations of the Chacoan Anasazi advanced far beyond those of their neighbors to the north at Mesa Verde and west at Kayenta.

The pottery, baskets, woodcarvings, and jewelry made in Chaco Canyon became more elaborate and sophisticated than artifacts made elsewhere. For example, the designs on jewelry and carvings became more complex. These artifacts were also frequently inlaid with turquoise and jet, a glossy black stone. Irrigation systems became more complex and ingenious, expanding far beyond the simple methods the Anasazi developed soon after they began farming.

Chaco Canyon's Beautiful House

The spectacular ruins of Pueblo Bonito (beautiful house), *above,* are only a faint echo of an architectural masterpiece, *opposite page.* The largest pueblo in Chaco Canyon, Pueblo Bonito was four or five stories tall and had 600 rooms and 32 underground ceremonial kivas. Built in the early A.D. 900's, the pueblo housed several hundred people.

Perhaps the most impressive accomplishment of the Chaco Canyon Anasazi was the construction of huge pueblos called *great houses.* The largest of these great houses, Pueblo Bonito, contained more than 600 rooms and at least 32 kivas and, at its tallest, stood 4 to 5 stories high. Indeed, until the 1800's, Pueblo Bonito was one of the largest "apartment houses" in the United States. Within a few kilometers of Pueblo Bonito are other great houses nearly as large. The precise shaping and fitting of the blocks used to construct these pueblos is one of the main reasons the ruins still stand.

At its peak, in about 1140, the complex of Chacoan settlements included at least a dozen great houses within the canyon, numerous smaller but spectacular pueblos called *outliers* outside the canyon, and hundreds of small villages. These settlements may have had thousands of residents, including about 5,500 inside Chaco Canyon.

Dozens of kilometers of roads linked the great houses to the outliers and to other large Chacoan villages. Traces of many of these roads are still visible. Photographs taken by high-flying aircraft and Earth-orbiting satellites have also revealed parts of the road system.

While the idea of roads connecting settlements is understandable, the reason for the Anasazi's roads is something of a mystery. The roads, which were broad—about 9 meters (30 feet) across—and carefully leveled, were traveled only by the Anasazi on foot. They had no vehicles or beasts of burden. The wheel, the horse, and cattle were not introduced to the Southwest until the coming of the

Spaniards in 1540, long after Chaco Canyon was deserted. Why bother to construct such elaborate roads only for foot traffic? Perhaps the roads were also used during religious ceremonies.

Archaeologists are still trying to determine the relationship of the great houses to the outliers, some of which were 160 kilometers (100 miles) from Chaco Canyon. One long-standing theory is that the outliers were support towns that provided food, pottery, and other goods for the great houses, which served as administrative and religious centers. This theory is based on the belief that all of the great houses were apartment houses. But in 1986, the results of a 15-year study of Chaco Canyon by a team of archaeologists working for the National Park Service challenged this idea. The team, headed by Stephen H. Lekson, noticed that trash heaps are conspicuously absent from a number of great houses. In addition, there are few hearths, and many of the rooms are small and featureless. The archaeologists concluded that some of the great houses were not dwellings at all but storehouses, mainly for crop surpluses, which may have been distributed to outlying communities during periods of drought.

Lekson and his colleagues also concluded that the great houses were the focus of a regional trading network dealing chiefly in turquoise, which the Anasazi mined, and pottery. This network encompassed not only the immediate region but also much of the Anasazi homeland and even central Mexico.

Trading Time

His wares around him, a trader from central Mexico displays a necklace decorated with a copper bell to residents of Pueblo Bonito. Archaeologists believe that such traders may have supplied the Anasazi with metal and shell jewelry as well as brightly colored macaws and other birds native to Mexico in exchange for pottery and turquoise, which the Anasazi mined.

By 1150, the impressive development in Chaco Canyon had come to an abrupt end. Tree-ring studies have revealed that beginning about 1140, the Southwest was struck by a severe drought. The Chaco Anasazi abandoned their great houses and moved south and east to areas where water was more plentiful. Although they settled mainly in the Rio Grande Valley of New Mexico, some also moved to an area now inhabited by Zuni Indians along New Mexico's western border.

Since the mid-1980's, some scientists have theorized that the Anasazi in Chaco Canyon may have helped to create their own environmental disaster. Years of intensive farming could have exhausted the sandy soil of the canyon. Cutting down many of the trees may also have contributed to an erosion of soil. During their occupation of Chaco Canyon, the Anasazi cleared large areas of forest for firewood and lumber. The construction of a single great house required up to 200,000 roof beams.

Between 1150 and 1200, people were on the move throughout much of the Anasazi homeland. The Grand Canyon and all the land west of the Colorado River in Utah and Arizona were deserted.

In the Kayenta region and at Mesa Verde, many Anasazi moved into cliff dwellings, pueblos built into rock overhangs in the canyon walls. The reasons for this move are still a puzzle, because some Anasazi in these areas continued to live in aboveground pueblos. The dark, chilly cliff dwellings were not as comfortable as the pueblos. Nor was water more accessible there. And there is no evidence of warfare or of attack by hostile neighbors.

Anasazi life in the cliff dwellings lasted only about 100 years. By 1300, these settlements were also deserted, probably chiefly because of another intense drought that began in 1276. Disease may also have forced the exodus. Turkeys, which the Anasazi kept in pens next to the living rooms of their cliff dwellings, are prime carriers of salmonella, a bacteria that can cause typhoid fever and other life-threatening diseases. It is possible that many people, especially children, died of salmonella poisoning and other diseases caused by unsanitary conditions. Archaeologists have, in fact, found an unusually high number of infant graves at sites dating from the late 1200's. Whatever the reason, the Kayenta Anasazi moved south to what are now Hopi areas in northern Arizona. The Mesa Verde Anasazi settled mainly in the Rio Grande Valley.

In their new homelands, the Anasazi continued their agricultural way of life. They built large pueblos and elaborate kivas decorated with beautiful, multicolored murals. The art of pottery making also reached new heights as the Anasazi discovered new glazes.

In 1540, another disaster—perhaps the greatest in their history—befell the Anasazi. In that year, a large column of armor-clad Spanish soldiers led by explorer Francisco Vásquez de Coronado reached Hawikuh, an Anasazi village in western New Mexico. When the Indians refused to submit to the invaders, the Spaniards killed many of Hawikuh's inhabitants and destroyed the village. Other Anasazi towns also suffered the same fate. The remaining Anasazi soon came under the domination of the Spaniards. Dispersed into widely separated areas, the Anasazi ceased to exist as a single group. Today, their descendants are the Hopi, Zuni, and other tribes of modern Pueblo Indians.

Despite nearly 100 years of exploration and study of the Anasazi, archaeologists still have much to learn about these amazing people. Threatening this investigation, however, is the widespread vandalism of Anasazi sites. Hundreds of sites are illegally destroyed each year by looters seeking pottery, jewelry, and other artifacts, which fetch high prices in art markets. Many other Anasazi sites are also lost to development—the construction of highways, dams, and shopping malls. These ancient sites and the artifacts found there are irreplaceable treasures. Once gone, they and the secrets they hold will be lost forever. And the ruined pueblos and abandoned cliff dwellings will stand as mute reminders of mysteries that will never be solved.

For further reading:

Cordell, Linda S. *Prehistory of the Southwest.* Academic Press, 1984.
Muench, David. *Anasazi: Ancient People of the Rock.* American West, 1974.
Williams, Barbara. *Let's Go to an Indian Cliff Dwelling.* Putnam, 1965.

Changing Views of Dinosaurs

In the following 34 pages, SCIENCE YEAR presents a special two-part section on dinosaurs. The first part explores how scientists have changed their views about the abilities and behavior of these "terrible lizards." The second part shows how artists have given us vivid images of dinosaurs that reflect these changing views.

Scientists carefully free dinosaur bones buried for more than 65 million years from the face of a rock at Dinosaur National Monument, *left*. What they learn from such fossils provides the framework for artists' reconstructions of these extinct reptiles, *above*.

New evidence has convinced most scientists that many dinosaurs once considered dull and plodding were actually agile, fast-moving, and even social.

New Discoveries About Dinosaurs

BY JOSEPH WALLACE

Imagine a world that is warm everywhere all year round. A world filled with strange plants and animals—without dogs or cats or most other mammals—and without flowering plants or familiar trees such as oaks or maples. A world where, if you have the time, you can walk from what is now the United States to Africa or China without getting your feet wet, because all the continents are joined together in one large land mass. If you can imagine this scene, you have a pretty good idea of Earth as it was 225 million years ago when dinosaurs first appeared.

Until they disappeared about 65 million years ago, dinosaurs dominated life on Earth for a breathtaking 160 million years. Yet until about 150 years ago, no one knew that dinosaurs had ever existed. So it is not surprising that *paleontologists* (scientists who study dinosaurs and other extinct creatures) still have a great deal to learn about these remarkable reptiles and their fascinating lives. Since the 1960's, new discoveries of dinosaur fossils and tracks and new interpretations of previous finds have dramatically changed scientists' thinking about such things as how fast dinosaurs could run, how they lived and behaved, their posture, and even whether some dinosaur species were the ancestors of today's birds. In addition, lively controversies have arisen about such issues as whether they were warm-blooded or cold-blooded and about the reason—or reasons—they died out. This intriguing mix of established fact, daring theory, and unsolved mystery has made the past 25 years a most exciting time for studying and learning more about dinosaurs.

Opposite page: A scientist examines casts of a dinosaur hatchling in its shell and a rare dinosaur nest with whole and broken eggs. The fossils, found in Montana, are among the discoveries that have helped revolutionize scientific thinking about dinosaurs.

Although no one knew about these extinct animals until the mid-1800's, the first recorded description of what turned out to be a dinosaur bone was published in 1677 by an English writer and professor named Robert Plot. In a book on the natural history of Oxfordshire, his home county, Plot included a drawing of a huge thighbone unlike any seen before. It was, we now know, the fossil thighbone of a meat-eating dinosaur called megalosaurus, which grew up to 9 meters (30 feet) long.

During the early 1800's, many more fossilized dinosaur bones were discovered, particularly in England. By that time, fossil hunters knew they were finding the remains of ancient reptiles of some kind. But until 1841, most scientists believed these reptiles had been gigantic lizards. In that year, British paleontologist Richard Owen concluded, after studying many fossils, that these creatures were so unlike any modern reptile that they deserved a name of their own. Owen named the ancient creatures *Dinosauria*, from two Greek words meaning *terrible lizards*.

Owen's pronouncement set off an enthusiastic hunt for fossils. Throughout Europe and the United States, scientists and amateur fossil hunters alike picked through quarries, examined canyon walls, and studied rocks turned up by road construction, searching for dinosaur bones.

No dinosaur hunters worked as hard or found as many fossils as a pair of American paleontologists, Edward Drinker Cope of Philadelphia and Othniel Charles Marsh of Yale University in New Haven, Conn. These two men never worked together. In fact, they were bitter rivals, whose "Bone Wars" fascinated and entertained Americans for years. Between 1860 and 1900, Cope and Marsh and their teams of fossil hunters scoured the Western United States—particularly Colorado, Montana, and Wyoming—turning up vast beds of dinosaur fossils. They often shipped hundreds of tons of bones to museums and universities in a single year, including the first remains of such now well-known dinosaurs as apatosaurus (formerly called brontosaurus), allosaurus, and triceratops.

Early in the 1900's, scientists expanded their search for dinosaur bones by mounting expeditions to Africa and Asia. They soon found that Europe and the United States didn't harbor all the interesting fossils. In 1907, for example, a German expedition recovered 250 tons of bones in Tanganyika (today named Tanzania). Less than 20 years later, American explorer Roy Chapman Andrews discovered new dinosaur species and the first dinosaur eggs in Mongolia's Gobi Desert. Today, new fossil beds are still being uncovered. In 1986, for example, a team of Argentine explorers discovered the first dinosaur fossils in Antarctica.

By studying fossilized dinosaur bones, tracks, teeth, and even skin, scientists have learned that dinosaurs were an amazingly varied lot. Evidence suggests that there were at least 400 species. Some

The author:
Joseph Wallace is a freelance writer and the author of *The Rise and Fall of the Dinosaur*.

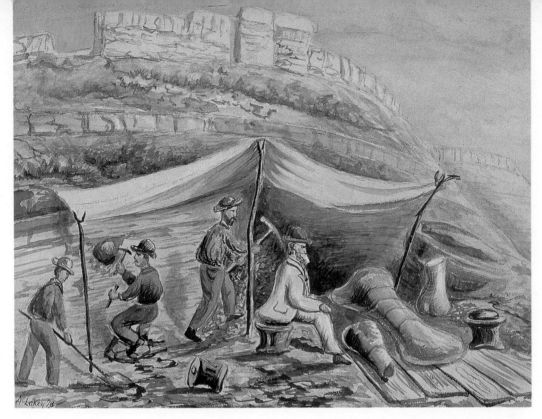

were smaller than a rooster; others weighed as much as 60 elephants and were tall enough to look over a four-story building. By studying the shape of dinosaur teeth, scientists discovered that some dinosaurs were plant-eaters and others meat-eaters. Meat-eating dinosaurs, like modern meat-eaters, had pointed, slightly curved teeth. In contrast, plant-eating dinosaurs had teeth that looked like blunt pegs.

By comparing the skeletons of dinosaurs to those of modern animals, scientists determined that all dinosaurs lived on land. Tracks and the positions of the leg bones told them that although dinosaurs were reptiles, they did not stand or walk the way living reptiles do. Nearly all living reptiles—such as turtles and crocodiles—walk with their legs sprawled to the side and their body touching the ground. Dinosaurs, in contrast, stood and walked with their legs straight under their body and their body off the ground, the way dogs and horses do.

By dating the rocks in which dinosaur fossils have been found, scientists know that dinosaurs first walked the Earth about 225 million years ago, during a geologic period called the Triassic Period, which began about 245 million years ago and lasted for some 37 million years. But only a few dinosaur species existed during this time, and nearly all of them were small as dinosaurs went, about the size of a modern horse. One of the largest and most common dinosaurs late in the Triassic was the plateosaurus, a long-necked plant-eater 8 meters (26 feet) long.

From the huge collections of dinosaur fossils dug up by fossil hunters, paleontologists have reconstructed skeletons, like that of the ferocious meat-eating albertosaurus at Chicago's Field Museum of Natural History, *above.* Such reconstructions are the chief means by which scientists learn about dinosaurs' size, weight, physical appearance, and posture.

After the Triassic came the Jurassic Period, which lasted until about 140 million years ago. During this period, the dinosaurs underwent a population explosion. Dozens of new species appeared, including the familiar apatosaurus, with its absurdly long and slender neck, and the ferocious, meat-eating allosaurus.

The heyday of the dinosaur, however, took place during the next period, the Cretaceous, which lasted until 65 million years ago. During this period, many groups of dinosaurs, including the fearsome tyrannosaurus and the three-horned triceratops, reached their greatest size, 12 meters (40 feet) and 9 meters (30 feet) long, respectively. Around the end of the Cretaceous, all the dinosaurs mysteriously became extinct.

Until the 1960's, most scientists believed that the dinosaurs were like today's reptiles in everything but size. They were seen as sluggish, slow-moving animals that plodded along dragging their tails behind them. Dinosaurs may have looked impressive, the scientists thought, but their lives were dull.

Today, dinosaurs have a much different image. Modern scientists, carefully studying both the bone structure of the dinosaurs and their footprints left behind in fossilized mud, have come to a new, much more entertaining conclusion: Far from being sluggish, many dinosaurs were active, fast-moving, and remarkably agile creatures.

This change in thinking began in 1964 with the discovery of the fossils of a fearsome dinosaur named deinonychus, which means *terrible claw.* The fossils of deinonychus, which lived 125 million years

ago, were found in Montana by paleontologists John Ostrom and Grant E. Meyer of Yale University.

Deinonychus was a finely tuned, beautifully designed, and very deadly hunting machine. It was 4 meters (13 feet) long and equipped with long, powerfully muscled hind legs built for speed and agility. Its arms ended in strong grasping hands tipped with sharp talons, and a curved claw sprouted from each foot like a scythe. Its large jaw was lined with daggerlike teeth.

In a 1969 report on his fossil find, Ostrom analyzed the types of weapons in deinonychus' arsenal—and the way each of them was probably used—to reconstruct the dinosaur's hunting technique. He concluded that deinonychus could race after its prey at great speeds. (Scientists later estimated, after studying tracks of deinonychus and similar dinosaurs, that the dinosaur could run at speeds greater than 48 kilometers per hour [kph] or 30 miles per hour [mph].) When it caught its victim, Ostrom speculated, deinonychus would rear onto one leg—using its stiff tail for balance—and disembowel its victim with the terrible claw on its foot. Few creatures would have been able to survive such an attack, especially since deinonychus apparently hunted in packs.

Ostrom concluded that deinonychus was "fleet-footed, agile, and quick," which he regarded as unusual characteristics for a cold-blooded reptile. Perhaps, Ostrom suggested, deinonychus was not cold-blooded like other reptiles, as scientists had long thought. Perhaps it could generate its own heat, the way today's birds and mam-

Dinosaur skeletons are still being found in bone beds—huge collections of dinosaur fossils, such as the one on display at Dinosaur National Monument on the Colorado-Utah border, *above.* This bone bed was once a bend in an ancient river where the bodies of dinosaurs that drowned or died along its banks collected.

Sluggish or Speedy?

Modern paleontologists study dinosaur tracks as well as dinosaur bones. They have concluded that many dinosaurs were fleet and agile, rather than slow moving as previously believed. By measuring the distance between tracks, *above right,* scientists can calculate the speed at which a dinosaur was moving. Tracks and the scythelike fossil claw, *above,* of a deinonychus led scientists to conclude that this dinosaur was a fierce and agile hunter, *opposite page,* that could chase its prey at speeds greater than 48 kilometers (30 miles) per hour and used its claw to disembowel its victims.

mals do. Cold-blooded animals have no built-in controls over their body temperature. In contrast, warm-blooded animals maintain a constant body temperature, regardless of their surroundings.

Many scientists considered Ostrom's theory ridiculous. Other paleontologists, however, decided that the sweeping—and unproven—theory that all dinosaurs were cold-blooded deserved a second look. Leading the charge was paleontologist Robert Bakker, now of the University of Colorado Museum in Boulder.

Why is this argument so important? According to Bakker, who believes all dinosaurs were warm-blooded, the debate goes to the very heart of the process of constructing an accurate picture of how dinosaurs lived. Dependent on the heat of the sun to regulate their body temperature, cold-blooded animals must live in or seek warm environments. Even then, most of them are active only at certain times of the day, seeking shelter at night and hiding from the heat of the sun at midday. Even under perfect conditions, cold-blooded animals don't have the energy or endurance to move very fast for more than a brief time.

Warm-blooded animals, however, can hunt or forage during both the heat of the day and the chill of the night and do so with far more energy and endurance than their cold-blooded kin. The hunting behavior of such mammals as wolves, which can tirelessly chase their prey for kilometers, is impossible for any cold-blooded animal. Therefore, Bakker argued that if dinosaurs were active, fast-moving creatures, they must have been warm-blooded.

Deinonychus and iguanodont (1985), an acrylic painting by John Gurche; collection of the artist

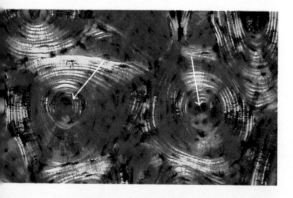

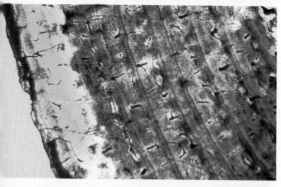

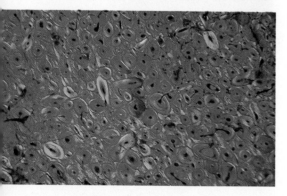

Warm-Blooded Dinosaurs?

Some scientists believe the structure of dinosaur bone tissue suggests that dinosaurs may have been warm-blooded. A microscope reveals that the bone tissue of adult human beings, *top* (greatly magnified), contains tiny channels (indicated by arrows) that carry blood vessels. The bone tissue of adult crocodiles, *center,* which are cold-blooded, is instead formed of bone that shows annual growth rings. Dinosaur bones, *bottom,* contain nearly as many channels (black dots) as those of human beings and other large warm-blooded animals.

Other evidence that dinosaurs may have been warm-blooded includes the structure of their bones. There are important differences between the bones of cold-blooded and warm-blooded animals. Most modern reptiles have slow-growing bones. It takes a crocodile 10 to 20 years to grow to its full weight of 90 kilograms (200 pounds), but a lioness can reach that size—nearly full growth—in just 2 years. Seen under a microscope, slow-growing bone appears solid. In contrast, the bones of most mammals and birds are riddled with microscopic channels. These channels contain blood vessels that carry minerals to and from the bone, enabling bones to grow and be repaired quickly.

In 1957, scientists discovered that many dinosaur bones also had these channels. More detailed studies of dinosaur bones were published beginning in 1968 by French paleontologist Armand de Ricqlès of the University of Paris. He found that dinosaur bones contained nearly as many channels as did bones of modern mammals. This suggested to him that dinosaur bones grew quickly and resembled those of warm-blooded creatures.

Bakker and other believers in the warm-blooded theory have also found support for their ideas in comparisons of the ratio of dinosaur predators to prey. Although warm-blooded animals have more energy and endurance than cold-blooded animals, these benefits exact a price. A warm-blooded lion must eat about 10 times as much food as a cold-blooded alligator. Therefore, warm-blooded predators must live in places where there are many animals to prey upon. Studies of dinosaur fossils found in an area of North America from Montana to Alberta suggest that the ratio of dinosaur predators to their prey was 3 predators for every 100 prey animals. This is closer to ratios found among warm-blooded animals than among cold-blooded animals.

Other scientists, however, dispute these findings. Ostrom himself points out that some modern reptiles, particularly sea turtles and crocodiles, have channels in their bones. Yet these animals are cold-blooded, which seems to poke a hole in the warm-blooded argument. In addition, some birds and small mammals have fairly solid bones.

Ostrom also argues that predator-prey ratios taken from the fossil record are not reliable evidence. The fossil record is incomplete to begin with. Only a few bones from the many animals that die become fossils. Most are destroyed by scavengers or weather. Many factors, including reproduction rates and environmental conditions, may have resulted in the bones of many more prey animals than predators becoming fossilized. Finally, paleontologists will never know for sure which animals in an area were in fact prey for the area's meat-eating dinosaurs.

Some paleontologists have also suggested that even large dinosaurs could have maintained a constant, fairly warm body temperature without being warm-blooded. They point out that temperatures during the age of the dinosaurs were warm and that large animals lose heat slowly.

Paleontologists may not agree that dinosaurs were warm-blooded, but deinonychus and similar dinosaurs have convinced nearly all paleontologists that dinosaurs were faster and more energetic than was previously believed.

Supporting this theory are studies of fossilized dinosaur footprints. In 1976, R. McNeill Alexander of the University of Leeds in England devised a formula to determine how fast the dinosaur was walking. It was based on the distance between two footprints and the size of the dinosaur that made them. Using this formula, Alexander and other scientists discovered that some dinosaurs, particularly small predators, could move at a fast clip. For example, velociraptor, a meat-eater 2 meters (6½ feet) long that ran on two legs, may have reached speeds of 56 kph (35 mph)—nearly as fast as a race horse. And even bulky apatosaurus, which weighed more than

Cretaceous Seaway (1983), a pastel on paper by Douglas Henderson; Museum of the Rockies, Bozeman, Mont.

Social or Solitary?

The discovery of clusters of dinosaur tracks has overturned the belief that all dinosaurs were solitary creatures. Dinosaur trails extending 210 meters (230 yards) along the Purgatoire River in Colorado, *below,* were made by five young plant-eating dinosaurs walking together along the shores of what was then a lake, *right.* Tracks also indicate that some plant-eating dinosaurs traveled in large herds, *opposite page,* perhaps migrating in search of food.

Maiasaura Herd, Aerial View (1983), a pastel on paper by Douglas Henderson; Museum of the Rockies, Bozeman, Mont.

Maiasaura and Hatchlings (1980's), a pastel on paper by Douglas Henderson; Museum of the Rockies, Bozeman, Mont.

10 big African elephants weigh, could move along at about 5 kph (3 mph)—about a person's normal walking speed.

Tracks have also helped paleontologists determine that dinosaurs did not walk with their tails dragging behind them but, rather, held them up. They came to this conclusion after realizing that dinosaur tracks would have been blurred if a tail had been dragged over them. This finding also supports the view that dinosaurs were active creatures, because it would have required energy to hold their tails up.

Tracks have also provided evidence for another turnabout in scientific thinking about dinosaurs. For a long time, paleontologists believed that dinosaurs, like living reptiles, were largely solitary creatures. Then, beginning in the 1940's, in Argentina, Canada, China, Germany, and the United States, scientists began finding large clusters of tracks made by plant-eating dinosaurs. The intriguing thing about these tracks was that they often pointed in the same direction. And because the tracks were found in the same layer of rock, scientists knew that they had been made at the same time. The conclusion seemed clear: Many plant-eating dinosaurs traveled in herds, perhaps migrating at certain seasons in search of food, much as today's African antelope do. A herd of hundreds of triceratops rumbling across the plains of the Western United States must have been an awe-inspiring spectacle.

The discovery that some types of dinosaurs lived in herds at least part of the time triggered new speculation about dinosaur behavior. Perhaps dinosaurs also engaged in other types of behavior scientists have observed in modern animals that live in groups. For example, among many animals that live in herds, the males fight to determine who will lead the herd during the mating season. Some paleontologists have speculated that pachycephalosaurs, or boneheaded dinosaurs, crashed their skulls, the bones of which were as much as 30 centimeters (12 inches) thick, in fights to determine leadership.

Despite such fascinating speculation, and the clues provided by tracks, paleontologists still knew little about the social life of dinosaurs until 1978. Then, a lucky visit to a souvenir shop in Montana by two paleontologists led to an exciting—and surprising—discovery. The owner of the shop showed some unusual dinosaur fossils to John R. Horner, now of Montana State University's Museum of the Rockies in Bozeman, and Robert Makela, a high school science teacher from Rudyard, Mont. The two men, who had spent many summers together hunting dinosaur fossils, immediately recognized the bones as those of baby dinosaurs. Such bones are the rarest of all fossil finds, because few such small, delicate bones survive long enough to become fossils. The bones, Horner and Makela soon realized, belonged to a previously unknown species of plant-eating hadrosaur (duckbilled dinosaur).

On the hillside near Choteau, Mont., where the bones had been found, the paleontologists discovered the remains of a fossilized mud nest about 2 meters (6½ feet) wide and 1 meter (3¼ feet) deep containing the fossilized skeletons of 15 baby dinosaurs. The bones were the first baby dinosaur fossils ever found in a nest.

Over the next few summers, Horner and Makela found thousands of baby hadrosaur fossils as well as more than 300 eggs—some broken, others intact. Never before had so many fossilized dinosaur eggs and baby dinosaur skeletons been found. But exciting as they were, these finds were only part of the story.

Many of the bones and eggs found on the hillside were inside nests that lay close to one another. Because the nests lay in the same rock layer, the fossil hunters concluded that the nests had been dug at the same time. They realized that 100 million years ago, this Montana hillside, now barren and windswept, must have contained a nesting colony of hadrosaurs. The dinosaurs and their eggs had probably been destroyed by a mud slide or ash from a nearby volcano, which then preserved them, allowing researchers 100 million years later to glimpse the surprisingly social private life and complex maternal behavior of a dinosaur.

More revelations were to come. Along with fossilized eggs and

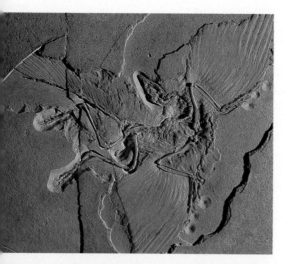

newborn dinosaurs, Horner and Makela found young dinosaurs of various sizes. Some measured less than 60 centimeters (2 feet) in length. But others were up to 2 meters (6½ feet) long—and therefore at least a few months old. (Adult hadrosaurs grew up to 9 meters [30 feet] long.) Crushed eggshells found at the bottom of the nests indicated that the juveniles had lived in the nests after hatching. In addition, the teeth of the juveniles were worn, evidence that they had been eating for a while. Horner and Makela concluded that the colony's adults, like modern birds, must have foraged for leaves and berries, then brought them back to the nest.

Why was this such a remarkable discovery? Because scientists had long believed that dinosaurs treated their young the way modern reptiles do. Nearly all lizards, snakes, and turtles lay their eggs and then abandon them. Even alligators, which guard their young, do not feed them. Only birds, mammals, and marsupials provide both food and protection to their babies. Yet the hadrosaurs of the Montana colony were apparently caring parents, protecting their young from predators and feeding them until they grew large enough to fend for themselves. Horner named this new type of hadrosaur *maiasaura*, which means *good mother lizard*.

The sizes of some maiasaura fossils in the nest were interpreted by believers in warm-blooded dinosaurs as evidence that the maiasaura grew relatively quickly. Some of the fossils found in the colony belonged to dinosaurs 2 meters long. If maiasaura were cold-blooded, it would have taken them about three years to reach that size. Therefore, either maiasaura were warm-blooded and so grew quickly, or they stayed in their nests for up to three years—an unlikely length of time.

In September 1987, paleontologists at the Tyrrell Museum of Palaeontology in Drumheller, Canada, reported finding more than 20 hadrosaur nests with eggs in southern Alberta. X-ray examination revealed that many of the eggs contained the fossilized skeletons of dinosaur fetuses about to hatch. The scientists also found the remains of young hatchlings as well as less mature embryos. The scientists surmised that all of them

Ancestors of Birds?
Most scientists believe that some types of small meat-eating dinosaurs were the ancestors of modern birds. Some scientists argue that archaeopteryx, *top,* whose fossils were first found in Germany in the mid-1800's, is the "missing link." Other scientists believe that protoavis, *above,* found in Texas in 1986, is the true ancestor of birds. Most scientists, however, believe the exact ancestors have yet to be discovered.

had died at the same time, probably drowned when a nearby river flooded its banks. Scientists hope knowledge of the growth rate of the fetal dinosaurs—determined by comparing their size to their estimated age—will shed new light on the warm-blooded-cold-blooded debate.

Whatever side they take in that debate, most paleontologists now accept another theory first proposed more than 100 years ago—that modern birds evolved from certain dinosaur species. According to this theory, the tiny sparrow fluttering at your backyard feeder is actually a distant relative of the fierce tyrannosaurus.

British naturalist Charles Darwin, who theorized that all species of plants and animals *evolved* (developed) from a few common ancestors, first theorized that birds had evolved from some type of reptile in his landmark book *On the Origin of Species* (1859). He noted that the bone structure of birds' wings closely resembles the front limbs of lizards, while other details of the skeleton are also similar. There was no fossil evidence for this connection, however, until 1861, when a remarkable discovery was made near Munich, Germany. In that year, workers at a limestone quarry found the fossilized skeleton of a creature that had the feathers of a bird but also looked like a small, fine-boned dinosaur. Scientists named this creature *archaeopteryx*, which means *ancient feather*.

In 1867, British scientist Thomas Huxley, a staunch defender of Darwin's theory of evolution, suggested that archaeopteryx was the "missing link" between reptiles—particularly dinosaurs—and birds—that is, a transitional animal with characteristics of both groups. Huxley noted that archaeopteryx closely resembled compsognathus, a meat-eating dinosaur with hollow bones and sharp teeth that was one of the smallest known dinosaurs. It was only about 60 centimeters (2 feet) long.

Today, many scientists agree with Huxley that some types of small meat-eating dinosaurs were the ancestors of birds. But the debate over the relationship between archaeopteryx and modern birds continues. Many scientists doubt that archaeopteryx was a direct ancestor because it had several features not found in modern birds.

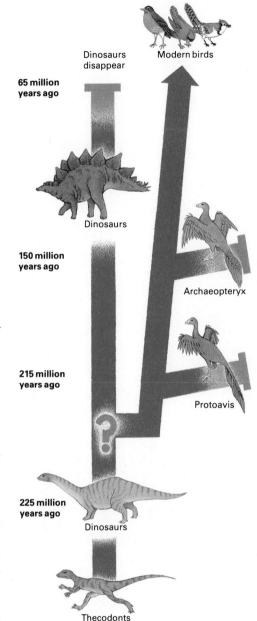

Dinosaurs disappear

Modern birds

65 million years ago

Dinosaurs

150 million years ago

Archaeopteryx

215 million years ago

Protoavis

225 million years ago

Dinosaurs

Thecodonts

What Became of the Dinosaurs?

Dinosaurs, which appeared about 225 million years ago, evolved from thecodonts, an early reptile. Birdlike dinosaurs probably evolved from still unknown types of small meat-eating dinosaurs and eventually evolved into modern birds. Early birds, such as protoavis and archaeopteryx, may have been side branches on the bird family tree. All the dinosaurs became extinct about 65 million years ago.

One of these scientists is paleontologist Sankar Chatterjee of Texas Tech University in Lubbock. Although Chatterjee believes that dinosaurs and birds are related, he argues that archaeopteryx was merely a side branch on the evolutionary tree. To prove that argument, however, it was necessary to find the real missing link.

In 1986, near Lubbock, Chatterjee discovered fossils of a creature he believes is the true ancestor of birds. The fossils were those of a crow-sized animal that seems to have been more birdlike than archaeopteryx. They were also 70 million years older. The creature, which was named *protoavis* (ancestral bird), lived 215 million years ago, near the very dawn of the age of the dinosaurs and long before any true birds existed. Protoavis had hollow bones and a well-developed wishbone for the attachment of flight muscles, features also found in birds. Yet, like compsognathus, it had tiny, needle-sharp teeth, and a dinosaurlike tail and hind legs. "I have no doubt that protoavis provides conclusive proof that dinosaurs and birds are closely related," says Chatterjee.

Many paleontologists are skeptical of Chatterjee's theory. They argue that some features of protoavis that Chatterjee labels as birdlike, such as its wide eye sockets, are simply characteristics commonly found in small animals.

Of all recent debates about dinosaurs, however, none has been louder than the disagreement over why these great reptiles vanished. From the fossil record, we know that about 65 million years ago at the end of the Cretaceous Period, they died out along with many other plants and animals during one of the most dramatic mass extinctions in the history of the planet.

Over the years, scientists have proposed many theories to explain the death of the dinosaurs. Some experts suggested that the great reptiles simply grew too large to feed themselves. Others speculated that mammals ate so many dinosaur eggs that the reptiles soon died out. These theories are now discounted.

Today, new extinction theories have become popular. Many are based on geologic evidence of the great changes affecting Earth during the Cretaceous Period. The climate gradually grew cooler. There were many volcanic eruptions. Areas that had once been desert were suddenly drenched with rain, while swamps and inland seas dried out. As adaptable as the dinosaurs were, they may not have been able to survive these drastic changes in their environment.

Bakker thinks that these changes caused the extinction of many of the plants that plant-eating dinosaurs depended on. As herds of dinosaurs wandered far in search of food, they mixed for the first time with other dinosaur species. This mixing may have resulted in some species transmitting new diseases to other species unable to fight off the strange germs. Great plagues may have decimated entire dinosaur populations.

Paleontologist J. Keith Rigby, Jr., of Notre Dame University in

Indiana is one of many scientists who argue that the dinosaurs' end was fairly commonplace. "I think that the dinosaurs just were unable to adapt to a cooler, changing Earth," he says. "As the Cretaceous Period progressed, fewer species and fewer individuals survived—until populations became so low that the dinosaurs died out."

The extinction theory that has received the most attention in the 1980's, however, is also the most dramatic. In 1979, a team of scientists headed by physicist Luis W. Alvarez of the University of California at Berkeley theorized that about 65 million years ago Earth was struck by an asteroid perhaps 10 kilometers (6 miles) in diameter. According to this theory, the impact created a vast dust cloud that blanketed the planet for months, blocking out the sun's rays and causing temperatures to plummet. Deprived of sunlight and subjected to cold, most plants died. They were soon followed into extinction by starving plant-eating dinosaurs. Unable to find plant-eating prey for food, meat-eaters also starved.

As evidence for their theory, the Alvarez team pointed to a layer of the element iridium they found in rock dating from 65 million years ago. Iridium is rare on the surface of Earth but more abundant in asteroids. The scientists theorized that the iridium layer formed when the dust cloud, which included particles from the comet, filtered back to Earth.

Since 1979, many studies have provided evidence supporting or challenging this theory. One of the main arguments against the theory is that there is no known impact crater of the right size and age.

Some scientists, including Bakker, doubt that there was a collision at all. Iridium is common in Earth's interior, they point out, and may have been brought to the surface by the enormous volcanic eruptions that occurred about 65 million years ago. Rigby and others believe that an impact did occur, but that it may have had little or nothing to do with the dinosaurs' death.

Warm-blooded or cold-blooded? Sluggish plodders or quick and agile hunters? Gradual extinction or sudden death from space? Few other scientific fields are so filled with controversy, with arguments, with out-and-out disagreements. Most dinosaur scholars wouldn't have it any other way. "The dinosaurs have been gone for 65 million years, yet studying them is more exciting than ever," says paleontologist Nicholas Hotton III of the Smithsonian Institution in Washington, D.C. "For scientists and the public alike, they're irresistible."

For further reading:

Charig, Alan J. *A New Look at Dinosaurs*. Facts on File, 1983.
Cobb, Vicki. *The Monsters Who Died: A Mystery About Dinosaurs*. Putnam, 1983.
Wilford, John Noble. *The Riddle of the Dinosaur*. Knopf, 1985.

Dryptosaurus (1897), a water color by Charles R. Knight; American Museum of Natural History, New York City

Dinosaurs and the Artist

Dinosaur art has changed greatly over the past century, reflecting advances in scientists' knowledge.

CHAS. R. K...

Preceding pages: An 1897 painting by pioneering dinosaur artist Charles R. Knight shows two dryptosauruses locked in mortal combat, a vision of ferociously agile dinosaurs that was very modern for its time.

Thanks to the skill of artists, almost everyone today has a pretty good idea of what dinosaurs looked like. Drawings and paintings of these ancient, awesome creatures, which became extinct 65 million years ago, add vivid reality to books and magazines; sculptures of dinosaurs make museum displays come alive. But accurately reconstructing a dinosaur for an illustration or a sculpture—adding flesh and muscle to breathe life into fossil bones—is a difficult and often painstaking task. The process involves, in varying degrees, hard evidence, educated guesses, and a good imagination.

Imagination often took the upper hand in the first dinosaur drawings and reconstructions made in the early 1800's. Paleontologists and artists at that time were trying to reconstruct an unknown type of animal, and, in most cases, they had only a few fossils to work with. As a result, these early efforts were often bizarre and terribly inaccurate by modern standards. For example, the first reconstruction of an iguanodon mistakenly had the creature's thumb bone attached to the end of its nose.

But our knowledge of dinosaurs has grown dramatically since the first dinosaur fossils were named in the 1820's. Fossil discoveries and the development of new techniques for unlocking their secrets have given scientists a much better understanding of the way dinosaurs looked and behaved. Not surprisingly, the images of dinosaurs in drawings, paintings, and sculptures have reflected these fascinating discoveries.

Two of the best early dinosaur artists were Benjamin Waterhouse Hawkins of Great Britain and Charles R. Knight of the United States. Both of these artists worked closely—as dinosaur artists still do—with paleontologists.

Waterhouse Hawkins worked with Sir Richard Owen, the British scientist who coined the word *dinosaur* (terrible lizard) in 1841. In 1851, Waterhouse Hawkins created the first life-sized dinosaur sculptures, including incorrectly assembled iguanodons, for an exhibit at the Crystal Palace in Sydenham in London. Although the Crystal Palace burned down in 1936, Waterhouse Hawkins' dinosaurs still stand on the grounds there today.

Knight, widely regarded as the grandfather of prehistoric life illustrations, collaborated for 30 years, beginning in 1896, with Henry Fairfield Osborn, later the president of the American Museum of Natural History in New York City. Discoveries in the 1870's of extensive beds of dinosaur bones in the American West gave Knight and other artists the opportunity to draw from complete skeletons with the bones in their proper order.

Today's dinosaur artists also begin with the bones. But artists now take other factors into consideration. For example, in the 1950's, artists, like paleontologists, began studying modern animals to determine how dinosaurs looked and behaved. Modern birds, reptiles, and even some mammals with features similar to those of dinosaurs, such as giraffes, elephants, and rhinoceroses, can provide clues to the way dinosaurs' muscles were attached to their bones. From these clues, artists can make some educated guesses about how these ancient creatures walked and moved.

Modern artists have also been able to draw on the new research findings and discoveries that have revolutionized scientific thinking about dinosaurs in the past 25 years. Studies by scientists have dispelled the idea that dinosaurs were sluggish, drab, solitary creatures. This has inspired artists to represent dinosaurs as looking sleeker, more streamlined, and more agile.

Artists are also depicting dinosaurs engaging in previously unheard-of activities, such as traveling in herds, hunting in packs, and caring for their young. In addition, advances in the study of ancient environments have enabled artists to place dinosaurs in more realistic settings.

Of course, artists must still deal with many uncertainties. The reconstructed dinosaur skeletons that delight museumgoers are not always trustworthy as artists' models. Many were assembled years ago on the basis of incomplete or inaccurate information. Some of the reconstructed skeletons are made up of the bones of several individuals of a particular species—or even of different species. And despite the discoveries of many rich fossil beds, some dinosaur species are still represented by only a few fossils, not enough to build an accurate picture of what they looked like.

Some questions about how dinosaurs looked may never be answered. For example, what color were dinosaurs? No one really knows because fossils of dinosaur skin are rare, and even those that exist provide few clues to their original color. How should artists depict dinosaur beaks, nostrils, eyes, and eyelids? Again, there are no certain answers because such soft tissue is almost never fossilized. Modern animals may help artists arrive at an educated guess, but no one knows for sure. Finally, artists—as well as paleontologists—may simply disagree on how to interpret fossil evidence in order to draw the details of a particular dinosaur.

Just as science benefits dinosaur art, dinosaur art may sometimes benefit science. For example, dinosaur illustrations and sculptures are often used to support new theories about dinosaur appearance and behavior. A then-startling drawing of a galloping deinonychus made in 1969 by paleontologist and artist Robert Bakker, now of the University of Colorado Museum in Boulder, was one of the opening shots in the revolution that led to scientific acceptance of dinosaurs as agile, active animals. In addition, artists researching particular dinosaurs by studying their fossilized bones and skin have discovered features overlooked by paleontologists.

But perhaps the greatest value of dinosaur art is that it enables us to become time travelers to an alien world and to view at a close—but safe—distance the sometimes terrifying, endlessly fascinating, and still mysterious creatures who ruled our world for 160 million years.

The Iguanodon's Transformation

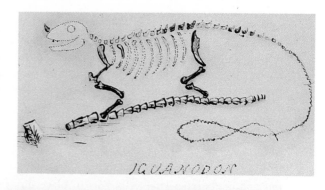

Early artists' depictions of dinosaurs were often based more on imagination than evidence. An 1830 sketch, *above right,* by Gideon Mantell, the English surgeon who reported the iguanodon's discovery, portrays this dinosaur as looking like a giant iguana. Mantell had only a few fossil bones to work with and wrongly guessed that one belonged on the end of the dinosaur's nose. This error was compounded in two iguanodon sculptures made in the 1850's by English artist Benjamin Waterhouse Hawkins, *right,* which showed the dinosaur as a fat rhinoceroslike animal with a horn. To celebrate the near-completion of the sculptures, the artist hosted a dinner in the unfinished shell of one of the statues, *below.* A 1986 painting by John Sibbick, *opposite page,* based on extensive iguanodon fossil finds, shows this dinosaur as a streamlined animal with an erect tail. The "horn" is now correctly positioned as a thumb spike.

Modern Iguanodons (1986), a painting by John Sibbick; collection of the artist

Detail of *Stegosaurus* (1901), an oil painting on canvas by Charles R. Knight; American Museum of Natural History, New York City

A Stegosaurus Puzzle: One Row or Two?

Not all first guesses about dinosaurs were wrong. Paleontologist Othniel C. Marsh, who discovered stegosaurus in 1877, believed this dinosaur had only one row of plates on its back. But a 1901 painting by Charles R. Knight, *left,* showed stegosaurus with two rows of paired plates. An 1899 drawing by Frank Bond, *below left,* showed an even more fanciful stegosaurus, with flat, overlapping plates and spikes on its back. After reanalyzing stegosaurus fossils, artist Stephen A. Czerkas concluded Marsh had been right and in 1986 created a stegosaurus sculpture with one row of plates, *below.*

Stegosaurus stenops (1986), a sculpture in resin by Stephen A. Czerkas; collection of the artist

Detail of *Triceratops* (1901), an oil painting on canvas by Charles R. Knight; Smithsonian Institution, Washington, D.C.

Claws & Teeth Against Horns & Beaks, a painting by Mark Hallett; © Mark Hallett 1984.

Daspletosaurus and Styracosaurus (1985), an acrylic painting by John Gurche; collection of the artist

From Still Lifes to Action Shots

New discoveries about dinosaurs have changed the way artists "pose" their reptilian subjects. The solitary, impassive vision of triceratops in Charles Knight's 1901 painting, *above left,* for example, has given way to Mark Hallett's 1984 depiction, *left,* of triceratops as an energetic animal that lived in herds. Spine-tingling prehistoric adventure comes to the fore in a 1985 painting by John Gurche, *above,* of a confrontation between a daspletosaurus and a styracosaurus, another horned dinosaur.

Jurassic Life of Europe (about 1870), an oil painting on canvas by Benjamin Waterhouse Hawkins; Museum of Natural History, Princeton University

A Tale of Two Tails

One of the most significant changes in the way artists have portrayed dinosaurs involves their posture. In early reconstructions, such as the 1870 mural by Benjamin Waterhouse Hawkins, *above,* dinosaurs were shown as lizardlike creatures that crawled along dragging their tails behind them. Based on better fossil evidence, a 1986 painting shows a mother mamenchisaurus and her baby, *right,* as sleek, streamlined animals that walked with tails held up.

Crossing the Flats, Mamenchisaurus, a water color on paper by Mark Hallett; Natural History Museum of Los Angeles County, Los Angeles;

Detail of *Chasmosaurus (= Pentaceratops) sternbergii Herd in Dry Cypress Swamp* (1977 and 1985), an oil painting on canvas by Gregory Paul; collection of the artist

Will Dinosaurs Show Their True Colors?

Artists must still rely on imagination and educated guesses for some aspects of dinosaurs' appearance, such as color, for which there is no direct fossil evidence. Dinosaurs were probably as brightly colored as modern animals, *opposite page.* They may have used color to attract mates or to frighten off an attacker, *right,* or as camouflage to hide from enemies, *below.*

Hypacrosaurus (1977), a painting by Eleanor Kish; National Museum of Natural Sciences, National Museums of Canada, Ottawa

Dinosaur Sculpture: From Tiny to Terrible

Greater realism and technical accuracy in dinosaur reconstruction extends to sculpture as well as painting. A 1975 sculpture shows a tiny protoceratops hatchling only 7.6 centimeters (3 inches) tall, *below,* struggling out of its shell. A ferocious allosaurus measuring 6.7 meters (22 feet) long, *opposite page,* is about to pounce on its victim. The allosaurus, created in the mid-1980's, was the first life-sized dinosaur sculpture with skin patterns based on actual fossilized skin impressions.

Protoceratops (1975), a sculpture in resin by Sylvia Czerkas; collection of the artist

Detail of *Allosaurus* (1984-1986), a sculpture in resin by Stephen A. Czerkas; Natural History Museum of Los Angeles County, Los Angeles

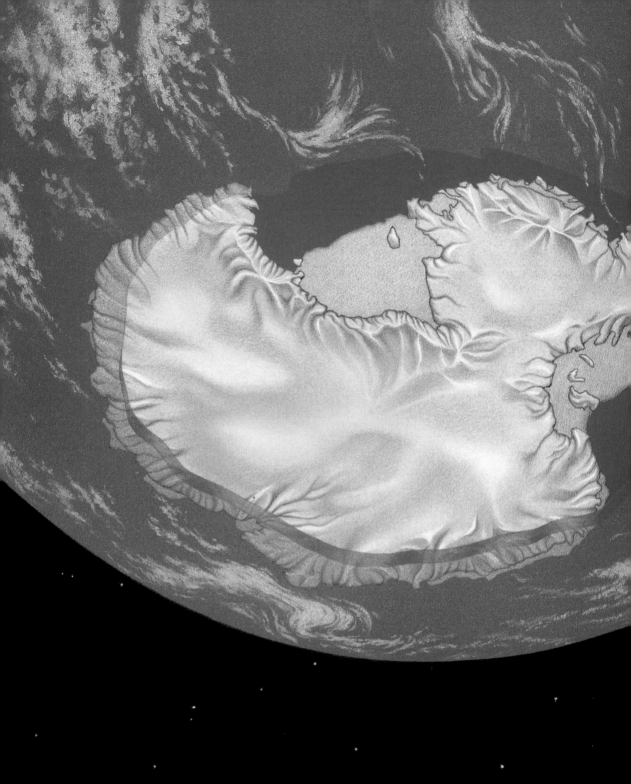

A drastic loss of ozone in the upper atmosphere over Antarctica is the first clear proof that this vital shield from ultraviolet rays is in danger worldwide.

The Hole in the Ozone Layer

BY RALPH J. CICERONE

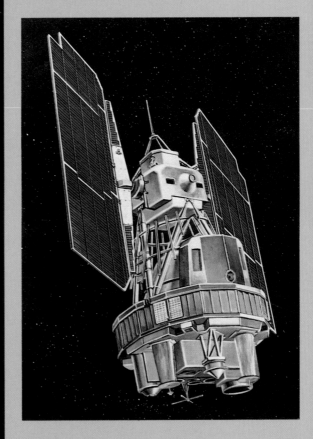

The author:
Ralph J. Cicerone is director of the Atmospheric Chemistry Division of the National Center for Atmospheric Research in Boulder, Colo.

Waiting for their plane at a New Zealand airport, a group of scientists were puzzling over a phenomenon with troubling implications for the entire world. A form of oxygen called ozone was mysteriously disappearing from the atmosphere over Antarctica to such a degree that researchers were talking about an "ozone hole"—a drastic thinning in the ozone layer that shields Earth from the sun's harmful ultraviolet radiation. The scientists were on their way to Antarctica to examine the conditions inside the hole and—they hoped—to pin down its causes.

A research expedition to frozen Antarctica is partly a wilderness adventure. In preparation for the project, the scientists had to learn how to cope with frigid winds and the darkness that prevails for all but a few hours a day from May through August. They also had to learn how to dress for survival in subzero temperatures and how to protect their scientific equipment from the extreme cold. Then they had to face the trip to Antarctica—an unusually difficult journey. Reaching McMurdo Station, a United States research base on Antarctica's Ross Island, involved a dangerous nine-hour flight from New Zealand. It was August 1987, when the scientists set out, but it was winter in Antarctica, and during winter Antarctica has only a brief period of daylight. They had to reach McMurdo by noon, while there was still some sunlight, because McMurdo's runway is on sea ice and has no lights. The group set off in two planes, and neither airplane carried enough fuel for a return flight. A decision had to be made at the midway point whether to continue to Antarctica or return to New Zealand—with no way of knowing whether a storm or fog would hit McMurdo before they arrived.

The expedition arrived safely, but the scientists were greeted by $-45°C$ ($-49°F.$) temperatures when they landed. During their two-month stay, the scientists learned to live with the dangers of extreme cold. They also gathered much important information about the damage to the ozone layer over Antarctica and the implications this may have for life on Earth.

Ozone in the upper atmosphere plays a crucial role in maintaining life on Earth because it absorbs ultraviolet light from the sun, providing a shield that prevents this radiation from passing through the atmosphere to Earth's surface. Ultraviolet radiation is biologically damaging. Scientists believe it causes human skin cancer and may suppress the human body's *immune* (disease-fighting) system. Ultraviolet radiation can also kill some small ocean-dwelling organisms, such as phytoplankton, and can harm crops, thereby reducing agricultural output.

The protective role of the ozone layer in the upper atmosphere is so vital that scientists believe life on land probably would not have evolved—and could not exist today—without it. If something were to cause this layer to disappear, life on Earth would be severely damaged. Eventually, the only remaining life might be found below the oceans' surface, where ultraviolet rays cannot penetrate.

In the atmosphere, molecules of oxygen and ozone together ab-

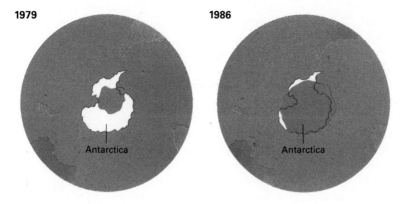

1979

1986

Antarctica

Antarctica

Each year since the mid-1970's, the ozone hole has grown larger during the Antarctic spring. In 1979, *far left*, the hole covered only part of Antarctica. By 1986, the hole extended over the entire Antarctic, *left*, which is larger than the continental United States, *below*.

Canada

United States

Mexico

sorb from 95 to 99.9 per cent of the sun's ultraviolet radiation. Only ozone, however, is effective at absorbing the most energetic ultraviolet light known as *UV-B*, which causes biological damage.

About 90 per cent of the ozone in Earth's atmosphere lies in the region called the *stratosphere* between 16 kilometers (10 miles) and 48 kilometers (30 miles) above Earth's surface. Ozone forms a kind of layer in the stratosphere, where it is more concentrated than anywhere else, but even there, it is relatively scarce. Its concentrations in the ozone layer are typically only 1 to 10 parts of ozone per 1 million parts of air, compared with about 210,000 parts of oxygen per 1 million parts of air.

Ozone also exists in the *troposphere*, the lowest part of the atmosphere, which extends from Earth's surface up to an altitude of 16 kilometers. In the troposphere, however, ozone is a pollutant, a component of smog caused by reactions between sunlight and car exhausts or industrial pollutants. High concentrations of ozone usually develop in large cities due to the reactions of nitrogen oxides and hydrocarbon gases from petroleum products burned as fuel. High ozone levels in smog can pose a health hazard to people with respiratory problems.

Until the early 1970's, scientists were more concerned about ozone pollution near Earth's surface than they were about ozone in the stratosphere. But since then, our understanding of ozone's role in protecting living things from harmful ultraviolet rays has grown. And so has our concern in the face of mounting evidence that the ozone layer surrounding Earth is thinning.

The first clear proof that the ozone layer is thinning came from frigid Antarctica. In 1985, atmospheric scientist Joe Farman and other members of the British Antarctic Survey released the results of 27 years of measurements of the ozone over Halley Bay, the site of a British research station on the Antarctic continent. Between the mid-1970's and 1984, the researchers found a 40 per cent decrease of ozone in the stratosphere over Antarctica. The decrease, however, occurred only in the months of September and October—springtime in Antarctica. These results were completely unexpected. No one had even conceived of such large and seasonal ozone losses due either to natural forces or to human causes. Yet the British results were convincing because their Antarctic ozone measurements, begun in 1957, had used reliable instruments.

Scientists measure ozone in several ways. The scientists at Halley Bay used a *spectrometer*, an instrument that breaks up sunlight into the rainbowlike range of colors known as the *spectrum*. Each color represents a certain wavelength of light. The spectrometer can be adjusted so that light of only a certain wavelength can pass through a special slit to be recorded by the instrument. We know what wavelengths correspond to ultraviolet light. We also know that ozone absorbs ultraviolet light more strongly at one wavelength than at another. By recording the ultraviolet light entering the slit at selected wavelengths, we can measure how much ultraviolet light is being absorbed and, therefore, deduce how much ozone is present. The greater the absorption, the greater the amount of ozone.

Ozone amounts vary naturally from day to day, from season to season, and from year to year. So proving that a sustained increase or decrease has occurred requires detailed observations over a long period of time. The British observations showed that regular variations took place from 1957 to 1974. But from 1975 through 1984, the observations disclosed that each spring there was less ozone than the spring before.

By 1986, scientists from the U.S. National Aeronautics and Space Administration (NASA) were able to confirm the British results. In 1978, NASA had begun using orbiting satellites to measure ozone. Instruments on the satellites determine the amount of ozone by measuring how much ultraviolet light from the sun is reflected back into space from Earth and the atmosphere. The difference between the amount given off by the sun and the amount reflected back by Earth and the atmosphere represents the amount of ultraviolet radiation absorbed by ozone in the atmosphere. NASA scientists examined their ozone data for the years 1979 to 1985 and found the same worsening springtime ozone hole over Antarctica. They also found that the hole covered the entire Antarctic continent, which is larger than the continental United States.

These alarming findings sparked the first of three expeditions specifically organized to investigate the ozone hole. The first group of scientists arrived at the McMurdo Station in mid-August 1986 and stayed until late October. Chemist Susan Solomon of the U.S. National Oceanic and Atmospheric Administration (NOAA) in Boulder, Colo., led the expedition of about 20 atmospheric scientists, which was called the National Ozone Expedition (NOZE). NOZE was sponsored by NASA, NOAA, the National Science Foundation, and the Chemical Manufacturers Association.

These scientists sent up balloons carrying meteorological instruments and also used ground-based equipment, such as special laser beams and spectrometers, to study the ozone layer. They measured ozone amounts and air temperatures in the stratosphere, as well as the numbers of condensed or frozen cloud particles and the concentrations of several key gases.

Two expeditions of scientists went to Antarctica in 1987, including the group that journeyed there in August. That effort, known as NOZE 1987, was similar to the 1986 expedition to McMurdo. There was, of course, no guarantee that the NOZE 1987 scientists would find an ozone hole, even though there had been one each previous year since 1975. But they found an even bigger, deeper, and longer-lasting hole.

Their findings were confirmed by the other 1987 expedition, called the Airborne Antarctic Ozone Experiment. This study was carried out entirely with aircraft. It was based in Punta Arenas, Chile, and was mounted simultaneously with the NOZE effort by about 150 other scientists and support personnel from five countries. From the Chile base, two NASA research aircraft carried instruments and scientists southward into the ozone hole. The aircraft, a converted DC-8 jet passenger plane and an ER-2 (a modified version of the U-2 spy plane), flew a total of 25 research missions covering about 175,000 kilometers (110,000 miles). The ER-2 often flew at altitudes as high as 19 kilometers (12 miles).

The DC-8 carried 7 instruments, along with a crew of scientists to monitor them. The ER-2 was equipped with 14 scientific instruments, all automated because there is no room for a scientific crew on that airplane. Meanwhile, NOZE scientists at several research stations on Antarctica launched research balloons that rose into the stratosphere.

Data from the instruments on aircraft, balloons, satellites, and the ground provided a clearer picture of the conditions inside the ozone hole. They showed that the ozone decline begins in August and accelerates in September and early October. When the hole is at its maximum depth, ozone concentrations decline about 50 per cent. At altitudes of 16 to 24 kilometers (10 to 15 miles) over Antarctica, an even greater loss of ozone was observed. During one day of observations in 1987, more than 90 per cent of the ozone at an altitude between 15 and 20 kilometers (9 to 12 miles) was gone.

The entire ozone hole drifts around the South Pole as part of a mass of extremely cold air called the *polar vortex*. Strong winds keep the vortex sealed off from the surrounding atmosphere as the vortex circulates around the South Pole, shifting position each day.

The air in the vortex is so cold that stratospheric clouds form. Elsewhere, clouds rarely form in the stratosphere because the air up so high is extremely dry. Water vapor is more abundant in the lower altitudes of the troposphere, so this is where clouds normally form. Because of the scarcity of water vapor, the air in the stratosphere must become extremely cold—about the temperature of dry ice, or

How Ozone Is Formed

Ozone is constantly being formed in Earth's atmosphere by the action of the sun's ultraviolet radiation on oxygen molecules.

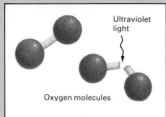

Oxygen molecules

Ultraviolet light

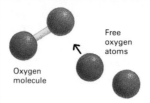

Oxygen molecule

Free oxygen atoms

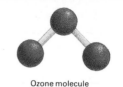

Ozone molecule

An ordinary oxygen molecule consists of two oxygen atoms. Ultraviolet light splits the molecules apart by breaking the bond between the atoms.

A highly reactive free oxygen atom then collides with another oxygen molecule.

The collision results in a temporary bond of three oxygen atoms to form an ozone molecule. Ozone is unstable, so ultraviolet light quickly breaks it up and the process begins again.

−80°C (−112°F.)—before water vapor can condense into ice particles to form clouds.

The data revealed that in late October the polar vortex breaks apart, and the hole begins to disappear. Air from the surrounding atmosphere rushes in, bringing ozone to the region where the vortex and the hole once existed.

From the Airborne Antarctic Ozone Experiment, scientists also learned that certain chemicals are present in abnormal amounts in the ozone hole. Chlorine monoxide, one of the principal chemicals suspected of destroying ozone, was present at concentrations 100 to 500 times greater than those found outside the ozone hole. The data showed an *inverse* (opposite) relationship between the amounts of ozone and the amounts of chlorine monoxide: the more chlorine monoxide, the less ozone.

This more detailed picture of the ozone hole has enabled scientists to analyze the various theories that attempt to explain its cause. We now know which theories can be supported by the observations and which cannot.

In order to understand these theories, it is necessary to know about the chemical and physical forces that control the ozone layer. Since the early 1970's, scientific understanding of these forces has been growing, but it is still far from complete. What we do know is that both natural processes and human activities can disturb the worldwide ozone layer.

First, let us examine the natural processes that produce and destroy ozone. Ozone molecules consist of three oxygen atoms (O_3). Normal oxygen in the air—the oxygen we breathe—is a molecule of two oxygen atoms (O_2). Ozone is produced in the stratosphere by the action of ultraviolet light from the sun on O_2 molecules. In 1930, British chemist Sydney Chapman was the first scientist to recognize that individual oxygen atoms are freed from their bonds in atmospheric O_2 molecules when struck by ultraviolet light. These free oxygen atoms then react very quickly with other oxygen molecules to form ozone molecules.

Because the sun gives off enormous amounts of ultraviolet radiation and because oxygen is the second most plentiful gas in the atmosphere after nitrogen, ultraviolet light continually creates more and more ozone. Measurements, however, show that ozone does not become increasingly plentiful. Chapman also recognized that some natural chemical reactions in the atmosphere can *destroy* ozone. One of these reactions occurs when a free oxygen atom combines with an ozone molecule to form two oxygen molecules. But this reaction alone cannot account for all of the natural ozone loss.

Not until the early 1970's were scientists able to identify additional mechanisms of ozone destruction. Then, scientists learned that small amounts of chemicals containing chlorine, nitrogen, or hydrogen can destroy ozone at a rapid rate because they act as *catalysts*. A catalyst is a substance that speeds up a chemical reaction while itself remaining unchanged. For example, two molecules containing nitrogen—nitric oxide and nitrogen dioxide—can participate as catalysts in ozone-destroying reactions repeatedly until each molecule has helped destroy more than 10,000 ozone molecules. Even though these nitrogen compounds are rare in the stratosphere, their destructive catalytic action counterbalances a large percentage of the sun's ozone production.

The destruction of ozone by nitrogen oxides is mainly a result of natural processes. A gaseous nitrogen compound—nitrous oxide—originates at Earth's surface where microbes process nitrogen-containing compounds in soil. Nitrous oxide rises into the stratosphere where nitric oxide forms from it and interacts with the ozone layer. The end result of these complex natural processes has been a balance in the rate of ozone production and destruction. Now we have evidence that human activities are upsetting that balance.

In 1974, chemists Mario J. Molina and F. Sherwood Rowland of the University of California at Irvine showed how a group of industrial chemicals called *chlorofluorocarbons* (CFC's) could destroy ozone. CFC's are widely used in packaging and insulating foams, as cooling fluids in refrigerators and air conditioners, as solvents in the electronics industry, and in most countries of the world as propellants in aerosol spray cans. The CFC molecules from these industrial products rise unhindered through the troposphere into the stratosphere, a journey that takes about 7 to 10 years. In the troposphere, there is no natural process for removing CFC's from the air. They are unaffected by the troposphere's normal air-cleaning mechanisms—such as rainfall.

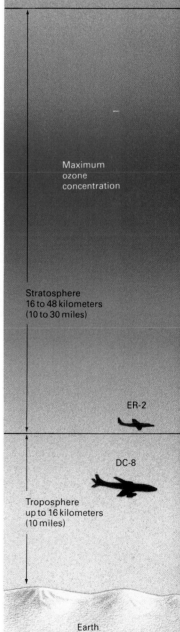

Where the Ozone Layer Is
About 90 per cent of the ozone in Earth's atmosphere is concentrated in a region known as the *stratosphere,* about 16 to 48 kilometers (10 to 30 miles) above Earth's surface.

Maximum ozone concentration

Stratosphere
16 to 48 kilometers
(10 to 30 miles)

ER-2

DC-8

Troposphere
up to 16 kilometers
(10 miles)

Earth

Probing the Atmosphere over Antarctica

Scientists used a variety of research tools to gather data on conditions in the ozone hole in 1987. These tools included a high-altitude airplane, the ER-2, *below;* a ground-based laser to measure the amount of ozone, *right;* and a balloon equipped with scientific instruments, *opposite page.* An instrument on the ER-2 detected abnormally high amounts of chlorine gas, indicating industrial chemicals caused the hole.

Once these chemicals reach the stratosphere, ultraviolet light can free chlorine atoms from CFC molecules. Chlorine—either as a single chlorine atom or combined with an oxygen atom to form chlorine monoxide—is an even more effective destroyer of ozone than nitric oxide. Each chlorine atom can carry out its destructive chain reaction from 10,000 to 100,000 times over 75 to 130 years before it finally reacts with other chemicals and becomes inactive.

Since 1974, scientists have been studying other industrial chemicals to evaluate their potential for harming the ozone layer. For example, laboratory studies show that bromine-containing gases can act as catalysts to reduce stratospheric ozone. Bromine is found in certain kinds of specialized fire extinguishers used in the computer industry and in some agricultural pesticides.

But what role, if any, do these chemicals play in the rapid seasonal loss of ozone over Antarctica? Many theories have been proposed.

Some maintain that chlorine from CFC's has caused the hole. Other theories propose that the hole is a result of various wind and weather conditions unique to Antarctica. Still others argue that the hole is due to electrically charged particles from the sun.

The findings from the recent Antarctic expeditions support the theory that chlorine is to blame. But the same findings also indicate that the rate of ozone destruction caused by chlorine is increased by meteorological conditions unique to Antarctica during the spring months of September and October. To begin with, the stratosphere over Antarctica is distinctive in the winter and spring. It is the coldest region of the entire stratosphere. The vortex that forms there is more regular and persistent than the vortex that forms over the Arctic, another cold region. There are far more polar stratospheric clouds in the Antarctic than in the Arctic. And where there are stratospheric clouds, there is less ozone.

How Ozone Is Destroyed by Chlorofluorocarbons

Chemicals called chlorofluorocarbons (CFC's) enter the atmosphere as a result of their use in industry. Scientists have learned that ultraviolet light reacts with CFC's to destroy ozone. This process may be responsible for the ozone hole over Antarctica.

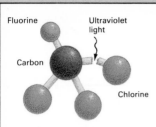

Chlorofluorocarbon molecule

A CFC molecule consists of atoms of chlorine, fluorine, and carbon. Ultraviolet light can break the bonds that attach chlorine atoms.

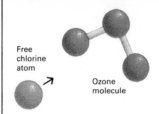

A free chlorine atom reacts easily with other molecules. When it collides with an ozone molecule, it can break up the molecule by stripping away an oxygen atom.

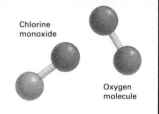

The chlorine atom combines with the oxygen atom to form chlorine monoxide. The other two oxygen atoms form pure oxygen gas.

Rare polar stratospheric clouds may be linked to ozone destruction. Such clouds can form in the stratosphere over Antarctica because of the extreme cold. In these clouds, nitrogen oxides can be trapped in icy cloud particles. Although nitrogen oxides alone can destroy ozone, they often combine with chlorine to form a compound that is harmless to ozone. But when nitrogen oxides are trapped in icy cloud particles, this compound cannot be formed, so more chlorine is available to destroy ozone.

Because of the strong associations between the stratospheric clouds and ozone loss, several groups of scientists in the United States and Europe began to investigate whether icy particles within the clouds could be a contributing factor. When certain chemicals are in the form of gases, reactions between them occur slowly. But when the same chemicals freeze, they have solid surfaces. For reasons that are not yet completely understood, the surfaces speed up the chemical reactions. Thus, the presence of icy particles in the clouds could contribute to the rapid loss of ozone. Also, when gaseous nitrogen oxides freeze, they are no longer able to combine with chlorine, thereby freeing chlorine atoms to destroy ozone.

In November 1987, chemists Mario J. Molina and Luisa Molina at the California Institute of Technology's Jet Propulsion Laboratory in Pasadena and Margaret Tolbert and David Golden, working independently at the Stanford Research Institute, showed through laboratory experiments that chemical reactions involving ice particles can free chlorine atoms from such chemicals as hydrogen chloride. At the same time, the researchers found that these particles can trap nitrogen dioxide gas, so that there is less of it in the atmosphere. These laboratory results support data from the expeditions that showed high amounts of atmospheric chlorine and small amounts of hydrogen chloride and nitrogen dioxide.

The exact manner in which chlorine is released in these chemical reactions and the precise chain of reactions that leads to ozone destruction, however, is still unclear. Finding out will enable us to measure the rate of ozone destruction so that we can predict how much the hole will grow.

Two of the uses of CFC's have been in packaging, such as fast-food containers, *top,* and as a refrigerant in refrigerators, *above.* In 1988, a group of packagers said they would stop using most CFC's.

Other theories that cannot yet be completely ruled out hold that wind circulation unique to the springtime Antarctic is the cause of the hole. Some meteorologists propose, for example, that ozone-poor air from the troposphere circulates into the stratospheric vortex and pushes out ozone-rich air from the vortex. The ozone-rich air then disperses into other regions of the atmosphere. Other meteorologists think that some as-yet-unknown event has cut off the normal supply of ozone to the South Pole from other regions of Earth's atmosphere. According to these theories, ozone is not being destroyed but is only being redistributed by natural causes. Data from the Antarctic expeditions, however, cast doubt on the idea that ozone-poor air is rising into the vortex from the troposphere. If this was happening, certain chemicals common to tropospheric air would also rise into the vortex, but scientists have not detected that happening. These theories shed light on why the hole occurs only during the Antarctic spring but not why the hole developed between 1975 and 1987. Why was there no hole between 1957, when the first Antarctic ozone measurements were made, and 1974? Another theory—that electrically charged particles from the sun lead to ozone destruction—was disproven by the Antarctic expeditions.

A Threat to Life in Antarctica?

If there is no ozone to block it, ultraviolet radiation from the sun could harm life on Antarctica. Seals, *below right,* and penguins, *right,* both feed on krill, *below,* which in turn feed on microscopic plants called phytoplankton, the base of Antarctica's food web. And phytoplankton are most vulnerable to ultraviolet rays.

The scientific quest to learn the cause of the ozone hole is vitally important. Without a clear knowledge of why this phenomenon is occurring, we will not be able to predict whether the hole will grow and spread northward or decline and fade away. Nor will we be able to predict whether other atmospheric regions, such as that above the North Pole, will develop a similar hole.

If the explanation involves CFC's, as is now thought, additional scientific research will be needed to evaluate how continuing CFC usage might affect the atmosphere and life forms on Earth. Such research, for example, should assess the impact of the hole on animal life in Antarctica. There is no evidence yet that ultraviolet radiation coming through the hole has damaged animal life there, possibly because of the low position of the sun in the winter sky. But if the hole lasts increasingly longer during each Antarctic spring, as the sun rises higher above the horizon, more ultraviolet radiation will penetrate the atmosphere. Animal life on and around Antarctica may be damaged both directly—by ultraviolet rays—and indirectly, through radiation damage to the food web. Human life is also a source of concern. Scientific researchers on Antarctica and people living in southern Chile could be endangered.

Scientists also need to explore whether other human-caused changes to the atmosphere may damage the ozone layer. For example, the burning of fossil fuels—such as coal and oil—has increased the amount of carbon dioxide and nitrous oxide in the atmosphere. CFC's, carbon dioxide, and nitrous oxide are all known as *greenhouse gases* because their presence in the atmosphere blocks heat radiation from escaping into space, thus warming Earth's surface and the troposphere, much like the glass in a greenhouse keeps the greenhouse warm. Greenhouse gases warm the troposphere, but because they prevent heat from escaping, they also cool the stratosphere. The cooling of the global stratosphere could create more stratospheric clouds like those occurring over Antarctica, and this, in turn, could increase the rate of ozone destruction.

The growing concern about CFC's and other artificial chemicals has already led to an international agreement to protect the ozone layer. On Sept. 16, 1987, representatives of 24 nations, including Australia, Canada, Great Britain, and the United States, met in Montreal, Canada, and signed a tentative accord agreeing to limit the production of CFC's and bromine-containing chemicals. The draft treaty, due to take effect in January 1989, calls for a freeze on the production of CFC's at 1986 levels and a gradual 50 per cent reduction in their use by 1999. The agreement provides for periodic reviews of new research results so that the regulations can be strengthened or relaxed, as needed. This feature recognizes that our knowledge about the ozone hole and its causes is still imperfect and that the future could hold more surprises. The U.S. Senate ratified the treaty on March 14, 1988.

On March 15, 1988, a panel of more than 100 scientists convened by NASA confirmed that ozone loss was a global problem and was not restricted to Antarctica. The panel reported a decline in stratospheric ozone ranging from 1.7 to 3 per cent over the Northern Hemisphere and a similar decline over the Southern Hemisphere between 1969 and 1986.

The panel's report called dramatic attention to the release of CFC's into the atmosphere because it stated that CFC's were the primary cause of the ozone hole over Antarctica and the likely cause of the ozone loss worldwide. In response to this finding, E. I. du Pont de Nemours & Company of Wilmington, Del., which manufactures one-fourth of the world's CFC's, announced on March 24, 1988, that it would soon stop producing these chemicals.

Although there is much we do not know, we have begun to see how human activities can disturb the delicate balance of life-supporting gases in this shell of air we call the atmosphere. We have discovered the potentially devastating consequences these changes may have for the entire planet. We need to make faster progress, however, in evaluating the impact of human activities and in setting safe and tolerable limits on those activities.

Once near extinction, the adaptable white-tailed deer have multiplied until they may harm themselves, their environment, and their human neighbors.

Has Success Spoiled the Whitetail?

BY JEAN M. LANG

Trees were bare and snow blanketed the ground as the helicopter hovered and dipped over the backyards of River Hills, Wis. Against the snow, the startled white-tailed deer were easy to spot, fleeing from one yard to the next. As the animals ran, their tails stood straight up, showing the flash of white on the underside that gives these deer, the most common deer in North America, their name.

River Hills, a prosperous suburb of Milwaukee, is overwhelmed with whitetails. Its spacious lots along the wooded banks of the Milwaukee River create an ideal haven for the deer.

The helicopter survey, in early 1986, tallied 159 deer roaming through the 14-square-kilometer (5.5-square-mile) village. By mid-1987, the herd had grown to 300 animals, and homeowners complained of damage to gardens and shrubbery.

The sheriff's office reported 36 costly collisions between deer and automobiles on village roads during 1987.

Accidents involving deer and cars take place regularly across the United States and Canada. In the first six months of 1987, motorists on Illinois state roads reported 2,385 collisions with deer, including 98 that resulted in injury to the motorist. Wisconsin and Pennsylvania each reported more than 32,000 deer accidents in 1986. And almost all the deer hit by cars are killed.

Cars are not the only vehicles involved in accidents with deer. In March 1987, a United Airlines 737 jet landing at Chicago's O'Hare International Airport hit a white-tailed deer on the runway. The deer was one of about 70 that—undaunted by thundering jets—had taken up residence on the grounds of one of the busiest airports in the United States.

White-tailed deer also are causing damage to food crops. For example, to the north of River Hills in picturesque Door County, apple growers struggle to keep whitetails from feeding on the leaves, fruit, and twigs of their orchards. In 1984, the growers reported $200,000 worth of damage by deer. Statewide, Wisconsin farmers claimed $37 million in crop losses due to deer in that year.

Concerns have also been raised about the relationship between deer populations and Lyme disease, a serious illness that produces symptoms similar to arthritis. One type of tick that infests deer may transmit Lyme disease to human beings.

From New Jersey to Florida and from Minnesota to Colorado, the white-tailed deer is coming into increasing conflict with human beings and their activities. Has the favorite wildlife animal of many Americans become a pest? Are its numbers out of control? And how has this shy creature come to be so bold in densely populated suburbs, on farmland, and even in busy airports?

Wildlife researchers say the answers are complex. The white-tailed deer, which has the scientific name *Odocoileus virginianus*, is thriving at population levels not seen in almost 100 years. At the same time, agricultural practices and suburban sprawl are destroying many of the wooded areas that provide whitetail habitats. Displaced from their natural environment, the deer become increasingly dependent on crops and gardens for food.

For a variety of reasons, North Americans have generally tolerated and even encouraged large populations of deer in their midst. A glimpse of an antlered buck, a graceful doe, or a spotted fawn is always a delight. In much of the United States, the whitetail is the only large wild animal that people see regularly. Whitetails also have great economic value as meat and trophy animals for hunters.

The white-tailed deer herd in the United States and Canada today numbers more than 18 million animals. This is a vast increase over the population of 350,000 to 500,000 deer that biologists estimate were scattered across the continent around 1900. But some scientists

The author:
Jean M. Lang is director of the Science Writing Program of the University-Industry Research Program at the University of Wisconsin in Madison.

The decline and recovery of the white-tailed deer

Hunters in the 1800's, *above,* killed so many white-tailed deer for meat and trophy animals that the deer were nearly wiped out. Today, game laws limit the number of whitetails that hunters can shoot, and the deer have adapted so well to human neighbors that they even make their homes in densely populated suburbs, *right.*

believe today's herd is only about half the number of deer present in the 1600's, before colonial times. And recent calculations for all of North America suggest that the early deer population numbered between 24 million and 38 million.

The Indian tribes of eastern North America depended heavily on the whitetail for meat and hides. Anthropologists who investigated the remains of refuse dumps left by Native Americans prior to European contact calculate that venison made up 50 to 90 per cent of the meat eaten by eastern tribes. The Indians also used deerskin to make containers, shelters, fishing gear, clothing, even glue.

After Europeans colonized eastern North America in the 1600's, they pressed westward, bringing great changes to the landscape and

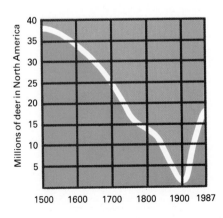

Before Europeans colonized North America in the 1600's, the white-tailed deer population may have numbered as many as 38 million. Hunters killed so many deer for food and for sport that the whitetail population dropped to fewer than 500,000 by 1900. After the passage of game laws to protect the deer, the number of whitetails rebounded to nearly half the former level.

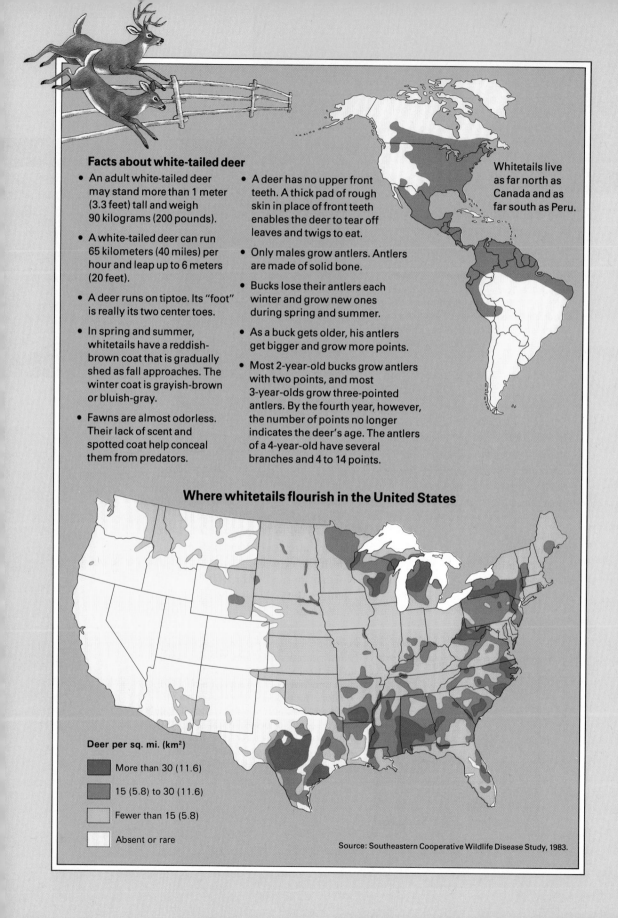

Facts about white-tailed deer

- An adult white-tailed deer may stand more than 1 meter (3.3 feet) tall and weigh 90 kilograms (200 pounds).

- A white-tailed deer can run 65 kilometers (40 miles) per hour and leap up to 6 meters (20 feet).

- A deer runs on tiptoe. Its "foot" is really its two center toes.

- In spring and summer, whitetails have a reddish-brown coat that is gradually shed as fall approaches. The winter coat is grayish-brown or bluish-gray.

- Fawns are almost odorless. Their lack of scent and spotted coat help conceal them from predators.

- A deer has no upper front teeth. A thick pad of rough skin in place of front teeth enables the deer to tear off leaves and twigs to eat.

- Only males grow antlers. Antlers are made of solid bone.

- Bucks lose their antlers each winter and grow new ones during spring and summer.

- As a buck gets older, his antlers get bigger and grow more points.

- Most 2-year-old bucks grow antlers with two points, and most 3-year-olds grow three-pointed antlers. By the fourth year, however, the number of points no longer indicates the deer's age. The antlers of a 4-year-old have several branches and 4 to 14 points.

Whitetails live as far north as Canada and as far south as Peru.

Where whitetails flourish in the United States

Deer per sq. mi. (km²)

- More than 30 (11.6)
- 15 (5.8) to 30 (11.6)
- Fewer than 15 (5.8)
- Absent or rare

Source: Southeastern Cooperative Wildlife Disease Study, 1983.

its wildlife. Clearing and fencing land, they steadily encroached on deer habitats while also hunting the whitetail for meat and hides.

Whitetail numbers steadily fell as the human population grew, especially after 1850. By 1900, when the white-tailed deer had been exterminated from much of its range, people realized that the animals had to be protected by law if the species was to survive.

For the following 85 years, deer-management policies focused on promoting the growth of the once-decimated whitetail population. Many states banned deer hunting indefinitely and launched programs to bring whitetails back into rural areas. Even though the deer's natural predators, such as wolves and mountain lions, had nearly disappeared from eastern North America, it still took many years for the deer populations to recover. In 1957, for example, Illinois had its first deer-hunting season in 56 years. Today, the whitetail is again found in healthy numbers from the Atlantic Coast west to the Rocky Mountains, and from the Arctic Circle in Canada south into Central and South America.

The comeback of the white-tailed deer was aided by the fact that it is one of the most adaptable large animals. With the ability to live in a variety of habitats, versatile food habits, a talent for quickly learning new behavior patterns, a high reproductive rate, and a rich genetic makeup, the whitetail has readily adapted to an increasingly urbanized environment.

Because the whitetail's needs are simple—adequate water and food, protection from frigid weather and deep snows, and cover in which to hide from predators—it can make its home in almost any terrain. The deer's range requirements are modest. In many parts of the Midwestern and Eastern United States, a whitetail may spend its entire life in an area of only 1 to 2 square miles (2.6 to 5.2 square kilometers). The deer's favorite habitats are areas biologists call *edge communities*, where one vegetation type, such as a forest, meets another, such as a meadow. These areas provide an abundance of food and cover for whitetails. Edge communities may occur in wooded acreage next to farmland; brushy land; lakeshores; suburban lots; and many city and county parks.

A taste for many types of plants also has helped the deer prosper in a changing landscape. Biologists have learned what whitetails eat by observing deer in confined preserves, by examining the stomach contents of deer killed on the road, and by accompanying tame deer as they browse in a natural environment. In Louisiana, for example, wildlife biologists have found that whitetails feed on at least 81 plant species. In Texas, a deer's diet may include cactus; in Florida, low-growing palm trees and persimmons; and in Michigan, cherries.

The whitetail's chief food is *browse*, a term that biologists use for the edible parts of woody plants, including leaves, flowers, fruits, and tender stems. The term *browse* also describes the deer's method of eating, which is to nibble here and there from many plants.

Despite its smorgasbord approach to dining, the white-tailed deer is discriminating and efficient at selecting the most nutritious diet. Because the nutritive value of a plant, and even different parts of the same plant, varies with the season, the whitetail switches frequently from one food to another as the year progresses. In early spring, the whitetail grazes on the first tender green grasses and herbs. A little later, it turns to browse and to broad-leaved plants such as buttercup and aster. In autumn, the deer's diet shifts to wild fruits and nuts, and, in agricultural areas, to corn and other grains. Acorns and other nuts are favorite autumn high-energy foods that the deer can store as fat to carry them through the active fall breeding season and, in northern areas, the winter's cold.

The deer's complex stomach allows it to digest plant tissues that many other animals cannot. A deer's stomach, like a cow's, has four chambers. The first chamber, called the *rumen*—where food collects immediately after being swallowed—contains millions of microorganisms that attack and predigest the food. After the food has been partly digested, stomach muscles send it back up into the deer's

Whitetails have multiplied so successfully that they are becoming a problem to their human neighbors. The deer destroy food crops, *left,* and cause highway accidents in which many cars are damaged and many deer are killed, *below.*

mouth. The deer rechews this food, called *cud*. The cud is then swallowed and goes to the other parts of the stomach to be completely digested.

The rumen microorganisms enable deer to live on the woody parts of plants that otherwise would be undigestible. Woody plant material, however, is low in nutrients. During severe winters or droughts, when deer can find only woody foods, they may slowly starve to death even though their rumens are full.

The way white-tailed deer raise their young and learn from one another are other important factors in the deer's success. Most white-tail fawns are born between May and early July. Fawns stay with their mothers for about a year, or until the doe's next fawns are born. Then the doe ignores her yearlings, as the 1-year-olds are called, or drives them away. These deer sometimes travel long distances. By tracking deer fitted with collars containing tiny transmitters that give off a steady radio signal, scientists have learned that some yearlings, particularly bucks, may travel 30 to 160 kilometers (20 to 100 miles) to establish new home ranges. After the doe's new fawns are weaned, however, her female yearlings—sometimes with fawns of their own—may rejoin her to form a three-generation family group. Except for a brief period during the mating season, males and females live in separate groups or alone.

During the year that whitetail fawns live with their mother, they learn much of the behavior they need to survive. For example, by copying their mother's behavior, they learn to eat a variety of foods. Orrin J. Rongstad, a wildlife biologist at the University of Wisconsin-Madison, notes that the mother can teach them new behaviors as well. If an adventurous doe ventures into an orchard or a wooded suburb, for example, her fawns will follow her—and will

In some areas, the white-tail population has increased beyond the environment's ability to support it. The deer themselves, like this starving fawn, suffer because there is not enough food for all the deer.

likely pass the habit of feeding there on to their own offspring. As the family multiplies, the habit may become a problem.

All it takes is for one doe in a family group to try something different, says Rongstad, and a large part of a local deer population may show the same behavior within a few years. Deer learn quickly. Biologists have noticed, for example, that whitetails in some areas are drawn to the sound of a chain saw. This signals to the deer that lopped-off branches will be available for browsing.

A high reproductive rate is another important factor in the whitetail's success. With a nutritious food supply, a doe will generally produce a single fawn in her first year of reproduction and thereafter will have twins every year, or occasionally triplets.

The whitetail's reproductive potential is illustrated by the experiences on the George Reserve, a wildlife study area in southern Michigan. The 464-hectare (1,146-acre) area was once the estate of wealthy industrialist Colonel Edwin S. George. In 1928, when all the whitetails in that region had been killed, George built a tall, deer-proof fence around his estate and brought in two bucks and four does. Five years later, after George had donated the land to the University of Michigan for research purposes, there were at least 160 deer on the reserve.

Working together with the deer's high reproductive rate is a rich gene pool. Genes, the basic unit of heredity, determine what characteristics an individual will have. Most genes have at least one alternate form, but some genes have three, four, or more. Different forms of the same gene are called *alleles*. When many of a species' genes have multiple alleles, the species as a whole has a large gene pool, or storehouse, to draw upon.

Genes *code for* (direct the production of) the hundreds of proteins made by an organism. Since 1968, scientists have examined the genes associated with some 35 of the proteins found in the blood and other tissues of white-tailed deer. By comparing the proteins of

Deer can learn from one another. A mature white-tail doe, *below,* leads a three-generation family group consisting of her fawns, her adult daughters, and their fawns into a new habitat. Deer may become pests when an adventurous doe leads her group into a park, a farm, or an orchard where food is plentiful.

Researchers follow a leashed deer, *above,* to see what it eats. Whitetails will eat a variety of foods—from apples in an orchard, *right,* to the contents of a bird feeder, *below.* This diverse diet has been a large factor in their success.

one whitetail with those of another, researchers can determine which genes the animals hold in common, how close their genetic relationship is, and how many different forms of the same gene exist in the population. They have found that 27 of those genes have at least two alleles, and that 11 genes have three or more alleles. Some biologists have suggested that whitetails may have the highest level of genetic variability of any large, hoofed animal.

Such genetic diversity helps the species quickly adapt to new or changing environments. It also ensures that some animals will survive epidemics or other crises and reestablish the population.

Considering all the factors operating in the whitetail's favor, the deer should be even more abundant than they are. What keeps them in check? Scientists have found that several forces work together to curb whitetail population growth.

For example, wildlife biologists have discovered links between the whitetail's reproduction and the quality of its diet. When the food supply is only marginally sufficient, females do not begin reproducing until they are at least 1½ years old.

With adequate nutrition, females may reach sexual maturity and breed at the age of 7 months. In Iowa, for example, where high-protein crops such as alfalfa, corn, and soybeans make up most of the whitetail's diet, 82 per cent of the females are fertile in their first year of life. Better-fed does breed earlier in the fall, deliver fewer stillborn offspring, and produce more twins. Their fawns also have higher survival rates.

In the early 1980's, wildlife biologists Louis J. Verme and John J. Ozoga of the Michigan Department of Natural Resources in Shingleton discovered another aspect of the relationship between diet and reproduction. They found that when does were on a poor diet, 72 per cent of their fawns were male. When does were on a good diet, only 43 per cent of their offspring were male. In addition, when does mated earlier in the breeding season—as is likely when

Scientists use various methods to study white-tailed deer. A special collar equipped with a radio transmitter, *above,* enables biologists to track the range of a deer. To estimate the future deer population, researchers take a blood sample from a doe, *right,* to find out if she is pregnant.

bucks are abundant—they produced more female fawns. When does mated later in the season—an indication of a shortage of bucks—their fawns were more likely to be male. Each of these self-regulating factors helps reduce the number of does when population levels are too high. And fewer does mean fewer fawns.

These built-in population controls, however, are weak ones. In the absence of hunting, life-threatening weather, and natural predators such as wolves, whitetails can multiply so rapidly that they consume all the available food and inflict extensive damage on the environment before their population is reduced by starvation or disease. A forest damaged by overbrowsing, for example, requires years to repair itself and in the meantime provides less food and cover to other wildlife species, especially birds and small mammals. Overpopulation is especially a problem when deer find their way into wooded areas, such as parks and arboretums, that are surrounded by urban landscape. Protected from hunters and predators on these "wilderness islands," the deer population explodes, causing serious damage to prized vegetation.

Weather—severe cold, deep snow, floods, and drought—can also be a major factor in keeping the deer population down. In northern areas, 20 to 25 per cent of a healthy herd may die during a particularly severe winter. Although many states provide supplemental winter feed for hungry deer herds, most biologists agree that this is not a good long-term solution. It does not solve the basic problem of a discrepancy between the size of the herd and the number of deer that the habitat can support.

Some people have suggested that deer problems would disappear if more wolves and other large predators were around. But predators other than human beings usually have only a moderate impact on the herd. Researchers find that an adult mountain lion may kill from 18 to 50 whitetails per year. A wolf kills an average of 15 to 20 deer annually. Even in remote wilderness areas, there are seldom enough wolves to control the deer population. Moreover, if enough wolves were brought into an area to significantly affect deer numbers, they would likely also prey on young livestock and even household pets—and probably frighten the local residents.

Most wildlife management experts believe that hunting, as a replacement for natural predators, is the most practical deer-management method. Hunting, however, must be carefully controlled to achieve the desired results.

State game managers carefully calculate the number and types of hunting permits allotted to different sectors of a state, based on each sector's whitetail population. The introduction of computers in the 1970's and 1980's has made such planning more effective. In 1982, U.S. hunters legally killed about 2.6 million whitetails.

In some areas, human settlement is too dense for hunting to be safe, or townspeople do not want to kill local deer even though they are pests. One solution is to relocate the deer to other areas. Relocation requires that deer be driven into a net or lured into a trap. Then they must be given tranquilizers to keep them quiet during the move. Trapping and tranquilization can be hard on the animals. Wildlife biologists claim this results in death from injuries or stress for about 25 per cent of the relocated deer. Relocation is also a costly process.

And transporting deer to a new range can make them vulnerable to predators, starvation, and accidents. Biologists followed the

State game managers weigh a captured whitetail. Information about the deers' size and condition in a particular area helps game managers plan hunting quotas that will maintain a stable, healthy deer population at levels the environment can support.

Feelings for and against deer hunting run strong. Hunters, *above,* regard hunting as a source of food, a fair contest between hunter and hunted, and a means of wildlife management. Opponents of hunting strap an effigy of a hunter to their car, *right,* to protest what they believe is a cruel practice.

movements of radio-collared black-tailed deer—close relatives of white-tailed deer—that were transported from San Francisco Bay's Angel Island to northern California in 1982. Within a year, 85 per cent of the radio-collared deer had died from hunting, accidents, and other causes. Of the 203 deer removed from the island, biologists believe, only a handful survived.

Another often-proposed strategy is to sterilize urban whitetails to stabilize their populations. Some biologists believe that small groups of deer in suburban areas could be trapped and given antifertility implants that would last up to three years. Treating 30 to 50 per cent of the females would stop population growth, but the use of implants is expensive and not yet tested.

Although the most efficient control continues to be hunting, opposition to hunting is on the rise. A national survey in the United States in the 1970's showed that about half the general public opposed hunting. Some animal-rights groups acknowledge the need to kill animals that are destroying their own environment. Other groups believe that all hunting is cruel. Sport hunting, they say, is immoral in an era when society no longer relies on wildlife for food. Acting on their principles, these organizations often go to court to block proposed hunts on public property.

Thomas A. Heberlein, a rural sociologist at the University of Wisconsin-Madison, has studied the sociology of hunters and hunting for many years. Heberlein attributes the widespread opposition to hunting to the fact that fewer people today grow up in rural communities or on farms, where the killing of livestock is a routine practice and the hunting of game is an accepted extension of that activity. But today the country is also home to many former city dwellers who seek its rural solitude and wildlife. Although their properties may be overpopulated with deer, many of these landowners forbid hunting. And they resent the disruption and endangerment that hunters briefly bring to the community.

Another source of friction, Heberlein says, is that some hunters have never been taught respect for property rights or the common courtesies of hunting. He believes that mandatory training courses teaching good manners, marksmanship, and responsible gun-handling are needed to increase public acceptance of hunters.

Mark A. LaBarbera, executive vice president of the North American Hunting Club, acknowledges "unsportsmanlike actions" by "a very small minority." But LaBarbera says, "The majority of hunters are safe, courteous, and ethical."

In addition, hunters make a major contribution to the economy. In 1980, hunting of all kinds contributed $8.5 billion to the U.S. economy, mainly for hunters' equipment, travel, and lodging. Millions of dollars collected annually from hunting licenses and special excise taxes on sporting goods fund wildlife restoration projects.

In many states, game managers are expanding the hunt with more licenses, longer seasons, or both, to bring deer numbers down to a stable and healthy level that will not harm the environment or cause damage to crops and gardens. Reaching this goal will require better hunter-landowner relations. Game managers agree that many of the deer that damage crops, invade suburbs, and are hit by cars come from nearby rural lands that are closed to hunting.

Deer nuisance problems will probably increase. As suburbs and farms push out into natural deer habitat, more deer will adapt to living where human population density is too high for hunting. Deer fences, repellents, or more creative solutions will be needed.

As we try to find ways to enable the white-tailed deer to coexist peacefully with human beings, however, we must keep in mind that "solutions" sometimes create more problems. In the case of the white-tailed deer, the initial problem was their near-extinction. The seemingly simple, straightforward solution to this problem—protecting the deer—resulted in an overabundance of whitetails. The deer themselves became a problem to society. And because the deer have adapted so well to a settled landscape, it may be—as Frank Haberland, game manager for the Wisconsin Department of Natural Resources, says—that "whitetail management has become, and will continue to be, more of a social than a biological problem."

For further reading:

Halls, Lowell K., ed. *White-Tailed Deer: Ecology and Management.* Stackpole Books, 1984.

McClung, Robert M. *Whitetail.* Morrow, 1987.

Wemmer, Christen. *Biology and Management of the Cervidae.* Smithsonian Institution Press, 1987.

An astounding scientific breakthrough promises to propel the electrical revolution into areas of technology that we can barely imagine—and beyond.

Plugging into Superconductors

BY ARTHUR FISHER

The author:
Arthur Fisher is science and technology editor of *Popular Science* magazine and author of the Special Report THE MICROCHIP—A MINIATURE MARVEL in the 1988 edition of *Science Year.*

Imagine that this is the year 2008.

■ A train whizzes along above its track on a cushion of electromagnetic force, completing its regular 320-kilometer (200-mile) run from New York City to Washington, D.C., in just 30 minutes.

■ A desktop computer in five minutes solves a problem in rocket design that took supercomputers five weeks to solve in 1988.

■ Underground cables made of exotic materials unknown in 1988 transmit electricity from the coal-rich Western United States to the power-hungry East—with minimal loss of power.

Can we look forward realistically to such amazing developments in a mere 20 years? The answer could very possibly be yes, according to chemist Alan Schriesheim, director of the Argonne National Laboratory, an energy-research facility near Chicago. Such technological miracles could be made possible by a scientific breakthrough he describes as being as important as the invention of the transistor or the laser. In 1986, 1987, and 1988, scientists discovered new groups of *superconductors*, materials that offer no resistance to the flow of electricity. The scientists who made the first of these discoveries, physicist K. Alex Müller and crystallographer J. Georg Bednorz of the International Business Machines Corporation (IBM) Research Center in Zurich, Switzerland, shared the 1987 Nobel Prize in physics for their work.

The excitement about the new superconductors centers on their ability to overcome electrical resistance. Because of resistance, some of the electric energy flowing through an ordinary conductor, such as a copper wire, is transformed into heat energy along the way. As a result, less electric energy emerges from the wire than went into it. This loss of energy does not occur in a wire made of a superconducting material.

Superconductivity itself is not new to scientists; it was first detected in 1911. But superconductors discovered before 1986 do not lose their resistance until they have been cooled to *critical temperatures* ranging from near *absolute zero* ($-273.15°C$ or $-459.67°F.$) up to $-250°C$ ($-418°F.$). These superconductors are expensive to use because they are very expensive to cool. Therefore they are used in only a few machines—such as high-powered atom smashers and sophisticated medical imaging devices.

The new materials are so exciting because they have critical temperatures higher than scientists had thought possible. These materials require much less expensive cooling equipment to reach these temperatures.

Most electrical equipment today still uses wires made of copper and certain other metals that are called *conductors,* because they conduct, or carry, electricity relatively efficiently. Two basic factors determine whether a material is a good conductor: first, the type of atoms that make up the material, and second, how the atoms are arranged. An atom of any material consists of one or more negatively charged particles called *electrons* orbiting a positively charged nucleus. How tightly the electrons are bound to the nucleus determines whether the material can conduct *electric current*, a stream of flowing electrons. In a good conductor, the electrons farthest from the nucleus are loosely bound. Certain metals, such as copper or aluminum, are examples of good conductors. When outside electric power is applied to these conductors, electrons are knocked out of orbit and flow as *free electrons* through the metal's *crystal lattice*.

The crystal lattice is the material's internal structure, made up of atoms joined together to create "building blocks" of the same shape, such as a cube or a prism. Flowing electrons collide with atoms in the lattice, and are also knocked off course by the normal vibrations of the lattice. The result is electrical resistance.

When flowing electrons are slowed or stopped, their energy of motion is transformed into heat energy. Thus, resistance causes wires to get hot and decreases the current flowing through wires.

In a superconductor, there is no heating effect and no loss of current because the electrons are not hampered in any way by the superconductor's crystal lattice. Scientists are still trying to determine why this is so in all cases.

Scientists do know, however, that the only way to chill a material to the −250°C critical temperature of pre-1986 superconductors is to cool it with liquid helium—a tricky operation and a very expensive one. The equipment required to refrigerate liquid helium and the insulation needed to keep it cold are costly, and liquid helium is high-priced. One liter (1.06 quarts) of it costs $3.

The new superconductors would not be nearly so expensive, however, because they have critical temperatures above the boiling point of liquid nitrogen, −196°C (−321°F.). So liquid nitrogen can be used to cool these superconductors below their critical temperatures. The difference, in practical terms, is enormous. Liquid nitrogen costs only 6 cents per liter and is much easier to handle than liquid helium.

Even more exciting is the possibility that scientists may one day discover materials that superconduct at room temperature. Such materials would require no refrigeration whatever, unleashing a technological boom of unparalleled dimensions.

A chapter in the electricity story

Today's progress in superconductivity, however, is but the latest triumph in the long history of the harnessing of electricity—a history that goes back to antiquity. For thousands of years, people knew electricity in guises that often mystified and terrified them— the awesome, occasionally fatal, power of the lightning bolt; the painful lash of the electric eel. The ancient Greeks observed that a piece of amber rubbed with cloth attracts bits of straw.

These phenomena went unexplored for centuries. Then, in 1600, William Gilbert, a physician to Queen Elizabeth I of England, found that many other materials, such as diamond, glass, sulfur, and wax, behaved like amber when rubbed. He called these materials *electrics*,

Glossary

Conductor: A material, usually a metal such as copper, that conducts, or carries, electric current relatively efficiently.

Critical temperature: The temperature at which a superconductor loses all its electrical resistance.

Electric current: A flow of electrons.

Electrical resistance: The property of a conductor that opposes the flow of electricity and changes electric energy into heat.

Electron: A negatively charged subatomic particle that orbits the nucleus of an atom.

Superconductor: A material that conducts electricity without resistance when cooled to its critical temperature.

a term based on *elektron*, the Greek word for *amber*. In 1846, another English physician, Sir Thomas Browne, coined the word *electricity* to mean whatever made "electrics" behave as they did when rubbed.

Later experimenters found that some materials, such as metals, could transfer electricity from one object to another, while other materials, such as wood, could not.

In the mid-1700's, Benjamin Franklin devised a theory to explain all these phenomena. Franklin said that electricity consisted of one moving "substance." He concluded that if one body had a surplus of this substance, and another body a shortage, the two bodies would attract each other. If both bodies had a shortage, or both had a surplus, the two would repel each other. And the transfer of electricity through a metal object such as a wire was merely the flow of "substance."

Franklin was correct. Today, we know that Franklin's "substance" is the electron. We call a surplus of electrons a *negative charge;* a shortage, a *positive charge.* The attractions and repulsions exerted by various objects when rubbed are phenomena of what we know as static electricity. And the flow of "substance" through a wire is the familiar electric current—a flow of electrons.

Scientists had to uncover one more fundamental phenomenon before electric current could be harnessed. Danish physicist Hans Oersted in 1820 made the key discovery—the relationship between electricity and magnetism. Oersted showed that a magnetic compass needle could be made to swerve if a current-carrying wire were nearby.

By the late 1820's, United States physicist Joseph Henry and later British physicist Michael Faraday discovered how to create current in a coil of wire by moving a magnet back and forth inside the coil. This laid the groundwork for the electromagnet and for the development in the 1870's of practical electric motors and generators—both of which use electromagnets.

The electric revolution begins

Meanwhile, electrical resistance—the obstacle superconductors overcome—was harnessed to play an important role in the practical uses of electricity. One of the earliest such uses was artificial lighting. In 1808, English chemist Humphry Davy showed how electric current from a battery could make a wire conductor so hot that it would glow—the first example of an electric light.

Other practical uses of electrical resistance centered around heating. Inventors discovered that impurities in wire would increase resistance and make the wire very hot. The toaster in your kitchen, for example, contains coils or wire made of an *alloy*—a metal mixture—called *nichrome.*

With the electrical revolution well underway in the 1880's, U.S. inventor Thomas A. Edison created the electronic vacuum tube, a device that led to the development of the field of electronics. By

Ordinary Conductivity and Superconductivity

Ordinary Conductivity: Resistance to Current

An electric *current* (a flow of electrons) encounters resistance in an ordinary conductor such as a copper wire. Flowing electrons strike atoms in the conductor, transferring energy to the atoms and thereby heating the conductor.

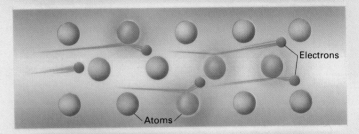

Electrons

Atoms

Useful Resistance

Resistance can be useful in some applications such as a space heater, whose glowing wires are made of a conductor designed to have high resistance and thus produce plenty of heat.

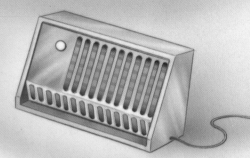

Wasteful Resistance

Resistance is a drawback in most cases. Resistance produces useless heat, for example, in cables that transmit electricity, resulting in a reduction of power.

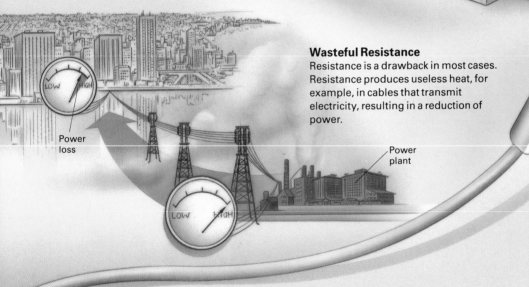

Power loss

Power plant

Superconductivity: No Resistance

Materials known as *superconductors* carry electricity without resistance when chilled to extremely low temperatures, making them useful in applications where resistance would be wasteful—provided the chilling process is not too costly.

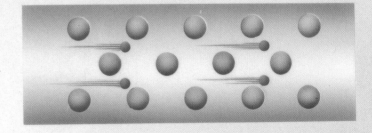

How Electricity Has Revolutionized Our Lives

Current flowing through ordinary conductors such as copper wires is responsible for the electric wonders that in little more than 100 years have radically changed the way people live. Electric light dispelled darkness; motors helped us to work; electronics brought about radio and TV broadcasting; microelectronics led to minicomputers. The discovery of "high-temperature" superconductors promises to continue this revolution far into the future.

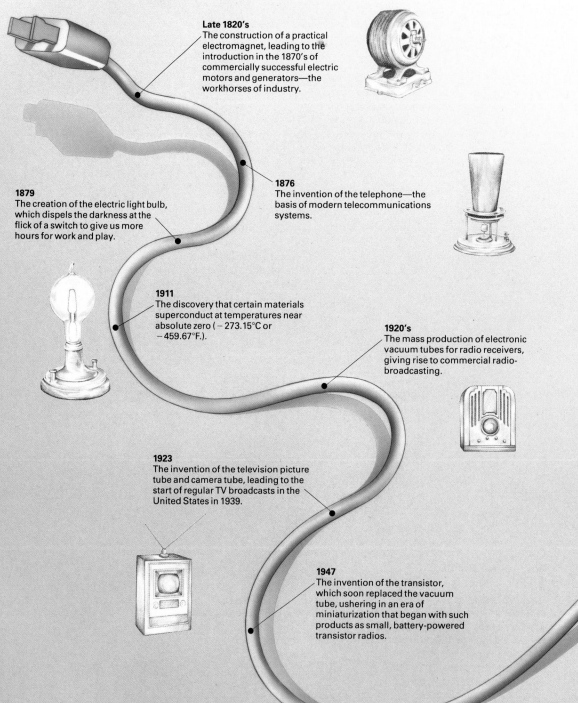

Late 1820's
The construction of a practical electromagnet, leading to the introduction in the 1870's of commercially successful electric motors and generators—the workhorses of industry.

1876
The invention of the telephone—the basis of modern telecommunications systems.

1879
The creation of the electric light bulb, which dispels the darkness at the flick of a switch to give us more hours for work and play.

1911
The discovery that certain materials superconduct at temperatures near absolute zero (− 273.15°C or − 459.67°F.).

1920's
The mass production of electronic vacuum tubes for radio receivers, giving rise to commercial radio-broadcasting.

1923
The invention of the television picture tube and camera tube, leading to the start of regular TV broadcasts in the United States in 1939.

1947
The invention of the transistor, which soon replaced the vacuum tube, ushering in an era of miniaturization that began with such products as small, battery-powered transistor radios.

1920, engineers had created vacuum tubes to broadcast, receive, and strengthen radio signals. That year marked the start of commercial radio broadcasting.

In 1947, three U.S. physicists—John Bardeen, Walter H. Brattain, and William Shockley—invented the *transistor*, a device that performs the functions of the vacuum tube, but is much smaller and less expensive. The three physicists received the 1956 Nobel Prize in physics for their work. During the 1960's, transistors largely replaced vacuum tubes and led to a host of new devices.

Over the past 100 years, the harnessing of electricity has revolutionized the way in which people live and work:

■ The electric light bulb dispelled the darkness, extending the hours people can devote to work and play.

■ Electric refrigerators, vacuum cleaners, dishwashers, and other appliances have saved untold hours of labor on household chores, while electric tools have enabled industry to produce goods quickly.

■ Electrical devices such as radio, television, and the telephone have enabled people half a world apart to communicate in an instant.

■ Electric circuits too small for the eye to see have brought about another electronic marvel—the computer.

The discovery of higher-temperature superconductors may make this revolution even more astounding.

A chilling discovery

The history of superconductors began in 1911 at Leiden University in the Netherlands. There, physicist Heike Kamerlingh Onnes was using liquid helium to chill various metals so that he could observe the effects of very low temperatures on them. In one experi-

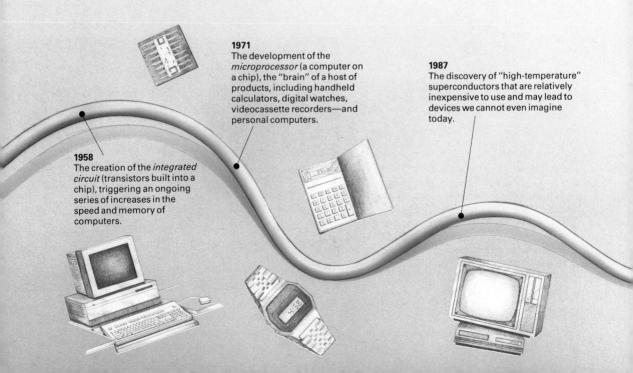

1971
The development of the *microprocessor* (a computer on a chip), the "brain" of a host of products, including handheld calculators, digital watches, videocassette recorders—and personal computers.

1987
The discovery of "high-temperature" superconductors that are relatively inexpensive to use and may lead to devices we cannot even imagine today.

1958
The creation of the *integrated circuit* (transistors built into a chip), triggering an ongoing series of increases in the speed and memory of computers.

0°C	32°F. Freezing
approximately −148°C	approximately 234°F. **1988**
−180°C	292°F. **1987**
−243°C	405°F. **1986**
−250°C	418°F. **1973**
−255°C	427°F. **1953**
−258°C	433°F. **1941**
−269°C	452°F. **1911**

Superconductivity's "Cold Rush"
Scientists are searching for materials that superconduct at ever-higher temperatures, *above*. After the discovery of superconductivity at −269°C (−452°F.) in 1911, there was little progress until 1987, when researchers found materials that have zero electrical resistance, *right*, when cooled to −180°C (−292°F.).

ment, he passed an electric current through mercury while he lowered the metal's temperature. To his amazement, he noted that all resistance to the current suddenly vanished at about −269°C (−452°F.). Soon after, he found that other metals, such as lead and tin, could also be turned into zero-resistance conductors.

Kamerlingh Onnes foresaw some of the implications of his discovery, including the construction of electromagnets with magnetic fields "as intense as we wish" and with no energy loss due to resistance. But another 50 years passed before useful supermagnets were built. A critical temperature of −269°C was so low that no practical electromagnet could be made of any of the early superconducting materials. Physicists searched for materials with higher critical temperatures, but their progress was tortoiselike. By 1941, 30 years after the discovery of superconductivity, the highest critical temperature researchers had achieved was −258°C (−432°F.) for a substance called niobium nitride. Another 32 years passed before an additional gain of 8°C was achieved—with a niobium-germanium alloy. And there progress in the search for higher critical temperatures stuck for years.

Then, in January 1986, came the breakthrough that turned the world of physics topsy-turvy. IBM scientists Müller and Bednorz uncovered a new class of superconducting materials with a record-

breaking critical temperature of $-243°C$ ($-405°F$.). The substance was a *ceramic*—a material that is neither a metal nor a plastic. (Bricks and dinner plates are two common examples of ceramic products.) The ceramic superconductor had a crystal structure made up of the chemical elements barium, copper, lanthanum, and oxygen.

Scientists accept an experimental breakthrough only after other researchers duplicate the initial work and verify the results. The IBM researchers published their results in the fall of 1986, and in December 1986 a team of scientists from the University of Houston and a group from the University of Tokyo announced that they had verified the results. This announcement launched a frantic race to improve on the work.

The "cold rush"

Researchers knew of hundreds of combinations of ceramic compounds containing so-called *rare earth* elements such as lanthanum that could be tested. Perhaps some would have even higher critical temperatures. Experimenters throughout the world climbed aboard the superconductor bandwagon. Soon, they had found materials with a critical temperature of $-220°C$ ($-364°F$.).

In March 1987 came another bombshell: The Houston team, led by physicist Paul C. W. Chu, published an article on a new ceramic compound of barium, copper, oxygen, and the rare earth element yttrium with the astounding critical temperature of $-180°C$ ($-292°F$.). They had broken a major barrier—inexpensive liquid nitrogen could cool this material to its critical temperature. A whole new world of technologies became a realistic possibility.

In early 1988, researchers announced even higher critical temperatures in ceramics that do not contain a rare earth element. In January, materials scientist Hiroshi Maeda and his colleagues at the National Research Institute for Metals in Tsukuba, Japan, reported a critical temperature slightly above $-173°C$ ($-279°F$.) in a material made up of bismuth, strontium, calcium, copper, and oxygen. In February, physicist Allen Hermann and chemist Zhengzhi Sheng of the University of Arkansas in Fayetteville announced that a substance containing an extremely poisonous element, thallium, in addition to calcium, barium, copper, and oxygen also has a critical temperature above $-173°C$. And in March, scientists at IBM's Almaden Research Center in San Jose, Calif., said that a material containing the same elements used by the Arkansas team had achieved a critical temperature of $-148°C$ ($-234°F$.).

Exactly how ceramics behave as superconductors is still a matter of debate. To find superconductivity in a ceramic compound seemed to fly in the face of what physicists knew—or thought they knew—about how superconductivity works.

The original theory of superconductivity is named the BCS theory for the last names of the three University of Illinois physicists who developed it in 1957—John Bardeen, Leon N. Cooper, and J.

Robert Schrieffer. The three scientists shared the 1972 Nobel Prize in physics for their achievement.

The BCS theory holds that low temperatures affect the behavior of free electrons flowing as current. Under ordinary circumstances, electrons repel one another because all electrons have a negative charge. According to the BCS theory, when the temperature of a superconductor drops below the critical point, the material's free electrons begin to act strangely. Aided by vibrations of the atoms that form the superconductor's crystal structure, they form so-called *Cooper pairs* (named after Leon Cooper), and these paired electrons do not repel each other but instead move in tandem. Cooper pairs sweep unhindered through the crystal lattice of a superconducting metal, encountering no resistance whatever.

So far, most physicists have had difficulty applying the BCS theory to ceramic superconductors. Many researchers think that the behavior of the ceramic superconductors must be linked somehow to their unusual crystal structure. The copper and oxygen atoms in these materials are stacked in flat layers (know as *planes* in geometry). In each "building block" of the crystal lattice, copper and oxygen form one or more layers, while the other elements make up the remainder of the block. The blocks are stacked one upon another like a deck of cards to fill out the crystal.

The critical temperature seems to depend upon the number of copper-and-oxygen layers per block—the more of these layers, the higher the critical temperature. The material with a critical temperature of −148°C has three consecutive layers made of copper and oxygen atoms in each block.

Payoff in electric power

Although scientists are not sure how the new superconductors work, the promise of superconductors is so clear that national governments, including the U.S. government, have begun pushing for rapid development of the new technology. The payoff may be awesome in applications ranging from the transmission of electricity along hundreds of kilometers of power lines to the operation of computer chips containing individual electronic components too small for the eye to see.

Superconducting power lines would cost too much to cool with liquid helium. Using liquid nitrogen as the coolant, however, would make a true coast-to-coast power grid practical. Electric utilities in the United States might be able to shut down an estimated 50 power plants that were built because it was not practical to transmit electricity over vast distances.

Nitrogen-cooled superconductors could also make the generation of electricity more efficient. Today's generators use electromagnets with copper coils to produce a magnetic field. Electrons flowing through these coils encounter resistance, producing useless heat. Because electrons do not encounter resistance in superconductors,

Cooking Up a Superconductor

A recipe for a "high-temperature" superconductor, *top,* calls for three inexpensive chemicals. Students at Jefferson Township High School near Dover, N.J., grind a mixture of these chemicals, *above left,* then bake pellets made of the mixture, *above* (in thimblelike cups). After a pellet cools, a student tests it, *left,* by chilling it with liquid nitrogen and lowering it toward a magnet. A superconductor rejects any other object's magnetic field, so the pellet floats in midair.

superconducting coils would not waste energy by producing heat. As a result, superconducting generators would be more efficient than today's generators. According to a Department of Energy study released in January 1988, the use of superconducting coils could cut energy losses in generators by 80 per cent.

Large superconducting electromagnets could also help make *fusion reactors* practical for nuclear power plants. In fusion reactors, which are still in the experimental stage, nuclei of two forms of hydrogen are heated until they *fuse* (join), liberating extra heat energy that can be tapped to produce electricity.

The promise and the problems

The new superconductors almost certainly will influence the design of future circular particle accelerators, or atom smashers. The size of an accelerator's circumference depends partly on the ability of its electromagnets to bend beams of charged subatomic particles whizzing through it. The stronger the magnetic fields generated by the electromagnets, the smaller the circumference required for a given energy level of beams. Some scientists have suggested using the new superconductors in the Superconducting Super Collider (SSC), an accelerator 85 kilometers (53 miles) in circumference that is scheduled to be built in the United States in the mid-1990's.

Transportation is one of the most attractive areas for high-temperature superconductor applications, notably *maglev* (magnetically levitated) *trains,* experimental vehicles that are held in the air above a track by powerful magnetic fields. Maglev trains can run faster than conventional trains because they produce no friction in wheel bearings or between wheels and the track.

Japan has been especially interested in maglev trains. In 1979, a Japanese maglev train using superconducting magnets that were cooled by liquid helium reached a speed of 517 kilometers (321 miles) per hour.

Superconducting magnets play a vital role in magnetic resonance imaging (MRI) machines, medical instruments that produce pictures of organs inside the body without exposing the patient to the risk of X rays or other radiation. Because the magnets have had to be cooled by expensive and cumbersome helium refrigeration units, however, their use has been confined to major hospitals and teaching centers. Refrigeration with much cheaper and simpler liquid nitrogen units could make MRI feasible for many smaller hospitals.

Computers and other electronic equipment may be among the first devices to benefit from the new superconductor technology. One of the keys to making faster, smaller, and more powerful electronic devices is to pack electric circuits closer together on *microchips*—flat crystals of silicon no bigger than a baby's thumbnail yet containing thousands of circuits. The closer together circuits are placed, however, the more difficult it becomes to get rid of the heat the circuits develop. Superconducting circuits would produce little

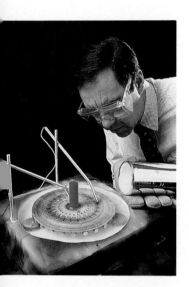

A scientist at Argonne National Laboratory near Chicago uses liquid nitrogen to chill an experimental electric motor that uses a "high-temperature" superconducting material. The two small pucklike disks sitting in a shallow bowl are composed of the superconducting material. They repel magnetic fields created by cylindrical electromagnets attached to the underside of a large aluminum plate above the bowl and make the plate rotate.

Researchers are studying computer-generated images to determine the complex crystal structure of "high-temperature" superconducting materials. In the image at left, atoms of yttrium are white; barium, green; copper, blue; and oxygen, red; yellow "pyramids" highlight a particular shape formed by some of the oxygen atoms. Researchers believe electric current flows without resistance in *planes* (flat surfaces) along the copper and oxygen atoms.

or no heat. By mid-1987, scientists at IBM and Stanford University in California had already developed experimental circuits made with thin films of ceramic superconductors.

None of these products will be possible, however, until certain technological problems involving the new superconductors are overcome. For example, the new superconductors are brittle and therefore extremely difficult to form into flexible wire. These brittle substances break if you try to wind them into coils of wire needed to make superconducting electromagnets. Robert A. Laudise, a chemist and director of materials research at AT&T Bell Laboratories, says, "We're going to have to learn how to do ceramic processing with a kind of finesse and control that we haven't been capable of before." Experts estimate that it will take at least five years to develop a practical superconducting wire made of a ceramic.

In addition, these new materials, to fulfill their promise, will have to carry large amounts of current without losing their superconducting abilities. Researchers are not at all certain that they can create materials that will be able to do this in the near future.

None of these doubts, however, can diminish the excitement over the future of superconductors. "I believe nature has been very kind and has given us all these wonderful phenomena to discover," said Chu in a talk at Drexel University in Philadelphia. "But I don't believe it is so kind as to let us hit everything right the first time."

For further reading:

Gleick, James. "In the Trenches of Science." *The New York Times Magazine*, Aug. 16, 1987.
Lemonick, Michael D. "Superconductors!" *Time*, May 11, 1987.
Maranto, Gina. "Superconductivity: Hype Vs. Reality." *Discover*, August 1987.

Don't be misled by how pretty some of them are,
plants—over millions of years—have evolved
many defenses to protect themselves against
insects and other plant-eating organisms.

The Wars
Between Plants
and Predators

BY IAN T. BALDWIN AND THOMAS EISNER

Everyone knows that plants are passive things. All day long they do little but grow leaves and flowers and suck fluids from the ground. Admittedly, plants can do some things that animals can't, such as trap sunlight and build their tissues from thin air. But when it comes to protecting themselves, they're a helpless lot. They just sit there, waiting to be eaten.

Everyone *knows* all that. But is it really true? Consider for a moment that some plants are covered with thorns or prickles. Eating those plants would be like chewing on barbed wire. Then there are plants such as poison ivy and stinging nettles. They wouldn't feel too gentle on the tongue, either. When you think about it, there are very few wild plants that we do eat. Most plants, in fact, taste terrible, and some will make you violently ill. Why is that? The answer is simple: Rather than being helpless and passive, plants protect themselves with a formidable array of defenses.

For millions of years, plants have been attacked by insects and other enemies, including fungi, bacteria, and plant-eating mammals. But becoming someone else's dinner is the worst of all fates for a

Opposite page: A tropical passionflower defends itself with tiny hairs that secrete a sticky, poisonous fluid. The hairs trap and kill ants and other crawling insects that would steal the flower's nectar without pollinating the plant.

119

plant—as it is for any organism—so plants have fought back. Some plants have evolved mechanical defenses, such as thorns, that make them all but impossible to eat. Many others have acquired chemical defenses. Several varieties of plants, for example, produce sticky substances that can trap an insect or glue its mouth shut. Certain plant chemicals repel predators, and a number of others are *toxins* (poisons) that kill or cause serious physical damage to organisms that eat them. These poisonous chemicals can kill the insect outright, interfere with its digestion, or disrupt its development.

But predators have pulled a few evolutionary fast ones of their own. Some insects, for instance, have acquired a resistance to certain plant toxins. Others have developed clever countermeasures to plant defenses, and a few insects have even adapted defensive plant chemicals to their own use.

The endless warfare between plants and predators is of great interest to scientists. For one thing, the protective compounds manufactured by plants are the raw materials from which we obtain many lifesaving drugs. Moreover, by gaining an understanding of the defensive strategies of plants, agricultural researchers may be able to produce crop plants that ward off insects and other pests without having to be sprayed with pesticides.

Scientists use a variety of instruments to study plant defenses, but some defenses are readily apparent to the naked eye. The protective strategy of the milkweed plant is a prime example. If you have seen a milkweed, you are familiar with the creamy liquid—called *latex*—that oozes from the plant when it is cut open. In addition to containing unpleasant or poisonous chemicals that discourage insects from eating the plant, latex forms a rubbery glue when exposed to air. An insect that munches on the milkweed's leaves is liable to get a mouthful of the rapidly congealing goo. That meal may be the last one the insect ever eats, because even if the chemicals in the latex don't kill it, its jaws are soon sealed shut.

Another sticky compound serving a similar function is the resin produced by many evergreen trees. The resin protects the trees from attack by fungi, bark beetles, and other pests.

The defenses of some plants are purely mechanical in character. Thistles, for example, have prickly stems and leaves that deter predators. In a pasture being grazed by sheep, grasses will be eaten almost down to their roots, while thistles stand untouched. Many other plants are covered with tiny hairs called *trichomes*. In addition to helping a plant regulate its temperature and water balance, trichomes play an important role in defense. Hooked or barbed trichomes can impale or immobilize an insect.

Other kinds of trichomes may be part of a plant's chemical line of defense. Resting on the surface of the plant and looking like microscopic trees or balloons, these *glandular trichomes* manufacture and store a variety of protective compounds. For example, glandular tri-

The authors:
Ian T. Baldwin is a doctoral candidate in biology at Cornell University in Ithaca, N.Y. Thomas Eisner is professor of biology at Cornell.

chomes on the leaves of the primula plant, a member of the primrose family, secrete irritating chemicals that repel insects.

Trichomes are just one of the plant structures in which defensive compounds are produced. Some plants—such as grapefruit, orange, and other citrus trees—manufacture repellents in their leaves and in the rind of their fruit. The chemicals, stored in oil glands, are the tree's way of protecting itself from predators, especially small insects, that would eat the fruit without scattering the seeds. (The dispersal of their seeds enables plants to spread to new areas.)

Repellent chemicals work in a variety of ways. Citrus repellents belong to the simplest class, which includes substances that cause itching and other sorts of physical irritation. Another such compound is produced by cat thyme, an herb related to mint. The leaves of this plant are covered with microscopic spherical capsules containing a fluid repellent. An insect biting into a cat thyme leaf breaks one or more of the capsules and gets a mouthful of the harsh chemical.

Some repellents are much more sophisticated in their mode of action. A particular species of wild potato, for instance, manufactures a chemical identical to one produced by an aphid—a small, juice-sucking insect that feeds on the plant. The aphid releases its chemical as an alarm to warn other aphids of predators. So when aphids sense the compound given off by the potato plant, they think it is an alarm, and they flee.

In addition to the many kinds of repellents, plants produce thousands of toxins that wreak havoc on predators' nervous systems, muscles, or internal organs. Many toxins are marked by their quick action; the most potent of these poisons can cause death in minutes. Some kinds of clover, for instance, manufacture compounds that, when the plant's leaves are damaged, break down to produce cyanide, one of the deadliest of all poisons. The quantity of cyanide produced is not enough to harm a grazing cow, but it is sufficient to kill an insect. Another well-known toxin is nicotine, the drug that gives tobacco its addictive qualities. Nicotine interferes with the transmission of nerve impulses and, in large-enough amounts, it is highly poisonous. An insect devouring a tobacco leaf may get a dose of nicotine sufficient to kill it.

Nicotine is found in tiny concentrations in many plant families, but it is produced in large amounts only in tobacco and other plants of the genus *Nicotiana*. Studies of *Nicotiana* plants provided one of the first proofs that many plant chemicals are indeed used for defense against predators.

Nicotine belongs to a large group of plant compounds called *alkaloids*, many of which are toxins. Other alkaloids include the deadly poison strychnine; the narcotic drugs cocaine and morphine, which are deadly in large doses; and the stimulant drug caffeine.

Biologists had known since the early 1900's that plants manufac-

How Plants Defend Themselves

Over millions of years, plants have developed a variety of defenses to protect themselves from predators, primarily insects. Those defenses can be grouped into four major categories: sticky substances that can trap an insect or cement its mouth shut; mechanical defenses, such as thorns; repellents; and poisons that kill predators outright or interfere with their digestion or development. Many plants defend themselves in more than one way.

Sticky substances

Mechanical defenses

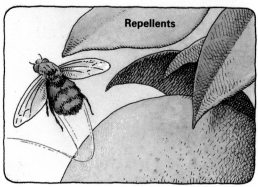
Repellents

Poisons

ture a variety of chemicals that have no apparent function in maintaining the life of the plant. But many scientists disputed the idea that such compounds had been evolved for defense, arguing instead that the substances were merely biochemical waste products.

The argument was largely settled in the 1940's and 1950's. One of the leaders in the study of plant defenses during that period was Ray F. Dawson, a biochemist at Columbia University in New York City. Dawson discovered that by grafting the tops of tomato and potato plants, which do not normally contain nicotine, onto *Nicotiana* roots, the plants' leaves accumulated nicotine. The nicotine was manufactured in the *Nicotiana* roots and transported to the tomato and potato leaves. Herbert Buhr, a plant researcher in West Berlin, West Germany, repeated Dawson's grafting experiments and carried them one step further. Buhr exposed the nicotine-laden plants to insects that usually feed on potato leaves and found that the leaves had become toxic to the pests. Later studies of plant chemicals confirmed that plants produce many compounds for no other apparent reason but defense.

A number of toxins have a delayed effect on the organisms that eat them. For example, some alkaloids hinder digestion by making it difficult for predators to utilize the carbohydrates in a leaf. Two other groups of compounds, the *tannins* and *proteinase inhibitors*, interfere with the digestion of proteins. Insects that feed on leaves containing any of these chemicals become malnourished and may die.

Still other toxic compounds disrupt the physical development of organisms. A striking example is a group of chemicals produced by a type of bugleweed, a flowering herb in the mint family. Scientists from the University of California at Berkeley, conducting research in Kenya, found that insects shunned the bugleweed. In fact, locusts swarming over a *savanna* (grassland) devoured every scrap of vegetation—except bugleweeds. To find out why the bugleweed was so unpopular, the investigators fed extracts of the plant to the larvae of various insects. As a consequence, the larvae developed several heads when they began the *metamorphosis* (change) into a *pupa* (the stage of life between the larval and the adult stages). The extra heads blocked the insects' mouthparts, and they starved.

The scientists determined that the bugleweed—like the wild potato with its aphid-fooling alarm scent—uses a form of chemical trickery. The compounds produced by the bugleweed closely resem-

Sticky Substances
A scientist, *left,* studies a milkweed, one of the plants that secretes a sticky substance for defense. When it is cut, the milkweed oozes a creamy liquid called *latex.* An insect that bites a milkweed leaf gets a mouthful of latex that seals its jaws shut, *above.*

ble predators' natural growth hormones. The fake hormones cause an insect larva's body to begin the metamorphosis process, but the normal steps are disrupted.

Most kinds of plants manufacture large amounts of protective chemicals at all times, but scientists discovered in the 1970's and 1980's that a sizable number of plants produce such compounds in quantity only when being attacked by predators. Like a villager rousing the townspeople to take up arms against an invader, these plants send chemical signals throughout their tissues, alerting every leaf and stem to shore up its defenses. This "summoning of the troops"—called an *inducible defense*—is similar to the protective response of the body's immune system to an invading germ.

Inducible defenses have been the focus of several studies. In the early 1980's, entomologist Jack Schultz of Dartmouth College in Hanover, N.H.—working with Ian Baldwin—studied oak trees that were being ravaged by gypsy moth caterpillars. They found that during the height of the attack, the concentration of tannin in the trees' leaves increased to three times its normal level. Tannin levels declined to match those of undamaged oak trees after the caterpillars stopped feeding and formed cocoons. Another researcher, biochemist Clarence A. Ryan of Washington State University in Pullman, detected a dramatic rise in the concentration of proteinase inhibitors in tomato leaves within 48 hours after an attack by potato beetles.

The discovery of inducible defenses raised two interesting questions. First, how do plants "spread the alarm"; that is, how is warning information transmitted throughout a plant? And second, why would a plant evolve an inducible defense in the first place? Why would it not just produce protective chemicals in high concentrations all the time?

Mechanical Defenses
A group of sheep, *below,* give a wide berth to a thistle plant. A close-up of the plant, *below right,* shows why: Its leaves and stems bristle with tiny thorns that discourage even the hungriest predator. Many kinds of plants use thorns, prickles, or sharp hairs for protection.

Repellents

Plants produce many chemicals that deter predators. The rind of the grapefruit, *left,* contains tiny glands filled with a fluid that evaporates in the air to repel insects. Squirted across a flame, the fluid ignites, *below,* showing that it is volatile and combustible. Such compounds require a great deal of energy to produce, leaving less energy for the plant to devote to growth and reproduction.

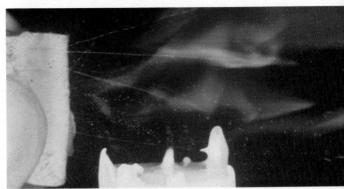

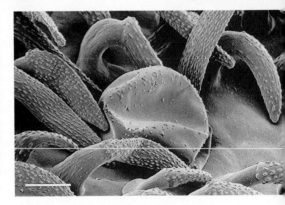

The strange-looking leaf of the cat thyme plant, an herb in the mint family, is covered with tiny spherical capsules, *above left.* The capsules are filled with an irritating repellent that is released when an insect bites into the leaf. A photomicrograph, *above,* shows a capsule that has collapsed after expelling its contents.

The answer to the first question is incomplete, but research is filling in some of the blanks. Some of the most interesting findings have come from Ryan's studies of tomato plants. Ryan discovered that when the plants' leaves were attacked by potato beetles, "fragments"—actually groups of complex compounds—from the torn cell walls circulated through the entire plant. He found that the fragments had somehow signaled cells to begin producing proteinase inhibitors. Ryan theorized that cell-wall fragments might be a universal defensive cue in the plant world, stimulating the manufacture of many kinds of protective substances.

In collaboration with other researchers, Ryan carried out an experiment in 1986 to test that theory. The scientists drilled a number of holes in the trunks of lodgepole pine trees growing in a forest. Into some of the holes they injected varying amounts of cell-wall material from insect-damaged tomato plants. Into other holes they

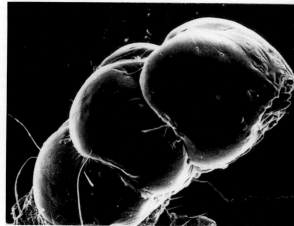

Poisons

Plants manufacture thousands of toxic compounds. The bugleweed, *above,* a flowering herb in the mint family, produces a chemical that disrupts the normal development of insects. A fall army-worm larva, *above right,* that fed on bugleweed leaves grew three heads when it began to change into a pupa. The extra heads blocked the larva's mouthparts, and it starved.

injected an inactive solution. Ryan and his colleagues found that wood tissues next to the holes that had been filled with cell fragments had increased their production of resin. The increase varied in proportion to the amount of cell material that had been injected: the more cell fragments, the more resin. The wood around the holes that received the inactive solution did not contain nearly as much resin as that around the other holes. These findings showed that cell-wall material can cause completely different protective responses in unrelated plant species.

Internal cues, such as cell-wall fragments, may be only one of the systems that plants rely on to activate their defenses. In 1983, Schultz's research team at Dartmouth conducted experiments indicating that undamaged plants can respond to airborne chemicals emitted from nearby plants under attack by predators.

Baldwin and Schultz grew 45 poplar seedlings in pots—one tree to a pot—in airtight chambers. Thirty of the trees were placed in one chamber and the remaining 15 in a second, smaller chamber. The researchers then simulated an insect attack on half the plants in the larger chamber by tearing their leaves. The remaining 15 trees in the larger chamber and the 15 trees in the smaller chamber were left undamaged. Fifty-two hours later, the scientists analyzed the level of *phenols*—the building blocks of tannins—in the leaves of all the seedlings. They found that both the damaged and undamaged plants in the large chamber had elevated concentrations of phenols in their leaves. They detected no increase in phenols in the trees isolated in the smaller chamber.

Because the plants were growing in individual pots and lacked root connections with one another, the investigators hypothesized that the damaged seedlings, in addition to sending internal cues to their own leaves, had released an airborne chemical signal. The chemical alerted the undamaged trees in the chamber to prepare for an invasion. Those trees then increased their production of phenols. Plants in the second chamber, cut off from the warning chemical, did nothing to bolster their defenses.

In 1987, Hampden J. Zeringue, Jr., a biochemist with the United States Department of Agriculture in New Orleans, reported a similar phenomenon in cotton. Zeringue found that when the leaves of cotton plants were attacked by a leaf-infesting fungus, the leaves of undamaged cotton plants growing nearby manufactured greater amounts of protective compounds. He concluded that the response must have been due to an airborne chemical emitted by the fungus-ridden leaves. Scientists now think that many kinds of plants may give off warning chemicals.

The answer to the second question—why plants evolve inducible defenses rather than produce a steady supply of defensive chemicals—may be a matter of economics. Scientists have found that protective chemicals are costly for a plant to produce. A plant that manufactures large amounts of such compounds is squandering resources, namely raw materials and stored energy from the sun, that it could otherwise use for growth or reproduction.

In 1986, Baldwin and his associates conducted an experiment at Cornell University in Ithaca, N.Y., to see whether plants really do "pay a price" for defense. They wanted to find out whether plants that are forced to maintain a high concentration of protective compounds produce fewer seeds.

The researchers worked with a species of wild tobacco that employs an inducible defense—the production of nicotine. They divided the laboratory plants into two groups. They treated one group of plants gently to prevent them from activating their defenses but simulated insect attacks on the other group by cutting the plants' leaves with scissors. Fresh injuries were inflicted on those plants every few days to keep nicotine production high.

Baldwin and his colleagues kept the number of leaves equal in both groups of plants. Because scissor-damaged plants in the second group had fewer leaves than the undamaged plants, the same number of leaves were removed from the first group of plants, but in such a way that the plants did not boost nicotine output. With some of the gently handled plants, the researchers cut the leaves and then applied a chemical that suppressed the manufacture of nicotine. With others, they peeled away leaf material slowly and carefully.

By the end of the growing season, the plants subjected to the simulated insect attacks had produced significantly fewer seeds than plants in the other group, even though plants in both groups had the same number of leaves to maintain. This result showed that a high level of defense must be paid for somehow. The research supported the theory that plants develop inducible defenses in order to conserve resources when there is no threat from predators.

Virtually all plants produce protective chemicals, either year-round or as an inducible defense. It may seem surprising, then, that

Responding to Attack

Just as the human body's immune system steps up its production of protective substances when the body is invaded by germs, many plants, such as the tobacco plant, manufacture defensive chemicals only in response to attack by insects and other predators.

As an insect chews on a leaf, fragments of damaged cell walls (purple dots) travel to other parts of the plant, causing cells to begin producing defensive chemicals (red dots). Within about 48 hours, the plant's leaves will be much less tasty—and perhaps even poisonous—to hungry insects. Cell-wall fragments may be just one of several warning substances used in this way by plants.

Some plants, including many varieties of trees, release airborne chemicals when attacked that warn neighboring plants of the danger. A tree being infested by leaf-eating insects produces defensive compounds (red dots) and also releases a chemical (blue dots) into the air. A nearby tree "perceives" the warning and begins producing its own defensive compounds. A more distant tree has not yet received the alarm and has therefore manufactured no defensive chemicals.

any plant gets eaten by predators, but of course many do. Unfortunately for plants—but fortunately for plant-eating animals—an impenetrable defense rarely lasts forever. As soon as a plant evolves a new defensive compound, predators begin evolving ways of getting around it. The never-ending struggle between plants and predators can thus be likened to the international arms race.

Insects, in particular, have evolved a number of countermeasures to plant defenses. The tobacco hornworm, for one, has developed a powerful "pump" in its intestines that excretes nicotine. With this protective addition to its physiology, the hornworm feeds freely on tobacco plants, consuming quantities of nicotine that would be deadly to other insects.

Some insects have evolved a biochemical resistance to certain harmful chemicals. The cabbage butterfly, for example, is one of several insects that feed on plants in the mustard family, which includes mustard, cabbage, and horseradish. These plants, though they are eaten by human beings, contain oils that are toxic to most kinds of insects. At some point in its evolutionary history, however, the cabbage butterfly developed the ability to break down mustard oils in its body.

Almost any plant defense can be overcome. Even with its gummy latex, the milkweed plant has fallen prey to a variety of insects. Several insects have "learned" to cut through the plant's latex veins with their jaws, then wait for the latex to empty from the veins. After that, the insect eats the leaf.

In the ultimate insult to plants, some insects not only are unfazed by plant defenses, they actually use those defenses for their own benefit. A certain species of grasshopper, for example, eats milkweed leaves and uses toxins from the leaves to help make a poisonous fluid that it sprays at predators. A similar theft of a plant defense has been perpetrated by the larva of the pine sawfly, which infests the Scotch pine tree. As it feeds, the sawfly larva ingests the tree's protective resin and stores it in its upper digestive tract. If the larva is beset by ants, it raises its head and regurgitates a bit of the sticky substance onto its attackers.

One of the most remarkable adaptations to a plant defense has been evolved by a species of assassin bug, an insect named for its murderous habits. The assassin bug catches insect prey with its forelegs, kills them with an injected venom, and then sucks out their blood and body fluids. The assassin bug has a special relationship with a wild plant called the camphor weed. The leaves and stems of the weed are covered with tiny glandular trichomes that produce droplets of a sticky secretion. The substance contains a number of compounds, including camphor, that repel insects. The assassin bug, however, is unaffected by the secretion, and the female actually harvests it for her own defensive purpose.

The adult female assassin bug gathers droplets of the secretion with her front legs. As soon as she has accumulated a sizable dab of the material, she transfers it to her second pair of legs and then to her belly. Later, when the female lays eggs, she uses her hind legs to coat the eggs with the secretion to protect them from predators. When the larvae hatch from the eggs, they scrape the secretion from the egg walls with their front legs. With this "glue" coating their forelegs, the larvae are equipped to catch their first prey.

Insects with the ability to feed on plants that are high in toxins sometimes reap a double benefit: In addition to having a source of food that most other insects cannot eat, they are themselves made poisonous to predators. One of the best examples of this phenomenon is the monarch butterfly. The monarch larva feeds on milkweed and stores the plant's toxic chemicals in its body. Those chemicals are still present in the insect's tissues when it emerges from its cocoon as an adult butterfly. Almost any kind of bird that eats a monarch gets sick within minutes, so birds learn to shun monarchs, which have a distinctive orange and black pattern on their wings.

The relative immunity from predators enjoyed by monarch but-

Ian T. Baldwin, one of the authors of this article, cuts the leaves of wild tobacco plants growing in a Cornell University greenhouse to test how such injuries cause the plants to increase their production of nicotine, a chemical toxic to insects.

terflies and certain other poisonous insects has led to a bit of evolutionary sleight of hand called *mimicry*. Mimicry is a trait, such as coloration, that makes an edible species of insect closely resemble an unpalatable species. The viceroy butterfly, for instance, has evolved coloration that is almost indistinguishable from that of the monarch. So birds avoid the viceroy just as they do the monarch.

Thus, the chemicals produced by plants often have far-reaching effects, and substances designed to do harm may be put to good use by their intended victims. Human beings, no less than insects, have benefited from plant chemicals. Throughout history, resourceful individuals have investigated the mysteries of the plant world in search of substances to cure disease and ease pain. The ancient Greeks extracted a compound from the bark of willow trees that was effective against headaches and many other kinds of pain. Today, a closely related chemical—acetylsalicylic acid, the active ingredient in aspirin—is still the most commonly used pain reliever. Many other medicines, including the heart stimulant digitalis and alkaloid drugs used to treat childhood leukemia and Hodgkin's disease, also come from plants. In fact, plant chemicals, or synthetic imitations of them, are used in more than 25 per cent of all pharmaceuticals.

Although many plant-derived substances used in medicine are classified as toxins, the difference between a toxin and a useful drug is often just a matter of dosage. A small dose of a powerful compound may be beneficial, while a larger dose will kill. Finding potential medicines and determining the amounts in which they can safely be administered requires years of painstaking work. Scientists think there may be thousands of valuable drugs still awaiting discovery, particularly in the world's tropical rain forests. Because those forests are rapidly being destroyed to make way for people, many plant species—and the chemicals they produce—are likely to disappear before botanists have even learned of their existence.

Agriculture may benefit as much as medicine from the study of

The Bugs Strike Back
Insects have evolved many ways of coping with the defenses of plants. Some insects, for example, have become resistant to certain toxic chemicals. Other insects have "learned" to evade plant defenses altogether. A beetle, *right,* bites through the latex veins of a milkweed plant. When the veins are empty of latex, the insect will eat the leaf.

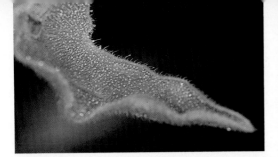

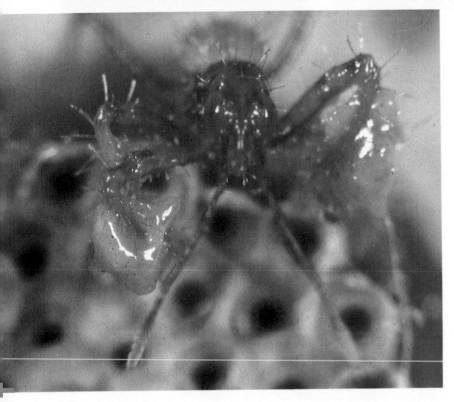

Some insects have adapted plant defenses to their own uses. The assassin bug harvests the sticky fluid secreted by the camphor plant, *above left*. The female assassin bug gathers the secretion with her forelegs, *above,* and uses it to form a protective coating on her eggs. When the larvae hatch, they scrape the substance from the egg walls until their forelegs are coated with it, *left*. The larvae use this "glue" to catch their first prey.

plant compounds. Many crop-eating insects have become increasingly resistant to pesticides, so researchers are looking for ways—perhaps through genetic engineering—to boost the natural defenses of plants, and at the same time avoid harming the environment. The goal is to develop plants that resist insects but are still tasty and safe for human consumption. As part of that goal, researchers hope also to thwart the remarkable ability of insects to overcome almost any plant defense. For eons, the war between plants and predators has been a stand-off, but soon—with a little help from agricultural scientists—crop plants may gain the winning edge.

For further reading:

Edwards, Peter, and Wratten, Stephen D. *Ecology of Insect-Plant Interactions.* Edward Arnold Publishers, London. 1980.

McDermott, Jeanne. "Biologists Begin Eavesdropping on 'Talking' Trees." *Smithsonian,* December 1984.

Rosenthal, Gerald A. "The Chemical Defenses of Higher Plants." *Scientific American,* January 1986.

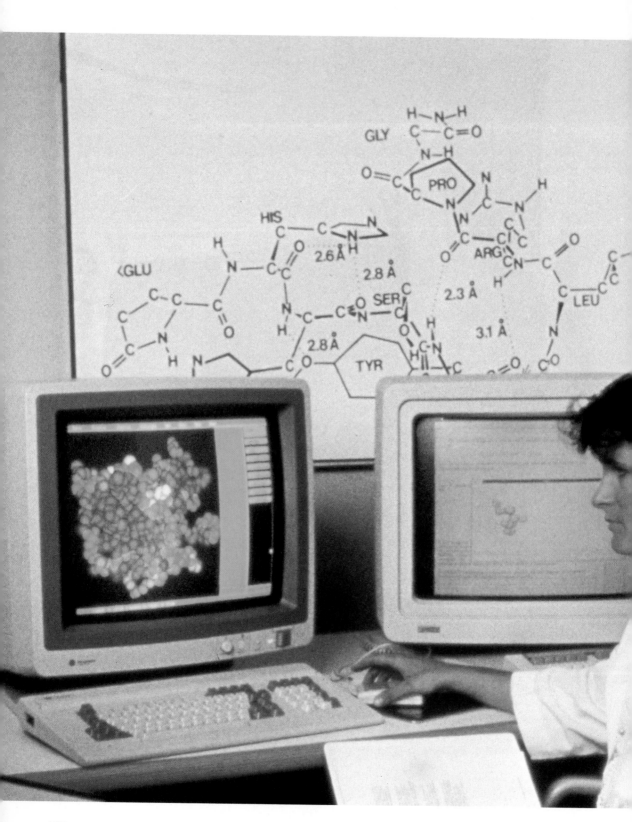

Sophisticated computer graphics software has given scientists a new, faster way to design more effective and safer drugs.

Using Computers to Design Drugs

BY DAVID A. KALSON

A woman seated at a computer pushes a button on the keyboard and glowing, needlelike branches displayed on the monitor sprout red, white, and purple grapes. She turns a knob and the image rotates. As the woman continues to twist knobs and push buttons, another bunch of grapes forms—a few grapes at a time—and then floats lazily toward the first bunch.

She watches the screen intently as the bunches move closer to each other and finally join with a precise fit—like two orbiting spacecraft docking with each other. The woman leans back in her chair and relaxes.

What is happening? Has she just won some sort of video game? In a sense she has, because what she is doing may lead to a major victory for hu-

A researcher at Polygen Corporation in Waltham, Mass., uses software made by that firm to create a precise image of a biological molecule—a crucial step in computer-aided drug design.

manity—the first drug able to cure *emphysema*, an often fatal disease of the lungs.

The woman is chemist Dagmar Ringe of Massachusetts Institute of Technology (M.I.T.) in Cambridge. She is one of a rapidly growing corps of scientists from many different fields who are using computers in their search for new, more effective, and safer drugs.

Each "grape" on her monitor represents an atom, and the "branches" are chemical bonds that hold atoms together in bunches known as *molecules*. One of the molecules closely resembles *lung elastase*, a protein created by the body to destroy damaged lung tissue. In emphysema victims, this protein functions abnormally, destroying healthy lung tissue. The other molecule represents the shape that a drug molecule must have to dock with lung elastase.

The location at which the druglike molecule docks is a crucial part of the elastase molecule's surface. This location, called a *binding site*, carries out the normal demolition work of the elastase molecule and is also responsible for the molecule's abnormal function of destroying healthy lung cells of an emphysema victim.

Normally, a protein "cap" fits into the binding site. The cap remains in place until the body needs to dispose of damaged lung cells. Then the cap comes off, enabling the elastase molecule to dock with a damaged cell by joining its binding site to a matching site on the cell surface. After docking occurs, chemicals in the elastase destroy the cell.

Elastase molecules of emphysema victims have abnormal caps that do not cover the binding site adequately. Scientists are not sure why the caps are abnormal. Cigarette smoking, air pollution, repeated infections, and heredity all may play a role. Without a suitable cap, elastase molecules are free to dock with any lung cells—including healthy ones—and destroy them.

Ringe plans to design an artificial cap to replace the abnormal natural cap. The druglike molecule she created on her screen is a preliminary design for such a cap.

The author:
David A. Kalson manages the Public Information Division of the American Institute of Physics and is the author of the Special Report CREATING IMAGES WITH COMPUTERS in the 1987 edition of *Science Year.*

Ringe's technological tools—a high-powered computer and sophisticated graphics software—are ideal for locating a particular binding site on the elastase surface and designing an artificial molecule that will bind to that site. These tools are ideal because shapes are the name of the game. Any design that docks with the elastase binding site must fit its shape exactly and so becomes a candidate for the drug that Ringe wants to design. In fact, all drugs work on this basic principle; they must have shapes that fit perfectly into the binding site of a particular biological substance—usually a protein.

Modern ideas of how drugs work grew out of discoveries made in the early 1900's. Before that, effective drugs were found only through trial and error—often supported by clever reasoning. British physician Edward Jenner, for example, in 1796 gave an 8-year-old boy the first vaccination—using material from a sore caused by

the minor disease cowpox—after reasoning that this would give the boy cowpox but would immunize him against the deadly disease smallpox. Jenner based his reasoning on the observation that dairy-maids who had caught cowpox did not catch smallpox.

German bacteriologist Paul Ehrlich in the early 1900's had the idea that certain destructive chemicals would attach themselves only to particular bacteria and would not affect other cells in the body. He developed this idea and—after testing some 3,000 compounds—in 1910 announced that arsphenamine, later marketed as *Salvarsan*, attaches itself to and destroys the bacteria that cause syphilis.

Ehrlich could not have explained the attachment in terms of a docking maneuver because scientists of his time knew very little about molecular structure. Chemists understood that atoms combined to form molecules, but they did not know how the molecules were shaped.

Another German scientist, physicist Max Theodor Felix von Laue, in 1912 found a way to determine the molecular shape of *crystals*—solid materials, such as rock salt, made up of an orderly arrangement of microscopic "building blocks" of a certain shape such as a cube or a prism. Von Laue exposed a crystal to a source of X rays after surrounding the crystal with photographic film. X rays struck atoms in the crystal, and *diffracted*—scattered in an orderly way that reflected the internal order of the crystal. The X rays that struck the film formed what scientists call *diffraction patterns*. After developing the film, von Laue analyzed the geometry of the patterns mathematically to determine the crystal's internal structure.

After von Laue's success, chemists began to use his technique of X-ray diffraction crystallography to determine the shapes of other molecules. Knowledge of molecular shapes enabled chemists to

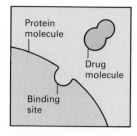

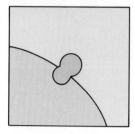

The Key to How Drugs Work

All drugs work by precisely fitting a certain spot called a *binding site* on a protein or other target molecule, *top*. The drug molecule performs a "docking maneuver" that connects it to the target molecule's binding site, *above*.

build models out of balls and pieces of wire and to use these models to study how molecules combine with one another.

But protein molecules presented special problems for crystallographers and model builders. Proteins are the most complicated molecules known. They are made up of long chains of *amino acids*, each acid consisting of 10 to 27 atoms. Only 20 different kinds of amino acids form the essential parts of proteins. Proteins are so complicated because their amino acids are linked together in billions of different sequences made up of about 500 to 50,000 atoms.

It was not until the late 1950's that X-ray crystallography first solved the structure of a protein. The work was done by molecular biologist John C. Kendrew of the University of Cambridge in England. The protein was *myoglobin*, which stores oxygen in muscles.

X-ray crystallography was—and still is—difficult to apply to the study of proteins because the technique is slow. It can take five years to determine the structure of a single protein. Even today, scientists know the structure of only about 300 of the more than 30,000 proteins that exist.

The X-ray analysis of proteins was a big step forward for drug designers, however, because it enabled them to use ball-and-wire models to locate binding sites. Once a particular binding site was located, a designer could build a model of a molecule with a shape that matched the binding site, then move this model about in space to represent the docking of the molecule with the protein.

The process was slow and awkward, because proteins are so complicated. It took months to build a typical ball-and-wire model of a protein. And because proteins contain so many atoms, many models occupied more than 1 cubic meter (35 cubic feet) of space.

In early 1964, Cyrus Levinthal, a biophysicist at M.I.T., came up with a faster and handier way to use crystallographic data. At that time, M.I.T. was developing Project MAC, a computer system that could display three-dimensional structures on a televisionlike screen. Project MAC had a feature that was advanced for its time: The user could enlarge and reduce the picture and manipulate it so that it seemed to turn in space. By manipulating a picture of a cube, for example, the user could "turn" the cube so that any of its six sides faced the user.

Kendrew had recently published photographs of the internal structure of myoglobin. After seeing Kendrew's pictures, Levinthal thought of using Project MAC to manipulate models of proteins. Levinthal developed a computer program based on the positions of the atoms in myoglobin. In a short time, he was able to display and manipulate an image of that protein. The science of molecular graphics had been born.

As this science matured in the late 1960's and the 1970's, it became far better than ball-and-wire modeling. To produce an image of a protein on a computer screen, designers merely punched in the

Using a Computer to Design a Drug

A computer graphics program at Genentech, Inc., a biotechnology company in South San Francisco, is being used to determine whether a molecule being considered for use as a drug will dock with a protein that may be involved in a digestive disorder.

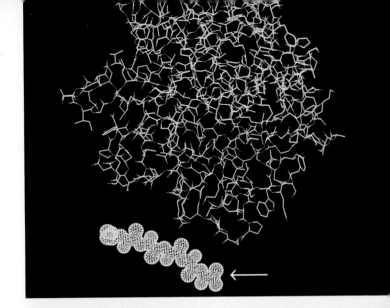

The shape and binding site of the large target protein, determined by bombarding it with X rays, is programmed into the computer and called up on the screen, *top photo.* Then the designer generates a molecule (arrow) that might fit the known binding site and thus act as a drug.

The computer graphics program allows the drug molecule to be maneuvered around the protein, *right,* in search of a possible docking position that will create a perfect fit with the binding site.

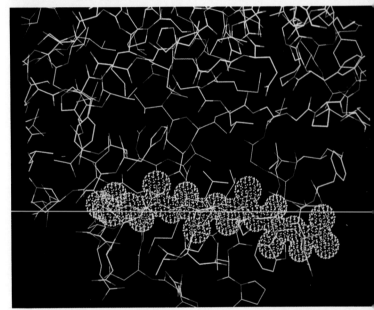

Once the molecule is docked firmly in place, *right,* the designer knows the drug will work. But the next step will be to use the computer program for examining other protein molecules in the body's vital organs to be sure the molecule does not fit their binding sites. Such a fit would mean the drug could cause harmful side effects.

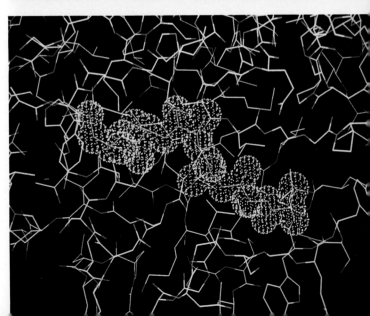

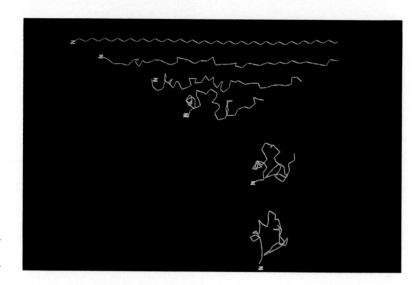

Researchers involved in computer drug design are trying to develop programs based on laws that determine how proteins fold. One such experimental program begins with a chain of *amino acids,* the building blocks of proteins, and uses a simple set of rules to make it fold in a particular sequence, *right.* The ultimate goal of protein-folding graphics programs is to eliminate the years-long process of analyzing each protein molecule with X rays.

locations of atoms as determined by X-ray crystallography. To locate binding sites, they manipulated the image so it could be viewed at various angles. To generate an image of a candidate for a drug molecule, the designers began by punching in the locations of atoms in known molecules or fragments of molecules. By manipulating the images of the protein and the molecule, the designers then represented the docking maneuver and tested the fit between the protein's binding site and the molecule.

Today's software is even more sophisticated. A researcher can call up molecular fragments from a database, for example, to construct an image of a molecule that might match a protein binding site and become a candidate for a drug.

Computer-aided drug design would become an even faster-paced and more fruitful technology if it did not have to rely on the slow method of X-ray crystallography for information concerning protein shape. Scientists could end this reliance by learning more about a molecular crumpling process known as *protein folding.* Whether produced in a living cell or in a test tube, a given sequence of amino acids always folds to assume the same shape.

Researchers are only beginning to learn the chemical laws responsible for folding. If these laws were discovered, scientists would build them into drug-design software. Then, instead of using data from X-ray crystallography, a drug designer would determine protein shape by applying this software to information available from a much faster technique called *protein sequencing*—a chemical snipping apart of a protein into its amino acids. To create an image of a particular protein, the designer would merely punch up that protein's amino acid sequence on the computer and then instruct the computer to apply the folding laws to this sequence.

No matter how advanced molecular graphics software becomes,

however, it will continue to focus on the docking maneuver. This maneuver will remain the focal point because it is crucial not only to all drug actions but also to the tactics used by *antibodies* (natural substances that fight harmful organisms) and by the disease-causing activities of viruses and bacteria.

Viruses, for example, begin their destructive work with a docking maneuver on cells. Viruses carry irregularly shaped binding sites that can dock with proteins on the surfaces of body cells. Once a virus protein docks with a cell protein, the virus's genetic material enters the cell and uses the cell's resources to produce more viruses. The new viruses then spread to other cells via the same tactic.

Drug designers might be able to create artificial antibodies that fit exactly into the binding sites of viruses and other harmful organisms. Antibodies frustrate viruses by docking with these sites, because a site that is attached to an antibody cannot dock with a cell. Antibodies also call up other immune cells to destroy the virus.

The design stage, however, marks only the beginning of an attempt to bring a lifesaving drug to the medical market place. After a well-fitting drug molecule is designed, a drug manufacturer must begin to think about creating the drug in the laboratory.

Manufacturers create most chemical drug molecules by modifying well-known drug compounds, rather than starting from scratch. Manufacturers make some protein drugs by *genetic engineering*, in which host bacteria, yeast, or animal cells are injected with genetic material that *codes for* (contains instructions for making) the protein. These biological "factories" then produce the protein that is used to make the drug.

After a manufacturer develops a drug, it determines whether it can produce the drug inexpensively enough to make the sale of the drug profitable. And before putting a new drug on the market, the manufacturer must test it.

Fewer than 2 per cent of the drugs being tested today will ever be marketed. A successful drug requires more than just a good fit into a binding site. For example, tests may show that a drug designed to fit into the binding site of a particular cell also fits into the binding sites of cells elsewhere in the body, causing an undesirable side effect. Or perhaps the drug is so unstable that it is broken down by body chemicals and does not reach a binding site intact.

Researchers first test a drug on cells grown in a laboratory. If the drug passes this test, they give it to animals to see whether it is safe and effective and to discover any side effects it may have. If the drug still seems to be a good candidate for the United States market place, the company may apply to the U.S. Food and Drug Administration (FDA)—a government agency—to conduct tests on people. Most such tests involve hundreds of patients and take up to a year. The entire procedure—from the design stage to FDA approval to sell the drug—may take 7 to 10 years and cost tens of millions of

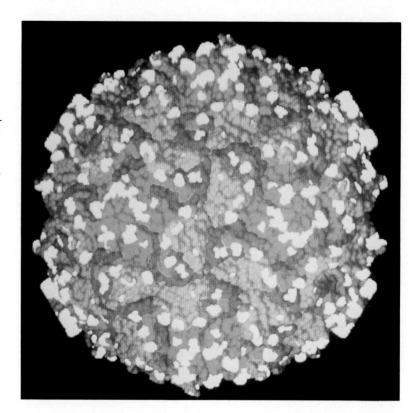

A computer-generated image of a *poliovirus, right,* the virus responsible for the crippling disease poliomyelitis, was created by researchers at the Massachusetts Institute of Technology in Cambridge. It may help researchers design another vaccine or a drug to treat the disease. The red, yellow, and blue areas represent three types of proteins. The white areas are the binding sites at which *antibodies* (natural substances that fight harmful organisms) dock to deactivate the virus.

dollars. No drug now on the market was designed exclusively on a computer, but many drugs that were designed largely with the aid of computers are now undergoing tests.

Drug companies, universities, and government research centers have acquired new computers and software with an enthusiasm and speed that is making computer-aided drug design one of the most fruitful and fastest-paced frontiers of science. One of the many incentives for drug companies is the fact that newly designed molecules can be patented and can generate enormous profits.

Artificial vaccines are one kind of drug that could one day be created with the aid of computers. Vaccines work by stimulating the body's disease-fighting immune system to make antibodies. This stimulation occurs because vaccines have binding sites that are identical, or nearly identical, to those of disease-causing organisms.

The first step in the design of an artificial vaccine for a virus is to obtain a picture of the virus's surface. This is an extremely difficult step, because viruses are made up of many different proteins and typically consist of millions of atoms.

In recent years, however, researchers have made notable progress in mapping virus proteins. In 1985, with computer graphics playing a large role, Michael G. Rossmann and his colleagues at Purdue University in West Lafayette, Ind., mapped rhinovirus-14, one of the viruses responsible for the common cold. That same year, Marie Chow of M.I.T. and James M. Hogle and David J. Filman of Scripps Clinic and Research Foundation in La Jolla, Calif., mapped the proteins of the poliovirus.

Computers are becoming increasingly important in the design of other kinds of drugs—high-blood-pressure medicines, AIDS drugs, artificial antibodies, anticancer drugs, and anti-inflammatories:

■ **Blood-pressure medication.** Computers have played their largest role to date in the design of drugs to counteract substances that cause high blood pressure. A natural substance in the body called *renin*, for example, plays a role in this disorder, so several drug companies are trying to design molecules that will dock with renin and deactivate it.

■ **AIDS drugs** are the objective of one of the most active areas of drug research. One way to prevent AIDS (acquired immune deficiency syndrome) would be to build small molecules that would dock at binding sites on surface proteins of the AIDS virus. Although scientists have identified the amino acid sequences of AIDS virus proteins, the shapes of the protein structures are still unknown.

■ **Artificial antibodies** are being designed by molecular biologists Richard Lerner and Alfonso Tramontano of Scripps and chemist Peter Schultz and his team of researchers at the University of California at Berkeley.

■ **Anticancer drugs** work by docking with cancer cells and then poisoning them. Unfortunately, the drugs also attack healthy cells. Researchers are using computers to search for a protein that is present only on cancer cells and with which a yet-to-be-designed anticancer drug could dock.

■ **Anti-inflammatory drugs.** Scientists at the Du Pont Company in Wilmington, Del., are using computers to help design a drug for the treatment of inflammation caused by arthritis. This drug would dock with a protein that is partly responsible for the inflammation. At present, such inflammation is treated with steroid drugs, which have numerous undesirable side effects, including the swelling of body tissues.

Computer-aided drug design seems certain to become even more efficient and creative than it is today as more is learned about proteins and better software is designed. With protein-folding software playing a major role, such old enemies of humanity as emphysema and cancer—as well as the new scourge of AIDS—may one day fall victim to drugs designed with the aid of computers.

For further reading:

Hogle, James M.; Chow, Marie; and Filman, David J. "The Structure of Poliovirus." *Scientific American*, March 1987.
Patrusky, Ben. "Biology's Computational Future." *Mosaic*, Vol. 16, No. 4, 1985.
Scientific American (special computers issue), October 1987.

A bold plan to seal eight people inside a closed
environment for two years may help solve
environmental problems on Earth and aid in the
design of future space colonies.

The Making
of Biosphere II

BY ELIZABETH PENNISI

An artist's conception envisions how Biosphere II will appear among the saguaro cacti in the southern Arizona desert.

In January 1990, if all goes according to plan, eight people will seal themselves into a huge glass-and-steel bubble. Cut off from the rest of the world, the bubble will sit like an alien being in a desert landscape. The bubble will enclose small-scale versions of a rain forest, an ocean, saltwater and freshwater marshes, a *savanna* (grasslands), and a desert. Is this part of a unique study in environmental science, or could it be a design for future space colonies on the moon or Mars? In the case of this experiment, the answer to that question is "both."

An ambitious group of scientists, architects, and entrepreneurs have designed the enclosure for this experiment: a 140,000-cubic-meter (5-million-cubic-foot) "greenhouse" being constructed on about 1 hectare (2.5 acres) of desert in southern Arizona. The eight people will live in the enclosure for at least two years. Scientists are calling this experiment Biosphere II because it is designed to be a miniature version of Earth's *biosphere*, the region where life exists.

In addition to the six different environments, an area will be set aside for farming and living quarters. Because they will grow their own food and their air and water will be recycled, the inhabitants of Biosphere II will be completely self-sufficient and will not need food, water, or air from outside the bubble. Only energy from sunlight will enter to heat the air and generate *photosynthesis*, the process by which plants convert carbon dioxide to food energy and give off oxygen in the process.

About 200 scientists from many fields of study have contributed knowledge and technical expertise to plan Biosphere II. Since 1984, a private company, Space Biospheres Ventures, has been designing and building Biosphere II at the base of the Santa Catalina Mountains, 56 kilometers (35 miles) north of Tucson. Funding for the $30-million project comes primarily from oil multimillionaire Edward P. Bass of Texas. The financial backers hope that their investment will lead to patents on new technologies developed for Biosphere II that may have other applications, not only for space travel but also for agriculture and for the monitoring and treatment of air and water.

Biosphere II will be the largest closed structure of its kind, but it is not a pioneer in its field. One attempt to create a closed environment for scientific study was made in 1967 by microbiologist Clair Folsome of the University of Hawaii in Honolulu. Folsome filled a round-bottomed glass flask about the size of a volleyball with water, sand, algae, and shrimp and then sealed it shut with wax. In effect, he created a miniature *ecosystem*—a system made up of a group of living things and their physical environment. Inside the flask, the shrimp, algae, and bacteria present in the sand were the living things, and the air, water, and sand were the environment. This closed ecosystem had its own food chain: The algae provided food for the shrimp, while waste matter from the shrimp, when decomposed by the bacteria, provided nutrients for the algae. Sunlight shining on the flask promoted photosynthesis in the algae. The oxygen given off by the algae was needed by the shrimp and bacteria. The shrimp and bacteria in turn produced carbon dioxide needed by the algae, establishing the balanced cycle required for this closed system to remain stable. Folsome was not sure whether his small closed system could survive. But the ecosystem that Folsome sealed in 1967 was still thriving in 1988.

The Soviet Union has also experimented with enclosed systems. The Soviet program began in the mid-1960's, according to James Bredt, former manager of Controlled Ecological Life Support Systems for the Life Sciences Division of the United States National Aeronautics and Space Administration (NASA). Soviet researchers lived in an enclosed system known as Bios located at a research institute in Krasnoyarsk, Siberia, for up to five months, according to Bredt. They raised about 80 per cent of their food.

The author:
Elizabeth Pennisi is a science writer based in Tucson, Ariz.

Biologist Clair Folsome of the University of Hawaii holds a closed ecosystem he created, consisting of air, water, sand, shrimp, algae, and bacteria. With energy from sunlight, this closed environment has all it requires to remain ecologically stable. Biosphere II's planners hope that their large-scale closed environment will remain sufficiently stable to support life.

Biosphere II, however, will be a much more ambitious experiment because it will attempt to re-create several major ecosystems found on Earth and make them self-contained enough to survive for perhaps 100 years or longer. And unlike the Soviets in Bios, the inhabitants of Biosphere II will ultimately depend entirely on the food they raise.

When completed, Biosphere II will cover an area of 9,100 square meters (98,000 square feet), the size of about two football fields. It will be divided into two attached sections. One section will contain a five-story domed house for living quarters and a 1,860-square-meter (20,000-square-foot) area for agriculture. The domed house will have apartments for Biosphere's eight inhabitants, along with a dining room, library, gymnasium, and laboratories.

The living quarters and farm area will open onto a second section 164 meters (539 feet) long by 44 meters (145 feet) wide, which will contain the six ecosystems. This section will be 24 meters (80 feet) high at one end, to accommodate a hill 15 meters (50 feet) high that is meant to resemble a rain forest mountain. At the base of the rain forest will be a lagoon and a small stream that flows through the savanna. A coral reef will separate the lagoon from the ocean, which will be divided into shallow and deep areas. At the ocean's edge will be saltwater and freshwater marshes. The desert will be at the opposite end from the rain forest. The glass-and-steel walls and roof and a stainless steel liner buried underground will completely encase both sections.

What Biosphere II Will Look Like

A test module, *right,* for the glass-and-steel structure that will enclose Biosphere II stands near the site of the planned Biosphere II on SunSpace Ranch near Tucson, Ariz. A floor plan, *below,* shows the living quarters for the eight volunteers who will occupy Biosphere II, the farm that will feed them, and the six ecosystems they will help maintain.

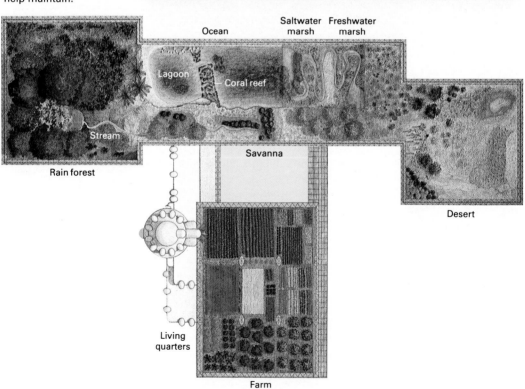

Ocean

Saltwater marsh

Freshwater marsh

Lagoon

Coral reef

Stream

Rain forest

Savanna

Desert

Living quarters

Farm

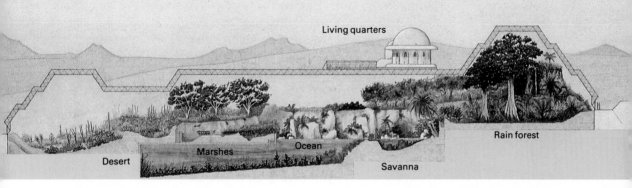

Living quarters

Desert

Marshes

Ocean

Savanna

Rain forest

A cross section of Biosphere II, *above,* shows the elevations of different environments. The desert will be at "sea level," while the rain forest will occupy the highest prominence.

Except for the energy from the sun, nothing will go in or out of Biosphere II for at least two years. As a result, air and water must be recycled and waste material broken down and made useful. For the most part, this will be accomplished by relying on cycles that occur in natural ecosystems. For example, Earth's atmosphere consists mostly of nitrogen and oxygen with traces of carbon dioxide and other gases. In Biosphere II, these gases will be continually recycled as plants supply oxygen needed by the animal inhabitants, and animals supply the carbon dioxide needed for plant photosynthesis to occur.

Earth's *nitrogen cycle* can also be duplicated in Biosphere II. In this cycle, certain kinds of bacteria in soil convert nitrogen gas in the air into compounds that can be used by plants. Other types of bacteria decompose plant matter and in the process release nitrogen gas back into the air. In Biosphere II, however, the gases in the air will have to be monitored carefully to make sure that an imbalance does not develop. Plants and some animals, for example, naturally give off toxic gases, such as methane and carbon monoxide. To control these gases, Biosphere's planners intend to pump air through special soil-filled, air-purification boxes containing microbes that devour these gases. The monitoring will be done by computers that keep track of data picked up by sensors located throughout the structure. The sensors will measure the amounts of gases in the air.

Waste material will also be recycled, mainly by artificial means. For example, water used for watering plants and for cleaning will be recycled as drinking water by passing it through various filters and soil beds containing microorganisms that break down harmful wastes. Animal waste, including that of the eight human inhabitants, will be recycled for use as fertilizer and fish food.

Another important recycling measure involves the rainfall needed for the tropical rain forest. The right "weather" will in part be achieved by the landscaping. Biosphere's desert and ocean will be at the lowest elevation, or "sea level," and the rain forest will be at the highest level. As sunlight warms the air above the desert, it will rise because warm air is buoyant. As it drifts over the ocean, it will collect moisture, and when the moist air reaches the top of Biosphere II above the rain forest, condenser coils on the ceiling will cool the air. This will cause a drizzling kind of rain or dew to fall on the forest below. The runoff from this rainfall will feed the lagoon and the stream that flows through the savanna into the marsh, and will eventually drain back to the ocean.

Biosphere's planners decided to include only tropical environments because, as with any greenhouse, they expect the enclosure to be warm and humid like the tropics. They included a number of different tropical habitats because they believe that each of these environments plays an important role in maintaining the stability needed for life on Earth. And they decided to include a wide variety of plant and animal life native to those habitats, because the greater the variety of life the less likely it will be that the failure of one plant or animal to survive will lead to the failure of other plants and animals. Biosphere's planners believe that the variety of life will make the ecosystems more stable.

A walk through Biosphere's ecosystems will be, in effect, a trip through all the tropics of the world. In a single day, Biospherians will be able to listen to tropical insect calls in a South American-like rain forest, wander through an African type of savanna, or slosh through a marsh whose plants were brought from the Florida Everglades. They can swim in an ocean or snorkel along a Caribbean coral reef and then dry off in a coastal desert like that found in Baja California Norte in Mexico.

They will also encounter about 300 land *vertebrates* (animals with backbones), including bats, songbirds, lemurs, snakes, and frogs. Each species will be brought in with a mate in the hope that they will breed. With them will come about 4,000 plant varieties along with microbes and soil—all the necessary components for rebuilding each ecosystem inside Biosphere II.

Considerable planning has gone into each of the ecosystems. A leading authority on tropical rain forests, Ghillean Prance, former senior vice president for research at The New York Botanical Garden in New York City, took on the task of selecting the plant and animal life that will make up Biosphere's rain forest. Prance and his colleagues will collect microbes found in soil from the Amazon jungle in South America. These microbes are needed to break down organic matter, such as leaves, that fall to the forest floor from the *canopy*—the crowns of trees that make up the top of the rain forest.

Botanist Tony Burgess of the United States Geological Survey designed the desert. Burgess modeled Biosphere's desert after the Vizcaíno Desert along the west coast of Baja California Norte in Mexico, which has moderate temperature variations and a high humidity. Not all of the Earth's deserts have low humidity. Some

A computer monitor, *above,* in a special laboratory set up for the planning of Biosphere II, keeps constant track of temperatures. Sensors mounted throughout Biosphere II will send data to computers so that the Biospherians can monitor temperatures in the various ecosystems and the balance of gases in the air. A researcher, *left,* inspects one of dozens of fish tanks where tilapia are being raised. These freshwater fish will be a prime source of protein for the Biospherians.

coastal deserts, such as the one in Baja and the Atacama Desert in Chile and Peru, are drenched in moisture from fogs that sweep in from the Pacific Ocean. The fog and mist rarely condense into rain, but the air contains a high degree of moisture, similar to the air in the tropics.

Ecologist Peter Warshall, a research scientist with the Office of Arid Land Studies at the University of Arizona, will select plant and animal life for the savanna. The savanna—60 meters (200 feet) long—will contain several types of African grasslands. The variety is a safeguard to help ensure that the savanna will thrive even if some grasses do not do well inside Biosphere II or if insects prefer some grasses to others and reduce the amount of those grasses. The savanna will be divided into two parts—a seep savanna, nourished by an underground waterflow created by running pipes under the soil, and a sparse, dry savanna.

Two termite mounds will rise 3 meters (9 feet) above the dry savanna's short grasses. The termites are the grass-eating kind normally found in African savannas. They will eat the savanna grasses and check their growth, which would otherwise overwhelm the savanna. The termite mounds will be imported in pieces from Africa along with a termite colony, and will then be reconstructed inside Biosphere II.

The saltwater and freshwater marshes will be among the more difficult environments to re-create. Marine biologist Walter Adey of the Marine Systems Laboratory of the Smithsonian Institution in

A Biosphere II researcher, *below,* examines the progress of plants cloned from plant tissues, rather than grown from seeds. The tissues are cultured in containers with nutrients rather than planted in soil. This method will allow the Biospherians to replace dead plants or to experiment with new ones in much less time than is required for growing plants from seeds.

Washington, D.C., came up with plans for the marsh areas. A single square meter of marsh can contain more than 100 species of plants and animals. So, instead of trying to collect these species one by one, Adey will simply dig up and transport parts of marshy areas with their plants, animals, and microbes attached.

In fact, Biosphere's watery environments will contain parts of a Caribbean coral reef and a mangrove swamp from the Florida Everglades. The coral reef will be 15 meters (50 feet) long and will separate the lagoon from the ocean. It will be constructed by making a base from a layer of limestone 4 meters (13 feet) thick taken from the ocean floor off the coast of Florida. Atop this limestone base, Adey will place coral-forming animals from the Caribbean Sea. The reef will also have algae and bacteria, which are vital to the coral, and other animal life, such as boring worms that will help recycle waste materials in the reef.

The ocean, also designed by Adey, will hold about 4 million liters (1 million gallons) of water, stocked with 150 kinds of fish and other types of marine life. Adey also designed tides and waves for the ocean and its nearby environments. Every eight seconds, a fan and compressed air from beneath the artificial ocean will generate a wave that will wash up on a beach. This kind of wave action helps replace oxygen in ocean water, which improves the productivity of ocean plants. Another system in Biosphere will make tides ebb and flow. When the ocean level rises, the nearby saltwater marsh will flood.

In a greenhouse at SunSpace Ranch, researchers experiment with various plants, *below left,* that may be grown on Biosphere's farm, while others sample a lunch of tilapia and green vegetables, *below.*

151

About 35 researchers, including biologist Carl N. Hodges, director of the Environmental Research Laboratory at the University of Arizona in Tucson, have helped develop Biosphere's farm. The farm will supply wheat, soybeans, sorghum, rice, and safflower and sunflower seeds. Other crops include beans, peas, potatoes, herbs, broccoli, and citrus fruit. Livestock will include chickens and goats. The farm area will also contain large tanks of water in which to raise a species of fish known as tilapia. Native to inland African lakes, this gray-and-orange species—called St. Peter's fish in Israel—grows fast, thrives in cramped conditions, and reproduces once a month. It will supply the Biospherians with half of their animal protein.

Shelves of test tubes and laboratory dishes will act as Biosphere's nursery. They will be used to *clone* plants. This is a technique whereby a single plant cell, grown in a special culture, rather than soil, develops into a whole plant. The laboratory will have a storage freezer full of plant tissue. When thawed, the cells from these tissues thrive in a growth media put in test tubes. They can be treated with hormones and chemicals to develop into clones, each an exact replica of the plant from which the cell originated. This type of agriculture is important to Biospherians because they have decided not to include some of the bees, wasps, and other insects that naturally pollinate crops and ensure seed production.

A Biospherian's weekly diet will consist of 227 grams (8 ounces) each of fish and chicken, a dozen eggs, and about 8 liters (2 gallons) of goat's milk. Daily rations of cereals, legumes, fruits, and vegetables will provide a total of 2,364 calories per day. Before their stay ends, 10 coffee trees will eventually supply fresh coffee beans.

Many crops will be close to harvesting when Biosphere II is sealed off in January 1990. But the Biospherians will also stock supplies to supplement what they grow, especially in the early stages. The group plans to begin partial closures of Biosphere II several months before the complete sealing off in order to work out any problems.

The eight volunteers who will inhabit Biosphere II will be selected from a group of candidates ranging in age from 20 to 50. They include a horticulturist, a botanist, a nutritionist, engineers, and computer experts. Most of the candidates have been working since 1986 to learn the techniques of tissue culture and agriculture. Each inhabitant will have to be part mechanic, part plumber, part farmer, part scientist, and part laboratory technician. According to current plans, they will work about four hours each day. They might spend this time weeding, harvesting, or planting in the agriculture wing. Or they might devote that time to making needed repairs and doing other maintenance chores. Another four hours will be devoted to scientific observation and research. Initially, they will need to observe each animal regularly to be sure it is healthy. They will keep a watchful eye on the ecosystems and have been taught to recognize subtle signs that an ecosystem is out of balance.

The inhabitants of Biosphere II will use computers to help monitor the environment. Throughout Biosphere, about 5,000 sensors will keep track of climate and growth conditions, and data from those sensors will be stored in computers as an information bank to help the Biospherians analyze problems.

Help with problems will also be available from scientists on the outside who will maintain communications by telephone. Television cameras may be set up at various locations so that outside consultants can watch an experiment in progress or get a close-up look at damage to plant life if any occurs. Information from the outside will be readily available to the inhabitants through radio and television.

In their leisure time, the Biospherians will be able to occupy themselves in a variety of ways, including exercising in the gymnasium, finding a book to read in the well-stocked library, or catching a favorite television program. "Cabin fever," however, will be an occupational hazard. But the volunteers are being selected in part because of their ability to live in isolation with just a small group of people. Of course, people can leave if a medical or other personal emergency occurs.

Even if Biosphere II is successful in Arizona, the project is still a long way from being attempted in space. Bredt, now retired from NASA, has pointed out that such a large-scale project is impractical for space missions because current rocket technology could not possibly launch the heavy and extensive components of Biosphere II to the moon or to Mars. Nevertheless, if colonies of space explorers are to be established there in the future, some type of biosphere will probably be essential, according to a 1986 report issued by the National Commission on Space, a study group of scientists and NASA officials appointed by President Ronald Reagan. In its report, *Pioneering the Space Frontier, Our Next 50 Years in Space*, the commission concluded that "to explore and settle the inner solar system, we must develop biospheres." The commission predicted that such colonies might be practical by the year 2025.

The experiment with Biosphere II may provide lessons that will one day be applied to future space colonies. But meanwhile, any immediate value of Biosphere II would probably lie in an improved understanding of tropical environments on Earth, such as what makes a biological system self-sustaining. Because the relationships between biological life and its physical environment are usually extremely complex and variable, biologists and ecologists often have difficulty understanding which relationships are essential to an ecosystem's function and stability. But since Biosphere II is artificial and self-contained, the scientists involved in this experiment believe they will have a unique laboratory in which they can both observe and control the interactions that occur in an ecosystem. "What can I learn by creating an ecosystem, rather than just observing one? That's the payoff," says Warshall.

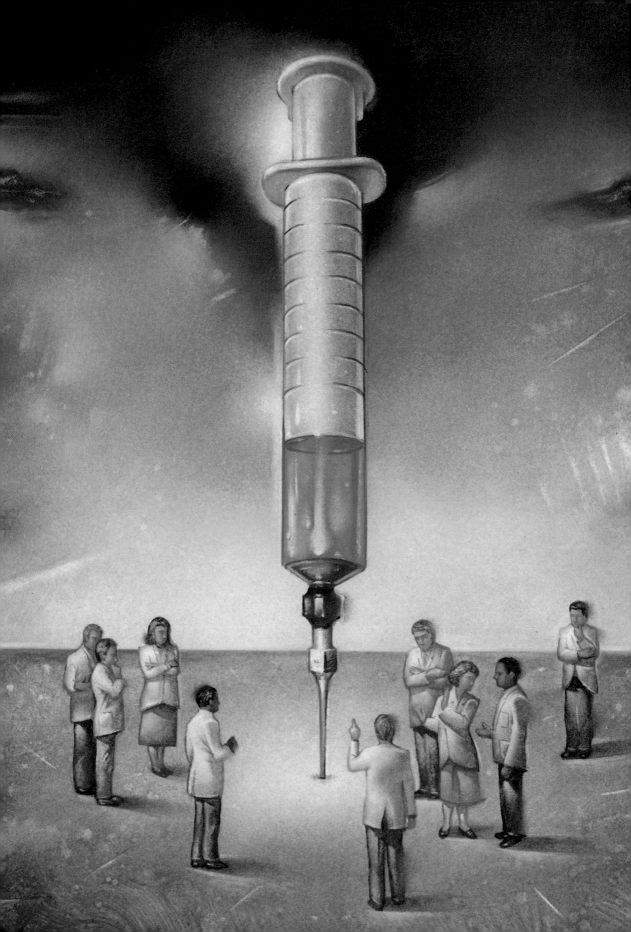

Despite the development of a number of experimental AIDS vaccines, the complexity of the AIDS virus has made the task more difficult than anyone expected.

The Search for an AIDS Vaccine

BY BEN PATRUSKY

Developing a vaccine against the virus that causes AIDS (acquired immune deficiency syndrome) was expected to be a pretty straight-forward job. After all, French and United States scientists had dis-covered the virus—in 1983 and 1984—less than three years after the disease had been identified. Their success had led many scien-tists to believe that creating an AIDS vaccine would be fairly easy.

The scientists had reason for their optimism—history. Science had already succeeded in creating a dazzling list of vaccines against other viral diseases, including rabies, polio, measles, rubella, hepa-titis B, and smallpox. Many scientists even believed that advances in molecular biology and genetic engineering technology would speed up the usually time-consuming task of building a vaccine. By 1988, however, it was apparent that despite the fairly rapid development of a number of experimental AIDS vaccines, the task was going to be more difficult than anyone had expected.

Glossary

Antibody: An immune-system molecule that locks onto a microbe's antigens and helps other parts of the immune system destroy the microbe.

Antigen: A molecule on the surface of a microbe or other invader that identifies it as foreign to the body.

Anti-idiotypes: Antibodies to antibodies that have the same shape as the antigens that stimulated the first set of antibodies.

Deoxyribonucleic acid (DNA): The molecule that makes up the genes of all plants, animals, and most viruses and carries the code for the various proteins that carry out an organism's life functions.

Gene: A segment of DNA that contains coded instructions for the production of a single protein.

Helper T cell: A type of white blood cell that orders the production of antibodies.

Retrovirus: A virus whose genes are made of RNA and that can insert a DNA copy of its genes into the genes of the cell it invades.

Reverse transcriptase: A protein in the AIDS virus's inner core that helps the virus make DNA copies of its RNA genes.

Ribonucleic acid (RNA): The molecule that carries out DNA's instructions for making proteins. The genes of some viruses are made of RNA.

The author:
Ben Patrusky is a free-lance science writer and a media consultant to several scientific institutions.

What has dampened the scientists' optimism are some discouraging facts revealed through an explosion of knowledge about the biology of the virus that causes AIDS. Scientists soon found that the AIDS virus—called the *human immunodeficiency virus* (HIV)—is unlike any other virus known to cause disease in human beings. First, it is one of a class of viruses whose genes can insert themselves into the genetic material of the cells they infect. Second, scientists discovered that the virus *mutates* (changes) quickly, producing a number of different AIDS virus types. "If you set out to dream up something nasty and rotten to stymie vaccine development, you couldn't think of anything worse than this AIDS virus," says virologist Maurice Hilleman of the Merck Institute of Therapeutics in West Point, Pa.

The need for an AIDS vaccine is urgent. An estimated 10 million people in 157 countries, mostly in Africa, are infected with the AIDS virus. The United States may have from 1 million to 1.5 million of that total.

Most people infected with the virus as yet show no symptoms of AIDS. Patients are diagnosed as having full-blown AIDS only when they develop one of several diseases—including Kaposi's sarcoma, an unusual form of skin cancer, and *Pneumocystis carinii*, a rare type of pneumonia—or damage to the nervous system. Other people infected with the AIDS virus may experience less severe symptoms, such as weight loss and fever.

Scientists still can't say for certain that every person infected with the AIDS virus will inevitably develop AIDS. But once diagnosed as having full-blown AIDS, few victims have survived longer than two or three years. Between 1981, when AIDS was first described, and mid-1988, more than 63,000 people in the United States had been diagnosed as having AIDS, and 55 per cent of the patients stricken with the disease—35,000 people—had died. The Centers for Disease Control in Atlanta, Ga., estimates that the number of new cases of AIDS diagnosed in 1991 will top 74,000, compared with 8,551 in 1985 and an estimated 21,000 in 1988 (in the Science File section, see PUBLIC HEALTH).

How the AIDS virus attacks the body

AIDS is so deadly because it attacks the immune system, the very system that normally protects the body against invasion by foreign microbes, such as bacteria and viruses. In 1981, physicians treating AIDS patients discovered that their patients had an abnormally small number of a type of white blood cell called *helper T cells*. This discovery was important because it helped to explain many of the symptoms resulting from damage to the immune system seen in advanced stages of AIDS.

Helper T cells serve as the control center of the immune system, regulating most of the system's functions. On sensing invasion by foreign microbes, helper T cells release chemicals that spur other cells in the immune system into action. For instance, helper T cells prompt another type of immune cell to manufacture and secrete molecules called *antibodies*. Antibodies recognize the invading microbes by their *antigens* (molecules on the surface of microbes that identify them as foreign to the body). The antibodies then attach themselves to the microbe like a key fitting into a lock. The helper T cells also attract immune cells called *macrophages* to the intruder. The macrophages—the scavenger cells of the immune system—surround and digest the invading microbes.

In AIDS, however, the helper T cells become the prey. That's because the AIDS virus attaches to a particular type of *receptor* on the surface of certain cells. (Receptors act as receiving stations through which substances gain entry into a cell.) Among the cells with this receptor are helper T cells and macrophages.

Another reason the AIDS virus is so deadly is that it can hide in the genetic machinery of the cells it infects. The AIDS virus belongs to a family of viruses called *retroviruses*. These viruses reproduce in a way opposite to the process that occurs in other viruses.

How the AIDS virus reproduces

The genes of plants, animals, and most viruses are made of deoxyribonucleic acid (DNA). DNA *codes for* (specifies the structure of) the various proteins that carry out the organism's life functions. When a cell makes a particular protein, it uses DNA as a blueprint for the appropriate gene. This blueprint is read by ribonucleic acid (RNA), which then directs the assembly of the protein.

In a retrovirus, however, the genetic information is encoded in RNA and the process moves in the opposite direction—from RNA to DNA. When an AIDS virus infects a helper T cell, its RNA is copied into DNA. The copying is done by a protein called *reverse transcriptase*, which the AIDS virus makes. The DNA copy of the genes of the AIDS virus then becomes a part of the cell's own genetic machinery.

The DNA copy may lie dormant in an infected cell for a very long time, even years, without causing noticeable symptoms. Scientists theorize that the AIDS virus DNA is activated when the cell tries to fight off another invading microbe—perhaps unrelated to the AIDS virus. The activated AIDS virus genes take over the cell's genetic machinery to make copies of the virus. The new AIDS viruses burst from the cell and infect other helper T cells. Eventually, the large number of AIDS viruses cripples the immune system.

For scientists seeking to prevent or interrupt this process with a vaccine, the AIDS virus has presented some unique problems. The purpose of an AIDS vaccine is the same as that of other vaccines—to stimulate the production of antibodies tailored to the antigens of a particular disease-causing microbe. Then if that microbe does attack, the immune system recognizes the antigens and quickly responds by making large numbers of antibodies. Most vaccines are

Milestones in AIDS Research

1981—Doctors in the United States begin reporting cases of a disease in which healthy young men fall victim to a variety of rare infections and cancers.

September 1982—The Centers for Disease Control names the disease *acquired immune deficiency syndrome* (AIDS) after researchers there discover that it causes a weakening of the body's disease-fighting immune system.

1983—Researchers led by Luc Montagnier of the Pasteur Institute in Paris discover a virus they believe causes AIDS.

1984—Two teams of scientists in the United States independently identify a virus that causes AIDS. The French and American discoveries are found to be the same virus.

December 1986 — Researchers headed by Daniel Zagury of the Pierre and Marie Curie University in Paris begin the first human tests of an experimental AIDS vaccine in France and Zaire.

August 1987—The Food and Drug Administration (FDA) approves the first human tests in the United States of an experimental AIDS vaccine developed by MicroGeneSys, Incorporated.

November 1987—The FDA approves human tests of a second experimental AIDS vaccine developed by Oncogen.

Late 1987—Jonas Salk, the developer of a polio vaccine, begins human tests of an experimental AIDS vaccine for people already infected with the disease.

April 1988—British health officials approve human tests of an AIDS vaccine manufactured by Viral Technologies Incorporated.

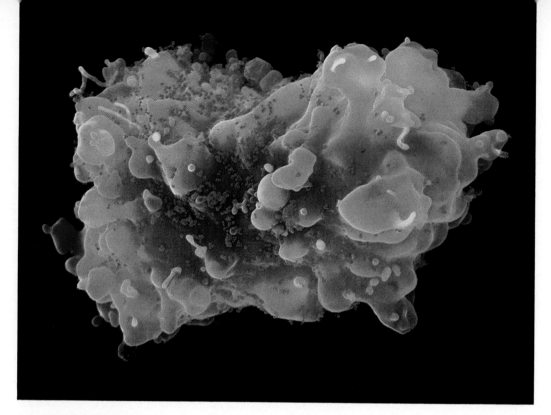

A powerful microscope reveals tiny AIDS viruses (blue and greatly magnified) swarming over a helper T cell, a special cell of the body's disease-fighting immune system.

made from killed or weakened viruses. These viruses can stimulate immunity without causing symptoms of the disease.

But a human vaccine has never been developed against a retrovirus. In addition, because the AIDS virus mutates and now exists in a variety of types, a vaccine effective against one type would not necessarily protect against others.

Researchers also faced a dilemma stemming from the AIDS virus's route of infection. Most other viral diseases are spread only by the virus. In AIDS, however, both the virus itself and virus-infected cells can transmit the infection. No previous vaccine has had to spur the body's immune system into combating such a two-pronged assault. And, of course, there was the basic problem that the AIDS virus targets the very cells—helper T cells—that orchestrate the body's counterattack against viral invasion.

Seeking a safe vaccine

One of the first decisions confronting AIDS vaccine researchers was the type of vaccine to make. For safety's sake, most scientists decided to avoid the most common type of vaccine, one made of killed whole viruses. They were concerned that some viruses would escape being killed and that live, potent AIDS viruses would find their way into a whole-virus vaccine. So, in 1984, a number of researchers decided to follow the route being used at that time to develop a vaccine against hepatitis B, a viral disease that affects the liver. The vaccine, approved for human use in 1986, consists of a noninfectious fragment of the hepatitis virus. The fragment, a protein antigen found on the surface of the virus, stimulates the immune system by provoking the production of antibodies. The vaccine was made using genetic engineering techniques—that is, by introducing the genes coding for the hepatitis protein antigen into harmless yeast cells. These cells made large amounts of the antigen, which was extracted and purified to make a vaccine. Researchers decided this approach might lead them to an effective AIDS vaccine as well.

The complexity of the AIDS virus, however, called for some new and ingenious strategies. The AIDS virus, like all viruses, consists of an inner core and an outer coat. Parts of the outer coat stick out from the virus like little spikes. These spikes serve as the virus's identifying antigens. Scientists found, however, that the AIDS virus's outer coat and antigens are not made of protein alone—as many viruses are—but rather of a glycoprotein, a mix of protein and sugars in about equal proportions. Scientists did not believe that the yeast or bacteria commonly used to genetically manufacture vaccines could produce the complex AIDS glycoprotein. This forced researchers to seek alternative "biological factories."

Three experimental vaccines

One research team, made up of scientists from MicroGeneSys, Incorporated, a biotechnology company in West Haven, Conn., and from the National Institute of Allergy and Infectious Diseases (NIAID) in Bethesda, Md., turned to insect cells. Using genetic engineering techniques, they inserted the gene for one of the AIDS glycoproteins into a virus that infects butterflies and moths. The virus carried the AIDS glycoprotein gene into the nucleus of the insect cell. The insect cells successfully produced large amounts of the glycoprotein. To make a vaccine, the scientists purified the glycoprotein, then mixed it with a chemical that boosts the glycoprotein's ability to stimulate an immune response. This chemical was needed because the immune response stimulated by a fragment of a virus is not as strong as the response stimulated by a whole virus.

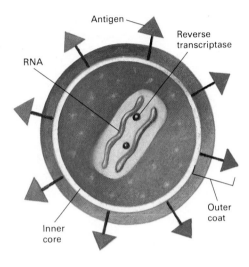

The AIDS Virus
The AIDS virus consists of an outer coat, an inner core, and genetic material called *ribonucleic acid* (*RNA*). Parts of the outer coat stick out like little spikes. These spikes serve as *antigens*. When the virus invades a person's body, the body recognizes the antigens as foreign to the person's immune system. A protein in the inner core, called reverse transcriptase, enables the virus to make *deoxyribonucleic acid* (*DNA*) copies of its RNA genes and insert them into the genetic material of the cell that it invades.

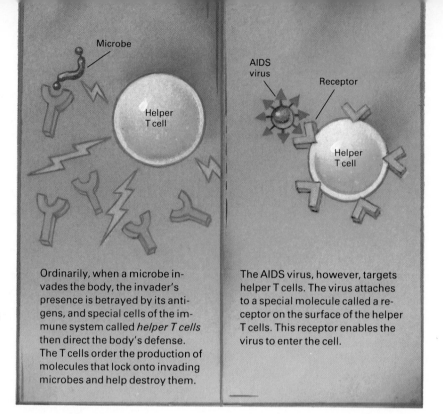

AIDS Attacks the Immune System

The AIDS virus is so deadly because it attacks the immune system, the body's defense against invasion by disease-causing microbes, such as bacteria and viruses.

Ordinarily, when a microbe invades the body, the invader's presence is betrayed by its antigens, and special cells of the immune system called *helper T cells* then direct the body's defense. The T cells order the production of molecules that lock onto invading microbes and help destroy them.

The AIDS virus, however, targets helper T cells. The virus attaches to a special molecule called a receptor on the surface of the helper T cells. This receptor enables the virus to enter the cell.

Two other teams—one at Oncogen, a company based in Seattle, and another at Pierre and Marie Curie University in Paris—tried a slightly different approach. They inserted the gene for one of the glycoproteins into a *vaccinia* virus, a large virus once used to inoculate against smallpox. The genetically engineered *vaccinia* virus was then used as the vaccine.

In tests of these three vaccines as well as four other experimental vaccines, researchers found that laboratory animals produced antibodies to AIDS. And when the scientists placed the antibodies in cultures containing human helper T cells, then added the AIDS virus, the virus did not infect the cells. The scientists theorized that the antibodies had attached to the virus and prevented it from attaching to the T cell receptors. Some research groups, including the Oncogen team, then tested their vaccine in chimpanzees. But when the immunized chimps were injected with the AIDS virus, the vaccine did not protect them.

The first human tests

In December 1986, the French team, headed by virologist Daniel Zagury, announced that they had injected their vaccine into 11 human volunteers who had been tested and found not to be infected with the AIDS virus. Among the volunteers was Zagury himself. The MicroGeneSys team also went directly to tests in human beings. Their tests were approved by the U.S. Food and Drug Administra-

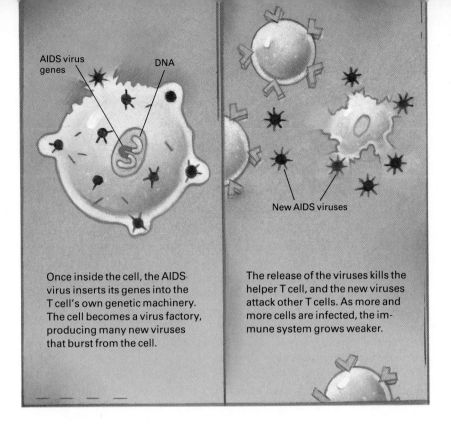

AIDS virus genes

DNA

New AIDS viruses

Once inside the cell, the AIDS virus inserts its genes into the T cell's own genetic machinery. The cell becomes a virus factory, producing many new viruses that burst from the cell.

The release of the viruses kills the helper T cell, and the new viruses attack other T cells. As more and more cells are infected, the immune system grows weaker.

tion (FDA) in August 1987 and began in September. Despite the problems with the chimpanzee tests, the FDA also approved the beginning of human trials of the Oncogen vaccine in November 1987. The scientists and government officials sanctioning the trials argued that the vaccine may have failed to ward off infection because the concentration of the virus to which the chimpanzees were exposed was very high and therefore overwhelmed what would normally have been an adequate level of antibodies.

All three vaccines were in the first stage of testing in 1988, being evaluated in a small number of volunteers. The first stage of testing is carried out to determine only whether the vaccines are safe and whether they stimulate the production of antibodies. In April 1988, Zagury announced that he had developed an immune response to the AIDS virus. That is, his immune system produced both antibodies and other immune cells that attached to the AIDS virus when they were mixed together in laboratory cultures. In May 1988, researchers testing the MicroGeneSys vaccine announced that 6 of 59 volunteers injected with the vaccine also produced antibodies that attached to the AIDS virus in laboratory tests. There was no evidence, however, that the antibodies or other immune system cells produced by Zagury and the MicroGeneSys subjects would prevent infection by the AIDS virus. Researchers also stressed that given the many uncertainties still surrounding the experimental vaccines, there was no way of telling when—or if—tests to establish whether the vaccines actually protect against AIDS will be undertaken.

Some researchers have criticized the rapid move to human trials. They argue that all the research groups should have done chimpanzee testing to be sure that the vaccines were safe and effective. Researchers testing the AIDS vaccines, however, argue that studies on chimpanzees or other laboratory animals would be useless, because AIDS affects only people. Even chimps, which can be infected with the AIDS virus, are not known to develop full-blown AIDS.

Many uncertainties

Aside from safety considerations, other questions have been raised about the true worth of these vaccines. Scientists are especially concerned about the tendency of genes coding for the antigens on the surface of the virus to mutate frequently. As a result, a vaccine effective against one type of AIDS virus may be ineffective against another. For this reason, some researchers believe that an AIDS vaccine will have to be made of antigens from several different types. The polio vaccine is such a mixture, containing three different strains of polio virus.

Something else worries researchers even more. No one really knows what kind of immune response an AIDS vaccine must provoke in order to provide future protection. That is, researchers don't know whether antibodies or other immune system cells play a more important role in fighting the virus. And if antibodies are the key, will antibodies to only a fragment of the virus's protein coat provide enough protection?

Determining the proper makeup and dosage of a vaccine against other diseases has been relatively easy. All scientists had to do was look at the amount and type of antibodies in the blood of people who survived the disease. But scientists have not yet found anyone who has recovered from an AIDS infection.

Researchers have found some clues, however, to how much antibody must be produced by analyzing the activity of antibodies against specific AIDS antigens at various stages of the disease—from initial infection to full-blown AIDS. For example, one significant antibody seems to be the antibody produced against a protein found just below the outer coat of the virus. Scientists have found that when levels of this antibody start to drop, patients begin to develop worsening symptoms of AIDS. The researchers are not sure, however, whether this antibody plays an important role in defending the body against AIDS or whether its decrease is merely an early sign of a weakening immune system. But because this inner protein is found in all strains of the AIDS virus, it has become the focus of vaccine research by an increasing number of scientists. In April 1988, health officials in Great Britain approved human tests there of a vaccine consisting of a synthetic version of the inner protein. The vaccine, manufactured using genetic engineering techniques, is made by Viral Technologies Incorporated in Washington, D.C.

Some research teams have gone even deeper into the AIDS virus

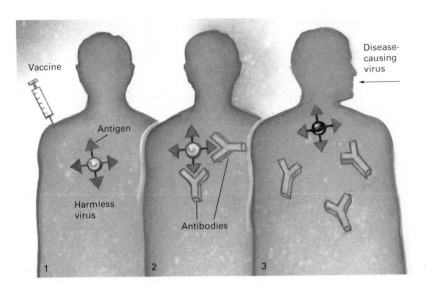

How a Vaccine Normally Works

A vaccine protects against disease by teaching the immune system the identity of a virus or other microbe before it actually invades the body. The vaccine, which consists of killed or weakened microbes or pieces of the microbe (1), stimulates the immune system to produce antibodies tailored to fit that microbe's antigens like a key fits into a lock (2). Then if the microbe later invades the body, the immune system is primed to quickly recognize and destroy it (3).

Labels in figure: Vaccine · Antigen · Harmless virus · Antibodies · Disease-causing virus

in a search for other chemicals common to all strains of the virus. They are focusing on reverse transcriptase, the enzyme that is used to make DNA from RNA. But some scientists believe this approach appears to be less promising.

Other vaccines and drugs

Scientists are investigating other strategies as well. A number of researchers, including a team led by Ronald C. Kennedy of the Southwest Foundation for Biomedical Research in San Antonio, are trying to develop a vaccine made of antibodies to antibodies. These vaccine antibodies—called *anti-idiotypes*—have a shape that is virtually identical to that of the AIDS virus antigen.

Kennedy and his team made the anti-idiotypes in a two-stage process. First they injected the AIDS antigen into laboratory animals. The antibodies to the AIDS virus that the animals produced were collected and injected into a second group of animals. These animals produced antibodies to the antibodies—anti-idiotypes— which had the same shape as the AIDS virus antigen that stimulated the first set of antibodies. As a result, these antigen look-alikes provoke the same immune response as the real AIDS antigen. But because they lack the virus's genes and other dangerous parts, they do not cause the disease. In March 1987, Kennedy reported that in laboratory studies, the antibodies to AIDS antibodies were able to neutralize various types of the AIDS virus.

Although most AIDS vaccine research is focusing on prevention, some scientists are also seeking to devise vaccines and other drugs that will boost the immune system of people already infected with the virus. In March 1987, for example, the FDA approved the use of zidovudine (formerly called azidothymidine or AZT), a drug that

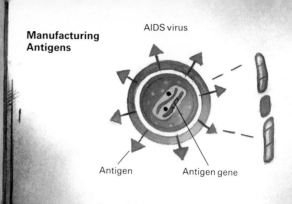

Manufacturing Antigens

AIDS virus

Antigen   Antigen gene

Making an AIDS vaccine from only part of the AIDS virus can eliminate the risk of triggering the disease. The process begins by removing from the AIDS virus the gene that *codes for* (specifies the structure of) part of the virus's outer coat, including antigens.

Attempts at Making an AIDS Vaccine

Scientists are trying several ways to create a vaccine that will provide immunity to infection by the AIDS virus, yet pose no danger of triggering the disease. Their approaches include manufacturing genetically engineered AIDS virus antigens, inserting AIDS genes into a harmless "carrier" virus, and creating a unique vaccine from antibodies to AIDS virus antibodies.

Harnessing the *Vaccinia* Virus

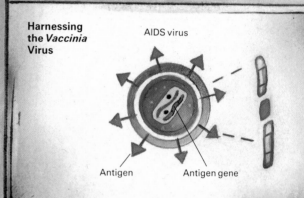

AIDS virus

Antigen   Antigen gene

Scientists are experimenting with adding the AIDS antigen gene to the *vaccinia* virus, which is used to inoculate against smallpox. This process also begins by removing the AIDS antigen gene.

Playing Tricks with Antibodies

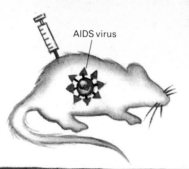

AIDS virus

An experimental vaccine made of antibodies to AIDS antibodies could prime the immune system to fight the AIDS virus. To create the first set of antibodies, the AIDS virus is injected into a laboratory mouse.

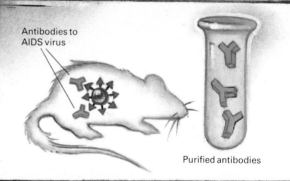

Antibodies to AIDS virus

Purified antibodies

The mouse's immune system produces antibodies against the AIDS virus. These antibodies are removed and purified.

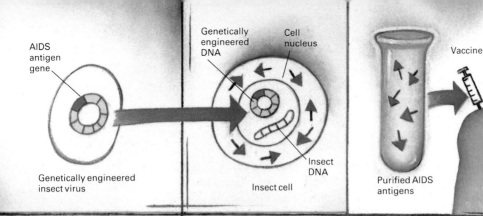

The AIDS antigen gene is inserted into a virus that infects insect cells. The virus is used to carry the AIDS antigen gene into the insect cell.

The AIDS virus gene then enters the insect cell's nucleus and causes the cell to manufacture great quantities of AIDS virus antigens.

The antigens are then extracted and purified to make a vaccine that is injected into the body. Scientists hope the synthetic antigens will stimulate the production of antibodies to the AIDS virus.

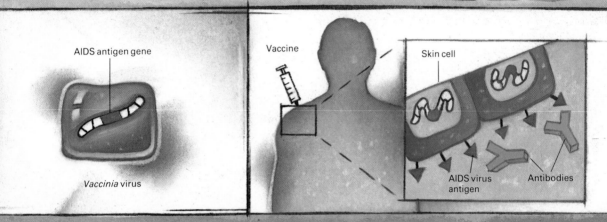

The AIDS virus gene is spliced into the genetic material of *vaccinia* viruses. The altered *vaccinia* viruses are then used to make a vaccine.

When injected into the body, the viruses infect skin cells, which produce AIDS virus antigens. These antigens may be able to stimulate the production of antibodies to the AIDS virus.

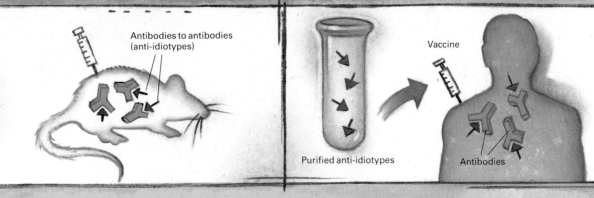

The purified antibodies are injected into a second mouse, which makes antibodies against the antibodies. They are called *anti-idiotypes*. These antibodies to antibodies mirror the shape of the original AIDS antigens.

The antigen look-alikes are extracted and purified to create a vaccine that may be able to stimulate the body's immune system to produce protective antibodies against the real AIDS virus.

apparently works by suppressing the ability of the AIDS virus to reproduce inside cells. Studies showed that the drug prolonged the life of some AIDS patients.

Other researchers are attempting to develop drugs that will prevent a person who is infected by the virus but has no symptoms of AIDS from becoming ill. One ingenious strategy involves the use of a decoy to attract the AIDS virus and block its action against helper T cells. The virus begins its attack against a helper T cell by attaching to a receptor on the surface of the cell. This process occurs in all types of the virus. Several research teams are investigating whether copies of the receptor given in large doses could prevent the AIDS virus from attaching to the helper T cell receptors. Laboratory studies have revealed that when the genetically engineered receptor is mixed with a culture containing the AIDS virus and healthy helper T cells, the decoy receptor fastens to the virus, preventing it from infecting the cells. Small-scale tests in human beings of a drug made of the decoy receptors were expected to begin in 1988.

Physician Jonas Salk, who in the 1950's developed the first polio vaccine, is taking a traditional approach. He is working with whole, killed AIDS viruses, which he believes pose little threat to people already infected. In tests on human volunteers, which began in late 1987, Salk has been investigating whether killed viruses can stimulate the production of antibodies and activity by other immune cells that would destroy the AIDS virus. Some scientists have criticized Salk's approach, arguing that the whole virus vaccine might overstimulate the damaged immune systems of AIDS patients, causing them to weaken sooner than they normally would.

AIDS vaccine ethics

Scientists testing the effectiveness of AIDS vaccines are also being confronted with difficult legal and ethical problems. For example, researchers are ethically bound to teach the volunteers how to avoid exposure to the AIDS virus. But how can a vaccine be adequately tested if people do not become exposed? How will the researchers know whether the vaccine works?

In addition, vaccine manufacturers may have difficulty obtaining liability insurance against adverse reactions to any vaccines. In 1976, the refusal of insurance companies to provide coverage to manufacturers of the swine flu vaccine forced the U.S. government to assume liability. By 1986, more than $4 billion in claims had been brought against the government for injuries and deaths blamed on the vaccine. In the case of AIDS, which has a much longer incubation period than flu—perhaps as long as 7 to 10 years—the claims could be substantially higher.

The long incubation period will also complicate efforts to determine whether the vaccine works. How long must researchers wait to establish that a volunteer is really protected?

To acquire enough statistical evidence to demonstrate effectiveness, vaccine researchers will also have to test large numbers of volunteers, ultimately numbering in the thousands. There are serious concerns about whether enough people in groups among which AIDS is most common—male homosexuals, intravenous drug abusers and their sexual partners, and newborn babies of infected mothers—can be found in the United States to serve as subjects. Many vaccine manufacturers may instead have to launch their trials in Africa, where infection rates are high. Considering how many vaccines are currently under development, manufacturers are sure to face difficult political as well as logistical and ethical problems.

AIDS can be prevented

Despite the many hurdles blocking the way to successful vaccine development, there is good news about the fight against AIDS that should not be overlooked or undersold. One means of preventing AIDS is already at hand—education. Public health officials repeatedly warn that AIDS cannot be caught by casual contact; infection results from an exchange of either semen or blood. In an overwhelming majority of cases, the AIDS virus has been transmitted through sexual relations or by sharing needles during intravenous drug use. Proper precautions or restraint will definitely keep the infection at bay. Thanks to education programs that have led to major changes in sexual practices, the rate of new infections among male homosexuals, previously the group most susceptible to AIDS infection, has dropped to almost zero in the United States. Drug abusers, who are generally less responsive to education programs, have replaced homosexuals as the primary victims of new infections. Despite the education efforts, however, many health officials believe that only a vaccine can stem the tide.

AIDS research has progressed—and continues to progress—at a dizzying pace, with new discoveries being reported continually. In March 1988, for example, researchers indicated that macrophages—the scavengers of the immune system—may play a central role in transmitting the AIDS virus to helper T cells and other body cells. Such discoveries may make the production of a vaccine easier or they may throw up new obstacles for vaccine researchers.

How soon will a vaccine be available? Perhaps the best answer is that no one knows, or—as virologist Maurice Hilleman said—"The likelihood of a successful vaccine is anywhere from zero to 100 per cent in no less than one year to an upper limit of eternity."

For further reading:

Surgeon General's Report on Acquired Immune Deficiency Syndrome, U.S. Department of Health and Human Services, 1986. To obtain a copy, call the American Social Health Association's toll-free Hot Line (1-800-342-7514).
Weisburd, Stefi. "AIDS Vaccines: The Problems of Human Testing." *Science News*, May 23, 1987.

Justly proud of its illustrious past, this renowned French research institution looks forward to another century of accomplishment in the fight against disease.

The Pasteur Institute at 100

BY ALEXANDER DOROZYNSKI

Late into the night of April 2, 1987, the plush Beau Rivage hotel in Geneva, Switzerland, buzzed with excitement as representatives of Sotheby's, a well-known London art firm, auctioned off the jewels of the late Duchess of Windsor. A Japanese businessman bid $3.15 million for a diamond ring, and actress Elizabeth Taylor picked up a brooch for $565,000. Not a single bauble was left when the sale ended the next day.

The $50 million raised by the auction went to the Pasteur Institute of Paris, one of the world's leading centers for the study of disease and the primary beneficiary of the duchess's will. She wanted to honor France, where she and her husband, the former King Edward VIII of Great Britain, had made their home after he re-

A bust of Louis Pasteur stands watch at the entrance of the institute's original building, which opened in 1888.

nounced the throne in 1936 to marry her. And she chose the Pasteur Institute as the most worthy symbol of that nation.

The windfall from the duchess's estate, an amount equal to half of the institute's annual budget, arrived as the institute was preparing the 1988 celebration of its 100th anniversary. This "birthday present" undoubtedly would have pleased Louis Pasteur, the great French scientist who developed the first rabies vaccine and for whom the institute is named. Pasteur had wanted the institute to remain an independent foundation, supported in part by voluntary contributions from the public it was dedicated to serve. The Windsor bequest came at just the right time to help the institute expand its activities and modernize its equipment and facilities. The funds have already been earmarked for several projects, including the construction of a research building for the study of viruses.

The Pasteur Institute is more than just a research facility; it is a national institution that plays an important role in France's health care system. In addition to conducting research on various infectious diseases, the institute has the responsibility of maintaining sufficient stocks of vaccines to handle a national epidemic. It also keeps track of a number of infectious diseases in France and other countries for the French Ministry of Health and the World Health Organization, an agency of the United Nations. The institute maintains links with 20 other Pasteur institutes the world over—offshoots of the original Paris laboratory—and its teaching center offers courses for several hundred students every year.

The institute was inaugurated on Nov. 14, 1888, in Vaugirard, then a suburb of Paris dotted with vegetable gardens and dimly illuminated by oil lamps. Visible in the distance from the newly constructed institute building—a slate-roofed brick structure embellished with white cornerstones—was the rising steel frame of a strange-looking structure, the Eiffel Tower, being erected for the 1889 World's Fair.

Louis Pasteur, the guest of honor at the institute's dedication ceremony, was at the peak of his public glory, but his best days of work and health were behind him. He was 65 years old and partially paralyzed from a stroke suffered 20 years earlier. Yet he would serve as the institute's first director until his death in 1895.

Pasteur's illustrious scientific career, which began when he was just 24, had led him from chemistry to microbiology to medicine. He had identified the role of *microbes* (microorganisms) in many diseases and in biological processes such as fermentation and decomposition. Armed with that knowledge, he developed *pasteurization*, the use of heat to destroy disease-causing microbes, or germs, in foods and beverages. Furthermore, realizing that germs posed a serious danger to medical patients, he urged physicians to always wash their hands thoroughly before treating patients and to sterilize all instruments and bandages. Pasteur also saved the French silk indus-

The author:
Alexander Dorozynski is a free-lance writer based in Paris.

A portrait of Pasteur, *left,* painted in 1885, depicts the scientist in his laboratory at work on a vaccine for rabies. In a painting depicting the early use of the vaccine, *below,* Pasteur, at left, holds a list of patients who have come for inoculations. Because Pasteur was not a physician, the vaccine was administered by a medical colleague, far right.

Alphonse Laveran

Elie Metchnikoff

Jules Bordet

Charles Nicolle

try by identifying a microorganism that was killing silkworms, and he produced a vaccine against anthrax, an infectious disease often fatal to sheep. Finally, in the early 1880's, Pasteur developed a vaccine against the deadly nerve-destroying disease rabies, spread by infected animals.

Pasteur did not discover vaccination; doctors had been vaccinating people against smallpox since about 1800. But Pasteur was the first to realize that vaccination was a general principle that could be applied to many diseases, not just smallpox. He found that microbes known to cause rabies, anthrax, and other diseases can be weakened in the laboratory and then given in a vaccine to an animal or human being. Though unable to cause illness, the "defused" microbe triggers an immune response—a protective reaction by the body's immune system. After that, if the actual disease-causing microbe enters the body, the immune system recognizes and overwhelms it.

Pasteur and his colleagues prepared the rabies vaccine from the spinal cords of rabbits that had died of the disease. The infected spinal cords were placed in flasks, preserved with a chemical, and exposed to sterile air. The action of oxygen on the spinal cords progressively weakened the rabies microbe, a virus, until it was incapable of causing disease.

Pasteur administered his new experimental vaccine to a number of dogs that had been bitten by rabid animals. Very few of the dogs developed rabies, and by trial and error, Pasteur was able to further improve the vaccine. By 1885, he was so sure of the preparation that he thought of testing it on himself or on condemned criminals. But on July 6 of that year, Joseph Meister, a 9-year-old boy who had been bitten by a rabid dog, was brought to Pasteur's laboratory. Assured by physicians that the boy would die if not treated immediately, Pasteur agreed he should be vaccinated, a treatment that involved a series of 12 injections of vaccine over a period of 12 days. In the final phase of the treatment, Joseph was injected with highly infectious material from day-old cultures.

Pasteur spent weeks torn between anguish and hope. But Joseph survived, and a few years later he was hired as a gatekeeper at the institute. Soon Pasteur successfully vaccinated another child, and the news spread rapidly that rabies had been conquered. Patients from throughout Europe crowded Pasteur's laboratory to receive the vaccine, among them a group of 19 Russian peasants who had been severely bitten by a rabid wolf. By late 1886, well over 2,000 people had been vaccinated against rabies, and the vaccine protected all but 10 of them. Most of the 10 people who developed rabies and died had received the vaccine too late.

In honor of Pasteur's service to the nation and to humanity, the Academy of Sciences, a French society for the advancement of the physical and biological sciences, decided to create a special establishment for the treatment of rabies, to be called the Institut Pasteur. An international campaign to raise funds for the institute was set up, and donations poured in from around the world. The gifts ranged from a few francs each from thousands of individuals to larger donations from business people and national rulers, such as the czar of Russia and the sultan of Turkey. In all, nearly 2.6 million francs (equivalent to about $8 million today) was raised.

Pasteur himself wrote the statutes of the institute. It was to be an independent foundation with, initially, four main departments: rabies, bacteriology (the study of bacteria), anthrax vaccine production, and physician education, in which doctors would be taught the applications of microbiology in medicine. Pasteur was named director for life.

The original staff of the institute consisted of scientists and physicians who had already worked with Pasteur. But there was a notable addition in 1892: Elie Metchnikoff, an eccentric, fiery, long-haired and bushy-bearded Russian bacteriologist with a great appetite for yogurt. Pasteur personally persuaded Metchnikoff to move to France to work at the institute. Metchnikoff discovered *phagocytosis*, the ability of certain kinds of white blood cells to engulf and "digest" bacteria and other foreign particles. He was also one of the pioneers of *immunology*—the study of how the body resists disease and how that resistance can be artificially enhanced.

Because Metchnikoff was married, he lived nearby and commuted to work each day. But the majority of the researchers were bachelors. They lived in small rooms on the top floor of the institute and took most of their meals in the dining hall, whimsically called *Le Microbe d'Or* (The Golden Microbe).

Under Pasteur's guidance, research flourished. Pasteur oversaw development of a successful treatment for diphtheria, a severe respiratory disease that was then the greatest killer of children in Western countries. Two institute bacteriologists, Emile Roux and Swiss-born Alexandre Yersin, showed that the disease was transmitted by a *bacillus*, a rod-shaped bacterium. In 1894, institute personnel began treating diphtheria-stricken children with an *antitoxin* extracted from the blood of horses that had been deliberately infected with diphtheria. (An antitoxin is a substance that neutralizes a toxin, or poison.) The horses' immune systems produced the antitoxin in response to the toxin released by the diphtheria microbes.

Daniel Bovet

François Jacob

André Lwoff

Jacques Monod

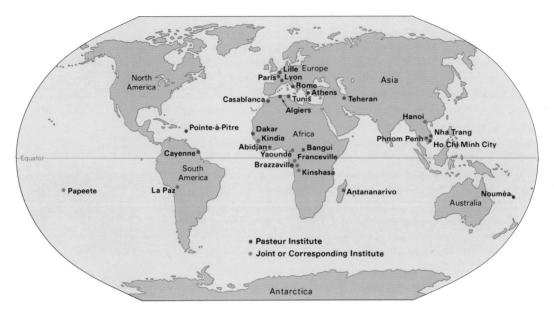

The far-flung domain of the Pasteur Institute includes the original Paris institute; institutes in Lille and Lyon, France; and 26 Overseas Pasteur Institutes, most of them in former French colonies in Africa and Asia. The foreign institutes were incorporated into national health care systems after the end of the colonial era in the mid-1900's, but 18 still bear the name of Pasteur. The other 8 are now known as joint or corresponding institutes.

The Pasteur "Empire"

Also in 1894, Yersin identified the bacillus that causes bubonic plague. For at least 2,500 years, this devastating and often fatal disease had been one of the greatest health threats facing humanity. A colleague of Yersin's, Paul Louis Simond, later proved that the plague bacillus is transmitted by fleas.

Pasteur died in 1895 at the age of 72 and was buried in an elaborate crypt in the basement level of the institute. Pasteur was succeeded as director by Emile Duclaux, a bacteriologist who had been one of his closest associates. When Duclaux died in 1904, the directorship passed to Emile Roux.

Under the leadership of Duclaux and Roux, the institute experienced some of its most productive and glorious years. By the beginning of World War I in 1914, researchers at the institute—Pastorians, as they had come to be known—had made a number of important contributions to the study and conquest of disease. Among other accomplishments, they had:

- Discovered the bacillus responsible for whooping cough, a childhood respiratory disease.
- Shown that fleas and lice are the carriers of typhus, an infectious illness that causes high fever and extreme weakness, and developed a typhus vaccine, the first vaccine made with a microbe that had been killed rather than just weakened.
- Begun to develop *antimicrobials*—drugs that destroy or weaken microbes in the body.
- Made pioneering studies of viruses, even though microscopes powerful enough to see a virus had not yet been invented.
- Found that polio is caused by a virus.
- Discovered *bacteriophages*, viruses that infect bacteria.

The work being conducted at the institute attracted international attention. In 1907, Alphonse Laveran, a pioneer in the study of malaria and other parasitic diseases, became the first Pastorian to be awarded the Nobel Prize for physiology or medicine. Metchnikoff received a Nobel the following year.

During those early years, the institute also continued a project outlined by Pasteur before his death: "We must train in the Paris establishment young scientists who will carry the mission in remote countries." Those remote countries were primarily the colonies of the rapidly expanding French colonial empire in Africa and Asia. The first in a series of Overseas Pasteur Institutes was created in Saigon, Vietnam, in 1890. It was followed in succeeding years by institutes in the African countries of Algeria, Congo, Madagascar, Senegal, and Tunisia and in the French Pacific Islands. Eventually, a network of 26 institutes was established. The overseas institutes were integrated into the national health care systems of their respective countries after the end of French colonial rule, but 18 still bear Pasteur's name. Two additional Pasteur institutes were created in France, one in Lille and the other in Lyon.

The Paris institute opened a nonprofit hospital in 1900, the first in the world specifically designed for the isolation of infectious patients. During World War I, the institute supplied antitoxins and vaccines to the civilian population, the Red Cross, and the armed forces of France and the United States. An institute physician, René Legroux, designed mobile laboratories for the diagnosis and treatment of infectious diseases on the battlefield.

The striking Pasteur Institute in Dakar, Senegal, *above,* is one of 12 overseas institutes in Africa.

But not all of the institute's efforts were devoted to saving lives. In April 1915, near the Belgian town of Ypres, the German army—in a flagrant violation of the rules of war—released a toxic gas that disabled 15,000 Allied troops. Some 5,000 of those soldiers, their lungs ravaged, died days or weeks later. In retaliation, the Allies began themselves to use poison gas, and Pastorians became involved in the production and testing of war gases at the institute.

After the war, with life back to normal, Pastorians embarked on another series of discoveries. Bacteriologist Albert Calmette and his colleague Camille Guérin developed a tuberculosis vaccine. Another bacteriologist, Gaston Ramon, showed that weakened toxins are capable of stimulating immunity and that an *adjuvant* (booster) can increase the effectiveness of a vaccine. A husband-and-wife research team, Jacques and Thérèse Tréfouel, developed anti-infection drugs called *sulfamides* and *sulfones*. And a microbiologist, André Lwoff, explained how biological substances called *growth factors* regulate the growth of an organism.

By the end of the 1920's, the Paris institute had grown considerably. It had 20 departments and several new buildings. With space at a premium, there was no longer a vegetable garden or a "Golden Microbe" dining hall. Some of the laboratories had been transferred to the remote suburb of Garches, where as many as 600 horses were kept for the production of the antidiphtheria serum.

The institute had also collected its third and fourth Nobel Prizes. The award went to Jules Bordet in 1919 for his research on the immune system and to Charles Nicolle in 1928 for his studies of typhus. Roux died in 1933 and was succeeded by his assistant director, Louis Martin, a bacteriologist.

With the start of World War II in September 1939, work at the institute was once again disrupted. After German troops entered Paris in June 1940, Joseph Meister—saved from rabies half a century earlier and still employed at the institute—committed suicide.

Most research ground to a halt during the war, but the production of vaccines, antiseptics, and antimicrobial drugs went on. With the help of Pasteur Vallery-Radot, Pasteur's grandson, the institute became the major supplier of drugs and other medicines to the underground resistance movement. Under the watchful eye of the Germans, however, the institute did not dare give away large amounts of the medications it produced itself. Instead, medical supplies were dropped by parachute in the countryside by British planes and smuggled to the institute. There, the supplies were sorted out and redistributed to various underground networks.

A drug that was then creating considerable excitement in medical circles was penicillin. Extracted from a mold called *Penicillium notatum*, penicillin was the first *antibiotic* (a germ-killing drug produced naturally by a living microorganism). Lwoff, director of the microbial physiology department, had received a sample of the *Penicillium* mold from its discoverer, British bacteriologist Alexander Fleming. The Nazis knew about Fleming's work and had somehow learned that a sample had been turned over to the Pasteur Institute. When they asked to "borrow" it, they were given instead a worthless strain of mold. German scientists cultured the mold in the vain hope of producing the miracle drug they had heard about.

Research on penicillin continued after the war ended in 1945, but the drug was still very scarce. The Pasteur Hospital developed a method to extract from the urine of patients about half the penicillin they had been administered the previous day. This so-called *pipicillin*, was actually purer than the original drug.

Lwoff, a physician, physiologist, microbiologist, and geneticist, was a leading Pasteur Institute researcher in the postwar years. He and two other Pastorians—physician Francois Jacob and biologist Jacques Monod—studied the genetics of bacteria and viruses. Their investigations shed light on the mechanisms by which the genes of all organisms are controlled. Among their many important discoveries, Lwoff, Jacob, and Monod learned that *structural genes*—those carrying the genetic blueprint for the production of proteins needed by an organism—are turned on and off by another class of genes, called *regulatory genes*. In 1965, the three scientists shared the

Most of the institute's original building is now a shrine to the past. Antique laboratory equipment from the early days of the institute is on display in a room that has been made into a museum, *above*.

Nobel Prize for their work, bringing to eight the number of Pasteur researchers who had been awarded Nobels. (In 1957, Daniel Bovet, a pharmacologist in Rome who had been at the institute from 1929 to 1947, became the seventh Pastorian to receive a Nobel. Bovet in 1937 produced the first of the antihistamines, drugs that relieve the symptoms of colds, hay fever, and certain other allergies.)

After more than 75 years of existence, the Pasteur Institute was still at the forefront of research. In other ways, however, the institute had fallen behind the times. The institute had neglected to look after its own financial interests. It had rarely patented the vaccines and medical treatments developed by Pastorians, and thus the fruit of their labors could be used the world over without any royalties being paid. As a result, the institute had been chronically short of money since the early 1930's. Revenue from the sales of antitoxins and vaccines, and from donations and occasional grants from the French government, were no longer adequate sources of income. Consequently, the money problems that began in the 1930's had grown worse, and the institute was seriously in debt. A key problem was that the institute was not geared for modern industrial production or marketing. Yet the institute found itself competing with a modern, dynamic pharmaceutical industry.

Beginning in 1971, the Pasteur Institute—under the guidance of

A modern biochemistry building, *right,* on the grounds of the Pasteur Institute in Paris is one of many new research facilities established by the institute in recent years. The institute has continued its emphasis on basic research, but it has also become a competitor in the French pharmaceutical industry. At a Pasteur-owned production plant, *below,* a worker clothed in sterile garments oversees the final step in the manufacture of a vaccine.

Jacques Monod, who in that year became its ninth director—put a drastic reorganization plan into effect. A modern plant for the manufacture of drugs was built in the Normandy region of northwestern France, and a separate production and marketing unit, named Institut Pasteur Production (IPP), was established. In addition, the staff of the Paris institute, numbering about 2,000, was trimmed.

But the plan did not work out as expected. The cost of the manufacturing plant far exceeded the original estimates, and as a result the institute found itself even more deeply in debt. Happily, the French government saved the day. Recognizing the institute's indispensable role in public health, research, and education, the government bailed it out financially and began supporting its operations on a regular basis. Since then, government funds have accounted for about half of the institute's annual budget.

The institute continued to make changes aimed at enhancing its success in business. In 1981, for instance, it created a scientific development office. In 1985, IPP was split into two independent units, Diagnostics Pasteur and Vaccins Pasteur, of which the institute owns 45 per cent of the stock. Thus, the century-old Pasteur Institute, while remaining an independent foundation, has become a full-fledged—and financially secure—member of the modern business world.´

Luc Montagnier, head of cancer virus research at the institute, holds a photomicrograph of a cell being attacked by the AIDS (acquired immune deficiency syndrome) virus. Montagnier's scientific team has been in the forefront of research on the deadly virus.

The institute today, situated in the southwestern part of Paris, is a blend of the old and the new, the traditional and the modern. In the original building, now largely abandoned by researchers, one gets a vivid sense of the institute's illustrious history. The busts of famous Pastorians cast their bronze or marble gaze over the main corridor, which occasionally reverberates with the footsteps of visitors to the cramped library. Now and then, the silence is broken by the chatter of schoolchildren guided through Pasteur's ground-floor apartment. On the floor below, in a crypt lined with mosaics illustrating Pasteur's major scientific achievements, visitors reverently contemplate the dark, somber marble tomb of the scientist who hoped his work would "seed other cultures."

Shelves of the museum on the second floor are lined with the original implements and specimens from Pasteur's experiments. There is also a strange-looking apparatus devised to take photographs through a microscope and an image of the anthrax bacillus, the first photomicrograph ever made.

Time seems suspended within the venerable old building, but that illusion evaporates as soon as one returns to the outside through the arched entryway. Nearby, the modern biotechnology building stands as a gleaming reminder that times have changed.

In many cases, the diseases being studied have changed as well. Much of the research at the institute these days is aimed at finding a cure for AIDS (acquired immune deficiency syndrome). This terrible, and apparently always fatal, disorder of the immune system was first recognized in 1981, in a number of homosexual men in the

United States. Since then, it has been discovered in intravenous drug users and in people who have received transfusions or other blood products contaminated with the virus that causes AIDS. The disease has since been discovered in France and other countries.

American and European scientists have worked long and hard to understand AIDS and develop a vaccine against it (see THE SEARCH FOR AN AIDS VACCINE, page 154). For the most part, AIDS researchers have cooperated with one another, and knowledge of the disease has advanced rapidly. One widely publicized incident, however, created some bad feelings between Pasteur Institute scientists and a group of American researchers.

The incident began in 1983, when Luc Montagnier, head of cancer virus research at the institute, reported that he and his colleagues had identified a virus as the likely cause of AIDS. In December of that year, the institute filed a patent application with the U.S. Patent and Trademark Office for a blood test to diagnose persons who had been exposed to the virus. In April 1984, virologist Robert C. Gallo and his associates at the National Cancer Institute (NCI) in Bethesda, Md., reported that they, too, had found a probable AIDS virus. The NCI filed its own application for a diagnostic-test patent.

When the NCI's patent was granted, while the Pasteur Institute's application was still pending, a costly legal battle ensued. The dispute went on for nearly three years but was finally resolved. In March 1987, United States President Ronald Reagan and French Prime Minister Jacques Chirac announced that the two sides had reached an agreement recognizing the respective contributions of both the Pasteur Institute and the National Cancer Institute.

Opposite page: Pasteur's somber marble tomb, located in an elaborate crypt in the basement of the original institute building, reminds visitors of the man who hoped his work would help ease human suffering throughout the world. The work he began continues today as the institute begins its second century.

Although AIDS research continues to receive high priority at the Pasteur Institute, AIDS is not the only disease being studied by institute scientists. The institute has developed a genetically engineered vaccine against the liver disease hepatitis B, and has research projects aimed at controlling cholera and a number of tropical diseases, including malaria.

Another area of research centers on how some bacteria become resistant to antibiotics by exchanging genetic material with other bacterial strains. Institute scientists also have been pioneers in *developmental biology*, the study of how an organism develops from a single fertilized egg cell. Developmental biology is leading to an understanding of genetic diseases, cancer, and diseases of the nervous system, which—along with AIDS and heart disease—are the greatest challenges facing medical science today.

And so, on the 100th birthday of the Pasteur Institute, the tradition of making contributions to human health continues. "The Pasteur Institute enters its second century with the same preoccupation for the future that it has had in the past," says former director Raymond Dedonder, "to pursue a mission of research in the service of public health."

Using a variety of advanced excavation methods, engineers are tackling some of the biggest tunneling projects ever undertaken, including a passageway under the English Channel.

Tunneling Under the Sea

BY JANICE LYN TUCHMAN

The possibility of joining England and France with a tunnel under the English Channel has obsessed visionaries for nearly 200 years. One scheme followed another throughout the 1800's and into the present century, but—despite a couple of tentative starts—a passage beneath the treacherous waters of the channel remained little more than a dream. Some dreams, though, eventually become reality, and it now appears that an English Channel tunnel—or "chunnel"—will be one of them. British engineers started tunneling toward France in late 1987, and French excavations began in early 1988. The chunnel's planners predicted that, if all goes well, high-speed trains will be racing between England and France by mid-1993.

Meanwhile, Japanese engineers in early 1988 were putting the finishing touches on the Seikan Tunnel, a railway corridor 53.9 kilometers (33.5 miles) long under Tsugaru Strait connecting the islands of Honshu and Hokkaido. That project, which was plagued with difficulties, took 24 painstaking years to complete.

Tunnels, whether through mountains or under rivers, are marvels of engineering. But no tunneling venture grips the imagination quite like the excavation of a passageway beneath the open sea.

Opposite page: A worker hangs onto the front of a giant tunneling "mole." Similar machines are being used to excavate a tunnel under the English Channel.

182

These mammoth undertakings are made possible by huge mechanical "moles" that bore through earth and rock, by laser guidance systems that make it easier to stay on course, and by methods for dealing with the problem of flooding. As the technology advances, engineers are contemplating the possibility of linking other land areas with subsea tunnels.

People started tunneling before they could write. As long as 15,000 years ago, prehistoric people in Europe used primitive tools to dig into hillsides in search of flint. In later times, the ancient Egyptians dug tunnels for the mining of gold and other metals and as corridors leading to rock tombs. The Romans, the greatest engineers of the ancient world, sometimes drove tunnels through mountains. But such projects relied on the backbreaking efforts of thousands of slaves, many of whom died of injuries or exhaustion.

The earliest known underwater tunnel was constructed about 2160 B.C. by the Babylonians in what is now Iraq. The tunnel, a pedestrian passageway connecting the royal palace of Babylon with a temple on the other side of the Euphrates River, was built during the dry season when the river was low. The builders diverted the river water and then dug a trench across the original riverbed. Within the trench, they constructed an enclosed corridor of bricks. After waterproofing the tunnel with an asphaltlike material, the Babylonian engineers returned the river to its natural course.

Very few underwater tunnels were attempted until comparatively modern times, because most rivers and other bodies of water could not be moved for the convenience of builders. Where water was wide and deep, boring a hole through the earth beneath it was the only way to dig a tunnel. And no one could figure out how to do that without the risk of being caught in a cave-in or flood.

In 1818, a French-born engineer named Marc Isambard Brunel patented a machine, the *tunneling shield*, that finally made underwater tunnel-building a practical possibility. The shield was a rectangular cast-iron construction containing tiers of open-ended compartments in which men could stand to hack out the earth ahead of them with picks and shovels. When the workers had cleared a meter or so of space, the shield was inched forward with large screw-operated jacks. The diggers then resumed their labors, while just behind them masons lined the tunnel with bricks.

The author:
Janice Lyn Tuchman is senior editor of *Engineering News-Record* magazine.

Using this method, Brunel was able to construct a tunnel 370 meters (1,200 feet) long under the River Thames in London, the first tunnel ever dug beneath the bed of a large, navigable river. But Brunel's solution to underwater tunneling had a serious flaw. Although his shield prevented the roof and sides of the tunnel from collapsing while they were being lined, the shield could do nothing to prevent floodwater from entering through the front of the tunnel. Flooding bedeviled Brunel's digging.

An underwater tunneling project is likely to proceed smoothly as

The Beach Hydraulic Tunnelling Shield.

The development of the tunneling shield in the late 1800's made underwater excavations possible. A tunneling shield—essentially a large metal cylinder in which men stood to hack out the earth ahead of them—was used, *above,* to tunnel under the St. Clair River between Michigan and Canada. The shield supported the walls of the tunnel until they were lined with cast-iron bands. High air pressure was maintained in the working area to keep water from entering through the face of the tunnel.

long as workers are digging through a layer of earth, such as clay, that forms an impenetrable barrier to water. But if the tunnelers suddenly encounter loose soil or soft, fractured rock, they are liable to be engulfed in a torrent of water, mud, and sand.

A British engineer, James Henry Greathead, perfected river-tunneling technology. Greathead worked for a London engineering contractor, Peter W. Barlow, who developed an improved shield shaped like a large, shallow cylinder. The cylindrical shape made it easier for the shield to be pushed forward through the earth. After adding his own modifications to Barlow's shield, Greathead in 1869 was able to construct a cast-iron-lined pedestrian tunnel under the Thames in just one year with no loss of life. Greathead avoided flooding problems by burrowing about 9 meters (30 feet) below the riverbed, twice the depth at which Brunel dug his tunnel. At that deeper level, he was able to dig through watertight clay.

But Greathead knew that engineers could not always depend on watertight soil when excavating under bodies of water; they needed a tunneling system that worked as well in porous ground as in clay. The answer, he concluded, was to combine the tunneling shield with compressed air in the working area. The pressure of the air on the tunnel walls would prevent water from entering the tunnel. Greathead proved the effectiveness of this approach in the construction of the first London subway tunnel, completed in 1890.

The use of compressed air with a shield quickly became standard for underwater tunneling. Although Greathead had pressurized only a small area at the front of the shield, most engineers pressurized nearly the entire tunnel. This was accomplished by first constructing a thick concrete wall, or bulkhead, near the tunnel entrance. Air was then pumped into the tunnel through pipes by powerful compressors. The bulkhead held the air within the tunnel.

Between 1888 and 1910, shields combined with compressed air were used to construct subway tunnels under the Hudson River in New York City and a railroad tunnel connecting Port Huron, Mich., and Sarnia, Canada, beneath the St. Clair River. The method had its drawbacks, however. Workers had to enter and leave the tunnel through an air lock—a steel chamber with a heavy door at each end—set into the bulkhead. Workers going into the tunnel entered the air lock and closed the door to the outside behind them. Air pressure within the chamber was then slowly raised to match the air pressure inside the tunnel. The door into the tunnel could then be opened. For workers leaving the tunnel, the steps were reversed.

These procedures, especially decompression when the workers left, had to be done gradually. Persons who underwent too-rapid decompression suffered ill effects, notably *decompression sickness*, or *the bends*. This painful condition, which is also experienced by deep-sea divers who surface too quickly, is caused when dissolved nitrogen in body fluids comes out of solution and forms bubbles.

Other forms of tunneling, particularly mountain tunneling, were also progressing rapidly in the late 1800's, stimulated by the expansion of the railroads. When rail builders came up against a river, they could often construct a bridge over it. But they couldn't build bridges over mountain ranges.

The first railroad tunnel through the Alps, the Fréjus Tunnel between Italy and France, was begun in 1857. The head engineer on the project, Germain Sommeiller, introduced several new tunneling techniques. His most valuable contribution to tunneling technology was the improvement of an excavation method known as *drill and blast*, which dated back to the 1600's and was still the only practical way of tunneling through rock. In the drill-and-blast technique, workers gouged holes in the rockface with a hammer and chisel. The holes were then filled with gunpowder, which was ignited with a fuse. The explosion shattered the rock to a depth of about 75 centimeters (30 inches). Sommeiller introduced an air-powered drill that sped up the boring of holes.

But it was in the excavation of the first major tunnel in the United States, the Hoosac Tunnel in western Massachusetts, that the drill-and-blast method was refined into a truly modern tunneling procedure. This railway tunnel, a passage about 7.5 kilometers (4.7 miles) long through the Hoosac Mountains, was started in 1851 and was beset with problems from the beginning. The work proceeded by fits and starts until the late 1860's, when the frustrated engineers at last got hold of just the tools they needed: nitroglycerin and a greatly improved air-powered drill.

Nitroglycerin, the forerunner of dynamite, far surpassed gunpowder in its ability to blow rock apart. Teamed with the new drill, which was more practical and reliable than the one developed by Sommeiller, the powerful explosive greatly speeded up progress of the work. The troublesome tunnel was finally completed in 1876.

Although the drill-and-blast method was a fairly effective way of boring through a mountain, it had limited applications in most underwater tunneling projects, where soft earth and the threat of floods necessitated the use of a shield. So, for most of the 1800's and 1900's, the technologies for tunneling through rock and tunneling beneath water remained largely separate.

The construction of underwater tunnels took a new turn in 1906. In that year, an American engineer, William J. Wilgus, began work on a railroad tunnel beneath the Detroit River to connect the cities of Detroit and Windsor, Canada. Using a method that harked back to the Babylonians, Wilgus dredged a trench across the river—without first diverting it, however—and then laid long sections of huge steel tubing in the trench. The tubes were connected end to end, weighted down with concrete, and covered with sediment from the riverbed. After water was pumped out of the tunnel sections, workers operating in normal air pressure completed their interiors.

Wilgus was not the first person to think of this idea—several schemes for an English Channel tunnel had proposed much the same thing—but he was the first to develop a workable procedure for carrying it out. By the mid-1900's, Wilgus' immersed-tube system had become the preferred method for building most underwater tunnels. A pair of highway tunnels in Chesapeake Bay, completed in 1964, and a subway tunnel under San Francisco Bay, which opened in 1974, are just two of the many projects that have used this technique.

But the immersed-tube method, too, has its limitations. The deeper or rougher the water, or the rockier the bottom, the more difficult it becomes to dig a trench and lay pipes.

For decades, underwater tunnelers and mountain tunnelers alike dreamed of having a machine that could gnaw its way through soil and rock. The first would-be tunnel-boring machine, or mole, made its appearance in 1856 at the Hoosac project. The huge, cumbersome apparatus, the brainchild of an American engineer named John Wilson, had a cutting face fitted with sharp blades. But a whole family of moles of the animal type might have made more progress against the rock; Wilson's contraption broke down after boring just 3 meters (10 feet).

A better machine was developed in 1881 by John Beaumont, a British military engineer. Beaumont's contrivance actually bored 2,400 meters (8,000 feet) under the English Channel in 1882. But that project—the only serious attempt at constructing a channel tunnel in the 1800's—was abandoned at the insistence of British military leaders, who argued that a tunnel would provide enemies on the European continent with a handy invasion route to England.

The first really effective tunneling mole was invented in the 1950's by an engineer in the United States, James S. Robbins. Put

The Tunneling "Mole"

Modern tunnel-boring machines, or "moles," have made tunnel digging faster and easier. At the head of the machine, a slowly rotating cutting face equipped with a number of steel disks grinds rock and soil into small pieces. The excavated fragments are carried on a conveyor belt to the rear of the machine and dumped into railcars for removal. As the mole advances, the operator guides the machine's movements with the aid of a laser beam projected down the length of the tunnel. Behind the mole, the tunnel's bare rock walls are lined with concrete. In the procedure shown below, which is being used in the English Channel tunnel, mechanical arms place precast concrete panels against the walls as workers bolt them into position. Powerful ventilation fans (not shown) keep air in the tunnel fresh for the workers.

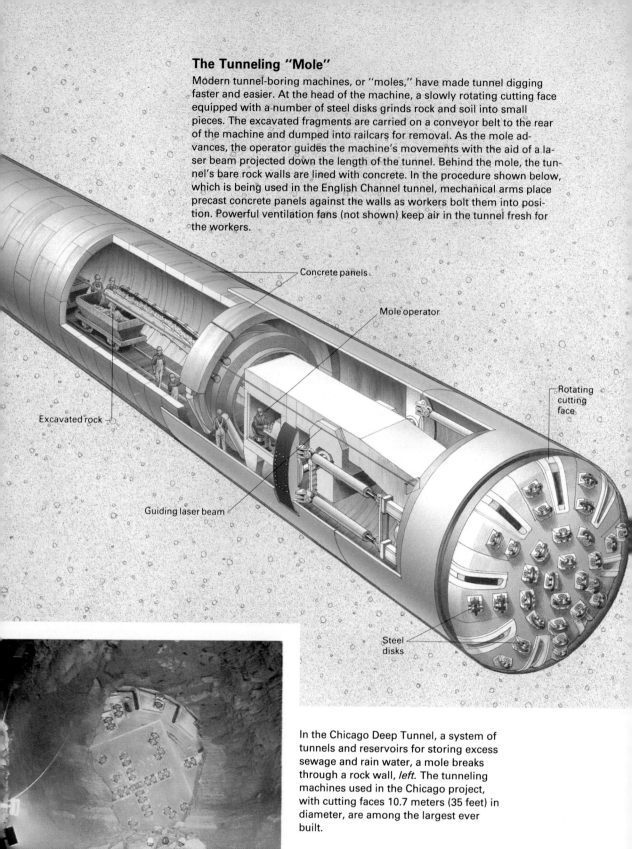

Concrete panels

Mole operator

Rotating cutting face

Excavated rock

Guiding laser beam

Steel disks

In the Chicago Deep Tunnel, a system of tunnels and reservoirs for storing excess sewage and rain water, a mole breaks through a rock wall, *left*. The tunneling machines used in the Chicago project, with cutting faces 10.7 meters (35 feet) in diameter, are among the largest ever built.

to work in 1952 on the construction of the Oahe Dam on the Missouri River near Pierre, S. Dak., Robbins' powerful machine drove through shale at a rate of 43 meters (141 feet) a day. Since then, moles—the great majority designed and built by the company Robbins founded in Kent, Wash.—have been used on almost every kind of tunneling project. As the technology has progressed, tunnel-boring machines have tackled ever-harder types of rock. The machines have also gotten larger. The biggest moles ever built for boring through hard rock have a cutting face 10.7 meters (35 feet) in diameter. They have been used in the Chicago area for the Deep Tunnel project, an extensive system of tunnels and reservoirs designed to hold excess sewage and rain water.

A tunneling mole exerts tremendous pressure against rock. Driven by powerful electric motors, the circular cutting head rotates five to eight times a minute, attacking the rock with up to 70 steel-alloy cutting disks set into the head. The cutting head is mounted on the front of a long body containing the motors and other apparatus, including a control panel for the operator.

A mole designed for the excavation of soft soil that could collapse is encased in a strong steel shield. If there is a flooding threat, the mole can be fitted with equipment that—much like Greathead's shield—can maintain a small area of high pressure at the front of the machine. Rather than using compressed air, however, the mole compacts the soil on the tunnel face so that water cannot pass through it. There are several ways of accomplishing this. A mole equipped with a *slurry shield*, for example, uses a wet, clay-containing mixture—called a *slurry*—which is forced between the cutting head and the face of the tunnel. Excavated soil mixes with the slurry and is carried away in pipes. The debris is separated out, and the slurry circulates back to the front of the machine.

A mole advances much like an inchworm. As the cutting head grinds away, it is pushed forward ahead of the machine by strong hydraulic cylinders. At the same time, two large appendages called grippers, located at the sides of the mole, push outward against the tunnel walls to hold the machine steady. After the cutting head has advanced a meter or so, it is stopped, and the grippers relax their hold. The cylinders then contract, moving the whole machine forward. Lastly, the grippers are again pressed against the walls, and the cutting head resumes its work. Scoops on the perimeter of the cutting head gather up the excavated rock or soil and drop it onto a conveyor belt, which carries the debris to railcars for removal. A ventilation system in the tunnel draws out dust and pumps in fresh air.

As the mole progresses, the tunnel is usually lined. (Hard-rock tunnels are often left unlined.) In some cases, preformed concrete panels are positioned on the tunnel walls by a mechanical arm on the back of the mole. The panels are bolted in place by workers. In

The Seikan Tunnel

Japanese engineers in 1988 completed work on the Seikan Tunnel, a railway tunnel linking the islands of Honshu and Hokkaido, *right.* The tunnel runs for 53.9 kilometers (33.5 miles), including a section 23.3 kilometers (14.6 miles) long beneath the floor of the Tsugaru Strait. Two sets of tracks in the tunnel, *below,* carry electric trains in opposite directions.

other tunnels, engineers prefer to finish the walls by coating them with a sprayable concrete mixture called *shotcrete*.

The operator of a mole controls the machine's movements with the aid of a laser guidance system. A laser beam—a narrow, intense beam of light—projected from near the tunnel entrance strikes a grid in front of the operator, showing any steering corrections that are needed. This highly accurate system is a great improvement over earlier methods of keeping a tunnel on course. Before the advent of the laser in the 1960's, tunnel builders had to rely on time-consuming surveying techniques to guide their excavations.

As effective as tunneling machines are, they are individually designed for specific digging conditions and thus suffer from a lack of flexibility. If engineers encounter unexpected situations, such as badly fractured rock or geologic faults, tunneling requirements may change abruptly. In such cases, engineers may turn to the drill-and-blast method. Although drill-and-blast has been refined, with better explosives and modern drills, it is essentially the same system devised by the builders of the Hoosac Tunnel. Over the years, however, tunnelers have learned to "fine-tune" the method to suit circumstances. If rock strata are unstable, for example, smaller amounts of explosive can be used and the tunnel advanced slowly.

A Seikan worker, *above,* uses a large drill to bore holes in the tunnel face. An explosive material placed in the holes blows out a small area of rock. Cracked, faulted rock beneath the Tsugaru Strait made it necessary for engineers to switch from tunneling moles to the drill-and-blast method.

In the excavation of the Seikan Tunnel, engineers decided to switch from tunneling moles to drill-and-blast after encountering mixed strata of weak, cracked, and faulted rock. Coping with the varied rock conditions became so difficult that the tunnel, which planners had predicted would be finished in 10 years, took more than twice that long to complete.

The biggest problem—and danger—was flooding. Even though the tunnel was being dug 100 meters (325 feet) below the floor of the Tsugaru Strait, fractures in the rock allowed water in some places to penetrate far into the seabed. Moreover, the strait is up to 140 meters (450 feet) deep along the tunnel route, so water would be forced into the tunnel under great pressure at any weak points. Using compressed air in the tunnel was out of the question; the high air pressure needed to keep water out of the tunnel would have been extremely hazardous to the health of the workers.

The Seikan engineers instead used a type of *grout* to control the inflow of water. This sealant, a mixture of cement and *water glass* (a compound of sodium, silicon, and oxygen), was injected with great force into holes drilled in the tunnel face. The grout then seeped into cracks in the rock and solidified, forming a barrier against water. Areas where heavy grouting would be necessary were identified by the drilling of long horizontal test borings along the planned excavation route. The engineers also dug a *pilot tunnel*—a small exploratory passageway beneath and in advance of the main tunnel—to confirm the geologic conditions ahead and to test various technologies, including grouting, for dealing with possible problems.

Wielding a long pipe, a worker lines a section of the Seikan Tunnel with *shotcrete,* a sprayable form of concrete, *above.* Shotcrete, which is often used in place of concrete panels, fills any cracks in the rock and strengthens the tunnel.

A Tunnel Under the English Channel

For nearly 200 years, engineers have dreamed of building a tunnel under the English Channel to link England and France. In 1988, construction on a channel tunnel—or "chunnel"— was underway at last in both countries.

One scheme proposed in the 1800's for a tunnel under the channel envisioned laying huge pipes on the sea floor, *above.* The plan also called for building ventilation towers at regular intervals. The channel tunnel now under construction is being dug beneath the bed of the channel by tunneling moles. In March 1988, three moles began boring toward England from a large vertical shaft in France, *right.* About three months earlier, British moles started tunneling toward France.

192

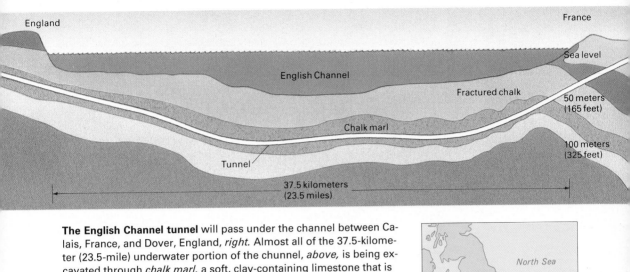

The English Channel tunnel labels: England, France, Sea level, English Channel, Fractured chalk, 50 meters (165 feet), Chalk marl, 100 meters (325 feet), Tunnel, 37.5 kilometers (23.5 miles)

The English Channel tunnel will pass under the channel between Calais, France, and Dover, England, *right.* Almost all of the 37.5-kilometer (23.5-mile) underwater portion of the chunnel, *above,* is being excavated through *chalk marl,* a soft, clay-containing limestone that is almost watertight. On the French side of the channel, however, part of the chunnel is being dug through fractured, water-filled chalk above the chalk marl. If the excavations proceed on schedule, high-speed electric trains, *below,* will begin carrying passengers and vehicles through the chunnel in 1993. The chunnel will consist of twin railway tunnels with a smaller tunnel between them for service and maintenance vehicles.

Map labels: North Sea, Ireland, Great Britain, Netherlands, London, Dover, Calais, Belgium, Channel Tunnel, English Channel, Paris, France, 0 200 Miles, 0 200 Kilometers

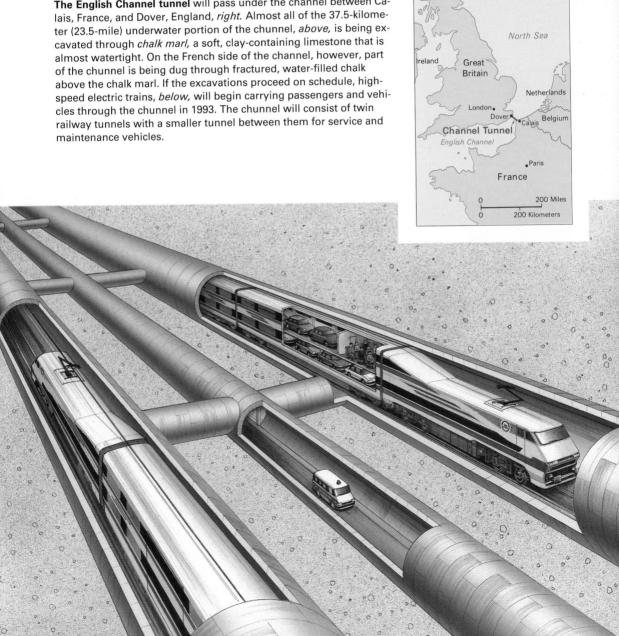

Despite the many precautions, water exploded into the tunnel four times. The worst flood occurred in 1976 in the service tunnel, a tunnel for ventilation and maintenance vehicles that was being excavated next to the main tunnel. When workers penetrated a zone of severely fractured rock, water poured in on them at a rate of more than 60,000 liters (16,000 gallons) a minute. Pumps in the pilot tunnel, which the workers quickly sealed off from the other areas by closing a heavy door, later succeeded in draining water from the interconnected main and service tunnels.

In March 1985, tunnelers punched through a wall of soft rock and greeted workers who had been digging from the other direction; after 21 long years, the excavation was complete. All that remained was to finish lining the tunnel with shotcrete and installing equipment for the trains. The project had resulted in 34 deaths and an estimated 700 injuries, but the toll could well have been higher considering the hazards involved. Construction experts consider the Seikan Tunnel one of the great engineering triumphs of the century. Its length of 53.9 kilometers—including a 23.3-kilometer (14.6-mile) section under the strait—makes it by far the longest tunnel ever built. The Seikan Tunnel opened on March 13, 1988.

On the other side of the world in 1988, work on the English Channel tunnel was progressing in earnest. The last attempt to build a tunnel, in the early 1970's, was terminated by the British government—not from a fear of invasion but because the project was deemed too costly. But in the 1980's, the money was "in the bank," and both Britain and France were committed to finally carrying the $8.5-billion venture through to completion. The two governments awarded the project to Eurotunnel, a private association of 5 banks and 10 construction companies.

The 50-kilometer (31-mile) chunnel will actually consist of three tunnels—two corridors for high-speed electric trains, with a smaller service tunnel between them. The tunnels will go underground near Dover, England, and Calais, France.

Work on the chunnel is expected to go much more smoothly than the Seikan project did. Nearly the entire 37.5-kilometer (23.5-mile) undersea portion of the tunnel will be dug through a layer of soft, clay-containing limestone called *chalk marl*. Besides being almost completely watertight, chalk marl is quite easy to excavate. The six tunneling machines—three British and three French—burrowing under the channel can bore through the chalk at speeds up to 4.5 meters (15 feet) an hour. As the machines advance, workers line the tunnel walls with concrete panels.

Tunneling on the French side of the channel is a bit more complicated than on the British side. Vertical test bores showed that the chalk marl is folded down near the French coast. In that area, the tunnelers must dig through a layer of fractured, water-filled chalk above the chalk marl. To prevent flooding in that part of the excavation, the French tunneling machines are equipped with slurry shields. Grout is also being used.

If all goes according to schedule, trains will begin using the chunnel in May 1993. Traveling at speeds up to 240 kilometers (150 miles) per hour, the trains—carrying motor vehicles and freight as well as passengers—will make the 385-kilometer (240-mile) trip from London to Paris in about 3¼ hours. The same trip now takes at least 6½ hours, including a channel crossing by hovercraft.

Originally, an automobile tunnel was also considered for the chunnel. That idea had to be scrapped, in part because existing ventilation systems would have been unable to cope with the exhaust fumes produced by tens of thousands of cars. Nevertheless, the British and French governments have committed Eurotunnel to investigate the possibility of constructing an auto tunnel adjacent to the chunnel by early in the next century.

By that time, new technologies will have emerged. In coming years, tunnel-boring machines that carve through rock with high-energy lasers, superhot jets of flame, or powerful streams of water may replace the mechanical mole. New procedures for stabilizing dangerous rock and soil are also being developed. Some engineers, for instance, are experimenting with the use of liquid nitrogen to freeze wet ground before it is excavated. And perhaps most intriguing of all, though it involves no digging, is the possibility of building "floating" tunnels across deep bodies of water. These steel-pipe tunnels—similar to those constructed by the immersed-tube method—would be anchored perhaps 20 meters (65 feet) below the surface of the water by heavy cables.

As tunnel-building technology advances, no tunneling idea seems too ambitious. Even before the Seikan Tunnel was finished, engineers in Japan and South Korea were studying whether it would be possible to link those two countries with a passage beneath the Korea Strait, a distance of about 180 kilometers (112 miles). At the same time, Spanish and Moroccan engineers were looking into the possibility of digging a 50-kilometer (31-mile) tunnel beneath the Strait of Gibraltar between Cadiz, Spain, and Tangier, Morocco. Tunnels have also been conceived to connect Ireland and England under the Irish Sea and to link Sicily with the Italian peninsula beneath the Strait of Messina. Norwegian officials have toyed with the idea of building a floating tunnel across a deep fjord. For the present, most of these ideas are little more than dreams. But for almost two centuries, so was a tunnel under the English Channel.

For further reading:

Beaver, Patrick A. *A History of Tunnels*. Citadel Press, 1973.
Free, John. "Chunnel for the Channel." *Popular Science*, May 1986.
Jackson, Donald D. "The Ins and Outs of a Dangerous and Boring Subject."
   Smithsonian, May 1986.

Scientists have developed a number of
ways to date the age of ancient fossils,
rocks, stars, and even the universe itself.

Finding Out
How Old
Things Are

BY FRANCIS REDDY

An anthropologist digs up a fossil bone and announces that it
belonged to an early type of human being who lived about 2 million
years ago. Geologists examine a fragment of meteorite and declare
that it along with Earth came into being about 4.5 billion years ago.
Astronomers look through telescopes to the distant reaches of space
and pronounce the universe itself to be between 10 billion and 20
billion years old.

How do scientists determine the ages of such ancient objects and
of events that took place so long ago? The methods needed to answer such questions have emerged over hundreds of years of scientific investigation. To determine the age of Earth and the universe,
scientists gradually developed some highly unusual "calendars" and
"clocks." Their methods included analyzing the layers of rock and
sediments found in Earth's crust, comparing *fossils* (the remains of
ancient plants and animals) found in those layers, logging the decay
of radioactive atoms, and studying the light from distant galaxies.

The task of charting Earth's history seems impossibly difficult, but
it is one of the most exciting and important in all of science. Its
focus is nothing less than our very origins: When did our planet
and life on our planet begin to exist?

During the late 1800's, a few scientists attempted to calculate the age of Earth, but no one had any certain idea of how old Earth was in years. By the late 1800's, scientists had assembled only a relative time scale for Earth's history based on studying *strata* (layers) of rock and the fossils found within the layers. This enabled them to determine which fossils were older and which were younger, even though they did not know how old any of the fossils actually were. Scientists had not even figured out what the fossils represented until the late 1600's.

Since the 1500's, scholars had been collecting fossils and were engaged in a lively scientific debate over what fossils might be. Danish physician Nicolaus Steno and English scientist Robert Hooke were among those who believed fossils were the remains of animals and plants that lived long ago. Steno became intrigued with the subject in 1666, when he noticed the similarity between the triangular teeth of a large white shark caught by local fishermen and certain triangular rocks then known as "tonguestones." He suggested that these "tonguestones" were really the fossilized teeth of ancient sharks.

How, asked other scholars, could shark's teeth and other kinds of sea life turn into solid rock? Steno and his supporters argued that the process of creating fossils began when dead creatures on the sea floor became covered with sediments of sand and clay. As the flesh decayed, the skeleton became covered by sediments that piled on top of it. In some cases, minerals infiltrated the air spaces in the skeletal bones, hardened, and helped preserve the fossil. The sediments that covered the fossils eventually turned into rock.

Secrets in the strata

In 1669, Steno found that this sedimentary rock builds up in layers over long periods of time, with the youngest layers on top and the oldest layers on the bottom. This discovery enabled scientists to learn the order in which geologic events occurred.

The layers of sedimentary rock, one on top of another, are apparent, for example, in the stratified walls of the Grand Canyon in Arizona. There the flow of the Colorado River has cut through and exposed the rock layers. The layers at the bottom of the canyon formed first, and higher layers formed later.

Of course, not all rock strata are as neatly arranged as those of the Grand Canyon. The slow but ceaseless movement of Earth's surface in some places causes once orderly strata to become a complex puzzle of different rock layers. For example, molten rock from below Earth's surface may intrude into cracks in much older rock, separating strata that actually formed one right after the other. The movement of the continents may also thrust old strata on top of newer strata. For example, a layer of sedimentary rock in Glacier National Park, Montana, that has been dated as being 1 million years old, lies atop rock layers that are just 100,000 years old. In other places, wind and rain have eroded away the uppermost strata.

The author:
Francis Reddy is a free-lance science writer, based in Milwaukee.

The complex jumble of rock layers at various places around the world made it difficult for geologists to piece together an overall picture of Earth's past. No single place on Earth has rock layers that cover all of geological time or even a major part of it. Therefore, it became difficult to determine whether a layer of limestone in England, for example, was older or younger than a similar limestone layer in France—or perhaps the same age.

Creating the fossil index

Fortunately, fossils provided the key to assembling that overall history. In the late 1700's, William Smith, an English civil engineer, showed that particular kinds of fossils were found only in certain layers of rock. Scientists concluded that finding the same kinds of fossils in layers of rock from two widely different locations meant that the layers of rock at those two locations probably formed at the same time. Scientists also learned that fossils found in the older, lower layers bore less resemblance to living things, indicating that they had existed long ago. Fossils appearing in the younger strata of rock most closely resembled living plants and animals, indicating that they were relatively recent remains. Thus, fossils provided a means of identifying the relative ages of rock layers.

Not long after Smith's discovery, French and English scientists used fossils to establish links between rock formations in each country. Fossils in the rock formations of one country matched those in rock formations of the other country. So the fossils showed that a part of both the French and English rock layers formed at the same time. By correlating fossil information from rock layers at many different sites around the world, geologists eventually assembled the *geologic column*—an overall picture of the sequence of rock layers from the oldest to the youngest.

Still, no one had any idea how long it took for these rock layers to form. Throughout the 1800's, geologists argued about whether geological processes occur slowly or quickly and disagreed about the age of Earth.

By the early 1900's, based on the fossil record, scientists had divided Earth's past into four eras—which they named the Precambrian, the Paleozoic, the Mesozoic, and the Cenozoic—the oldest being the Precambrian and the most recent the Cenozoic. Each era, except the Precambrian, was subdivided into periods. These included, for example, the Silurian Period of the Paleozoic Era, whose rock layers contained fossils of the first land plants, and the Triassic Period of the Mesozoic Era, whose layers contained the first dinosaur fossils. But no one knew precisely how long the eras had lasted. This would be like historians knowing that World War I came long after the Revolutionary War in America but not knowing the years in which the wars took place. Geologists had succeeded in the relative dating of fossils, but they wanted an absolute dating technique, a means of determining how old a rock was in terms of years.

Dating with atomic clocks

They soon got it—in the form of an "atomic clock." In the 1890's, French physicist Antoine Henri Becquerel and his young research assistant Marie Sklodowska Curie discovered that atoms in certain elements are unstable. These atoms decay, or change, into lighter elements and give off radiation in the process. They found, for example, that uranium decays through a series of elements into lead. Curie called this spontaneous emission of radiation *radioactivity*. Scientists also discovered that atoms in radioactive elements decay in a regular and predictable way, so they can be used as atomic clocks. These clocks are based on the *half-life* of a radioactive element, the time it takes for half of the atoms in a sample of the radioactive element to decay into another element. By knowing the half-life of a radioactive element and the amount of that element and its decay product in a particular rock, geologists can compute the age of the rock.

For example, imagine a sample of rock that contains *isotopes* (different nuclear forms of the same chemical element) of both uranium and lead. Atomic physicists have calculated that it takes 4.5 billion years for half of the atoms in the most common isotope of uranium (U-238) to decay into a certain isotope of lead. By measuring the amounts of these isotopes and their ratio to each other in a rock sample, geologists can calculate the age of the rock.

American chemist Bertram B. Boltwood dated several uranium minerals by this method in 1905. His calculations showed that the minerals were up to 2.2 billion years old. But Boltwood's results were not generally accepted by other scientists.

Scientists discovered other atomic clocks, with different half-lives. These included radioactive isotopes of carbon and potassium and rarer radioactive elements such as rubidium. These elements provided additional ways of dating rock samples and the fossils they contained.

The long half-lives of uranium and another radioactive element called thorium, which has a half-life of 14 billion years, enabled scientists to date billion-year-old rocks. But the isotope carbon 14 (C-14), with a half-life of about 5,700 years, allowed scientists to date objects that were only thousands of years old. The C-14 dating technique was like finding a "second hand" on the atomic clock.

This C-14 technique was developed in 1947 by American chemist Willard F. Libby. Libby discovered that C-14 is created in the upper atmosphere when an isotope of nitrogen absorbs cosmic rays from outer space. Because Earth's atmosphere is constantly bombarded by cosmic rays, this process creates a continuous supply of radioactive carbon in the air. This radioactive carbon combines with oxygen to form radioactive carbon dioxide, which with stable carbon dioxide is used by plants in photosynthesis and then taken in by animals that eat the plants. As a result, all living plants and animals contain C-14, and this serves as the basis for an atomic clock after they die.

Fossil skeleton of extinct animal.

Imprint of a
fern in rock.

Fossil shell of
extinct sea creature.

What a Fossil Is

A fossil is an imprint or the actual remains of a plant or animal that lived in the past. In the case of dinosaurs, for example, the fossil could be a footprint, an egg, a bone, a tooth, or the entire skeleton preserved by the process illustrated below.

A dinosaur dies in a river or a lake and sinks to the muddy bottom.

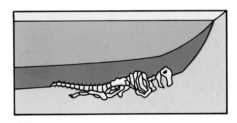

Layers of sediment bury the dinosaur. Its flesh decays, but the sediment layers help preserve the bones.

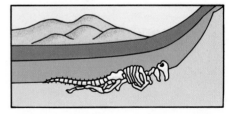

Over millions of years, the lake evaporates, and the muddy sediment hardens into rock.

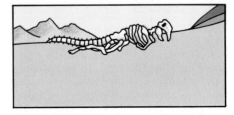

Eventually, the sedimentary rock erodes away, revealing the dinosaur's fossilized skeleton.

In a living organism, there is a known ratio between C-14 atoms and ordinary carbon atoms called carbon 12 (C-12). But when an organism dies, it no longer takes in air or food containing C-14. Consequently, the C-14 to C-12 ratio changes thereafter as the C-14 decays back to nitrogen. A bone or a piece of dead wood, for example, in which the ratio of C-14 atoms to C-12 atoms has changed by a half, would be 5,700 years old—the half-life of carbon 14. Archaeologists have used this clock to date animal and plant tissue, wood, bone, charcoal, and cloth samples that they uncover during their excavations. Because of its short half-life, however, this method of dating is useful only for objects that are no older than about 40,000 years.

In the 1950's, physicists determined the half-life of another radioactive element, potassium 40, which decays to a stable form of the inert gas argon. Potassium 40 is commonly found in rocks, has a half-life of 1.3 billion years, and can be used to date objects at least 100,000 years old. Skeleton fragments of one of our earliest human ancestors, found in Tanzania in 1986, were determined to

Dating Fossils

Fossils and the rock layers in which they are found gave scientists the first relative time scale for the history of Earth. This index also helps date newly found fossils. Other dating methods can arrive at more precise dates.

Prehistoric human being

Eohippus

Dinosaur

Fern

Eurypterid

Trilobite

Stromatolites

Much of Earth's land surface holds *sedimentary rocks* (rocks that build up in strata, or layers, as in Arizona's Grand Canyon, *above*). By studying the layers and the fossils found in them, scientists succeeded in the *relative* dating of fossils—that is, in determining the order in which the fossils were created, *right*. Scientists know that trilobites lived long before dinosaurs because they are found in much deeper layers. They also know that if they find a previously unknown fossil in the same layer as a trilobite, the new fossil also lived long before the age of dinosaurs.

Holocene Epoch 10,000 years ago	**Cenozoic Era**
Pleistocene Epoch 2,000,000	
Pliocene Epoch 5,000,000	
Miocene Epoch 24,000,000	
Oligocene Epoch 37,000,000	
Eocene Epoch 58,000,000	
Paleocene Epoch 66,000,000	
Cretaceous Period 144,000,000	**Mesozoic Era**
Jurassic Period 208,000,000	
Triassic Period 245,000,000	
Permian Period 286,000,000	**Paleozoic Era**
Pennsylvanian Period 320,000,000	
Mississippian Period 360,000,000	
Devonian Period 408,000,000	
Silurian Period 438,000,000	
Ordovician Period 505,000,000	
Cambrian Period 570,000,000	
Precambrian Time 4,500,000,000	

Atomic "clocks"

Based on the radioactive decay of elements, atomic "clocks" enable scientists to estimate the actual age of fossils and rock layers, *left.*

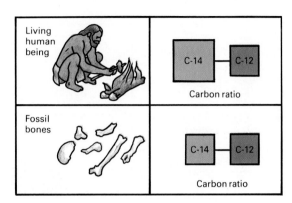

Radiocarbon dating of fossils less than 40,000 years old measures the ratio of radioactive carbon 14 (C-14) to carbon 12 (C-12), *above.* When a plant or animal is alive, it takes in both C-14 and C-12 atoms. Once the organism dies, it stops taking in any form of carbon. The C-14 in the organism then decays into nitrogen, while the amount of C-12 remains unchanged. So the greater the ratio of C-12 to C-14 that scientists detect, the older the fossil.

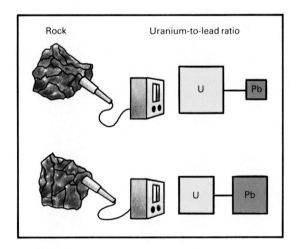

Rock dating uses the same principle to date a rock sample containing isotopes of uranium (U), *above,* which decay into lead (Pb) isotopes. Scientists know that half of a certain uranium isotope will decay in 4.5 billion years, so they use the uranium-lead ratio to date rocks billions of years old.

Looking Back in Time

Astronomers use the behavior of light to date very distant objects in the universe, even the universe itself. The more distant an object is, the longer it takes for its light to reach us. Therefore, astronomers know that the farther out they look into space, the farther back they see in time.

The Speed of Light

Light travels at a constant speed of 299,792 kilometers (186,282 miles) per second, *right,* covering 9.46 trillion kilometers (5.88 trillion miles) per year (a *light-year*).

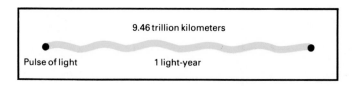

The Spectrum of Light

Astronomers also analyze the *spectrum* (band of colors) of light, *right,* given off by distant stars and galaxies. The spectrum consists of a rainbow of colors ranging from the shorter wavelengths of blue to the longer wavelengths of red.

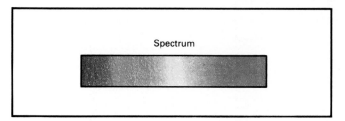

Red Shift

Dark bands known as *absorption lines* can be seen in the spectrum of a star at rest, *at top, right.* The lines correspond to particular elements in the star. If a star is moving away from an observer, the absorption lines will be shifted toward the red end of the spectrum, *at center, right,* similar to how sound waves become longer as the source of sound moves away. The farther away an object is, the greater is its red shift. In 1987, astronomers detected a quasar, *below* (arrow), that may be the most distant known object in the universe. Its light took more than 12 billion years to reach us. By searching for the most distant detectable objects, astronomers try to establish the age of the universe itself.

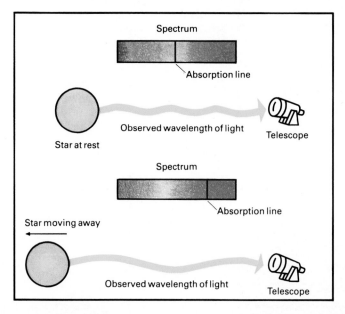

be about 2 million years old by potassium-argon dating of the rock layers in which the fragments were discovered.

Potassium and another radioactive element—rubidium—often occur together in the same minerals, giving geologists two independently running clocks to compare. Rubidium 87 has a half-life of about 50 billion years and is used to date objects between 50 million and 4.5 billion years old.

The discovery of atomic clocks gave scientists the means to arrive at absolute ages for the layers in the geologic time scale. The variety of those clocks enabled them to date rocks and fossils of different ages. As a result of radioactive dating, scientists now believe that our planet formed about 4.5 billion years ago. They base this age primarily on the radioactive dating of meteorites, which scientists think are unchanged fragments of the material that originally formed Earth, its moon, and the other planets.

In addition, the radioactive decay of potassium and rubidium from samples of lunar rock returned by the Apollo moon missions in the 1960's indicated that rocks on the moon's surface formed between 3.7 billion and 4.5 billion years ago. The oldest rocks known to have solidified on Earth have been dated as 3.8 billion years old. Scientists have also found evidence that primitive life formed on Earth at least 3.5 billion years ago by dating rocks from a region in Australia where fossils of microscopic bacteria were found. In contrast, the fossil-dating technique painstakingly assembled by geologists in the 1700's and 1800's gave us ages for only a relatively brief period—about the last 600 million years or just 13 per cent—of our planet's history. Radioactive dating revealed just how ancient our planet is.

The link between distance and age

Meanwhile, astronomers had been gathering evidence that indicated stars and other objects far away must be very old. In 1838, as geologists hotly debated the latest "guess-timates" for Earth's age, German astronomer Friedrich Wilhelm Bessel discovered a means of directly measuring the distance to the stars. By measuring the movement across the sky of a star known as 61 Cygni, Bessel calculated it to be some 700,000 times farther from Earth than Earth is from the sun. To express such great distances, astronomers adopted a measurement based on the speed of light. The speed of light never changes. A beam of light travels about 9.5 trillion kilometers (5.9 trillion miles) in one year. Astronomers call this a *light-year*. Bessel's calculations placed 61 Cygni about 11 light-years from us. This marked an important step toward determining the ages of objects in space.

The next major breakthrough came in 1908, when Henrietta S. Leavitt, a research assistant at Harvard University, began her study of a particular type of "variable" star that periodically appears to change in brightness. These stars were called *Cepheid variables*. Leav-

The Stellar Clock

Astronomers use the mass of a star and the rate at which it consumes hydrogen in its nuclear fires to determine the lifetime of the star. The more massive a star is, the hotter it is, and therefore the quicker it will consume its hydrogen and enter a stage in a star's life known as the *red giant stage.*

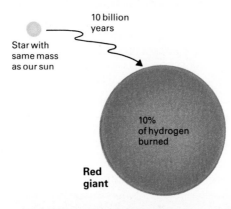
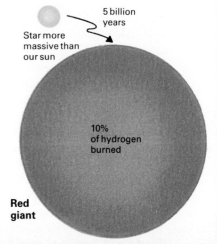

Star with same mass as our sun

10 billion years

10% of hydrogen burned

Red giant

Star more massive than our sun

5 billion years

10% of hydrogen burned

Red giant

Dating Red Giants

A star with the same mass as our sun, *right,* will burn 10 per cent of its hydrogen in about 10 billion years. The star then expands and becomes red. A star more massive than our sun, *far right,* will reach this *red giant* stage sooner—perhaps in 5 billion years.

Dating Star Clusters

Scientists can use this knowledge about red giants to determine the ages of stars in a cluster like the globular cluster at right. They have found that many of these red giants consumed 10 per cent of their hydrogen about 9 billion to 15 billion years ago, making that the age of the oldest known stars in our Milky Way galaxy.

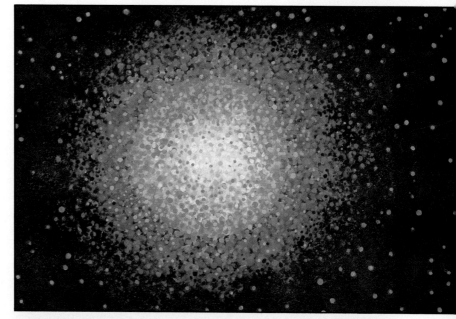

Dating the Milky Way

Globular clusters shown at right, above and below the disk of the Milky Way galaxy, probably formed at the same time as our Galaxy. The clusters are about 9 billion to 15 billion years old, so the Galaxy itself must be that old.

disk

Milky Way galaxy

itt established a direct relationship between a Cepheid's *intrinsic brightness* (how brightly it actually shines) and the length of time required for it to complete one cycle from faint to bright to faint again. Her calculations showed that this property of the Cepheids makes them powerful astronomical "yardsticks" because it gives astronomers a means of distinguishing between a star's intrinsic brightness and its *apparent brightness*. A star's apparent brightness depends on how far away it is from Earth. If two stars have the same intrinsic brightness, but one star is farther away from Earth than the other, the apparent brightness of the more distant star will be less. Assuming that all Cepheid stars behave the same way, an astronomer could measure the cycle of variable light to calculate the intrinsic brightness of a Cepheid and determine its distance in relation to other stars whose distance had already been determined.

In 1924, another American astronomer, Edwin Hubble, identified a Cepheid in what was then known as the Andromeda nebula. Hubble showed that Andromeda was at least 100,000 light-years away and was a separate galaxy of comparable size to our own. It is now known as the Great Andromeda Galaxy. Astronomers believe this galaxy is 2.2 million light-years away.

Light arriving today from Andromeda actually left the galaxy 2.2 million years ago. So we see the galaxy as it looked more than 2 million years ago. Andromeda, therefore, is at least 2.2 million years old, and astronomers believe it is much older.

Looking back in time

Astronomers realized their telescopes were time machines: The farther out they looked in space, the further back they were seeing in time. At distances beyond about 10 million light-years, however, Cepheids become too faint to see. With more powerful telescopes, astronomers could peer deep into the universe. But without an accurate means of determining how far away a very distant object was, there was no way to determine how ancient it was.

Earlier, in 1912, American astronomer Vesto M. Slipher had examined the light from dozens of galaxies through a special instrument attached to a telescope. The instrument, called a *spectrometer*, spreads light into the rainbow of colors known as the *spectrum*. Slipher noted that the light from the galaxies was shifted toward the red—or longer—wavelength end of the spectrum. This phenomenon, called *red shift*, occurs when a cosmic object is moving away from an observer. A similar and more familiar phenomenon called the *Doppler effect* occurs with sound waves. As a speeding object moves away from us, any sound waves coming from the object are stretched, and this seems to cause a lowering of the pitch. For example, the pitch of a train whistle seems higher as a train approaches (because the waves are compressed or shortened) and lower after it races past (because the waves grow longer). Similarly, the greater the speed of a receding object in space, the more the wavelengths of light coming from it are stretched or shifted to the longer wavelengths of the red end of the spectrum. Slipher's measurements of the galaxies' red shifts indicated that the galaxies were moving away from us at incredible speeds—hundreds of kilometers per second.

In 1929, Hubble discovered that there was a relationship between a galaxy's red shift, or speed, and its distance from Earth. Hubble found that the distance of a galaxy was directly proportional to how fast it was speeding away. The more distant the galaxy, the greater its speed away from us. Everywhere in space, galaxies were moving away. So Hubble concluded that the universe is expanding.

Hubble's discovery of the expanding universe provided a means of estimating the age of the universe. If the galaxies are receding from one another due to the universe's expansion, then there must have been a time when all of the matter in the galaxies was packed together. And the length of time that the universe has been expanding could be determined if it has been expanding at a constant rate.

The chief problem has been that we cannot be sure that the universe has always been expanding at a constant rate. Many astronomers think that the expansion of the universe has slowed over billions of years due to the force of gravity exerted by matter within the universe. How much it has slowed depends on how much matter there is, and astronomers still do not know this. In addition, there is uncertainty about the current rate of expansion. For both of these reasons, astronomers have been able to calculate only a maximum age for the universe of about 20 billion years and a minimum age of about 10 billion years.

How old are the stars?

Astronomers also found a "stellar clock" for determining how old the oldest stars are in our galaxy, the Milky Way. In 1938, American physicist Hans A. Bethe found that stars are powered by nuclear energy produced when four hydrogen atoms *fuse* (combine) to form a helium atom. Following up on this work, astrophysicists described how stars age. They found that when a star exhausts a certain percentage of its hydrogen fuel, it begins to consume helium in its core. Then its outer layers of gas expand so that the star becomes much larger in size and its color changes from blue to red. When a star reaches this unstable state—known as a *red giant*—it reveals its age.

The red giant phase tells astronomers that a star has consumed every gram of hydrogen in about 10 per cent of its mass. Knowing how much hydrogen has been converted to helium, astronomers can calculate the total amount of energy the star has given off during its lifetime. And knowing how bright the star is, which is a measure of how rapidly the star releases energy, astronomers can then calculate its age. They simply divide the total amount of energy given off by the rate at which the star releases energy as light.

Once they were able to determine the age of stars, astronomers set out to find the oldest stars in the Galaxy. In the 1960's, a group of astronomers completed careful calculations of the ages of stars in *globular clusters*, collections of hundreds of thousands of stars. The astronomers determined that the stars in these clusters were the most ancient stars in the Galaxy, having burned their nuclear fuel for at least 9 billion and perhaps as long as 15 billion years. Since these clusters formed at the same time as the Galaxy itself, astronomers concluded that galaxy formation occurred about 9 billion to 15 billion years ago.

Still a third astronomical clock involves radioactive dating. Astronomers believe that radioactive heavy elements were created in *supernovae*—the explosions of extremely massive stars. Radioactive elements could not have been present in the first generation of stars that existed in the Galaxy, because these stars contained only the light elements hydrogen and helium. Heavier elements could have been manufactured only when those first stars exploded.

Of course, no one witnessed those first supernovae explosions, but astronomers Geoffrey and Margaret Burbidge, Fred Hoyle, and William Fowler, working at the California Institute of Technology in Pasadena in the 1950's, used calculations to theoretically show how much uranium could have formed in those first supernovae. They determined that about 1.65 times as much U-235 as U-238 was created during the period of those first explosions. But U-235 decays about seven times faster than U-238, and measurements of uranium samples on Earth show that U-235 now represents only about 0.71 per cent of all natural uranium compared with 99.28 per cent for U-238. Knowing the decay rates of U-235 and U-238, the astronomers calculated that these heavy radioactive elements formed nearly 10 billion years ago.

Comparing the "calendars"

Since these original estimates were made, astronomers have realized that there are other pairs of isotopes to compare for this kind of very ancient dating, such as the ratio of thorium 232 to U-238. The thorium isotope has a half-life of about 14 billion years, which is closer to the length of time being investigated and is about three times longer than the half-life of U-238. Using this method, astronomers believe that the heavy radioactive elements formed from 10 billion to 20 billion years ago. It is this agreement on the age of the universe—arrived at by three independent methods—that gives astronomers confidence that they have narrowed the range of possible ages for the universe.

Through patience and ingenuity, scientists have developed a set of tools that allow them to determine the ages of many ancient objects, including the planet on which we live. Astronomers, however, hope to improve on their methods until they can chart a time sequence for the universe: When did it begin and when did the stars and galaxies first form?

Science File

Science Year contributors report on the year's major developments in their respective fields. The articles in this section are arranged alphabetically.

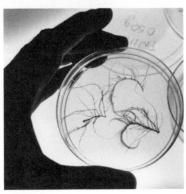

Agriculture

A severe drought, the worst in about 50 years, gripped much of the United States in the spring and summer of 1988. Crops withered, and in July 1988 the American Farm Bureau Federation near Chicago estimated that 25 to 50 per cent of the crops in some Midwestern states had been lost. Still, most agricultural experts said that because of large grain surpluses in storage, food prices in the nation's supermarkets would most likely rise only 1 or 2 per cent by early 1989.

The drought varied in intensity from one region of the United States to another. The hardest-hit areas were the northern Great Plains—especially Minnesota, Montana, and the Dakotas—and the Southeast, particularly Tennessee, Georgia, and North and South Carolina.

Scientists were uncertain why the United States was so hot and dry in 1988. Some blamed the drought on a global warming trend—the so-called greenhouse effect—but others said it was probably due to normal climatic variation. See Environment.

Killer bees. Agricultural scientists in 1987 and 1988 were taking action to head off the invasion of Africanized honey bees into the United States. The bees—known as "killer bees" because of their highly aggressive nature—are the descendants of African honey bees taken to Brazil in 1956 for experimental purposes.

Twenty-six swarms of the African bees escaped from a Brazilian laboratory in 1957 and began interbreeding with European honey bees, the kind used in commercial honey-making operations. The "Africanized" offspring of those matings have the same aggressive characteristics as the pure African strain. The bees attack human beings or animals they perceive as threats.

Bee blockade. The killer bees, spreading northward during the past three decades, had reached the Isthmus of Tehuantepec in southern Mexico by late 1987. Because the isthmus, with a width of about 190 kilometers (120 miles), is the narrowest part of Mexico, it was considered the best place to make a stand against the bees.

Two researchers test techniques that may help disrupt the mating of Africanized, or "killer," honey bees expected to reach the United States from Mexico by late 1989. A scientist with the U.S. Department of Agriculture (USDA) tracks a swarm of honey bee drones on radar, *below right,* to learn the bees' mating patterns. Another USDA researcher, *below,* inspects a trap that will be suspended from a balloon to catch bees.

The United States and Mexican governments in September 1987 established a "bee-regulated zone" across the isthmus. Within the zone, U.S. and Mexican scientists began measures aimed at stopping—or at least blunting—the northward progress of the bees.

The main thrust of the program was an effort to dramatically reduce matings between Africanized honey bees and European honey bees. In many areas, the bee experts kept European drones confined in specially constructed hives, and captured African drones in traps. After they trapped and killed most of the Africanized drones in an area, they released European drones to mate with European queens.

Scientists were also monitoring hives to find and remove Africanized queens. In addition, the Mexican government offered rewards for information on the locations of Africanized bee colonies. Any colonies found were destroyed.

By February 1988, the bees had advanced about 160 kilometers (100 miles) past the original barrier area on the isthmus. The scientists continued their efforts, but many experts doubted that the insects could be stopped entirely; they predicted that swarms of killer bees would reach Texas by late 1989 or early 1990. If that happens, eradication efforts will begin in the United States. Some scientists think that prompt and vigorous action against the invasion could prevent killer bees from overwhelming European honey bee colonies in the Southern States.

Pest control remained a high priority in agricultural research in 1987 and 1988. Because conventional pesticides are potentially hazardous to the environment and to human and animal health, scientists continued to explore a number of new ways to combat weeds and insects.

In December 1987, Robert J. Kremer, a microbiologist with the United States Department of Agriculture (USDA) in Washington, D.C., reported that *rhizobacteria* (root-dwelling bacteria) that infect weed seedlings could replace some chemical herbicides. He said the microorganisms interfere with certain weeds' life processes—for example, by producing poisons that travel to the leaves and reduce the manufacture of chlorophyll.

Kremer said he had identified strains of rhizobacteria that attack velvetleaf, cockleburs, and several other common weeds. In greenhouse tests on velvetleaf—a pest that infests fields of cotton, corn, soybeans, and a number of other crops—one strain of the bacteria reduced weed growth by 88 per cent.

The report recommended further studies of rhizobacteria to determine exactly how the microorganisms attack weeds. Kremer cautioned that scientists must also find out whether these bacteria have any harmful effects on crop plants.

Chemical pesticides will undoubtedly continue to be used against crop pests for some time to come, but researchers in 1987 and 1988 were developing chemicals that are less environmentally harmful. Some of these new compounds contain synthetic imitations of natural antipest substances found in plants. Because the artificial chemicals are identical to those found in nature, they do not harm the environment.

Researchers were also developing and testing a number of pesticides that are targeted to protect plants against specific species of insects or weeds. Such chemicals act by attacking a particular biochemical function in the targeted organism or by making the organism supersensitive to its environment. Some chemicals, for example, greatly increase weeds' sensitivity to light, causing them to wither and die.

Most of these new compounds are structured so that they break down after a few hours in the environment. Thus, they do not build up in the soil or contaminate ground water.

Improved livestock production. A new method for producing livestock with identical features was nearing commercial application in the United States and Canada in 1988. The technique, called *cloning*, enables livestock breeders to produce numerous animals from a single embryo.

Cloning begins with the mating of two prize animals with certain desired characteristics, such as lean meat.

A flea beetle, *top right,* and a spurge hawkmoth caterpillar, *top left,* feed on leafy spurge, a weed infesting U.S. farmland. The insects were imported from Europe in the 1980's to help control the weed. In Montana, a scientist counts insects on leafy spurge, *above;* the white cages are used to test herbicides' effects on the insects.

When the fertilized egg from the mating has divided into an embryo of up to 32 cells, the embryo is removed from the female's uterus. In the laboratory, the embryo is divided.

In one technique, the embryo is separated into individual cells, and the nucleus of each cell is fused with an unfertilized egg cell from which the nucleus has been removed. The fused cells are then placed into the wombs of surrogate mother animals, where they develop normally. All of the animals produced from an embryo are genetically identical.

Cloning will eventually enable livestock growers to produce entire herds of cattle or flocks of sheep with the same characteristics, such as a uniformly high quality of meat or superior resistance to diseases and pests.

While research on cloning progressed, scientists at Iowa State University of Science and Technology in Ames were testing a chemical called *alpha keto isocaproate* (KIC) to improve livestock. KIC occurs naturally in animals' bodies in small amounts.

The Iowa State researchers reported in February 1988 that larger amounts of KIC, given to young cattle, increased the animals' muscle mass by 15 per cent and reduced their fat content by 20 per cent. The chemical works by preventing the breakdown of protein as an animal grows.

Computer program for farmers. A computer program that enables farmers to combine data on plant growth, weather, and pest control was being evaluated in 1988 by agricultural scientists at Mississippi State University. The program—introduced in 1987 by the scientists in cooperation with the USDA and researchers at other state universities—provides advice on crop management that results in lower production costs, reduced pesticide use, and savings of energy and labor.

Seventy-two farmers tried the program in 1987. The farmers made simple tests and observations in their fields and fed the information into a desktop computer. Following their computers' guidance, the farmers saved an average of about $250 per hectare (2.4 acres). [James E. Halpin]

See also GENETICS. In WORLD BOOK, see AGRICULTURE.

Anthropology

Pieces of burnt flint found in Israel have provided evidence that anatomically modern human beings lived in the Middle East twice as long ago as most anthropologists had believed. The finding was reported in February 1988 by a team of scientists headed by physicist Helene Valladas of the Institute for Low-Level Radiation in Gif sur Yvette, France. The flint flakes, dated to about 92,000 years ago, were found in a cave called Qafzeh, near Nazareth, in the same geologic layer in which the fossilized bones of modern-looking human beings—*Homo sapiens sapiens*—were found in 1973. The flakes were probably chips that fell into a hearth or campfire as chunks of flint were being shaped as tools.

The researchers dated the flakes using *thermoluminescence*, a technique used mainly to date pottery. Thermoluminescence is based on the knowledge that, over time, naturally occurring radiation displaces subatomic particles called electrons at a known rate in some mineral substances, such as clay and flint. When the substance or an object made from it is heated—such as when clay pots are fired—the electrons are knocked back into their original positions, giving off light in the process. As time passes, however, electrons again are displaced. By heating pieces of pottery and measuring the amount of light emitted, scientists can determine the time that elapsed since the pottery was originally fired and, thus, the age of the pottery. Thermoluminescence can also be used to date flints that have been burnt. According to Valladas and her colleagues, the flints—and the fossils found in the same layer in the cave—are about 92,000 years old.

Some scientists have questioned the accuracy of Valladas' date, however. They argue that the flints may not have been originally heated to a high enough temperature to return all the displaced electrons to their original places. If so, the flints would appear to be much older than they are, according to the amount of light they gave off when reheated. If Valladas' date is correct, however, it indicates that ana-

A computerized tomography (CT) scan in October 1987 of an ancient prehuman fossil skull revealed apelike features previously hidden by rock in which the skull is encased. The so-called Taung skull, found in 1924, *below,* is from a child who lived in Africa between 2 million and 3 million years ago. The CT images, *below right,* revealed that the teeth and sinus cavities are more apelike than humanlike.

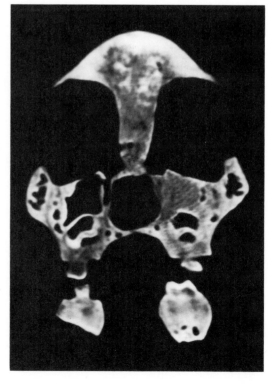

The Mother of Us All?

Where and when did modern human beings first appear? For decades, proposed answers to that question have stirred up considerable controversy among anthropologists who study the fossils and tools left by our ancient ancestors. Now scientists who investigate our genetic makeup are influencing the debate. According to a genetic study published in 1987, every person living today can trace his or her maternal ancestry to one woman who lived in Africa about 200,000 years ago.

The study was done by a team of scientists headed by biochemist Rebecca L. Cann of the University of Hawaii in Honolulu. The genetic material the scientists analyzed was mitochondrial deoxyribonucleic acid (mtDNA), a type of DNA found in small amounts outside the nucleus of cells. MtDNA, which is involved in producing energy for cells, is passed from generation to generation only through the female line. The DNA in the cell's nucleus—which carries the instructions for an organism's structure and life processes—contains genes from both parents.

For their study, the scientists gathered mtDNA from 147 people in the United States with ancestors from Africa, Asia, Europe, Australia, or New Guinea. They then used chemical "scissors" to cut the mtDNA at specific sites and compared the segments. The differences in the segments reflected random genetic changes called *mutations* that occurred over time.

The researchers identified two general categories of mtDNA. One consisted of mtDNA from people only of African descent. The other category consisted of mtDNA from people with roots in any of the five areas. Cann and her colleagues found the greatest number of mutations in the mtDNA of people in the exclusively African group. This finding suggested that Africans have been around longer and so their mtDNA had more time to change.

The scientists also used a computer to create a mtDNA "family tree." Tracing backward, they charted the minimum number of mutations needed to determine the last common ancestor of the people in the study. In this way, they calculated that the people in the Africa-only group had only African ancestors. In contrast, those in the other group had at least one African ancestor. From this, the scientists concluded that modern human beings had emerged first in Africa and then later spread to other parts of the world.

To determine when the last common ancestor of the modern people in the study lived, the scientists theorized that mtDNA mutates at a rate of 2 to 4 per cent every million years. At that rate, it would have taken about 200,000 years for the mutations in the modern mtDNA to accumulate. Therefore, the scientists concluded that the ancestral woman who has become known as "mitochondrial Eve" lived about 200,000 years ago.

Cann emphasized that mitochondrial Eve was not the only woman alive at that time. She was, however, the only woman alive 200,000 years ago whose descendants included some females in every generation to pass along the mitochondrial genes.

The role of genetics in the study of human evolution has been widely debated since the

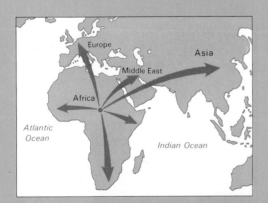

The mtDNA study supports the theory that modern human beings evolved in one place—probably Africa—about 200,000 years ago and spread out from there.

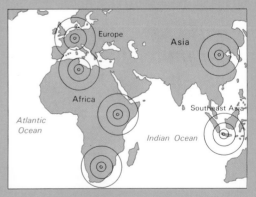

A competing theory holds that modern human beings evolved in several places from a common ancestor that lived as long as 1 million years ago.

early 1960's when the first research in this area was reported. The level of the debate rose significantly in 1967, when scientists at the University of California at Berkeley published a study suggesting that chimpanzees and human beings split from their common ancestor just 5 million years ago. The 5-million-year date was nearly 10 million years later than the date for the split accepted by most anthropologists at that time. Since then, fossil finds have supported the later date. But disagreements over the use of genetics in anthropology persist.

Cann's research has come in for its share of criticism as well. Some scientists believe that Cann's calculations of the mtDNA mutation rate are too high and that mitochondrial Eve lived much earlier. Other scientists challenge Cann's conclusion that mitochondrial Eve lived in Africa. For example, geneticists at Emory University in Atlanta, Ga., agree with Cann that mitochondrial Eve lived about 200,000 years ago. But their studies of mtDNA gathered from 700 people on four continents led them to suggest that she may have lived in Asia. Using a different method of slicing mtDNA and categorizing the fragments, they found that mtDNA differs according to race. The Emory researchers claim that the type most similar to the mtDNA of apes occurs more often in Asians. So they concluded Asia was a likely place for the origin of modern human beings.

Cann's research is also influencing the debate about how modern human beings evolved. One group of anthropologists contends that modern human beings—*Homo sapiens sapiens*—first appeared in one place—probably Africa—sometime between 100,000 and 200,000 years ago and spread to the rest of the world. According to this theory, earlier types of human beings, such as Neanderthals, who lived in Europe, the Near and Middle East, and Asia, became extinct as modern human beings flourished. Some anthropologists also believe there was some intermixing between Neanderthals and *Homo sapiens sapiens*.

Other anthropologists, however, argue that different groups of primitive human beings evolved into *Homo sapiens sapiens* from a common ancestor that lived perhaps 1 million years ago. These different groups were the ancestors of the various modern racial groups. Cann's finding that mitochondrial Eve lived in Africa about 200,000 years ago supports the first theory.

New fossil finds will, no doubt, lead scientists to a better understanding of the origins of modern human beings. It seems clear, however, that genetic studies of modern populations will also play an important role in attempts to solve this intriguing puzzle. [Bruce Bower]

tomically modern human beings appeared in the Middle East about 50,000 years earlier than most previous estimates.

The finding also challenges the theory that Neanderthals—an early form of *Homo sapiens*—were direct ancestors of modern-looking human beings. Fossil evidence indicates that Neanderthals, who lived in Europe and Asia from about 100,000 to 35,000 years ago, arrived in the Middle East about 60,000 years ago. The new research, however, suggests that Neanderthals were not direct ancestors because they arrived in the Middle East more than 30,000 years after *Homo sapiens sapiens*.

Valladas' finding also bolsters the argument that the subspecies *Homo sapiens sapiens* evolved in Africa about 200,000 years ago and then spread from there. The Qafzeh fossils are only slightly younger than fossils found in Africa dated at about 130,000 years old. Many anthropologists believe that these are fossils of *Homo sapiens sapiens*. Some scientists, however, argue that *Homo sapiens sapiens* evolved in many places from different groups of early human beings whose common prehuman ancestor existed up to 1 million years ago (see Close-Up).

Neanderthal pelvis. The discovery in Israel of the most complete Neanderthal pelvis yet found has challenged a theory that Neanderthals were more mature at birth than modern human infants. The pelvis, part of an adult male skeleton dating from 50,000 to 55,000 years ago, was described in June 1987 by anthropologist Yoel Rak and his colleagues at Tel Aviv University in Israel. The pelvis was found in a cave called Kebara on Mount Carmel, about 30 kilometers (18½ miles) south of Haifa.

Previous studies based on fragmentary remains had suggested that the central cavity in Neanderthal pelvises was larger than that in modern human beings. In females, the central cavity forms part of the birth canal through which babies are born. Some scientists had speculated that the central cavity was larger because Neanderthals, like nonhuman primates, may have given birth to more developed infants, with larger heads. Modern human infants

Rocking the anthropological world, a second
"Lucy" is discovered in southern Uganda.

are more immature at birth than other primate babies.

Rak reported, however, that the central cavity in the Neanderthal pelvis is the same size as the cavity in modern human beings, though the shape is different. According to Rak, the unusual shape of the Neanderthal pelvis is related to the way these primitive human beings stood and walked.

Stone Age dwarf. An analysis of the skeleton of a Stone Age dwarf found in Italy suggests that, contrary to popular belief, prehistoric people may have cared for the handicapped and infirm, instead of abandoning them. The analysis of the bones was published in November 1987 by a team of scientists headed by anthropologist David W. Frayer of the University of Kansas in Lawrence. The skeleton, which was radiocarbon-dated to about 11,000 years ago, was found in the mid-1960's in a cave near Casenza in southern Italy.

According to Frayer, the skeleton is that of a 17-year-old male who suffered from a rare inherited form of dwarfism known as acromesomelic dysplasia. He stood from 1 to 1.3 meters (3 to 4 feet) tall and had a high, bulging skull and a small face. The bones of his legs were about half normal length, so he probably would have tired after walking even short distances. The bones of his forearms were especially short and so curved that it would have been impossible for him to completely straighten his arms. Like modern people with this type of dwarfism, the prehistoric dwarf probably had normal intelligence.

The dwarf, who lived before the development of agriculture in Europe, was one of a band of nomads who roamed the mountains of southern Italy hunting wild animals and gathering plants. According to Frayer, the dwarf's survival to age 17 indicates that he was accepted and cared for by his group, despite his difficulty in traversing the region's rugged terrain and his limited ability to hunt and gather food.   [Charles F. Merbs]

In WORLD BOOK, see PREHISTORIC PEOPLE.

Archaeology, New World

Important new information about prehistoric Indian life on the southern coast of New England was reported in May 1988 by archaeologists Francis P. McManamon of the National Park Service and James W. Bradley of the Massachusetts Historical Commission. Their investigations of a 1,000-year-old Indian burial site at the Cape Cod National Seashore in Massachusetts produced evidence supporting the theory that the Indians of this region lived in permanent settlements instead of leading a seminomadic existence, as some archaeologists have argued.

The burial site, located on Indian Neck, a peninsula of the outer cape, is an *ossuary* (a mass grave) about 1.3 meters (4 feet) across and 30 centimeters (1 foot) deep. The bones in the ossuary, which was discovered in 1979, were radiocarbon-dated to the A.D. 900's or 1000's.

In the ossuary, the archaeologists found the remains of 56 people of all ages and both sexes. Although the bones appeared to be lying in the grave in a jumbled mass, an examination of their position revealed that they had been carefully placed there. For example, most of the skulls had been placed along the eastern and western edges of the ossuary.

The discovery that the bones were no longer connected at the joints led the archaeologists to conclude that the flesh had been removed from the bones before they were placed in the ossuary. The bodies were probably buried first in temporary graves or exposed aboveground. Then, after the bodies had decomposed, the bones were placed in the ossuary.

Because the bones had few signs of physical injury or infectious disease, the archaeologists theorized that the ossuary was not the result of a massacre or epidemic. Instead, it was probably a part of the Indians' usual burial practices.

The ossuary at Indian Neck also provided insights into the Indians' way of life. Some archaeologists have theorized that these Indians generally lived inland, visiting coastal areas only occasionally during the summer. Other archaeologists argued that they made summer visits on a regular basis, mainly for the purpose of gathering shellfish. Yet a third group of archaeologists proposed that the Indians, beginning as early as 2500 B.C., lived along the coast the year around.

The Park Service archaeologists reported that their findings support the third theory. They noted that ossuaries were usually built only by settled people, such as the Huron Indians of Ontario.

The ossuary findings supported earlier evidence for year-round occupation that came from a study of the growth rings in the shell of a certain type of clam called a *quahog* found in *middens* (trash mounds) elsewhere in the Cape Cod area. The study was conducted in the early 1980's by archaeologists Mary E. Hancock and Alison Dwyer, also of the Park Service.

Each year of their life, quahogs lay down a new band of shell. Shell added during the early winter is translucent. Material added during the late winter and spring, when the clam grows faster, is opaque with fine growth lines. By examining and counting these lines, scientists can determine the season—and sometimes even the month—in which a clam was harvested. Hancock and Dwyer discovered that most of the clams they studied had been collected in winter, suggesting that the Indians lived near the coast throughout the year.

Columbus' lost colony. The discovery in Haiti of the first Spanish settlement in the New World—a village founded by explorer Christopher Columbus in 1492—was reported in November 1987 by archaeologist Kathleen A. Deagan of the Florida State Museum in Gainesville. The settlement, named La Navidad, was established on Dec. 26, 1492, two days after the *Santa Maria*, Columbus' flagship, ran aground off the northern coast of what is now Haiti.

The colony apparently was founded on the site of a village inhabited by Taino Arawak Indians. In January 1493, Columbus departed for Spain, leaving 39 crew members at La Navidad. When he returned to Haiti 11 months later, he found the settlement burned and its Spanish occupants killed. Columbus sailed on and knowledge of the location of the colony was soon lost.

Archaeology, New World

Continued

Deagan and her colleagues believe they have found the remains of the settlement near the town of En Bas Saline, Haiti. At the site, the archaeologists discovered pieces of European pottery and the bones of European animals dating from the late 1400's.

Many of these artifacts were found in a large pit—later filled in—that may be evidence of a well and thus support the idea of a European presence at the site. If the pit, which had been dug down to the present water table, was a well, it represents something unknown in the Caribbean before the arrival of Europeans.

A tooth found in the well—from a domestic pig—has provided another link between the site and the *Santa Maria*'s crew. Archaeologist Jonathon Ericson of the University of California at Irvine studied the levels of the element strontium in the tooth. Small amounts of strontium, which is naturally present in soil, enters plants as they grow—and the bones of animals that eat them.

Scientists have discovered that soil levels of strontium vary by region. As a result, Ericson was able to determine that the pig probably was raised near Seville, Spain, a city close to the port from which Columbus set sail.

Early human remains. The discovery in Kansas of what may be the oldest known human skeletal remains in the New World was announced in April 1988 by geologist Wakefield Dort of the University of Kansas in Lawrence. The discovery was made at a site along the Kansas River near Bonner Springs, a town west of Kansas City. At the site, Dort and anthropologist Lawrence D. Martin, also of Kansas, found the bones of several people together with the bones of animals that became extinct more than 10,000 years ago.

The scientists dated the human bones with a dating technique called electron spin resonance (ESR), discovered in the late 1970's. ESR is a complicated technique based on the measurement of the amount of naturally occurring radiation absorbed by buried objects, such as bone, containing *calcite*, a type of mineral. The level of

A combination flute and maraca, *right,* top, and an ocarina, right, made in the shape of a woman holding a bird are among the ceramic musical instruments whose discovery in ancient Maya tombs in Belize was reported in January 1988. The instruments date from between A.D. 600 and 900. Maya musicians played the ocarina by blowing air through the mouthpiece against a wedge-shaped piece called a tone edge (shown in diagram at far right), which created air currents that swirled into the instrument. By covering the tone hole, the musician varied the ocarina's pitch.

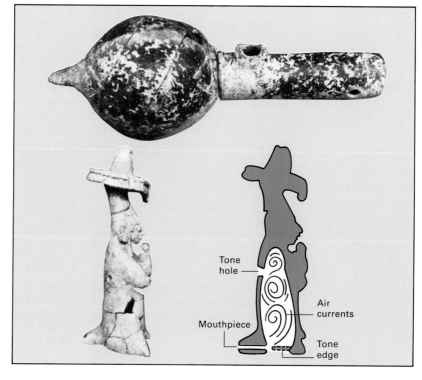

Tone hole

Mouthpiece

Air currents

Tone edge

Archaeology, New World

Continued

radiation increases with age. Using ESR, the scientists calculated the human bones are about 15,400 years old. But Dort cautioned that further research is needed to confirm this date.

Ancient Maya metropolis. A review of nearly a decade of excavations at the ancient Maya city of El Mirador in Guatemala was published in September 1987 by archaeologist Ray T. Matheny of Brigham Young University in Provo, Utah. The ruins, which lie 360 kilometers (225 miles) north of Guatemala City, were first seen by archaeologists in the 1930's. Constructed in 150 B.C., El Mirador represents the largest collection of civic and religious buildings known to have existed at that time in the territory occupied by the Maya.

Excavations at the site—which have revealed an elaborate city built with superb engineering skills—have challenged long-held beliefs about the development of Maya civilization. El Mirador was built more than 500 years before Maya civilization reached its peak. Previously, most archaeologists believed the early Maya did not have the skills or organization for a project as elaborate as El Mirador.

El Mirador encompassed an area of 16 square kilometers (6 square miles). At the site, Matheny has found large pyramids, platforms, temples, and plazas. One pyramid rises 18 stories and covers 18,000 square meters (22,000 square yards), about the size of four football fields. The structures, which were made of limestone blocks, were covered with stucco and then painted red. Some were also decorated with elaborate jaguar masks made of stucco.

For unknown reasons, El Mirador began to decline about A.D. 150. A few hundred years later, another group of Maya occupied the city, though the city never regained its earlier prominence.   [Thomas R. Hester]

In the Special Reports section, see THE ANASAZI OF THE SOUTHWEST; FINDING OUT HOW OLD THINGS ARE. In WORLD BOOK, see COLUMBUS, CHRISTOPHER; INDIAN, AMERICAN (Indians of the Eastern Woodlands); MAYA.

Archaeology, Old World

Israeli archaeologists excavating the oldest and largest underwater prehistoric site in the Middle East continued to discover the remains of buildings, tools, and human and animal bones in 1987, according to a report published in January 1988. The site, called Atlit-Yam, consists of the ruins of an 8,000-year-old village now lying 12 meters (40 feet) under the Mediterranean Sea off Israel's northern coast.

The remains were discovered in 1984 after a fierce storm swept away much of the sand that had buried the village. The site, which now lies more than 400 meters (1,300 feet) offshore, once lay about 305 meters (1,000 feet) inland. When the village was inhabited 8,000 years ago, sea levels were lower because Earth's climate was colder and massive amounts of seawater were trapped in glaciers.

The Israeli archaeologists excavating Atlit-Yam uncovered an area measuring about 100 by 300 meters (330 by 990 feet). They found the remains of 12 structures, including walls, pits, and four houses. The archaeologists excavated one of the houses, a rectangular stone structure measuring 9 by 5 meters (30 by 17 feet). The scientists believe that other walls attached to the house are the remains of courtyards and storage pits.

Based on artifacts found at the site, the archaeologists concluded that Atlit-Yam was a farming village. These artifacts included hoes, sickle blades, and other farming tools; many grinding and milling stones; and the remains of domesticated wheat and lentils. The presence of the bones of deer, pigs, and gazelles, however, indicates that the people of Atlit-Yam were also hunters.

In addition, the archaeologists found the bones of cattle and goats. Although these bones resemble those of wild forms of these animals, the archaeologists believe the bones were from domesticated animals because they found complete skeletons. This probably would not have been the case if the animals had been hunted and butchered in the wild. In addition, the archaeologists discovered a large con-

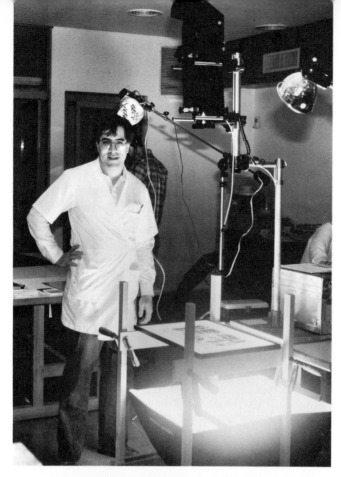

The 2,000-year-old *Genesis Apocryphon, above,* a Dead Sea Scroll still largely unread 40 years after its discovery in Israel, was unrolled for study in early 1988. To decipher the text of the badly deteriorated scroll, a scientist photographed it using infrared film and special lighting, *top.* The infrared pictures clearly revealed letters indistinct or invisible to the naked eye.

centration of cattle bones in one of the courtyards, suggesting that this area was used for slaughtering the animals.

Most of the five human skeletons found at the site showed signs of health problems, including tuberculosis, arthritis, dental problems, bone fractures, and high fevers developed during childhood. In addition, the ear canal of one of the individuals contained a bony growth like those frequently found in modern-day scuba divers. The archaeologists theorized that these remains may be those of the world's oldest known skin diver.

Ancient Egyptian boat. In October 1987, Egyptian and United States scientists used advanced technology to view the disassembled remains of an ancient Egyptian boat without excavating the chamber in which it has been sealed for 4,600 years. The chamber is near the base of the Great Pyramid at Giza, Egypt.

To see inside the chamber, the scientists drilled a hole through a slab of rock 1.5 meters (5 feet) thick that covered the chamber and then inserted a miniature video camera. Televised pictures revealed the piled-up sections of the disassembled wooden boat, which were covered with reed mats. The boat's wooden planks appeared to be in excellent condition. The scientists also saw inscriptions on the chamber's walls made by ancient workers.

The chamber is similar to a nearby pit excavated in 1954 in which archaeologists found the perfectly preserved remains of another disassembled wooden boat. That boat was assembled and is now on display near the pyramid. Some scholars believe the reconstructed boat, which is 43 meters (142 feet) long, was buried at the death of Pharaoh Khufu, called *Cheops* by the Greeks, about 2583 B.C., and was intended to transport him in the afterlife. There are no plans to assemble the second boat. After viewing the chamber, the scientists sealed the drill hole, leaving the chamber intact.

Another objective of the project was to obtain a sample of the air in the chamber. The scientists hoped that an analysis of the ancient air would help them determine how Earth's atmosphere has changed over the past 4,500 years. For this reason, they used a spe-

Archaeology, Old World

Continued

A scientist in October 1987 views televised images, *below,* of the disassembled remains of an ancient Egyptian boat sealed in an underground chamber for 4,600 years. To explore the chamber without excavating it, scientists drilled a hole through the chamber's stone ceiling and inserted a miniature television camera. The disassembled boat is believed to be similar to another boat, *below right,* found in 1954 in a nearby chamber and assembled for display.

cially designed drill to penetrate the chamber. The drill, based on technology developed for moon exploration, prevented fresh air from entering the chamber. An analysis of the air sample, however, revealed that it had been tainted by outside air.

Pyramids discovered. The discovery of two buried and previously unknown ancient Egyptian pyramids was reported in April 1988 by a team of French archaeologists. The pyramids, located about 27 kilometers (17 miles) southwest of Cairo, Egypt, were detected by ground-penetrating radar, which allows scientists to identify buried structures.

The scientists who found the pyramids reported that the structures date to between 2420 and 2280 B.C. The pyramids are fairly small structures, about 12 meters (40 feet) high and with a base 25 meters (82 feet) long and 20 meters (65 feet) wide. The discovery of the pyramids brings the number of known ancient Egyptian pyramids to 85.

Celtic tomb. The results of excavations at an apparently undisturbed Celtic burial mound near Stuttgart, West Germany, were reported in November 1987 by Jörg Biel, an archaeologist with the West German government. Discovered in 1978, the mound, called the Hochdorf mound, was constructed about 550 B.C. The Celtic people, who inhabited this part of western Europe between 600 and 450 B.C., buried their chieftains in large mounds around the mountain fortresses in which they lived.

Archaeologists have excavated many of these mounds. In nearly all cases, however, the mounds had already been looted by grave robbers seeking the beautiful and costly artifacts they often contained. The Hochdorf mound, which escaped the looters, has thus provided archaeologists with new examples of Celtic art and artifacts as well as new insights on Celtic burial customs.

Inside the mound, archaeologists found the skeleton of a man about 2 meters (6 feet 6 inches) tall. He was about 40 years old when he died. A

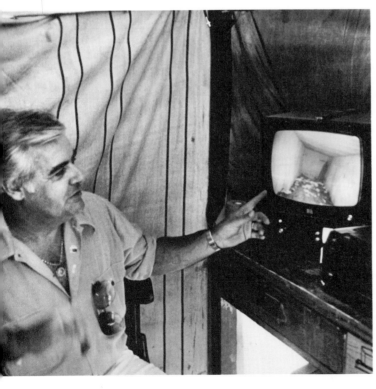

Archaeologists excavating the circus of the ancient city of Carthage, *above right,* in mid-1987 uncover a structure that may have been a souvenir stand. The circus, an arena for chariot races and other sporting events, was used from the A.D. 100's to the 400's. Among the items found at the circus were curse tablets, *right,* made of sheets of lead. The lead sheets were covered with curses intended to bring bad luck to the charioteers, then rolled up and thrown onto the track.

Archaeology, Old World

Continued

golden hoop around his neck symbolized his status as a chieftain. A small bag on his chest contained a wooden comb, an iron razor, five amber beads, and three iron fishhooks.

The tomb consisted of two chambers. The outer chamber, built of oak logs, measured 7.5 by 7.4 meters (24 feet 6 inches by 24 feet 3 inches) and was about 2 meters deep. The wooden inner chamber, which contained the skeletal remains and many artifacts, was 4.7 meters (15 feet 6 inches) square and was about 1 meter (3 feet) deep. To protect the grave from robbers, the tomb's builders filled the space between the walls and roofs of the two chambers with large rocks.

Other objects found in the grave included textiles, arrows, and numerous gold vessels and figurines. Among the most exciting finds were a highly decorated reclining throne, a two-horse wagon, a large bronze kettle decorated with lions, an iron drinking horn, and a decorated golden bowl.

Black Death cemetery. Excavations of the largest cemetery ever found in

England for victims of the Black Death—bubonic plague—that swept through that country in the mid-1300's were reported in March 1988 by archaeologist Peter Mills. The plague killed about 600,000 people in England, about one-third of the nation's population.

Although the cemetery, found in London near the Tower of London, contained 1,500 skeletons, the only object found was one belt buckle. Grave robbers probably stripped the corpses of any valuables.

The archaeologists excavating the cemetery removed each skeleton, washed it, and cataloged it at the Museum of London. These skeletons represent a cross section of the population of medieval London, and by studying them, archaeologists hope to learn about the general health and other physical characteristics of the people of that time.   [Robert J. Wenke]

In the Special Reports section, see FINDING OUT HOW OLD THINGS ARE. In WORLD BOOK, see BUBONIC PLAGUE; CELTS; EGYPT, ANCIENT.

Astronomy, Extragalactic

More observations of the enormous and puzzling arcs found in three clusters of galaxies in 1987 were reported by French astronomers in January 1988. Genevieve Soucail and colleagues of Toulouse Observatory used the 3.6-meter (142-inch) Canada-France-Hawaii telescope atop Mauna Kea on Hawaii and the 3.6-meter European Southern Observatory telescope at La Silla, Chile, to make detailed observations of one of the arcs that appears near a cluster of galaxies known as Abell 370. Their findings supported the theory that the arcs are optical illusions formed by a *gravitational lens*, the gravitational field of a massive object that deflects or magnifies light from a more distant object. In this case, light from the more distant object is being bent by the gravitational field of the cluster and spread out into the image of an arc.

Soucail's group observed that everywhere along the arc, the same amount of energy was being given off, indicating that its light was coming from a single object, as predicted by the grav-itational lens theory. If the light was not coming from a single object, some portions of the arc would have given off more energy than other portions. The astronomers determined the energy distribution by studying the *spectra* (color patterns) of the arc's light.

They also determined that the single object producing the light was more distant than the cluster of galaxies. They came to this conclusion by studying *red shift*, a shift in the wavelength of light given off by an object toward the longer, or red, wavelength of the spectrum. Light is shifted toward the red end of the spectrum when the source of the light is moving away from an observer.

This phenomenon is called the *Doppler effect* and is similar to the apparent change in tone of a train whistle, for example. As the train approaches the listener, the sound waves are compressed and the pitch of the whistle seems higher, but as the train moves away, the sound waves are stretched and the pitch of the whistle seems lower. The greater the red shift,

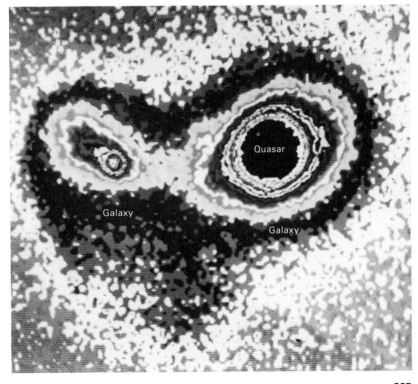

A computer-enhanced image of two colliding galaxies may explain what triggers the formation of *quasars,* the most energetic objects in the universe, astronomers reported in January 1988. Astronomers at Kitt Peak National Observatory near Tucson, Ariz., who obtained the image of the galaxies—one of which contains a quasar at its center—theorize that the collision disrupts the orbits of stars. The stars fall into the center and provide the energy source for the quasar.

225

The Lessons in a Supernova

Throughout 1987 and on into 1988, astronomers followed the explosion of the brightest supernova in 383 years. Known as Supernova 1987A, this cataclysmic explosion of a massive star became visible from Earth on Feb. 23, 1987. It has since shed light on how stars evolve, demonstrated how heavy chemical elements originate, and helped us understand what happens when a giant star dies.

Astronomers now agree on the identity of the star that exploded. Known by its star survey number as Sanduleak −69 202, it was one of many bright blue stars in the Large Magellanic Cloud, a galaxy neighboring our own Milky Way galaxy and one that is visible only from the Southern Hemisphere. The Large Magellanic Cloud is about 160,000 *light-years* from Earth. (A light-year is the distance light travels in one year, about 9.46 trillion kilometers [5.88 trillion miles].) Before this bright blue star exploded, it was about 20 times more massive and about 100,000 times brighter than the sun.

Because of its enormous mass, Sanduleak −69 202 passed through numerous stages of nuclear burning in its core, first converting hydrogen to helium, then helium to carbon and oxygen, carbon to neon and magnesium, oxygen to silicon, and, eventually, silicon to iron. After an iron core of about 1.4 times the mass of the sun had formed in the middle of the star, no further energy could be obtained from nuclear reactions.

The core collapsed to a density about 100 trillion times greater than the density of Earth, compressing a mass greater than that of the sun into a region only about 50 kilometers (30 miles) across. The core then sprang back, producing a shock wave that traveled through the rest of the star, heating it and ejecting the star's outer material at great speeds. The collapsed core—all that remained of the star—became a *neutron star*, an extremely dense mass comprised chiefly of subatomic particles known as *neutrons*. Over the next 10 seconds, as the neutron star cooled and shrank to a diameter of only 20 kilometers (12 miles), it gave off a flood of subatomic particles called *neutrinos*. The glowing ashes of the rest of the star rushed into space and released the energy created by the shock wave.

The supernova was so bright that even at a distance of 160,000 light-years, it was about as bright as the relatively nearby stars in the Big Dipper, which are visible in the Northern Hemisphere. The peak brightness of the supernova was about 200 million times that of our own sun. Bright as it was, however, the light energy of the supernova was less than 0.01 per cent of the energy that the supernova gave off in the form of neutrinos. We now know that for 10 seconds, the supernova emitted an energy in neutrinos that was approximately equal to all the energy emitted by all the stars, galaxies, and

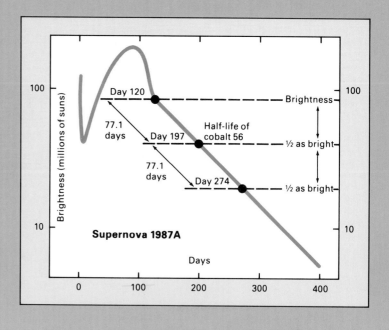

Measurements of the brightness of Supernova 1987A detected the radioactive decay of the heavy element cobalt 56. This confirmed the theory that heavy elements are produced in supernovae explosions. On the 120th day after the explosion, the supernova was almost 100 million times as bright as our sun. About 77 days later, its brightness declined by one-half, corresponding exactly to the 77.1 day *half-life* of cobalt 56—the time it takes for half of the atoms in a sample of cobalt 56 to decay. On the 274th day—another 77 days later—the brightness again declined by half, confirming the presence of cobalt 56, which decays into iron—one of the most abundant heavy elements.

quasars in the entire visible universe. Supernovae are the most powerful explosions known.

Observations of Supernova 1987A have also confirmed that heavy elements are created in supernovae explosions. In November 1987, a telescope carried to a high altitude by the *Kuiper Airborne Observatory*, an airplane equipped with astronomical instruments, showed that such heavy elements as iron, cobalt, nickel, silicon, carbon, oxygen, and others had been produced in the explosion. The plane flew at a high altitude so that the telescope could detect *infrared* (heat) radiation from the supernova. Earth's atmosphere blocks much of this radiation and prevents it from reaching Earth's surface.

Further information on the production of heavy elements came from instruments in space. Since late 1987, instruments on the Soviet Union's space station, *Mir*, and a Japanese satellite, *Ginga*, have studied the X-ray emissions of the supernova, which are unable to penetrate Earth's atmosphere. Gamma rays, radiation of even shorter wavelength than X rays, have also been detected.

Beginning in August 1987, a United States satellite normally used to study the sun—the *Solar Maximum Mission Observatory*—detected gamma rays characteristic of the decay of cobalt 56. This form of cobalt is radioactive, and it has a *half-life* of 77 days—that is, half of the atoms in a sample of cobalt 56 will decay into another element in 77 days. These observations were subsequently confirmed in October 1987 by sensitive gamma-ray detectors carried on high-altitude balloons that flew out of Alice Springs, Australia. The cobalt decays to iron, one of the most abundant heavy elements in nature.

Thus, the observations confirm a theory, first proposed in the 1940's, that supernovae explosions create heavy elements. The iron and other elements in our bodies originated in a supernova explosion that happened long before the sun was formed. The gas that formed the *solar nebulae*—out of which came the sun and planets—had traces of iron, oxygen, carbon, silicon, and other heavy elements made in supernovae. So supernovae, in effect, made life on Earth possible.

Supernova 1987A has been by far the most extensively studied supernova in history. Observations of this spectacular explosion have involved the collaboration of scientists from all over the world. And emerging from these observations, consistent with previous theory, is the picture of a titanic explosion in the core of a massive star, the ejection of material heated to high temperature by a shock wave, and the creation of heavy elements from lighter ones in the fiery interior of a star.   [Stan Woosley]

the faster an object is moving away and, therefore, the farther away it is.

The red shift of Abell 370 indicates that it is about 6 billion *light-years* away. (A light-year is the distance light travels in one year, or 9.5 trillion kilometers [5.9 trillion miles].) The red shift of the single object whose light has been bent into the shape of an arc indicates that it is about 12 billion light-years away. The spectra also indicate that this object is a spiral galaxy.

Lens and mass. Arcs may be a common occurrence in the universe, according to a January 1988 report. Most arcs, however, are dim and cannot be detected. Astrophysicists Scott A. Grossman and Ramesh Narayan of the University of Arizona in Tucson ran computer simulations of clusters of galaxies acting as gravitational lenses. The two astronomers predicted that several medium-sized arcs would exist near every long arc discovered, though observations have not yet been able to detect any other arcs near Abell 370.

The discovery of a gravitational lens is important to astronomers because the lens provides a means of determining the total mass of the cluster and the mass of some of the individual galaxies located near the cluster's center. The mass of the cluster can be deduced from the strength of the gravitational field causing the lens effect.

In the case of Abell 370, the total mass is about 60 times greater than the amount of visible mass that can be observed through telescopes. This great difference is typical in the observation of clusters and is presumed to be due to the presence of *dark matter*—the invisible substance, which may be unlike any known form of matter, that makes up most of the mass of galaxies and clusters of galaxies. The detection of other giant arcs in other distant clusters of galaxies should provide astronomers with a powerful tool for investigating the distribution of mass in the universe, particularly the distribution of dark matter.

Red shift record. The discovery of the most distant object yet found in the universe—a quasar that is more than 12 billion light-years from Earth—was reported in December 1987 by astronomers Stephen J. Warren, Paul Hew-

Astronomy, Extragalactic

Continued

Astronomer Susan M. Simkin of Michigan State University displays a photograph of Markarian 348, the largest known galaxy in the universe, with a diameter of 1.3 million light-years. Simkin and her colleagues reported on their findings about the galaxy at a conference in China in June.

itt, and Michael J. Irwin of the Institute of Astronomy in Cambridge, England, and Patrick C. Osmer of Kitt Peak National Observatory near Tucson, Ariz. The quasar's distance was determined by its red shift of 4.43, which means that its light has been shifted 443 per cent toward the red—or longer—wavelength end of the spectrum.

Astronomers once thought that there might not be any detectable objects in the universe with a red shift greater than about 3.5. Over the past several years, however, this barrier—the so-called *red limit*—has been broken repeatedly with new record red shifts being set every few months. Since 1987, three quasars have been found with red shifts exceeding 4.0. The new record-setting quasar, designated Q0051-279, is moving away from Earth at 93.4 per cent of the speed of light.

The astronomers plan to continue searching for distant objects and hope to find quasars with red shifts greater than 5.0 within a few years. Since the farther out we look in space, the further back we look in time, the discoveries of such distant objects will tell us what the universe looked like at an early age. This will help astronomers test theories of when and how quasars and galaxies began to form.

Huge, distant supercluster? Growing evidence that the universe contains enormous *superclusters*—clusters of clusters of galaxies that are hundreds of millions of light-years in diameter—was reported by two groups of astronomers in November 1987 and March 1988. The evidence also indicates that superclusters consist of many shells, or bubbles, and that galaxies cluster together along the edges of the shells, while the interiors of the shells are vast voids of mostly empty space separating one galaxy cluster from another.

Many superclusters are so distant that they cannot be directly observed. But their existence can be inferred from other observational evidence.

The idea of superclusters. The existence of one vast supercluster, which would be the largest structure in the universe, was first proposed in 1986 by astronomer Peter Jakobsen of the European Space Agency (ESA). Jakobsen

based his proposal on similarities in the spectra of two distant *quasars*—extremely bright and energetic objects—that were widely separated in the sky.

Specifically, Jakobsen found that the quasars each had four sets of *spectral lines* (distinctive patterns in their spectra) that matched. The matching spectral lines were *absorption lines*, dark vertical lines in the spectra that correspond to certain elements. The lines actually represent certain wavelengths of light missing from the spectrum.

Indirect evidence. Absorption lines are not given off by the quasars' light. Instead, as the light from the quasars travels toward Earth, some of it is absorbed by material in its path. For example, heavy elements such as carbon, silicon, and magnesium are found in some galaxies. If light from a quasar passes through such a galaxy before the light reaches Earth, instruments on telescopes will detect patterns of dark lines in the quasar's spectrum corresponding to the heavy elements that absorbed the light. Furthermore, the absorption lines will have their own red shift—distinct from the red shift of the quasar's light—enabling astronomers to calculate the distance of the intervening galaxy.

It was highly unusual for four matching absorption lines to appear in the spectra of two widely separated quasars at the same red shifts. Some astronomers suggested that it was just a random coincidence. But Jakobsen theorized that the light from the two quasars passed through the same series of galaxy clusters. As the light from each quasar passed through a galaxy, it acquired a distinctive pattern of absorption lines at a particular red shift, or distance. Since there were four series of absorption lines, the astronomers deduced there were four series of galaxies.

Since the distances of the four galaxies in the spectra of one quasar matched the distances of the four galaxies in the spectra of the other quasar, Jakobsen concluded that each series of galaxies was connected somehow. The galaxies with the same red shifts were members of a single cluster of galaxies. Thus, the scientists concluded that four clusters of galaxies stretch in front of the two qua-

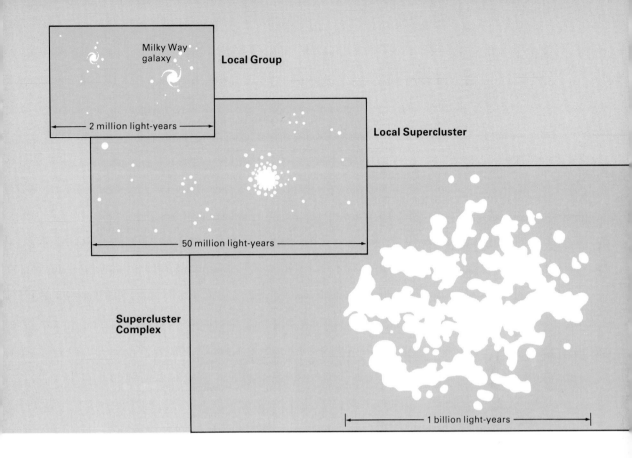

Milky Way galaxy

Local Group

2 million light-years

Local Supercluster

50 million light-years

Supercluster Complex

1 billion light-years

Astronomy, Extragalactic

Continued

Astronomers in November 1987 reported the discovery of a structure, or grouping of galaxies, about a billion light-years wide. It includes our Milky Way galaxy, which is part of a grouping called the Local Group. This, in turn, is part of the Local Supercluster, which contains many clusters of galaxies. And this, in turn, is part of the vast, newly discovered Supercluster Complex, which includes about 60 superclusters.

sars and between the two quasars and Earth. These clusters of clusters of galaxies form a supercluster that is hundreds of millions of light-years in diameter.

Seeking real superclusters. Because the hypothetical supercluster is too far away for its clusters of galaxies to be seen with telescopes, some astronomers suggested that a test of Jakobsen's hypothesis was to look at the spectra of other quasars in the same region of the sky as the pair of quasars that Jakobsen studied. If the same absorption features were seen in the spectra of these other nearby quasars, this would be further evidence for the existence of a supercluster.

In November 1987, astronomers Wallace L. W. Sargent and Charles Steidel of California Institute of Technology (Caltech) in Pasadena reported that absorption lines in a third nearby quasar did indeed match the features seen in Jakobsen's original pair.

Still more evidence was reported in March 1988 by Jakobsen and M. A. C. Perryman of the ESA and Stefano

Christiani of the European Southern Observatory in Garching near Munich, West Germany. The astronomers observed four more quasars in the same region of the sky where the initial pair are located. Their spectra showed several more sets of common absorption line features, again supporting the hypothesis that there is an intervening supercluster between these quasars and Earth. The probability that these common absorption features are simply coincidences is less than 1 in 50, according to a statistical analysis by the astronomers.

The clusters also seem to be spaced at a fairly equal distance from each other and are separated by much larger regions that are nearly empty of matter. This finding is similar to a 1986 report of bubblelike structures in the universe in which galaxies appear to be on the surfaces, or outer shells, of the bubbles, while the bubble interiors are empty. [Stephen S. Murray]

In the Special Reports section, see FINDING OUT HOW OLD THINGS ARE. In WORLD BOOK, see ASTRONOMY.

Astronomy, Galactic

Two new methods for determining the age of our galaxy, the Milky Way, were reported between June 1987 and June 1988. They came up with very different ages.

One of the techniques was based on the time required to produce the amounts of heavy elements observed in the Galaxy. It was reported by astrophysicists John J. Cowen of the University of Oklahoma in Norman; Friedrich Thielemann of Harvard University in Cambridge, Mass.; and James W. Truran, Jr., of the University of Illinois in Urbana-Champaign in December 1987.

Astronomers believe that very few heavy elements existed when our Galaxy and the first stars in it formed. The Galaxy contained mainly hydrogen and helium gas. The heavy elements were created later by nuclear reactions in the interiors of stars. These reactions fused the nuclei of lighter elements to create heavier elements. When the most massive of these stars exploded as supernovae, they released the heavy elements into space. Eventually, these heavy elements became part of the stars we observe today.

The researchers believed they could arrive at an age for the Galaxy by determining how long it took to create the amount of heavy elements known to exist today by analyzing the *spectra* (range of colors) of starlight. Each element has its own distinctive pattern of *spectral lines*, or bands in the spectrum.

Knowing the rate at which nuclear reactions produce heavy elements and using calculations to deduce how many supernova explosions have occurred in the Galaxy, the researchers concluded that it took 13.5 billion years to produce the amount of heavy elements observed today. They then inferred that our Galaxy is about 13.5 billion years old.

A younger age. A group of astronomers headed by Donald E. Winget of the University of Texas in Austin reported in April 1988 that they used a different dating method and found a much younger age for the Galaxy. The scientists based their findings on the known cooling rate of *white dwarfs*— dying stars that can no longer produce energy through nuclear reactions.

As white dwarfs age, they become cooler and dimmer, because they slowly lose the heat stored in their interiors from the nuclear fires that once burned there. Winget's group studied many white dwarfs in the vicinity of the sun. The researchers measured the temperature and brightness of the white dwarfs by using scientific instruments attached to telescopes. They determined that there was a temperature and brightness limit below which no white dwarfs could be found.

Winget's group concluded that the oldest white dwarfs were those that had reached this point of lowest temperature and dimness. Knowing the rate at which white dwarfs cool, they calculated that it took 9 billion years for the oldest white dwarfs to reach that point. They then inferred an age for the Galaxy of about 9.3 billion years. (In the Special Reports section, see FINDING OUT HOW OLD THINGS ARE.)

How big is the Milky Way? The Milky Way galaxy may not be as large as was previously thought, according to a report in June 1988 by a team of astronomers headed by Mark J. Reid of Harvard-Smithsonian Center for Astrophysics in Cambridge, Mass. In November 1985, the International Astronomical Union had agreed on a new standard for the size of the Galaxy and had placed the sun at a distance of 27,700 *light-years* from the galactic center. (A light-year is the distance that light travels in one year, about 9.5 trillion kilometers [5.9 trillion miles].) Based on new measurements, Reid's group estimated that the sun is about 23,100 light-years from the galactic center.

The new estimate was reached by analyzing the distance from Earth to a star-forming region near the center of the Galaxy. Using radio telescopes, the astronomers observed the *apparent motions* of young stars in this region—that is, the rate at which the stars appeared to move across the sky in relation to other stars. They then compared the apparent motions with the actual speed of the stars as determined by the *Doppler effect*. The Doppler effect is a change in the length of a wave as the source of the wave moves closer or farther away. The astronomers measured the Doppler effect in radio waves

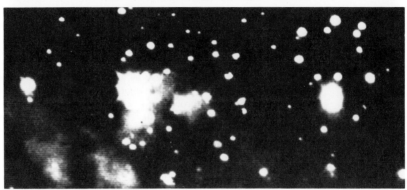

A dark cloud of gas and dust viewed through an optical telescope, *above right,* appears to have few stars. But an *infrared* (heat) detector in October 1987 revealed many young stars in this gas cloud, *below right,* in the constellation Orion. Although the dust prevents their visible light from shining through, the stars' heat warmed the cloud so that the stars appear as bright spots on the infrared image.

Astronomy, Galactic

Continued

given off by the stars. By measuring changes in wavelength, the astronomers determined the speed at which the stars were moving away from the radio telescopes. By comparing the apparent motions and the actual speeds of the stars, the astronomers estimated the stars' distances from the sun.

If the new result is accepted, astronomers will have to revise their estimate of the diameter of the Galaxy. And this could lead to revisions of distances to other galaxies.

An unusual pulsar. In July 1987, a team of British and American astronomers reported the discovery of the first pulsar to be found in a *globular cluster,* a ball-shaped cluster containing hundreds of thousands of stars densely packed together. The new *pulsar*—a rapidly rotating star that gives off regular pulses of radio waves—is also only the fourth to be found with a rotation rate of more than a hundred times per second. This pulsar spins at a rate of 328 times per second. Other pulsars rotate as slowly as once every 4 seconds.

Astronomers believe that pulsars are *neutron stars*—the remains of supernova explosions in which the cores of the stars consist almost entirely of densely packed subatomic particles known as *neutrons.* Astronomers also theorize that the four fastest-spinning pulsars rotate much more quickly than other pulsars because some external force caused their rotation to speed up after they initially formed. These pulsars probably gained new matter from a companion star in a *binary system*—a system of two stars that orbit each other. The addition of new matter would cause the pulsar to spin more rapidly.

The newly found pulsar in the globular cluster, however, does not have a binary companion, so it is difficult to understand how it could have gained the added matter needed to increase its spin. The researchers suggested that either the binary system has since been disrupted so that the companion star no longer exists, or the pulsar captured matter when it collided with another star.

231

Astronomy, Galactic

Continued

The new rapid pulsar will serve as a beacon for astronomers who want to know more about globular clusters. Astronomers now know little about these clusters because they are so far away and so densely packed that it is hard to observe their structure.

Analyzing how the pulsar moves through the cluster will help reveal how stars are distributed in the cluster. This is because slight variations in the pulsar's rotation rate are caused by slight changes in the pulsar's path, or motion. The slight changes in motion, in turn, are due to the gravitational force of matter acting on the pulsar.

Brown dwarf. What may be the first strong observational evidence for the existence of brown dwarfs was reported on Nov. 10, 1987, by astronomers Benjamin M. Zuckerman of the University of California at Los Angeles and Eric E. Becklin of the University of Hawaii in Honolulu. Brown dwarfs are thought to be objects with properties that lie between those of a planet and a star. Astronomers theorize that brown dwarfs might be objects that

failed to evolve into stars. As a result, they might be too hot and too massive to be considered planets and yet not be hot and massive enough to undergo nuclear reactions and be considered stars.

Zuckerman and Becklin set out to search for brown dwarfs by using an infrared telescope because such objects would produce infrared radiation. Also, they chose to search for brown dwarfs by looking near the positions of known white dwarfs. White dwarfs give off most of their radiation as visible light, so any excessive amounts of infrared radiation would indicate the existence of a nearby companion brown dwarf.

The astronomers' search turned up only one possible brown dwarf. In the constellation Pisces, they found a white dwarf that gave off 10 times more infrared radiation than white dwarfs normally give off, indicating the possible presence of a companion brown dwarf.   [Theodore P. Snow]

In WORLD BOOK, see ASTRONOMY; MILKY WAY.

Astronomy, Solar System

Evidence of *cometesimals* (small comets) in the inner solar system was reported in December 1987. Comets are composed of rock and ice. They are about 1 to 10 kilometers (0.6 to 6 miles) in diameter. The orbits of some comets take them into the *inner solar system*, the region that includes the planets Mercury, Venus, Earth, and Mars. Scientists have assumed that the original building blocks of such comets, ranging from tiny grains to boulders of rock and ice, were long ago swept out of the solar system as the sun and planets formed.

Space scientists Thomas M. Donahue and Támas I. Gombosi of the University of Michigan in Ann Arbor and Bill R. Sandel of the University of Arizona in Tucson reanalyzed data from the *Voyager 1* and *2* spacecraft that flew from Earth toward Jupiter in 1978. The spacecraft carried instruments that detected *ultraviolet radiation*—light of wavelengths shorter than that detectable by the human eye. One particular set of ultraviolet wavelengths represents radiation given off by

hydrogen atoms. A possible source of hydrogen atoms in space is the breakdown of water from icy objects.

From the intensity and distribution of the radiation pattern measured by the *Voyager* spacecraft when they were still near Earth, the scientists concluded that a large amount of water was being released in the region of the solar system near Earth. The amount of water is most naturally explained by the existence of a large number of boulders containing ice—possibly remnants of the building blocks of comets that were previously thought to have been swept away.

Formaldehyde in comets. Halley's Comet contains a complex *polymer* (chain of molecules) of formaldehyde, according to an international team of scientists who analyzed data from spacecraft that flew past Halley's Comet in 1986. Formaldehyde is a colorless—but pungent—gas that is often used to preserve biological specimens. Molecules of formaldehyde contain two atoms of hydrogen and one each of carbon and oxygen, which are com-

Astronomy, Solar System

Continued

A supercomputer simulates an eclipse of the planet Pluto by its moon, Charon, *below*, in a demonstration presented in January 1988 by astronomers at the University of Hawaii in Honolulu. Charon passes over Pluto's equator, *below right*, and casts a shadow over the planet's north pole (white area at right). Pluto is tilted so that its polar areas appear on each side of the pictures. The eclipses, though they cannot be seen clearly from Earth, have allowed astronomers to calculate the size of Pluto and its moon.

mon elements in *interstellar space*—the space between the stars.

Two separate analyses of data from the European Space Agency's *Giotto* spacecraft were reported in August 1987 by astronomer Walter F. Huebner of Southwest Research Institute in San Antonio, Tex., and a team of scientists from the United States, West Germany, and France, headed by David L. Mitchell of the University of California at Berkeley. The scientists studied readings from a *mass spectrometer*, an instrument that measures the masses of atoms or molecules in a sample. In this case, the instrument measured the mass of fragments of molecules in the gas-and-dust cloud surrounding the *nucleus* (core) of Halley's Comet. Previously unnoticed in the data were regular patterns of mass which are similar to portions of certain polymers. The scientists identified the chemical source of these fragments as a form of polymerized formaldehyde. The number of these fragments led the scientists to conclude that formaldehyde is present in small amounts in

the nucleus of Halley's Comet. The quantity of formaldehyde may equal 1 per cent of the comet's water, which is the comet's most abundant molecule.

The existence of formaldehyde in comets yields important clues to the origin of these icy bodies. Astronomers had previously detected formaldehyde in interstellar gas. Its presence in Halley's Comet suggests that either the building blocks of comets originated in interstellar space or chemical processes similar to those that take place in interstellar space occurred in the *solar nebula*—the cloud of gas and dust from which the sun and planets formed. Understanding the origin of formaldehyde in Halley's Comet may lead us to a deeper understanding of how the solar system—and our Earth—formed.

New eruptions on Io. A new hot spot on Jupiter's satellite Io erupted in 1985, according to a report in August 1987 by a team of astronomers led by Jay D. Goguen of the Jet Propulsion Laboratory of the California Institute of Technology in Pasadena. Io was found to have active volcanoes when

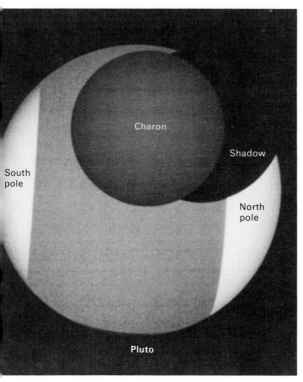

South pole

Charon

Shadow

North pole

Pluto

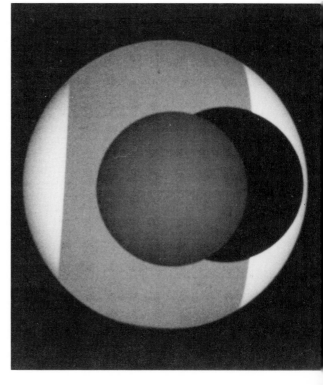

Voyager 1 and *2* flew through the Jupiter system in 1979. Instruments on the spacecraft detected *plumes* (columns) of volcanic gas and lava flows, and possibly lakes of molten material.

Io's vigorous activity is thought to be a result of mutual tidal forces between Jupiter and the moons Io, Europa, and Ganymede. As the moons orbit Jupiter, the mutual gravitational forces act much like the gravitational forces in the Earth-moon system, which in part cause the ebb and flow of ocean tides on Earth. The tidal forces distort Io's interior and cause melting of rock.

Goguen's team observed a series of rare events in 1985 called mutual eclipses, in which astronomers on Earth could see Jupiter's satellites pass in front of each other. Telescopes that detect *infrared* (heat) radiation were trained on Jupiter's moons when Io was blocked from view several times by Ganymede and Callisto. Infrared telescopes were used because the volcanic material is not hot enough to glow as visible light but can be detected as infrared light.

As Ganymede or Callisto moved in front of Io, as seen from Earth, individual hot spots were covered at different times, so that the brightness of each eruption could be separately determined. The eclipses occurred slowly enough that Goguen's team could actually measure the size of the eruptions as they disappeared and reappeared during each eclipse. Normally, it is difficult to detect individual hot spots from Earth-based telescopes because Io is so far away. In addition to known hot spots, the team observed an eruption that lasted for several weeks in an area not known for volcanoes.

Io continued to surprise scientists with the unpredictability of its activity. In September and October 1987, Goguen and astronomers Robert Howell and William Sinton of the University of Hawaii in Honolulu observed two more volcanic outbursts on Io. The next set of moon eclipses will occur in 1991, and the United States *Galileo* spacecraft is expected to reach Jupiter in the mid-1990's.

Venusian plate tectonics. Portions of the surface of Venus may be moving in a manner similar to the spreading of the sea floor on Earth, according to a January 1988 report by geologists Larry S. Crumpler and James W. Head III of Brown University in Providence, R.I.

Decades of study of Earth's geological features have indicated that the *crust*, the outer layer of our planet's surface, is divided into a number of rigid *plates*. The movement of these plates, known as *plate tectonics*, is responsible for continental drift and the occurrence of earthquakes and volcanoes near the plates' edges. These studies have also shown that undersea volcanoes form new crust along long chains of undersea mountains, called *midocean ridges*. As new crust rises from volcanic vents, the sea floor spreads out on either side of the ridges.

Crumpler and Head reported that the Aphrodite Terra region of Venus has features similar to Earth's midocean ridges. Aphrodite Terra is a broad highland region that stretches for 20,000 kilometers (12,400 miles) across the surface of Venus.

The geologists analyzed data recorded by a radar instrument on board the *Pioneer Venus 1* spacecraft. By bouncing radio signals off the surface of Venus during the spacecraft's orbit of the planet in 1980, this instrument measured differences in elevation on the surface. The geologists found fracture patterns on Aphrodite similar to the fracture patterns found near the midocean ridges on Earth. In addition, the surface features on either side of the main ridge of Aphrodite are remarkably alike, almost like a mirror image, which is also a characteristic of our planet's midocean ridges. Finally, patterns of high elevation, valleys, and faults in the Aphrodite region suggested spreading of the Venus crust. Crumpler and Head estimated the spreading rate to be roughly several centimeters (about one to two inches) per year, comparable to spreading rates on Earth.

Scientists have debated for years whether plate tectonics occurs on Venus, a planet similar to Earth in size and density. Crumpler and Head identified features that suggest similar geological processes on Earth and Venus. [Jonathan I. Lunine]

In WORLD BOOK, see ASTRONOMY; COMET; HALLEY'S COMET; VENUS.

Books of Science

Here are 25 outstanding new science books suitable for the general reader. They have been selected from books published in 1987 and 1988.

Archaeology. *The Cave of Lascaux: The Final Photographs* by Mario Ruspoli contains photographs of the prehistoric wall paintings of Lascaux Cave in southwestern France. The book also tells about the people who painted the murals some 17,000 years ago and about the world they inhabited. (Abrams, 1987. 208 pp. illus. $45)

Lines to the Mountain Gods: Nazca and the Mysteries of Peru by Evan Hadingham investigates the civilization that constructed the Nazca lines, elaborate geometric designs in the Peruvian desert, more than 2,000 years ago. Hadingham believes that the lines are closely tied to the builders' attitude toward the spiritual and material resources of the harsh land they inhabited. (Random House, 1987. 307 pp. illus. $22.50)

Archaeology and Language: The Puzzle of Indo-European Origins by Colin Renfrew argues that modern linguistics and archaeology can be used to help us understand when and how the peoples and cultures of Europe emerged. (Cambridge Univ. Press, 1988. 346 pp. illus. $29.95)

Astronomy. *Darkness at Night: A Riddle of the Universe* by Edward Harrison explores the question of why the sky is dark at night. Harrison also presents the various answers that have been proposed and how these are related to space, time, the nature of light, and the structure of the universe. (Harvard Univ. Press, 1987. 293 pp. illus. $25)

Exploring the Southern Sky: A Pictorial Atlas from the European Southern Observatory (ESO) by Svend Laustsen, Claus Madsen, and Richard M. West displays some of the impressive astronomical photographs made at the ESO, an observatory on Cerro La Silla in Chile. (Springer, 1987. 274 pp. illus. $39)

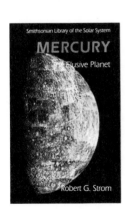

Mercury: The Elusive Planet by Robert G. Strom documents current knowledge about the planet Mercury, much of it obtained by the U.S. *Mariner 10* spacecraft during its 1973-1975 mission. Strom also tells of the in-flight mechanical problems experienced by *Mariner* and how they were handled by controllers on Earth. (Smithsonian In-

stitution Press, 1987. 197 pp. illus. $19.95)

Meteorites and Their Parent Planets by Harry Y. McSween, Jr., introduces the reader to the various kinds of meteorites, including chondrites, achondrites, and iron meteorites; describes the parent bodies from which they originate; and tells the events that launch them on their journey to Earth. (Cambridge Univ. Press, 1987. 237 pp. illus. $24.95)

Biology. *The Balance of Improbabilities: A Scientific Life* by Henry Harris is the autobiography of Harris, an Australian-born cell biologist who conducts research on cancerous cells. Harris shows the excitement that can lead people to devote their lives to science. (Oxford Univ. Press, 1987. 245 pp. illus. $35)

Eggs: Nature's Perfect Package by Robert Burton. This profusely illustrated book is devoted to eggs, to the animals that lay them, the nests that shelter them, and the care they receive from parents. (Facts on File, 1987. 158 pp. illus. $22.95)

Computer Science. *The Media Lab: Inventing the Future at MIT* by Stewart Brand shows how scientists at the Massachusetts Institute of Technology in Cambridge use computers to link all forms of communications media, including television, telephones, recordings, films, newspapers, and books. (Viking, 1987. 285 pp. illus. $20)

Thinking Machines: The Evolution of Artificial Intelligence by Vernon Pratt focuses on the work of three mathematicians, Gottfried W. Leibniz of Germany and Charles Babbage and Alan M. Turing of England, each of whom planned and built a calculating machine. (Blackwell, 1987. 254 pp. illus. $24.95)

History of Science. *Who Got Einstein's Office?: Eccentricity and Genius at the Institute for Advanced Study* by Ed Regis. The Institute for Advanced Study in Princeton, N.J., founded in 1930, has been the home of many of the great figures of modern physics, including Albert Einstein of Germany, Wolfgang Pauli of Austria, and Murray Gell-Mann and J. Robert Oppenheimer of the United States. This book is an informal history of the institute, the people who work there, and their achieve-

Books
of Science

Continued

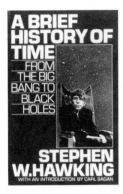

ments. (Addison-Wesley, 1987. 316 pp. illus. $17.95)

To Infinity and Beyond: A Cultural History of the Infinite by Eli Maor. Philosophers and mathematicians have dealt with the puzzles and paradoxes of the infinite for more than 2,000 years. Maor unfolds the story of infinity through the ages, explaining concepts of infinity in mathematics, geometry, art, and philosophy. (Birkhäuser, 1987. 275 pp. illus. $49.50)

Natural History. *Drylands: The Deserts of North America* by Philip Hyde describes and illustrates with large, beautiful photographs the geography and wildlife of the five major North American deserts—the Great Basin, Mojave, and Painted Desert of the United States, and the Chihuahuan and Sonoran deserts of Mexico. (Harcourt Brace Jovanovich, 1987. 173 pp. illus. $59.95)

The Natural History of Lakes by Mary J. Burgis and Pat Morris includes chapters on the various kinds of lakes, the plant and animal communities that live in them, and why they need to be conserved. (Cambridge Univ. Press, 1987. 218 pp. illus. $29.95)

A Naturalist amid Tropical Splendor by Alexander F. Skutch describes the author's experiences during half a century of research in the tropics, surrounded by fascinating birds and unusual plants. (University of Iowa Press, 1987. 232 pp. illus. $22.50)

Tracks in the Sky: Wildlife and Wetlands of the Pacific Flyway by Peter Steinhart shows how marshes, deltas, and tidelands serve as refuges for millions of migratory birds. (Chronicle Bks., 1987. 166 pp. illus. $35)

Paleontology. *Extinction* by Steven M. Stanley evaluates the rock and fossil record for what it tells us about the mass extinctions of species. Stanley concludes that global climatic changes and the shifting of Earth's crustal plates explain most of the great extinctions. (Scientific Am. Lib., 1987. 242 pp. illus. $32.95)

Life Pulse: Episodes from the Story of the Fossil Record by Niles Eldredge argues that evolutionary change takes place in spurts, or "pulses," and that extinction of species offers opportunity for the rise of new species. (Facts on File, 1987. 246 pp. illus. $19.95)

Physical Science. *A Brief History of Time: From the Big Bang to Black Holes* by Stephen W. Hawking considers where the universe came from, how and why it began, whether it will come to an end, and if so, how. Hawking, one of the world's leading theoretical physicists, discusses space and time, the expanding universe, subatomic particles, and the forces of nature. In the People in Science section, see STEPHEN W. HAWKING. (Bantam Bks., 1988. 198 pp. illus. $18.95)

Molecules by P. W. Atkins explains what molecules are and why they behave as they do. Atkins includes sections on the functions of molecules in fuels, color, taste, smell, pain, and sight. (Scientific Am. Lib., 1987. 197 pp. illus. $32.95)

Space Technology. *Heroes in Space: From Gagarin to Challenger* by Peter Bond tells the story of U.S. and Soviet space missions from their beginning in 1961 through the explosion of the space shuttle *Challenger*, in which all seven crew members were killed, in 1986. Bond describes the spacecraft and crews of both nations. (Blackwell, 1987. 467 pp. illus. $24.95)

Zoology. *Elephant Memories: Thirteen Years in the Life of an Elephant Family* by Cynthia Moss tells how the elephants in the Amboseli National Park in Kenya fared in their struggles with droughts, poachers, disease, injuries, tourism, and researchers. Each chapter covers a year and discusses an aspect of elephant life such as mating, birth, and social organization. (Morrow, 1988. 336 pp. illus. $22.95)

The Red Ape: Orang-utans and Human Origins by Jeffrey H. Schwartz is an account of recent discoveries in the study of human and ape ancestry, advancing the author's view that orangutans are the closest living relatives of human beings. (Houghton Mifflin, 1987. 337 pp. illus. $18.95)

Running with the Fox by David Macdonald details the behavior of the red fox in both urban and rural environments. Macdonald summarizes 15 years of research during which he learned much about the foxes' behavior, body language, cubs, territory, and even whether they make good pets. (Facts on File, 1987. 224 pp. illus. $23.95)   [William G. Jones]

Botany

Small holes called *domatia* dot the underside of leaves of the mirror plant, an ornamental shrub, *below right.* Found on at least 1,000 other species of plants, domatia serve as homes for many kinds of mites. These tiny animals, *below,* relatives of spiders and ticks, apparently protect plants by feeding on destructive insects and fungi. Many botanists think pesticides might actually harm a plant by killing mites along with insects.

One of the most clear-cut examples of a hormone's action in a plant was reported in September 1987. Botanist Bastiaan J. D. Meeuse of the University of Washington in Seattle, working with researchers from E. I. du Pont de Nemours & Company in Wilmington, Del., found that a tropical plant called the voodoo lily uses a chemical similar to aspirin to raise its temperature.

A hormone is a substance that is made in one part of an organism and transported to another part of the organism where, in small amounts, it controls some aspect of growth or biochemical activity. Although the first plant hormone was discovered in 1926, plant scientists have found few instances in which the action of a hormone can be clearly traced.

The voodoo lily has male and female flowers that grow around the bottom of a long, cylindrical organ. The upper portion of this fleshy column is called the appendix.

When the female flowers become receptive to pollen, the appendix absorbs oxygen from the air and rapidly increases its temperature, becoming as much as 14 Celsius degrees (25 Fahrenheit degrees) warmer than the surrounding air. This heat causes compounds in the appendix to evaporate, producing a smell like that of dung or rotting meat. The odor attracts flies, which bring pollen from other voodoo lilies to the female flowers.

Scientists had long puzzled over the voodoo lily's ability to raise its temperature so quickly. In 1975, Meeuse and his students obtained an extract from voodoo lily flowers that caused a phenomenal production of heat when applied to pieces of tissue cut from the appendix. But it took another 12 years for Meeuse to identify the active compound in the extract as *salicylic acid*, part of the aspirin molecule.

Salicylic acid is found in many plants, and botanists had discovered responses to the chemical in species other than the voodoo lily. But the voodoo lily is the only plant known to use salicylic acid as a true hormone.

Hemoglobin in plants. Scientists have known for several years that the root

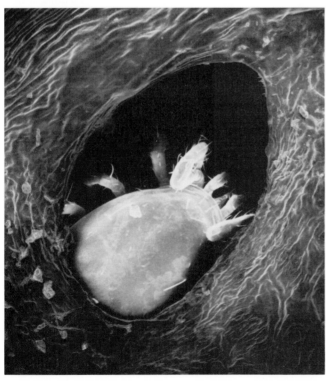

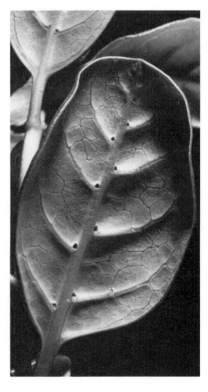

Botany

Continued

cells of plants with *root nodules* contain the oxygen-carrying molecule hemoglobin. (Root nodules are structures containing bacteria that convert gaseous nitrogen into a form usable by the plant.) In January 1988, botanist W. James Peacock and his colleagues at the Commonwealth Scientific and Industrial Research Organization in Canberra, Australia, reported finding hemoglobin in the roots of a plant that does not form root nodules.

Hemoglobin, the red part of blood, carries oxygen in many animals, but researchers are not certain what function it has in plants. It may provide oxygen to bacteria in root nodules. But for the plant without nodules studied by the Australian scientists a different explanation was required.

The plant is the trema, a member of the elm family. Not only does this plant form no root nodules, it produces only tiny quantities of hemoglobin. Such small amounts of hemoglobin, according to the researchers, would not be enough to provide oxygen to the plant or to any organisms, such as bacteria, living in the plant.

The researchers speculated that the plant may use hemoglobin to monitor the level of oxygen in its roots. The discovery of hemoglobin in this plant suggests that hemoglobin genes may be present in all plants.

Ozone and ethylene. Ozone in the upper atmosphere absorbs harmful ultraviolet light and is thus considered beneficial, but when this corrosive form of oxygen is close to the ground it endangers human health and damages plants. In June 1987, Horst Mehlhorn and Alan R. Wellburn, plant physiologists at the University of Lancaster in England, reported that ozone's harmful effect on plants might depend upon the presence in the plants of another gas, *ethylene.*

Since the late 1950's, botanists have been studying the role of ethylene in plants. This colorless, flammable gas, which acts as a hormone, is normally produced in small amounts by a plant. But when plants are subjected to stresses, such as drought, low temperatures, or exposure to ozone, their rate of ethylene production markedly increases. This can lead to the premature loss of leaves.

Mehlhorn and Wellburn exposed a group of newly sprouted pea seedlings to ozone for seven hours a day for three weeks. At the end of that time, the seedlings were producing only small amounts of ethylene and showed no visible signs of leaf injury. Continuous exposure to ozone had apparently caused the seedlings to become less sensitive to the gas.

The researchers also subjected a second group of seedlings to the same concentration of ozone, but for just one seven-hour period when the plants were three weeks old. Those seedlings produced much more ethylene than the first group, showing that sudden exposure to ozone is likely to cause a stronger response. Those plants suffered extensive leaf damage.

To demonstrate that the ozone damage depended on the presence of ethylene, the scientists treated another group of pea seedlings with a compound called AVG, which inhibits the synthesis of ethylene in plants. As the researchers had predicted, AVG-treated plants were not damaged by sudden exposure to high concentrations of ozone.

Leaf pores and carbon dioxide. Much as animals use oxygen in their life processes, plants use carbon dioxide (CO_2). Plants absorb CO_2 from the air through tiny pores called *stomata* on their leaves. In June 1987, botanist F. Ian Woodward of the University of Cambridge in England reported that plants vary the number of their stomata in response to the amount of CO_2 available to them.

Woodward grew several kinds of plants in chambers in which he could regulate the concentration of CO_2. He found that as he decreased the level of CO_2 in the chambers, the plants developed leaves with more stomata. Conversely, when CO_2 levels were raised, the plants produced fewer stomata.

Woodward also examined dried leaves collected over the past 200 years. He discovered that leaves from the 1700's and 1800's, when there was less CO_2 in the air than there is now, had up to 40 per cent more stomata than leaves of the same species have today. [Frank B. Salisbury]

In WORLD BOOK, see BOTANY; PLANT.

Chemistry

Modern chemistry met ancient folk medicine in January 1988 when chemist Elias J. Corey and his colleagues at Harvard University in Cambridge, Mass., reported that they had *synthesized* (produced in the laboratory) pure samples of a chemical compound called ginkgolide B. Nature produces this compound—along with similar substances—in the leaves of the ginkgo, or maidenhair tree.

For 5,000 years, Chinese people have made medicines from various parts of the ginkgo. Today, Europeans spend some $500 million annually on ginkgo-derived medicines to treat blood-circulation problems in elderly individuals. To date, however, the United States Food and Drug Administration (FDA)—a government agency—has not approved ginkgo-derived medicines for sale in the United States.

The FDA has not approved these medicines because they have not been shown to be safe and effective in tests on human beings. The medicines are difficult to test because chemists have been unable to separate sufficient amounts of a specific compound from other substances in the leaves and thus cannot obtain a pure sample of the desired compound, such as ginkgolide B, for testing. As a result, researchers often cannot determine whether a good —or a bad—reaction to a test is caused by the compound being tested or by another substance that nature has mixed in with it.

The pure ginkgolide B manufactured in the laboratory, however, will be much easier to test than a natural extract. The results—good or bad— clearly will be caused by ginkgolide B. Furthermore, if ginkgolide B turns out not to be as safe and effective as hoped, researchers can use techniques developed by Corey and his colleagues to synthesize and test a variety of similar compounds.

Chemical stealth. Prospects for the development of military "stealth" aircraft that cannot be detected by radar took an unexpected turn in August 1987, when chemist Robert R. Birge of Carnegie-Mellon University in Pittsburgh reported the discovery of chem-

A laser beam, *below,* is used to vaporize a metal rod, *below right,* and produce clusters of 2 to 100 iron atoms. Chemists at Argonne National Laboratory near Chicago study such clusters in an effort to understand how clusterlike substances called *catalysts* speed up reactions while remaining essentially unchanged.

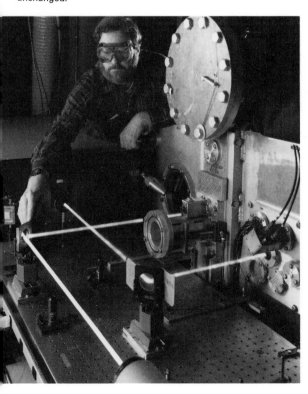

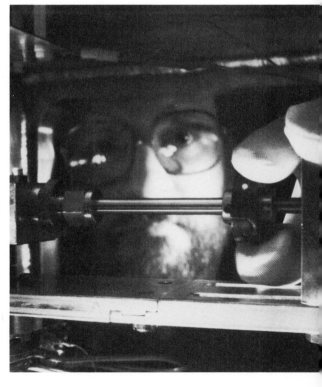

Chemistry

Continued

icals that absorb rather than reflect radar beams. Such chemicals, if used in paint applied to an airplane, would make the craft "invisible" to radar. Military researchers have been trying for years to find ways to prevent radar from detecting aircraft. The United States already has built aircraft whose winglike shape and special coating make them less obvious to radar. But radar scans of varying wavelengths could spot these aircraft.

The new chemicals, called *Schiff base salts*, can convert radar of different frequencies into heat, so the beams do not bounce back to detectors. A paint containing a mixture of such chemicals could absorb a wide range of wavelengths, foiling even radar systems that used varying wavelengths. The United States military cannot use the new chemicals yet, because scientists do not know how to mix the chemicals in paint without destroying their ability to absorb radar beams.

Surprisingly, the research leading to the discovery of the chemicals was not a defense project. Rather, Birge was studying the chemistry of vision. He used Schiff base salts as a model for *rhodopsin*, a pigment found in the retina of the eye. Rhodopsin changes its structure when it absorbs light.

Frog formula. The first evidence of *antibiotics* (disease-fighting biochemicals) produced by a *vertebrate* (an animal with a backbone) was reported by biochemist Michael Zasloff of the National Institutes of Health in Bethesda, Md., in August 1987. Antibiotic drugs are produced from bacteria and fungi. Zasloff theorized that the antibiotics produced by vertebrates act as a first line of defense against infections by working before the immune system goes into battle.

The study of disease-fighting chemicals is not Zasloff's regular research specialty. He discovered them while investigating how genetic material determines the development of animals. In gathering genetic material, he removed the ovaries of African clawed frogs that are kept in tanks. He then extracted immature eggs from the frogs' ovaries and put the frogs back

"Now that we've come up with a sweetener 650 times sweeter than sugar, we're working on a sourer 475 times sourer than a lemon."

A researcher at Argonne National Laboratory near Chicago adjusts one of 600 fine wires in a unique new detector that can map the exact locations of atoms in small molecules. As charged atoms are beamed through, the wires detect their positions and flight times, and send this data to a computer for mapping.

into their tanks. But although the tanks contained harmful bacteria, the frogs healed without even showing signs of inflammation.

Once Zasloff realized that something unusual was going on, he began to investigate the chemistry of the frog's skin. He found two proteinlike molecules that kill bacteria, yeast, protozoa, and other infectious microorganisms.

The molecules also seem to "ignore" normal animal cells. Because the chemicals seem to kill only harmful organisms, scientists may test them as anticancer drugs. Presently used drugs that work against cancer cells also attack healthy tissue, causing such side effects as nausea and a loss of hair.

Reaction pictured. The first "snapshots" of chemical reactions were reported in August 1987. Chemical physicist Ahmed H. Zewail and his colleagues of California Institute of Technology (Caltech) in Pasadena took the "pictures" with a "camera" having a speed approaching one-millionth of one-billionth of one second—the time it takes light to travel a distance equal to 1 per cent of the thickness of a human hair.

Zewail's "camera" was made up of a beam of molecules, a pulsed laser, and a device that measured the energy level of two laser pulses. The first laser pulse struck the beam of molecules, providing them with enough energy to react chemically. The second laser pulse, emitted a tiny fraction of a second later, also struck the molecules, and a detector showed how much of the energy of this pulse was absorbed and reemitted by the molecules. This amount of energy depended upon the wavelength of the second pulse and upon the stage of the reaction process. So by varying the time interval between the laser pulses and the wavelength of the second pulse, the Caltech scientists determined precisely the status of the molecules at each moment of the reaction process. In this way, they recorded the "birth" of molecules.

The researchers "took pictures" of simple molecules such as cyanogen iodide—which contains only three atoms—breaking apart or combining with other molecules. Such pictures will give chemists a better understanding of how reactions occur, enabling

Researchers at AT&T Bell Laboratories in Murray Hill, N.J., discovered in mid-1987 that an electronic device called a scanning-tunneling microscope, *below,* used to take pictures of very small objects such as the surface of a crystal, could alter the chemistry by moving an atom on the crystal. Pictures taken with the microscope show an area before, *inset,* left (arrow), and after the device moved an atom into it, *inset,* right (arrow).

Chemistry

Continued

researchers to develop more efficient chemical processes.

Very tiny rulers. To measure something very small requires a ruler with very small distances between the measuring lines. There is no ruler, however, that can measure distances on the next generation of electronic microcircuits, some of which are expected to have parts a few billionths of a meter across. But in January 1988, researchers from the University of Minnesota in Minneapolis and Brookhaven National Laboratory in Upton, N.Y., reported that they had come close to making such a ruler.

Minnesota chemist Larry L. Miller and his colleagues attached iridium atoms, which served as ruler markings, to rodlike molecules. The scientists then looked at the molecules with a scanning transmission electron microscope. The atoms showed up as spots a few billionths of a meter apart.

Unfortunately, the distances between the spots were not uniform enough to enable the molecules to be used as rulers, and the molecules were too flexible. The researchers are working to find a way to get the iridium atoms to attach at more precise intervals, and to make stiffer molecules.

Artificial blood vessels. Chemist Debra Wrobleski of Los Alamos National Laboratory in New Mexico in August 1987 announced progress toward the development of plastic blood vessels. Blood tends to clot on the surface of plastics, so surgeons cannot now use plastic tubes to replace damaged blood vessels. Instead, they must use healthy vessels from their patients. In coronary by-pass surgery, for example, they use vessels from a patient's leg to replace damaged arteries of the heart.

The key to making plastic that does not promote clotting lies in modifying the plastic's surface. The first step in this process is to place the plastic into a chemical solution that softens its surface. Chemists then add to this solution certain compounds that make the plastic less likely to react with blood to form clots. Then the solution is diluted, so the surface hardens as the compounds attach to it.

Chemistry

Continued

Wrobleski has attached compounds that forestall clotting somewhat. Scientists need to do more research, however, to find compounds that would work well enough for use in patients.

Water for space colonists. New measurements of the amount of hydrogen contained in moon rocks indicate that colonizing the moon may be less expensive than previously thought. A major expense for a moon colony would be obtaining enough oxygen to breathe and water to drink.

Of the two substances, oxygen would be easier to obtain. The analysis of moon rocks collected in 1969 during the *Apollo 11* mission revealed that moon rocks are full of oxygen. Calculations indicated that mining moon rocks and heating them to release oxygen would be less expensive than transporting oxygen from Earth.

There is no water in moon rocks, however, and water is much too heavy to shuttle from Earth, so colonists would have to create water by combining hydrogen with oxygen obtained from moon rocks. Scientists have thought that moon rocks contain almost no hydrogen, so they concluded that bases on the moon would have to import hydrogen from Earth.

In December 1987, however, chemist Roberta M. Bustin of Arkansas College in Batesville announced that moon rocks contain a significant amount of hydrogen. Bustin and Everett K. Gibson, Jr., a planetologist with the National Aeronautics and Space Administration, heated moon rocks and measured the amount of hydrogen gas that came out of the rocks. Bustin concluded that the hydrogen liberated from 1 kilogram (2.2 pounds) of lunar rocks and soil, when combined with the appropriate amount of oxygen, would make about 14 drops of water.

Bustin concluded that mining and heating moon rocks to obtain hydrogen for residents of the moon would be less expensive than shuttling hydrogen from Earth.   [Peter J. Andrews]

In the Special Reports section, see THE HOLE IN THE OZONE LAYER. In WORLD BOOK, see CHEMISTRY.

Computer Hardware

The personal computer (PC) industry moved quickly in 1987 and 1988 to adopt the 32-bit *microprocessor chip*, which handles larger chunks of information at a much higher speed than its predecessors. A microprocessor performs a PC's arithmetic and logic functions. A *32-bit* microprocessor handles 32 bits of data at a time. (Bits are the 0's and 1's of the binary digital language that computers use.) Earlier PC's had 8- or 16-bit microprocessors.

Most of the new 32-bit PC's used the model 80386 processor made by Intel Corporation of Santa Barbara, Calif. To upgrade the performance of earlier PC's, several manufacturers, including Intel, also offered 80386-equipped circuit boards.

Powerful portables. Compaq Computer Corporation of Houston, the first major manufacturer to market an 80386-equipped microcomputer, stayed on the cutting edge of PC design by introducing in September 1987 two machines, including a portable computer that operates more rapidly than do other PC's with 80386 micro-processors. A computer operates by sending pulses of electricity through electric circuits. The interval between the beginning of one pulse and the beginning of the next is one *cycle*. Most 80386-equipped PC's operate at a rate of 16 million cycles per second. By contrast, Compaq's new PC's operate at 20 million cycles per second.

Compaq's Portable 386, which sells for $7,995, weighs 9 kilograms (20 pounds), and has a hard disk drive with up to 100 million *bytes* of storage capacity, the equivalent of 50,000 typewritten pages. (One byte is one letter, numeral, or other single symbol.)

The other leading supplier of microprocessors, Motorola Corporation of Schaumburg, Ill., began to ship its MC68030 32-bit microprocessor in October 1987. This chip promises to greatly increase the speed of such already swift computers as the Macintosh II, a product of Apple Computer Incorporated of Cupertino, Calif. The Macintosh II now uses an earlier 32-bit Motorola microprocessor, the MC68020.

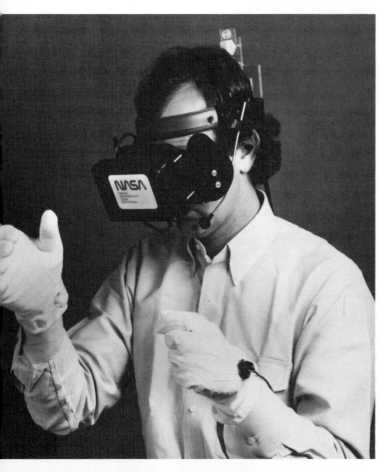

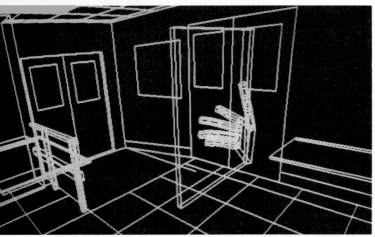

An electronic glove on the hand of a researcher at NASA Ames Research Center at Moffett Field, California, *top,* allows him to directly control a computer-generated image, *above,* displayed on tiny TV screens in his "goggles." When the researcher moves his hand, the image of the hand moves in exactly the same way.

New printers. Apple Computer launched three new laser printers in January 1988 to replace its current Apple LaserWriter line. The three new models, with prices ranging up to $6,699, incorporate Canon's upgraded SX engine, which gives improved printing and a much longer operating life. The LaserWriter IISC is the least expensive model at $2,799, and is Apple's first laser printer not to include Adobe Systems' PostScript—a page description programming language that provides high-quality text and graphics for desktop publishing.

CD memory. CD-ROM technology, which adapts for computer data storage the 12-centimeter (4¾-inch) compact disc (CD) favored by music enthusiasts, got a boost in March 1988, when Apple became the first major computer hardware company to offer a CD-ROM drive, the $1,199 AppleCD SC. (*ROM* means *r*ead *o*nly *m*emory, the kind that a computer can "read" but cannot modify.) A CD-ROM disc can hold huge amounts of text, sound, or pictures—even moving pictures. A typical such disc can store as many as 275,000 typewritten pages. Yet another virtue of the CD-ROM is that data can be accessed randomly and quickly. Apple says the average time to retrieve data anywhere on the disc is under half a second with its player. CD-ROM drives that are IBM-PC compatible have been available from Hitachi Limited of Japan and N.V. Philips of the Netherlands since 1984, but neither firm makes computers.

More RISC. Meanwhile, *reduced instruction set computing* (RISC) microprocessors gained increasing attention. RISC processors cannot handle as many kinds of *software* (program) instructions as ordinary processors, called *complex instruction set computing* (CISC) chips. RISC processors, however, execute instructions much more quickly. In April 1988, Motorola announced 32-bit 88000 series microprocessors that carry out 17 million instructions per second (MIP's). By contrast, Compaq's Deskpro 386, built around the CISC technology of Intel's 80386 microprocessor chip, handles about 3.5 MIP's.   [Ronald D. Scibilia]

In WORLD BOOK, see COMPUTER; COMPUTER, PERSONAL.

Computer Software

The single most-talked-about computer software of 1987 and 1988 was HyperCard, a program introduced in August 1987 by Apple Computer Incorporated of Cupertino, Calif., for its Macintosh computers. HyperCard is a kind of database that ties together text and graphics.

The basic unit of a HyperCard database is called a *card*. The cards are grouped into *stacks*. Pieces of information on various cards are linked together to enable the user to move quickly from data on one card to related data on another card.

The basic starting point of Hyper-Card is Home Card. It contains the various icons, or symbols, representing the existing stacks of cards. To jump from stack to stack or from one card to another, the user moves a mouse to point a cursor at the icon or words representing the card or stacks, and then clicks the mouse. Operators can use the ready-made stacks that come with HyperCard, modify them, or create their own stacks without learning a computer language.

Information is entered onto cards in "fields" that the user creates. There are two types of fields—background and card. A background field is common to all cards in a stack; card fields are only for information on a particular card. Background can be text, pictures, or fields for entering information. One type of background is an *address card* format, an image of a card like the cards that are used in a Rolodex file system.

The invention of HyperCard gave rise to several new "stackware" products, such as a program called Business Class, introduced by Activision Incorporated of Mountain View, Calif. This program arranges information about various countries on cards. For example, a card on Great Britain shows a map of the country. Beneath it is a series of "buttons," icons that indicate climate, currency, ground transportation, holidays, and other information for travelers. Clicking the mouse with the cursor pointing at one of these buttons brings the card with that information to the screen.

HyperCard, a new type of software for Macintosh computers, arranges data as "stacks" of "cards," beginning with Home Card. Using a mouse to point a cursor at a picture representing a stack, then clicking the mouse button, brings up cards of information, such as addresses or favorite restaurants, left. Commercial stackware, such as Business Class, right, contains stacks of information about various countries. Pointing and clicking at the buttons on the bottom of each card makes the computer retrieve the desired information, such as time or climate.

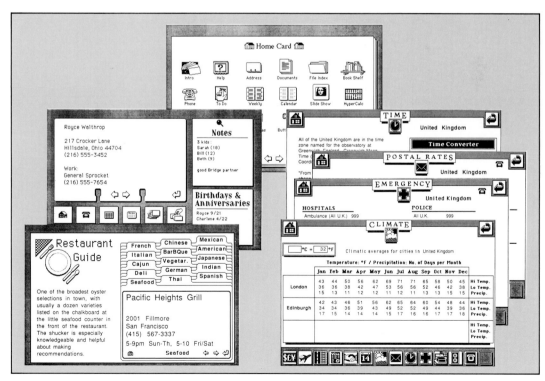

The Attack of the Computer Viruses

A strange diseaselike phenomenon is attacking computers, especially on college campuses. Computer experts began sending out warnings in late 1987. Minicomputer users were complaining of data disappearing from their diskettes for no apparent reason. Programmers began to find strange messages buried in the code in which computer programs are written. Even worse, the electronic scourge was contagious, spreading from one minicomputer to another. This form of sabotage became known as "computer virus."

■ In late 1987, computer users at George Washington University in Washington, D.C., began mysteriously losing data from their disks. Programmers in the university's computer lab examined a damaged disk and found a cryptic message written on it. The message read, "Welcome to the dungeon. . . . Beware of this computer VIRUS. Contact us for vaccination. . . ." It included two names, an address, and three telephone numbers in Lahore, Pakistan.

■ In January 1988, computer scientists at Hebrew University in Jerusalem, Israel, discovered and dismantled a virus containing a command to delete all the files on the university's massive computer network, including information on government and military installations.

■ In March 1988, there appeared the first virus in commercial software. This virus merely startled users by producing a message on the screen calling for universal peace. Nevertheless, the presence of the virus showed that even shrink-wrapped software purchased legally is not safe from "infection."

A computer virus is a small computer program designed to do mischief by deleting data, producing messages, altering information, or even destroying hardware. Viruses are easy to sneak past many users of computers because the viruses, like legitimate programs, are written in a computer-programming language, a type of code made up of letters, numbers, and other symbols. A programming code gives instructions to the computer "behind the screen," so most users never see such codes. Furthermore, even programmers—individuals who work with programming codes—must look hard to find the simplest viruses.

A virus spreads by burying itself deep within the computer's *disk operating system* (DOS), the set of instructions that acts as a "traffic cop" inside a computer, coordinating the activities of the disk drive, the keyboard, the monitor, and the electronic chip that performs the machine's arithmetic and logic operations. This DOS must run every time the computer is turned on.

The virus then gives commands to make room for a copy of itself on every data diskette, or on every program stored on the hard disk in

A renegade programmer creates a computer virus, or code, that can alter or destroy data. The virus is inserted into a regular program, such as a database, and spreads in two basic ways: by an infected floppy disk inserted into another computer; or by transmittal by modem over telephone lines to an electronic bulletin board, where it is picked up by other computer callers. The virus infects the operating system and program disks of any computer it comes in contact with, and these pass the virus on to still other computers.

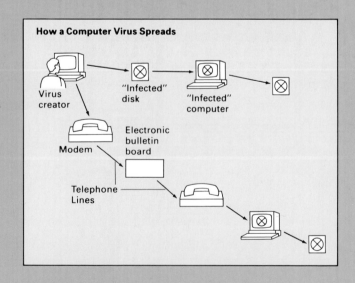

How a Computer Virus Spreads

Virus creator

"Infected" disk

"Infected" computer

Modem

Electronic bulletin board

Telephone Lines

the infected computer. Every time a new diskette is used to store data or copy a program, the virus goes along. When that diskette is introduced into a "clean" computer, it spreads the virus to that machine's DOS. When data from that newly infected computer are stored on a clean diskette, the virus spreads there, too. And thus it multiplies. Because viruses often are designed to do their dirty work at a later time, when some date or event acts as a trigger, they are likely to spread among a group of users before they do anything to make their presence known.

In many cases, viruses spread through the illegal copying of software sold on diskettes. Industry experts believe, however, that viruses are transmitted mainly through electronic bulletin boards—public forums run by commercial database services. Electronic bulletin boards enable users with telephone link-ups to communicate with one another and trade *public domain*, or free, software.

According to Fred Cohen, a professor of computer science at the University of Cincinnati in Ohio, computer viruses are so easy to write that "anybody can do it." Cohen is generally credited with developing the first computer virus as part of his research on computer security for his doctoral thesis in 1983. Cohen says that it is possible in some programming languages to write a virus in as few as 11 characters.

Once a virus has been discovered, it is easy to write a simple program that deletes the virus. Creators of viruses, however, can just as easily upgrade their viruses to override such a program. Furthermore, some viruses can change the characters in their code every time they reproduce, making it almost impossible to stop them.

By the spring of 1988, a number of small companies had rushed to the market place with various types of hardware and software designed to detect viruses and prevent them from infecting computer systems. In addition, by early 1988, computer magazines began to warn their readers to be wary of public domain software, and to avoid sharing and copying diskettes that belong to people they do not know well. They also advised users to put their operating systems on separate diskettes, and to use the diskette's *write protect tabs*, devices that prevent anything from being added to a diskette.

Some industry observers feared that computer viruses could have a chilling effect on the free flow of data and slow down the growth of the information age. Others, however, suspected that the main result of the computer-virus outbreak would be an end to the illegal copying of software.   [Christine Winter]

CD memory. Software experts expect HyperCard to increase the use of compact discs (CD's) to store computer data. These CD's are the familiar 12-centimeter (4¾-inch) discs used to record music. Computer information stored on a CD is called *read-only memory* (ROM) because a computer can "read" the data but cannot change it.

CD's would make a good storage medium for large stacks of HyperCard index cards because a CD can hold an astounding amount of data—the equivalent of 275,000 typewritten pages or 2,000 highly detailed images. A HyperCard user could search through the data quickly.

Software firms in 1987 and 1988 introduced a wide range of programs on CD-ROM. These included medical databases, book catalogs, encyclopedias, dictionaries, and art libraries.

An operating system designed to take full advantage of the tremendous computing power of 80286 and 80386 microprocessor chips made its debut in December 1987—four months ahead of schedule—when International Business Machines Corporation (IBM) released a system called OS/2 1.0. IBM and Microsoft Corporation of Redmond, Wash., developed this system. An operating system functions as a "traffic cop" between a computer's hardware and its *applications software*, such as programs for word processing, spreadsheets, and databases, by controlling the flow of data among the various parts of the computer.

IBM's OS/2 and other OS/2 systems for 80286 and 80386 chips produced by Intel Corporation of Santa Clara, Calif., will be used in personal computers manufactured by such major firms as Compaq Computer Corporation of Houston, and Tandy Radio Shack of Fort Worth, Tex., as well as IBM. The older MS-DOS operating system that has been used with the machines cannot handle as much memory as the chips can.

In fact, even after the introduction of OS/2 1.0, a great deal of computing power went untapped. Applications software designed for OS/2 systems was still largely in the design and testing stage in 1988. [Ronald D. Scibilia]

In WORLD BOOK, see COMPUTER; COMPUTER, PERSONAL.

Deaths of Scientists

Notable scientists and engineers who died between June 1, 1987, and June 1, 1988, are listed below. Those listed were Americans unless otherwise indicated. An asterisk (*) indicates that a biography appears in THE WORLD BOOK ENCYCLOPEDIA.

*Brattain, Walter H. (1902-Oct. 13, 1987), physicist who shared the 1956 Nobel Prize in physics with John Bardeen and William Shockley for inventing the transistor, a tiny device used to control the flow of electric current. The transistor made possible the miniaturization of computers and other electronic equipment.

Cool, Rodney L. (1920-April 16, 1988), physicist who helped prove the existence of subatomic particles called *quarks.* He served as a professor of high-energy physics at Rockefeller University in New York City from 1970 until his death.

Cournand, André F. (1895-Feb. 19, 1988), French-born physician who shared the 1956 Nobel Prize for physiology or medicine with Dickinson W. Richards, Jr., of the United States and Werner Forssmann of West Germany for developing *cardiac catheterization,* a method of exploring the interior of the heart with a slender, flexible tube called a catheter.

Downie, Allan W. (1901-Jan. 26, 1988), Scottish bacteriologist who played a leading role in ridding the world of smallpox.

Draper, Charles S. (1901-July 25, 1987), aeronautical engineer who developed navigation and guidance systems for nuclear submarines and missiles, the Atlas and Titan rockets, and the *Apollo* spacecraft that took astronauts to the moon and back.

Fagg, Bernard (1915-Aug. 14, 1987), British archaeologist who in the 1940's discovered the Nok civilization of Africa. The Nok culture, which produced some of the oldest sculptures found in black Africa, flourished in what is now Nigeria from about 500 B.C. to A.D. 200.

*Feynman, Richard P. (1918-Feb. 15, 1988), physicist who shared the 1965 Nobel Prize in physics with Sin-itiro Tomonaga of Japan and Julian S. Schwinger of the United States for developing an improved theory of *quantum electrodynamics* (the interaction of electrons and electromagnetic radiation). The theory enabled scientists to predict the effects of electrically charged particles on each other in a radiation field. Feynman also worked on the Manhattan Project, a top-secret U.S. government project that produced the first atomic bomb in 1945.

Fuchs, Klaus (1911-Jan. 28, 1988), German-born physicist convicted of giving United States and British atomic bomb secrets to the Soviet Union in the 1940's.

Killian, James R., Jr. (1904-Jan. 29, 1988), engineer who served under President Dwight D. Eisenhower from 1957 to 1959 as the first full-time presidential science adviser, laying the groundwork for the U.S. space program. Killian earlier had been president of the Massachusetts Institute of Technology in Cambridge from 1948 to 1959.

King, Charles G. (1896-Jan. 21, 1988), chemist who isolated vitamin C from the juice of lemons in 1932. He served as a professor of chemistry at Columbia University in New York City from 1946 until his death.

Leloir, Luis Federico (1906-Dec. 3, 1987), Argentine chemist who won the Nobel Prize for chemistry in 1970 for his discovery of compounds called *sugar nucleotides,* which are involved in the storage of chemical energy by living things.

Levine, Philip (1900-Oct. 18, 1987), Russian-born physician and serologist who identified the Rh factor in human blood in the early 1940's, greatly increasing the safety of blood transfusions. He also developed means of preventing the miscarriages and infant deaths that may result from *Rh hemolytic disease,* a disorder caused by Rh incompatibility between the blood of the baby and that of the mother.

Li, Choh Hao (1913-Nov. 28, 1987), Chinese-born biochemist who discovered and later synthesized human pituitary growth hormone. He also discovered, in 1978, the natural painkiller *beta endorphin,* a morphinelike substance produced in the brain.

*Medawar, Sir Peter B. (1915-Oct. 2, 1987), British zoologist who shared the 1960 Nobel Prize for physiology or medicine with Australian physician Sir Macfarlane Burnet. Medawar proved

Richard P. Feynman

Luis Federico Leloir

Sir Peter B. Medawar

Deaths
of Scientists

Continued

Isidor Isaac Rabi

Patrick C. Steptoe

Georg Wittig

Burnet's theory of *acquired immunological tolerance*, which showed that rejection of transplanted tissues could be prevented. Their work paved the way for modern organ transplant surgery.

Murphy, William P. (1892-Oct. 9, 1987), physician who was awarded the 1934 Nobel Prize for physiology or medicine along with George Minot and George H. Whipple for developing the liver treatment for a blood disease called *pernicious anemia*. The treatment—which consisted of feeding patients 0.2 kilogram (0.5 pound) of liver daily—cured the disease, which had previously always been fatal.

Mylonas, George E. (1898-April 15, 1988), Turkish-born archaeologist recognized as an international authority on ancient Greece. Mylonas served on the faculty of Washington University in St. Louis, Mo., from 1933 to 1969. He also directed excavations at Mycenae, Greece, that filled in large gaps in the history of the area's Bronze Age, from about 1550 to 1100 B.C.

Neddermeyer, Seth H. (1907-Jan. 29, 1988), physicist whose research led to the discovery in 1937 of subatomic particles called *muons*. He also worked on the Manhattan Project, where he developed the *implosion trigger* that set off the first atomic bomb in 1945. The trigger used conventional explosives to compress a core of fissionable material, causing the nuclear explosion.

Panofsky, Hans A. (1917-Feb. 28, 1988), German-born atmospheric scientist who contributed to our understanding of air turbulence and the transport of air pollutants. He taught at Pennsylvania State University in University Park from 1945 to 1982.

Rabi, Isidor Isaac (1898-Jan. 11, 1988), physicist, born in Austria-Hungary, who won the 1944 Nobel Prize in physics for his work on measuring the magnetic properties of atoms, molecules, and atomic nuclei. His research led to the development of extremely precise atomic clocks and *nuclear magnetic resonance imaging*, a technique used in medical diagnosis.

Ruska, Ernst (1906-May 27, 1988), West German electrical engineer who shared the 1986 Nobel Prize in physics with Gerd Binnig of West Germany and Heinrich Rohrer of Switzerland. Ruska was honored for his invention

in 1931 of the electron microscope, which uses beams of electrons instead of beams of light and has much higher power than an ordinary microscope.

Slotta, Karl H. (1895-July 17, 1987), German-born biochemist who discovered the female hormone *progesterone* in 1935.

Steptoe, Patrick C. (1913-March 21, 1988), British obstetrician and gynecologist who pioneered the technique of *in vitro fertilization*, in which eggs are removed from a woman's ovaries, fertilized in a laboratory with her partner's sperm, and returned to her uterus. Steptoe and his partner, Robert G. Edwards, were responsible for the birth in 1978 of the world's first "test-tube" baby, Louise Joy Brown. Their research made parenthood possible for thousands of otherwise infertile couples.

Strömgren, Bengt (1908-July 4, 1987), Swedish-born Danish astronomer who gained world recognition for his research into the chemical composition of stars. He also studied the matter that occupies the space between stars.

Williams, Roger J. (1893-Feb. 20, 1988), biochemist who discovered the growth-promoting vitamin *pantothenic acid*. From 1939 until his death, he served as a professor of chemistry at the University of Texas in Austin. He founded and directed the Clayton Foundation Biochemical Institute, a research center at the university that discovered more vitamins and their variants than any other laboratory in the world.

Wittig, Georg (1897-Aug. 26, 1987), West German chemist who shared the 1979 Nobel Prize for chemistry with Herbert C. Brown of the United States for developing a method of linking carbon and phosphorus to synthesize biologically active substances. The technique made possible the mass production of hydrocortisone and other important drugs as well as compounds used in many industrial processes.

Worrell, Eric (1924-July 13, 1987), Australian naturalist who founded the Australian Reptile Park near Sydney.

Wright, Sewall (1889-March 3, 1988), geneticist who established a mathematical basis for the theory of evolution.   [Sara Dreyfuss]

249

Dentistry

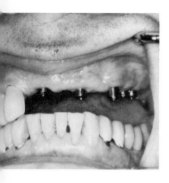

Screw-in dental fixtures made of titanium offer an alternative to dentures and bridges. The fixtures are implanted in the jaw-bone, *top,* wherever natural teeth are missing. An artificial tooth is then fitted over each metal implant, *above.*

The theory that the reduced flow of saliva that comes with age may promote cavities on the *roots* of teeth—the parts of teeth covered by the gums and jawbone—in the elderly was reinforced by a January 1988 report by dental researchers at the University of Rochester in New York. Dentists had long reported an increase in root cavities among patients who lacked salivary flow due to various medications, disease of the *salivary glands* (glands in the mouth and cheeks that produce saliva), or damage to the salivary glands due to radiation treatment for head or neck tumors.

The University of Rochester researchers reported an animal study suggesting that saliva may help prevent decay of tooth roots. The researchers removed the salivary glands from rats and fed the animals a high-sugar diet to promote tooth decay. The scientists also infected the rats with two species of bacteria that cause dental decay, *Actinomyces viscosus* and *Streptococcus mutans.*

The experiment lasted six weeks. As might be expected, decay of the tooth *crowns* (the parts of the teeth that appear above the gumline) developed extensively and rapidly during the six weeks. What was surprising was that decay on the root surface became evident within a few days of beginning the study and increased with time. The researchers concluded that removal of salivary glands greatly enhanced the development of root cavities in the animals, which normally do not develop such cavities.

Altered tetracycline. A modified form of the antibiotic tetracycline may reverse gum disease, according to research reported in August 1987. Dentists have long used tetracycline to treat *periodontal disease*, infection of the gums and jawbone that may destroy the tissue supporting teeth, causing them to loosen and fall out. Tetracycline inhibits the growth of a number of microorganisms that cause periodontal disease.

A group of dental investigators at the State University of New York at Stony Brook have pointed out that tetracycline helps cure periodontal disease not only as an antibiotic but also in another way unrelated to fighting infection. Tetracycline blocks the action of *collagenase*, an enzyme suspected of destroying collagen, which makes up periodontal tissue.

In August 1987, the Stony Brook research group, headed by oral biologist Lorne M. Golub, reported that they had succeeded in modifying the tetracycline molecule to remove its antibiotic properties but retain its anticollagenase activity. They fed the modified tetracycline to diabetic rats that had high levels of tissue-destroying collagenase. The drug produced a 55 per cent decrease in collagenase activity in the animals.

Later, the researchers produced similar findings with human gum tissue. The scientists believe that modified tetracyclines may prove useful in the treatment of not only gum disease but also other conditions, such as rheumatoid arthritis, that involve the breakdown of tissues due to excessive amounts of collagenase.

The effect of cigarette smoking on gums was investigated by dental researchers at the Karolinska Institute in Stockholm, Sweden, who reported their findings in two articles in autumn 1987. The researchers studied 242 professional musicians between the ages of 21 and 60, 76 of whom were smokers. The scientists found that, compared with nonsmokers, the smokers had more loose teeth and more and deeper *periodontal pockets*, the gaps formed when the gums pull away from the teeth.

The investigators used dental X rays of both groups to compare the height of supporting bone between the teeth. The results showed that the amount of bone support was significantly less in smokers, compared with nonsmokers.

The researchers pointed out that their results cannot be explained by inferior dental care among the smokers because all the participants had a high standard of oral hygiene. In addition, there was no significant difference between the smokers and the nonsmokers in the accumulation on their teeth of *plaque* (a film of food particles and bacteria). The investigators concluded that smoking alone damages the tooth-supporting bone and gum tissue. [Paul Goldhaber]

In WORLD BOOK, see DENTISTRY.

Drugs

A new drug that rapidly dissolves blood clots in patients suffering a heart attack was approved in November 1987 by the United States Food and Drug Administration (FDA). Studies show that the drug, called *tissue plasminogen activator* (t-PA), often can halt a heart attack or prevent serious damage to the heart. Sold under the trade name Activase, t-PA was developed by Genentech Incorporated of South San Francisco, Calif.

Doctors believe that many heart attacks are triggered by the formation of blood clots in the narrowed portions of the arteries that carry blood to the heart muscle. The clot blocks the flow of oxygen-rich blood, preventing the heart muscle from receiving enough oxygen to continue pumping effectively. As a result, a portion of the heart muscle dies. T-PA rapidly dissolves the clots.

In December, the results of a study confirming t-PA's effectiveness in treating heart attack patients were published by a team of researchers headed by cardiologist Alan D. Guerci of Johns Hopkins School of Medicine in Baltimore. The researchers administered the drug to 72 heart attack victims. A control group of 66 heart attack patients received a *placebo* (inactive substance) instead. According to the report, t-PA opened obstructed arteries in two-thirds of the patients who were treated with the drug within four hours of the start of a heart attack. Patients receiving t-PA also suffered less damage to the heart.

Anticholesterol drug. The use of a new drug that may reduce the chances of suffering a heart attack was approved by the FDA in September 1987. Lovastatin, marketed by Merck Sharpe & Dohme of West Point, Pa., under the trade name Mevinolin, lowers levels of cholesterol, a fatty substance, in the blood. Reducing cholesterol levels can reduce the risk of heart attack, because it is cholesterol that builds up in plaque that causes the narrowing of arteries. Doctors emphasized that lovastatin works best when the patient also follows a low-cholesterol diet.

Technicians at Genentech, Incorporated, inspect vials of Activase, a new drug approved in November 1987 to halt heart attacks. Many heart attacks are triggered by the formation of a blood clot in the arteries that carry blood to the heart muscle. Activase quickly dissolves the clot and restores blood flow to the heart.

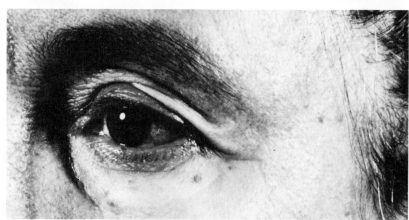

Wrinkles caused by sun damage, *above right,* nearly disappear, *below right,* in a patient treated with Retin-A, a drug long used in the treatment of acne. The drug stimulates cell growth, causing the skin layers to thicken. Researchers believe this thickening tightens and smooths skin, reducing wrinkles.

Drugs

Continued

Acne drug dangers. In May 1988, the FDA ordered severe restrictions on the distribution of an acne drug linked to severe birth defects. The drug, isotretinoin, which is manufactured by Roche Laboratories in Nutley, N.J., and sold under the brand name Accutane, has been on the market since it was approved by the FDA in 1982. The FDA reported 62 documented cases of birth defects caused by the drug. An FDA study, criticized by Roche as flawed, estimated that the total number of birth defects related to the mother's use of Accutane was 900 to 1,300 between 1982 and 1986.

At the time it approved the drug, the FDA issued strict guidelines for its use. Roche had also conducted an extensive education campaign, warning of the danger of birth defects. The new measures include asking doctors and their patients to sign a consent form indicating they are aware of the dangers of the drug and that the patients are avoiding pregnancy.

Steroid challenge. In September 1987, two groups of researchers inde-pendently reported studies challenging the use of corticosteroids, synthetic versions of a steroid produced by the adrenal glands, in the treatment of shock due to severe infection. Steroids are powerful drugs capable of altering the functioning of nearly all the body's organ systems. Many physicians routinely give steroids to patients with severe infection.

One group of researchers headed by Roger C. Bone of the University of Arkansas for Medical Sciences in Little Rock studied 382 patients suffering from massive infection. Half the patients received methylprednisolone, a type of corticosteroid. The other half received a placebo. The researchers found that high doses of methylprednisolone did not prevent the patients from going into shock, improve the condition of patients in shock, or prevent death from shock. In fact, after two weeks of treatment, the death rate among patients who received methylprednisolone was higher than among the patients who received a placebo.

The second study, conducted at 10

Drugs

Veterans Administration medical centers around the United States, reached the same conclusion as the first study.

Smoothing wrinkles. A drug that has long been used to treat acne can also reduce wrinkles caused by sun damage, according to research reported in January 1988 in the *Journal of the American Medical Association* by scientists at the University of Michigan Medical Center in Ann Arbor. The drug, tretinoin, is sold under the brand name Retin-A.

The researchers tested the drug on 30 white people aged 35 to 70, all of whom showed signs of premature skin aging—wrinkling, roughness, discoloration, and freckles—caused by exposure to sunlight. All the subjects rubbed a cream containing tretinoin on one forearm and a cream without the drug on the other. In addition, half the subjects rubbed a cream with tretinoin on their face. The other half used a face cream without the drug.

After 16 weeks, the researchers found that tretinoin had reduced fine wrinkling, discoloration, and rough-

ness on the arms of all 15 patients treated with the drug and on the faces of 14 of them. Although the drug caused mild to moderate redness in the skin of nearly all the patients, this irritation seldom lasted longer than several weeks. The researchers also found that tretinoin stimulated cell growth in both the outer and underlying layers of the skin, causing these layers to thicken. It is believed that this thickening tightens and smooths the skin. The researchers suggested that the drug may also improve skin wrinkled by the normal aging process.

An accompanying editorial in the *Journal*, however, cautioned that the test involved only 30 subjects at one medical center and that the improvements were often subtle. The editorial also noted that the researchers did not establish whether the improvements are permanent or whether the drug must be used continuously. The long-term effects of tretinoin are also unknown.   [B. Robert Meyer]

In WORLD BOOK, see CHOLESTEROL; DRUG; STEROID.

Ecology

Unusual climatic disturbances can have far-reaching ecological effects, according to a report in December 1987. Ecologists H. Lisle Gibbs of the University of Michigan in Ann Arbor and Peter Grant of Princeton University in New Jersey reported that the event known as El Niño caused a population explosion among certain birds of the Galapagos Islands in 1982-1983.

El Niño is a warm current that occurs about every two to seven years in the Pacific Ocean off the west coast of South America. The southward-flowing water replaces the cold Peru Current that normally flows north along the South American coast. The current is called *El Niño*—Spanish for *the child*—because it usually occurs around Christmas. The name refers to the Christ child.

The 1982-1983 El Niño was the most extreme of this century. It not only caused a severe reduction in the number of fish in Peruvian and Ecuadorean waters but also had global effects, including climatic changes in various parts of the world.

During the 1982-1983 El Niño, the Galapagos Islands, about 970 kilometers (600 miles) west of Ecuador, received about 10 times their normal rainfall. The heavy rains caused a dramatic increase in the amount of food available to the islands' birds.

Gibbs and Grant studied two species of Darwin's finches, island birds named for British naturalist Charles R. Darwin. The finches eat the seeds of various plants and feed caterpillars to their young. Both seeds and caterpillars were in great abundance after El Niño rains.

The finches responded to these increased resources by producing more young. The birds continued to nest and breed for a full nine months, three times longer than their usual breeding season. During that time, female finches laid five times as many eggs as they do in most other years. By the end of 1983, the number of the two types of finches in the islands was estimated at 1,900, compared with about 450 in 1981.

The researchers said the number of

finches in the islands probably increases after each El Niño. Thus, they concluded, the Galapagos' bird population may be determined mainly by the effects of El Niños.

Bleached coral reefs. Another unusual effect of the 1982-1983 El Niño was the "bleaching" and mass death of coral reefs in the eastern Pacific, a phenomenon that most biologists think was a direct result of the abnormally warm water. In late 1987, scientists reported bleaching among many coral reefs of the Caribbean Sea.

The natural color of corals results from the presence of algae in their tissues. The corals provide nutrients to the algae, and the algae supply the corals with sugars and oxygen—products of photosynthesis—that enable the corals to grow faster. But, for reasons that are not yet understood, corals evict their algal "guests" when confronted with environmental stress, such as water pollution or an increase in ultraviolet light. With its algae gone, a coral takes on a white, bleached appearance. It also becomes weaker and may die.

The Caribbean bleaching episode began in mid-1987 in the Florida Keys. It soon spread to the coast of Colombia, and by November, reefs throughout the entire Caribbean Basin were affected. Soon after that, most reefs began to regain their color, and by January 1988 scientists reported that the worst was over.

Biologists did not know what caused the bleaching. Because the problem occurred so quickly and over such a wide area, they ruled out water-borne germs or pollution. Most biologists believed that the bleaching—like the episode that occurred in the Pacific in response to El Niño—was due to a rise in water temperature. Water temperatures in the Caribbean were unusually high in summer 1987.

Diversity of habitats. In efforts to preserve species of plants and animals, it is better to provide a large number of moderately sized habitats than just a few large habitats. That conclusion emerged from research reported in February 1988 by ecologists James F. Quinn of the University of California at Davis and Susan P. Harrison of Stanford University in California.

Their findings may serve as guidelines for the design of national parks in the United States and elsewhere.

The researchers examined data from 100 censuses of plant and animal populations in land areas of various sizes. The data clearly showed that the combined land area of a group of relatively small habitats contains a greater total number of species than does the land area of one much larger habitat.

The scientists noted, for example, that three national parks—Big Bend in Texas, North Cascades in Washington, and Redwood in California—with a combined area of 5,100 square kilometers (1,965 square miles) have two more mammal species than Yellowstone National Park in Wyoming, which has an area of about 9,000 square kilometers (3,460 square miles). One reason for that difference is that the three smaller parks contain a greater variety of habitats—desert, alpine, and coastal forest—than does the larger park.

In planning strategies for wildlife conservation, therefore, the study suggested that the best course of action is to create the largest possible number of reserves. But Quinn and Harrison cautioned against making reserves too small or establishing only small reserves, because biologists have found that species confined to limited areas are more likely to become extinct.

Controlling ragwort. Biological controls in Oregon have greatly reduced the growth of ragwort, a pasture weed poisonous to livestock, according to researchers at Oregon State University in Corvallis in March 1988. The scientists, led by insect ecologist Peter B. McEvoy, reported that the weed was brought under control by two insects imported for that purpose.

Ragwort is a problem in the Northwestern United States and much of Canada. In 1960 and 1971, the state of Oregon imported two insect predators of ragwort—the cinnabar moth and the ragwort flea beetle, respectively—from Europe in an effort to combat the weed without using herbicides. The moth eats the plant's leaves, and the beetle chews tunnels in its stems and roots.

Studies in the early 1980's showed that the number of ragwort plants in

Studying the Wood Stork
A family of wood storks nest in a cypress tree at Big Dukes Pond in central Georgia. University of Georgia ecologists study the endangered birds to learn about their feeding and nesting habits by examining a feeding site (inset, left) and watching nesting storks from an elevated blind (inset, right).

Ecology

Continued

Oregon had declined by 93 per cent six years after the flea beetles were introduced, but there was no proof that the decline was caused by the beetles. McEvoy and his colleagues wanted to learn whether the beetles and moths were really keeping ragwort under control and whether the two insects in combination were more effective than either insect alone.

For their study, the researchers transplanted a number of ragwort plants to a meadow. They protected half of the plants from insects by placing them in cages and spraying them with insecticide. They exposed the other plants to cinnabar moths and ragwort flea beetles.

More than half of the plants exposed to the insects died, while the remaining weeds in that group produced less than half as many flowers and seeds per plant as the protected ragworts. This result demonstrated that the insects are effective at controlling ragwort.

In a second experiment, the scientists tested the effects of the insect species individually. They divided a field of transplanted ragworts into four groups: a group protected from both insects; a group exposed to both insects; a group exposed to only cinnabar moths; and a group exposed to only ragwort flea beetles.

The plants in the first two groups fared the same as the plants in the previous experiment; the protected weeds thrived, while most of the ragworts exposed to both insects died. In the last two groups, however, the results of the second experiment were different. In neither of those groups was insect damage sufficient to control the weeds.

Flea beetles killed many small, non-flowering ragworts but had little impact on adult plants. The moths damaged flowering plants, but the plants were able to regrow the injured parts. McEvoy and his associates thus concluded that it is the combined feeding of the two insects that kills or stunts the weeds.   [Paulette Bierzychudek]

In the Special Reports section, see The Making of Biosphere II. In World Book, see Ecology.

Electronics

Inch-Mate, made by Digitool Corporation of Aspen, Colo., calculates in feet, inches, and fractions of an inch, making it a handy device for carpenters and other workers who need to make non-metric measurements and calculations.

Manufacturers of electronic products for consumers improved their goods in two ways in 1987 and 1988. First, they reduced the size of certain critical parts of these products, enabling the manufacturers to introduce a host of portable devices, including battery-powered color television sets and miniature digital audio compact disc (CD) players. Second, manufacturers improved the quality of consumer products such as videocassette recorders (VCR's) and camera-recorders. Manufacturers also introduced home video systems that produce three-dimensional (3-D) images.

Miniature CD's. The technology for building tiny CD's led to the introduction of new CD products. A miniature CD measures 7.6 centimeters (3 inches) across and holds up to 20 minutes of sound, compared with a regular CD, which measures 12.1 centimeters (4¾ inches) in diameter and holds up to 75 minutes of sound. Because of its 3-inch diameter, the music industry calls the new disc *CD-3*.

The new CD-3 disc allows manufacturers to build battery-powered portable players small enough to fit in a pocket. The first such player, introduced in March 1988 by Sony Corporation of America in New York City, measures about 9.5 centimeters (3¾ inches) square and 3.8 centimeters (1½ inches) thick. Including its rechargeable batteries, the player weighs about 400 grams (14 ounces).

Another advantage of CD-3 discs is their price. Full-sized, album-length CD's often costing $12 or more are still too expensive for many people. By contrast, record companies plan to issue one to four hit songs on each CD-3 disc, and charge about $4 per disc.

Pocket-sized TV's with flat liquid crystal display (LCD) screens instead of picture tubes have been on the market for several years, but only in black and white. In early 1988, the first practical color-LCD TV's became available from Sony; Sharp Electronics Corporation of Mahwah, N.J.; and, under the brand name Magnavox, NAP Consumer Electronics Corporation of Knoxville, Tenn. These sets

Electronics

Continued

cost as much as $600 for a model with a 7.6-centimeter screen. The LCD screen is only about 3 millimeters (⅛ inch) thick.

Sharper video. By the spring of 1988, VCR's made for consumers were producing images nearly twice as sharp as those possible in 1986. This increased sharpness was due mostly to improvements that enabled the recording tapes to hold more information.

The sharpness of a video image depends upon the number of *lines of horizontal resolution* in the picture. Imagine a row of vertical bars running like fence posts from the left side of your TV screen to the right. The more of these lines there are, the closer together they will be—and therefore the sharper the image they will produce.

In conventional VHS and 8-millimeter video systems, the image has about 240 lines of horizontal resolution. Beta VCR's deliver about 300 lines, and an ordinary TV broadcast produces a picture with as many as 330 lines.

The latest generation of VCR's produces pictures that are even sharper.

For example, the Super VHS format introduced in late 1987 by JVC Company of America in Elmwood Park, N.J., provides up to 440 lines of horizontal resolution. Sony's ED-Beta, scheduled to go on sale in the United States in mid-1988, offers up to 500 lines.

3-D video. The first 3-D video systems were introduced in 1987 and 1988. In late 1987, Sega Electronics, Incorporated, of San Diego, put 3-D video games on the United States market. For home movies, Toshiba America, Incorporated, of Wayne, N.J., planned to sell a 3-D camera-recorder in the United States in mid-1988. The Toshiba unit costs about $2,850.

Human beings perceive real-life objects in three dimensions—height, width, and depth. We see depth because of the separation between our eyes. Each eye sees an object from a slightly different perspective, and the brain somehow combines what the two eyes see to create an image that corresponds to the three-dimensional shape of the object.

An electronic price tag, *right,* produced by Telepanel, Incorporated, of Markham, Canada, displays a grocery item's price per unit for cost comparison when a shopper presses a button, *below right.* When the price of an item changes, the store's computer instructs the tag to display the new price.

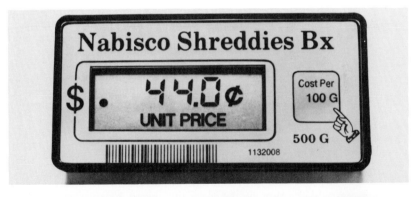

Electronics

Continued

Film and video cameras that have a single lens cannot convey the dimension of depth because they take pictures from only one perspective. And an ordinary television set cannot convey depth because it displays an image created by a single-lens camera.

A TV image created by two cameras spaced apart—like our eyes—can convey the illusion of depth, however, provided your left eye sees only the image created by the camera on the left, and your right eye sees only the image created by the camera on the right. To restrict vision in this way, manufacturers have developed a system that enables your eyes to "take turns" viewing images created by two cameras.

The system consists of a videotape of a 3-D motion picture or 3-D video game, a pair of special eyeglasses, and an adapter box that controls the TV set and the glasses. The "lenses" of the glasses are actually LCD panels that alternate between being clear and opaque.

A 3-D video image is created by two cameras recording the action from different perspectives. The image appears in 3-D on the TV screen because a computer chip in the adapter box instructs the TV to display the image from the left camera and then the image from the right camera. The display alternates between the two perspectives every one-sixtieth of a second.

The computer chip also controls the special LCD eyeglasses. In some models, the control signals are electric pulses that travel by wire to the eyeglasses. In other models, the signals travel on a beam of infrared light. In either case, the pulses make the left panel clear and the right panel opaque whenever the TV screen is displaying a scene for the left eye. The opposite happens when the screen shows a scene intended for the right eye. This switching occurs so rapidly that the brain combines the two images as if the eyes were seeing both images at once. [Stephen A. Booth]

In WORLD BOOK, see ELECTRONICS; TELEVISION; VIDEOTAPE RECORDER.

Energy

Sunrayer, an automobile built by General Motors Corporation, topped a field of 25 solar-powered racing cars from seven nations in November 1987 to win the Pentax World Solar Challenger Race in Australia. The competition, held to stimulate the development of solar-energy devices, covered the 3,030 kilometers (1,880 miles) from Darwin in the Northern Territory to Adelaide in South Australia.

Each car had solar cells mounted on it to collect energy from the sun's rays and convert the energy into electricity. Most of the electricity flowed to an electric motor that propelled the car. The remainder charged batteries, which provided extra power for acceleration and hill climbing, and for driving when the sky was cloudy. The cars also used battery power early and late in the day to supplement the reduced solar energy striking the cells.

According to the rules of the race, the cars were driven only from 8 A.M. to 5 P.M. each day until the race was completed. In addition, the solar cells could charge the batteries each day for two hours before the start of the day's run and for two hours after the run.

The race began on November 1. On November 6, Sunrayer completed the course about 960 kilometers (600 miles) ahead of its nearest competitor. The vehicle's elapsed driving time was 44 hours 54 minutes, and its average speed was 67.5 kilometers (41.9 miles) per hour.

The teardrop-shaped vehicle measured 6 meters long, 2 meters wide, and 1 meter high (19.7 by 6.6 by 3.3 feet). The car and driver weighed 260 kilograms (573 pounds).

The solar cells covered an area of 8.4 square meters (90 square feet), and could deliver approximately 1,500 watts of power at 150 volts. Hughes Aircraft Company of El Segundo, Calif., designed the solar array, using the type of solar cells mounted on satellites built by Hughes.

The car's batteries contained 68 rechargeable silver-zinc cells, each providing a total of 102 volts. They weighed a total of 27 kilograms (60 pounds), 20 per cent of the weight of

Energy

Continued

conventional lead-acid batteries with the same capacity.

The Sunraycer used a braking technique that fed energy into the batteries. When the driver took his foot off the accelerator, the left rear wheel, which normally was turned by the electric motor, began to turn the motor. The motor acted as a generator, producing electricity that flowed into the batteries.

The framework of the racing car was welded aluminum tubing, and the body was made of a lightweight plastic.

Electricity from tires. An unusual power plant in California in November 1987 demonstrated a technology that may solve a major problem for most communities—the accumulation of tires in dumps. Artificial rubber tires are not biodegradable, and when they are buried in landfills, their buoyancy eventually makes them rise to the surface. There are about 2 billion tires in dumps in the United States, and more than 200 million are added annually.

The $41-million Modesto Energy Plant, the first plant in the United States to burn whole tires to make electricity, was dedicated in Modesto, Calif., on November 10. General Electric Corporation designed, built, and operates the plant for the Oxford Energy Company of New York City.

The plant is located near the largest tire dump in the United States. The dump contains about 35 million tires. The plant will consume nearly 5 million tires annually, generating 14.4 megawatts of electricity—enough to meet the needs of 15,000 households.

The process by which the plant burns tires has been used for more than 14 years by a West German firm. Conveyors carry tires to two boilers, where they burn at temperatures exceeding 1100°C (2000°F.). At such high temperatures, the burning tires do not emit the foul-smelling black smoke produced when rubber burns at lower temperatures. The boilers produce steam, which drives a turbogenerator to produce electricity.

The plant's pollution control system was designed to remove 99.9 per cent of the particles in the smoke, 95.6 per

Sunraycer, a sleek vehicle covered with solar cells and built by General Motors Corporation, won a race for solar-powered automobiles held in Australia in November 1987. Sunraycer covered the 3,030 kilometers (1,880 miles) from Darwin to Adelaide at an average speed of 67.5 kilometers (41.9 miles) per hour.

"The electricity is off in the whole area. Find out what happened."

cent of the gaseous sulfur dioxide, and 70 per cent of the nitrogen oxides. Oxford Energy will recover all by-products produced in the tire combustion for recycling. The firm will sell steel from steel-belted radial tires, for example, for scrap; and zinc compounds recovered from ash will be resmelted into zinc metal.

Unconventional nuclear reactor. Scientists at Argonne National Laboratory near Chicago in 1987 and 1988 continued to develop the Integral Fast Reactor (IFR), an experimental nuclear reactor designed to prevent a disaster in the event of an accident affecting its *core*, which contains nuclear fuel. One of the main dangers of a conventional reactor is that the core might overheat, melt or burst through structures designed to contain it, and release radioactive substances into the environment.

The fuel of a conventional reactor is made up of pellets of radioactive *uranium oxide*. Pressurized water cools the fuel. The reactor is housed in a *pressure vessel*, a tanklike structure with steel walls at least 15 centimeters (6 inches) thick.

Both the fuel and the coolant of the IFR are unconventional, however. The fuel consists of cylinders made of an *alloy* (a metal mixture) of uranium, plutonium, and zirconium. Heat flows through this alloy much more efficiently than through uranium oxide, so the IFR operates at a relatively low temperature. Furthermore, experiments in 1987 showed that even if the fuel produced four times the amount of power for which the reactor is designed, the fuel would not begin to melt. In addition, Argonne researchers say that if the fuel cylinders start to overheat, the cylinders will swell and deform, causing the heat-producing nuclear reaction to stop.

Liquid sodium cools the IFR's core, entering at a temperature of about 345°C (653°F.) and leaving at about 510°C (950°F.), well below sodium's boiling point—881°C (1618°F.). The reactor operates at atmospheric pressure, so it does not need to be surrounded by a thick pressure vessel.

Energy
Continued

Testing reactor overpressure. Engineers at Sandia National Laboratories in Albuquerque, N. Mex., in July 1987 intentionally pressurized a scale model of a nuclear reactor *containment building* until the model leaked. A containment building is a nuclear power plant's final barrier to the release of radioactive materials into the environment. It is made of reinforced or prestressed concrete and stands an average of about 60 meters (200 feet) high. The structure at Sandia was one-sixth the size of a containment building—the largest and most complex model of a nuclear power plant ever built. It stood 11.3 meters (37 feet) tall, and contained more than 1,200 recording devices, including cameras and instruments to measure heat, pressure, warping, and cracking.

The Sandia engineers pressurized the model to obtain data to improve computer programs that predict what would happen to a full-sized structure if an accident caused a great deal of pressure to build up inside it. Sandia built the model to withstand an *over-pressure* (pressure above that normally exerted) of 317 kilopascals (kPa), or 46 pounds per square inch (psi). By comparison, the highest overpressure in the containment building at the Three Mile Island nuclear power plant near Harrisburg, Pa., during the 1979 accident there was 193 kPa (28 psi).

Before the test, the engineers analyzed the model, using special computer programs from France, Great Britain, Italy, the United States, and West Germany that predict how reactors will behave. The programs predicted failure at pressures from about 900 to 1,300 kPa (130 to 190 psi).

The researchers tested the model by pumping nitrogen gas into it and gradually increasing the gas pressure. Only when the pressure reached 952 kPa (138 psi) did the pressure sensors indicate that the structure was leaking. Engineers in the five countries will use the test data to modify the computer programs.   [Marian Visich, Jr.]

In WORLD BOOK, see ENERGY; NUCLEAR ENERGY; NUCLEAR REACTOR; SOLAR ENERGY.

Environment

Severe drought and high temperatures hit the Midwestern United States in 1988. Such conditions can be expected for the next 10 years and beyond, according to a National Aeronautics and Space Administration (NASA) scientist. In June 1988, NASA climatologist James E. Hansen declared, "the greenhouse effect is here." The *greenhouse effect* refers to a build-up of carbon dioxide and other gases in Earth's atmosphere that prevent *infrared* (heat) radiation from the sun escaping into space, and this creates higher temperatures. Other scientists said that higher temperatures and drought are natural climate variations. See AGRICULTURE.

The disappearance of ozone from the upper atmosphere emerged as one of the greatest concerns involving the environment during 1987 and 1988. A historic treaty designed to protect ozone in the upper atmosphere from further destruction by industrial pollutants was signed by representatives of 24 nations and the European Community (EC) on Sept. 16, 1987, in

Montreal, Canada. Ozone is a form of oxygen. It is concentrated in the stratosphere about 16 to 48 kilometers (10 to 30 miles) above Earth's surface, where it absorbs the sun's ultraviolet radiation. Ultraviolet radiation is thought to cause skin cancer.

By June 1988, 31 nations and the EC had agreed to the treaty, which requires the signers to cut their use of industrial pollutants known as *chlorofluorocarbons* (CFC's) by 50 per cent by 1999. CFC's can destroy ozone, according to laboratory studies. CFC's are widely used as refrigerants, as aerosol propellants, and in the manufacture of packaging and insulation.

Global ozone loss. Atmospheric scientists since 1985 have called attention to a drastic thinning of the ozone layer that occurs over Antarctica in the spring and has become known as the *ozone hole* (in the Special Reports section, see THE HOLE IN THE OZONE LAYER). On March 15, 1988, a panel made up of more than 100 scientific experts convened by the National Aeronautics and Space Administration

Environment

Continued

issued a report showing for the first time that the thinning in stratospheric ozone occurs not only over Antarctica but also over the Northern and Southern hemispheres. The study covered the years between 1969 and 1986. It found that between 1978 and 1985, the amount of stratospheric ozone over much of the two hemispheres decreased by 2.5 per cent. Such a decline is not as drastic as the 50 per cent decline that occurred over Antarctica during the months of September and October 1987, but it is nevertheless of great concern.

Radon inside. Results of the largest U.S. study of indoor radon levels were released by the EPA in August 1987. Radon is a radioactive gas created by a chain of reactions that begins with the radioactive decay of uranium. The survey focused on 11,600 houses in 10 states. It found excessive levels of radon in about 1 in 5 of the houses. Lifetime exposure to such levels of radon carries a 1 in 100 risk of developing lung cancer.

Radon usually seeps from slate, granite, phosphate, or rock containing uranium. Although radon becomes harmlessly diluted when it mixes with outdoor air, it can accumulate to toxic levels when it seeps into buildings that are not well ventilated. The EPA estimated that each year between 5,000 and 20,000 lung cancer deaths in the United States may be linked to long-term inhalation of radioactive particles known as *radon daughters* that are created as radon decays.

Based on the findings of the EPA survey, Sheldon Myers, director of EPA's Office of Radiation Programs, warned that the cancer risk posed by radon pollution is "much, much higher" than that of any other known air pollutant.

On Jan. 5, 1988, the National Research Council (NRC), an arm of the National Academy of Sciences, issued the results of an independent study that confirmed the EPA's findings. The NRC study also reported that cigarette smokers face the highest lung cancer risk from radon. Smokers exposed to excessive levels of radon are

Pollution-control workers use vacuum hoses to suction diesel fuel that spilled into the Monongahela River near Pittsburgh, Pa., in January 1988. A huge fuel-storage tank collapsed, fouling the river with millions of liters of diesel fuel.

Environment

Continued

10 times more likely to develop lung cancer than nonsmokers.

Acid rain. A panel of experts who coordinate U.S.-funded acid-rain research issued a report in July 1987 on its five-year study of acid rain. Acid rain is rainfall with a high acid content, usually as a result of industrial pollution.

The National Acid Precipitation Assessment Program panel confirmed that sulfur dioxide and nitrogen oxides given off by burning fossil fuels, such as from coal-burning power plants, can acidify lakes. A high acid content in lake water can kill fish and other aquatic species. The panel's report also said, however, that it had found little evidence of such damage in the United States. Even where lake acidification had occurred, such as in New York's Adirondack Mountains, only a few lakes were affected, the panel reported. The study found no evidence of regional lake acidification in the Western United States and little or no effect of acid rain on agricultural crop yields.

Acid rain's major effects are not limited to acidity, according to a study reported in April 1988 by researchers with the Environmental Defense Fund in New York City. The nitrates that are carried by acid rain are nutrients. When excessive levels of these nutrients enter water, they overfertilize algae and other microscopic plant life. This causes *algal blooms*—an overgrowth of these plants—which quickly consume most of the oxygen in the water. Other life forms may then begin dying from oxygen starvation.

The new study focused on acid rain's nitrate effects on Chesapeake Bay. The bay is the largest U.S. estuary and a primary breeding ground for oceanic fish from Maine to North Carolina. The study charged that the EPA and others had largely ignored or underestimated acid rain's contribution to the increasing problem of algal blooms along the U.S. East Coast. The study's calculations showed that acid rain contributes at least one-fourth of all human-caused nitrogen pollution in the Chesapeake. Several other areas along the East Coast showed similar high contributions of nitrates from acid rain.

Toxic troubles. A voluntary agreement to end the production and sales of chlordane, heptachlor, and other chemically related pesticides in the United States was announced on Aug. 11, 1987, by the U.S. government. Velsicol Chemical Corporation of Rosemont, Ill., the only U.S. manufacturer of these chemicals, worked out an agreement with the EPA to ban these pesticides after a study conducted by Velsicol showed that they can contaminate the interiors of buildings for at least a year. These pesticides are used to kill termites, but studies show that they are also capable of causing liver damage and nerve disorders in animals and may cause cancer in human beings.

Asbestos continued to be a troublesome issue. The EPA on Feb. 29, 1988, announced the results of a study indicating that about 1 in 5 commercial and public buildings in the United States contain asbestos, a cancer-causing agent. Most of the asbestos identified in this survey was contained in heat-insulating wraps covering pipes and other heating-system components.

Lead also is a toxic chemical that can pose a serious health hazard. A new U.S. regulation, which took effect in June 1988, requires water suppliers to tell their customers how much lead is in their water, how the lead got into the water-supply system, and whether the levels of lead in the water pose a serious health hazard.

But there was still some question about what constitutes safe levels of lead. Several studies conducted in 1986 and 1987 linked low-level lead exposures to minor hearing losses, diminished scores on intelligence tests, elevations in blood pressure, and a range of other symptoms. These studies found adverse effects from blood lead levels that were considerably below levels that the U.S. government considers acceptable for children. According to toxicologist Ellen Silbergeld of the Environmental Defense Fund in Washington, D.C., an estimated 88 per cent of U.S. children have lead levels in their blood near the levels found to cause adverse effects in the recent studies.   [Janet Raloff]

In WORLD BOOK, see ENVIRONMENTAL POLLUTION.

263

Genetic Science

The first patent for a genetically engineered animal was issued in April 1988 by the United States Patent and Trademark Office. The patent was awarded to Harvard University in Cambridge, Mass., for a strain of mice that were engineered to contract cancer easily.

The mice were developed by two Harvard geneticists, Philip Leder and Timothy A. Stewart. The researchers isolated a gene known to cause cancer in many mammals, including human beings. They made many copies of the cancer gene (*oncogene*) and injected them into fertilized mouse eggs.

The mice that developed from the eggs had multiple copies of the oncogene in their cells and thus were highly susceptible to developing cancer, especially breast tumors. The mice passed that trait on to their offspring. The new breed of mice will be used in various kinds of cancer research.

Although most geneticists praised the patent office's action, some members of Congress were critical of it. The Senate and the House of Repre-sentatives in mid-1988 were considering legislation forbidding further animal patents until Congress has had time to consider the economic and moral issues involved with patenting forms of life.

The Harvard patent was permitted under a 1980 decision of the Supreme Court of the United States. The court ruled that newly created life forms are equivalent to inventions and so have the right to a patent. By 1988, the patent office had issued a number of patents for genetically engineered bacteria, but the Harvard patent was the first granted for a higher form of life.

Second genetic code. Scientists at Massachusetts Institute of Technology in Cambridge announced in May 1988 that they had deciphered a second genetic code that cells use in the production of protein molecules. The code, worked out by geneticists Ya-Ming Hou and Paul Schimmel, reveals how a type of ribonucleic acid (RNA) assembles proteins from building blocks called *amino acids*.

RNA molecules are the workers in

Geneticist Philip Leder of Harvard Medical School in Boston shows off the world's first patented animal—a mouse genetically engineered to develop cancer easily. In April 1988, the U.S. Patent and Trademark Office granted Harvard a patent for such mice, which will be used in cancer research. Leder and his associate, geneticist Timothy A. Stewart, inserted multiple copies of a cancer-causing gene into the genes of the mouse, which it will pass on to its offspring.

the manufacture of proteins. When a protein is needed by a cell, coded instructions for the making of that protein are copied from *deoxyribonucleic acid* (DNA)—the master molecule of heredity, and the material genes are made of—into a type of RNA called *messenger RNA*. The messenger RNA then moves into the cytoplasm, the main part of the cell. There, the RNA molecule's coded instructions are "read" by a number of smaller RNA molecules called *transfer RNA*.

The transfer RNA molecules are bound to amino acids and assemble them in the order specified by the messenger RNA. There is at least one kind of transfer RNA for each of the 20 types of amino acids used to make proteins, and each form of transfer RNA binds to just one kind of amino acid.

Geneticists have understood the coding system used by messenger RNA and DNA since the 1960's. But they had been unable to decipher the transfer RNA code—that is, how a particular transfer RNA molecule always binds to the same kind of amino acid.

Hou and Schimmel found that just one tiny segment of a transfer RNA molecule determines the molecule's function. In some cases, the difference between one transfer RNA molecule and another is a single *base*. Bases are a component of building blocks called *nucleotides*.

DNA and messenger RNA use three-base units—called *codons*—to specify amino acids, and scientists had thought that transfer RNA's coding system might be more complicated than that. That it turned out to be simpler surprised most geneticists.

Breaking the transfer RNA code should be a boon to genetic engineering, making it easier for scientists to manufacture tailor-made proteins for use as drugs or for other specific purposes. The new code may also enable geneticists to identify genetic diseases caused by errors in the functioning of transfer RNA.

Gene map. A "map" giving the location of many human genes was reported in October 1987 by researchers at Collaborative Research, Incorporated, in Bedford, Mass., and the Whitehead Institute for Biomedical

Research in Cambridge, Mass. While city maps, for example, show the location of streets, parks, and buildings, this map shows the location of genes, *chromosomes* (threadlike structures that carry the genes), and pieces of DNA.

The map developed by the researchers, called a *linkage map*, traces various disease-causing genes to particular pieces of DNA. These pieces, called *genetic markers*, show up in some people's DNA but not in other people's. The markers occur at known places in chromosomes and serve as genetic signposts.

If the DNA of a person with a genetically caused disease contains a marker that is also present in the DNA of close relatives who have the same disease—but is absent in the DNA of close relatives who do not—then the disease-causing gene probably lies near that marker.

The linkage map identifies 404 markers on the 23 pairs of human chromosomes. The scientists identified 306 of the markers by studying the DNA of three generations—children, parents, and grandparents—in 21 families. The inheritance of particular diseases and their associated markers were traced in the DNA of each generation. The other 98 markers had previously been identified by other researchers making similar genetic studies.

In addition to allowing scientists to zero in on particular genes, linkage maps may prove useful as a diagnostic tool. But to be truly useful, many scientists believe, a linkage map should contain several thousand markers. When it becomes possible to map large numbers of markers in a person's DNA, doctors should be able to determine an individual's susceptibility to diseases in which genes play a role, including heart disease and many forms of cancer. Individuals could then modify their life styles to reduce the chances of developing these diseases.

The map created by Collaborative Research and the Whitehead Institute could perhaps serve as a framework for a very ambitious project that is being urged by many geneticists. The goal of the project would be to learn the complete sequence of DNA nucleotides in the approximately 100,000

265

A New Law-Enforcement Tool: DNA Fingerprints

The introduction of scientific evidence is common in courts of law, especially in criminal cases. Bits of human tissue—blood, semen, skin, or hair—are often presented in a trial to link the accused person to the crime. But such evidence usually shows just a probability of guilt, not a certainty. What prosecutors have needed is a way to analyze tissue samples that proves guilt beyond a shadow of a doubt.

In 1987 and 1988, they got it: an investigative technique called DNA "fingerprinting." Like regular fingerprinting, which relies on the fact that no two people have exactly the same pattern of lines on their fingertips, DNA fingerprinting is based on differences in people's DNA, or *deoxyribonucleic acid*. DNA is the complex molecule, found in all the cells of the body, that carries the genetic code.

DNA fingerprinting was pioneered in the early 1980's by Alec Jeffreys, a geneticist at the University of Leicester in England. Jeffreys and his colleagues noted that everyone's DNA contains many sections in which the sequence of *nucleotides*—the building blocks of DNA—is repeated over and over. These repetitive sequences, however, vary in number and length from one person to another. It is this variability in repetitive sequences that makes DNA fingerprinting possible.

To make a DNA fingerprint, DNA is first isolated from a tissue sample, such as a bit of blood, semen, or skin. The DNA is then chopped into millions of pieces with chemical "scissors" called *restriction enzymes* that cut the DNA molecule at specific sites. The pieces of DNA are then placed in a gel between positive and negative electric poles and exposed to an electric field. Because the pieces of DNA are negatively charged, they move through the gel toward the positive pole. The smaller pieces of DNA move more rapidly than the larger fragments, so the DNA becomes separated according to size, forming a series of bands. But these bands are not visible in the gel.

Next, the DNA is transferred, using a gentle "blotting" technique, from the fragile gel to a membrane made of a more durable material, such as nylon. The membrane is then immersed in a solution containing radioactively tagged *probes*—short strands of DNA that match the repetitive DNA sequences. The probes and the repetitive sequences join together, much like the two halves of a zipper.

Radiation from the probes is used to make the repetitive-sequence DNA bands visible. The nylon membrane is placed against a sheet of X-ray film that absorbs radiation from the probes for several days. When the film is devel-

British geneticist Alec Jeffreys, the inventor of DNA fingerprinting, examines the distinctive pattern of bands that make up DNA prints. The prints are made by cutting apart *deoxyribonucleic acid* (DNA)—the molecule of heredity—with special enzymes and separating them by size with an electric field. The chance that any two people, except identical twins, will have the same DNA fingerprint is about 1 in 10 billion.

oped, it displays an image of the DNA bands. That pattern of bands is the DNA fingerprint.

A DNA fingerprint can be made from blood that is several years old or from material that would probably be insufficient for other types of analysis, such as a single hair. The DNA fingerprint produced from such specimens, collected from a crime scene or from a victim's body, is compared with a suspect's DNA print, made from DNA isolated from a sample of the accused person's blood. If the two DNA prints match, the suspect is most certainly guilty of the crime. The probability that any two DNA prints would match by chance alone is about 1 in 10 billion. Only identical twins, whose DNA is also identical, would have matching DNA prints.

DNA fingerprinting has been gaining favor in the criminal courts, though it still is more widely used in Great Britain than in the United States. In England, DNA fingerprinting convinced police that a man who had been arrested for the 1986 rape and murder of a young girl was in fact innocent of the crime. Police then decided to check the DNA prints of several thousand men living in the small town where the crime was committed. On the basis of that evidence, another man was arrested and convicted of the crime.

In the United States, DNA fingerprinting has been introduced in several cases, including a rape trial in Orange County, Florida, that resulted in a guilty verdict. But American courts, which require new investigative techniques to be certified as "reliable and trustworthy" by the scientific community, have moved cautiously in accepting DNA fingerprinting. Because of the growing interest in the potential uses of this technique, however, at least two U.S. companies began offering DNA fingerprinting services in 1987. In addition, law-enforcement officials in some states have proposed storing the DNA prints of convicted criminals in a computer.

DNA fingerprinting has a number of potential applications. For example, the procedure provides a way of establishing *paternity* (identity of the father) in child-support cases. It can also be used to prove the pedigrees of animals, such as show dogs; to identify missing children; and to confirm that cell lines used in laboratories have not become contaminated with cells from other sources.

The technique's most important application, however, will most likely continue to be in establishing guilt or innocence in criminal investigations. As one U.S. legal expert commented, "What [conventional] fingerprinting was to law enforcement at the end of the 19th century, DNA analysis will be at the turn of this century and beyond."   [David S. Haymer]

human genes. Because there are about 3 billion nucleotides, the task would be enormous. Scientists disagree as to whether the information gained from the project would be worth the cost and effort.

Gender genes. Scientists have long been interested in isolating human genes that determine the sex of an individual. In December 1987, geneticist David C. Page of the Whitehead Institute reported identifying a small portion of the Y chromosome—one of the two human sex chromosomes—that appears to be crucial in this process.

Page and his associates studied the genetic material of people with abnormal sex chromosomes. Human males normally have one X and one Y chromosome, while females have two X chromosomes. Certain rare individuals, however, differ from that pattern. For example, about 1 in 20,000 men has two X chromosomes and only a small piece of the Y. That small piece, attached to one of the X chromosomes, is apparently enough to produce male characteristics. Other rare individuals have an X and a portion of the Y chromosome and are female. Although they often are normal in other respects, people with genetic defects of this sort are usually infertile.

By carefully examining the chromosomes of such people, the researchers identified a small part of the Y chromosome that was always present in males and always absent in females. One 12-year-old girl had more than 99 per cent of the Y chromosome in her cells but apparently lacked the crucial piece identified by the scientists.

Page and his colleagues found that this tiny region of the Y chromosome contains a gene, but the role that gene might play in the process of sex determination was uncertain. To their surprise, the researchers subsequently found a similar gene on the X chromosome. That discovery, the scientists said, showed that the genetic factors deciding an individual's sex may be more complicated than anyone had expected. They said much work remains to be done before the X and Y chromosomes are fully understood.

Cancer-gene findings. Scientists in England and the Netherlands reported in October 1987 that they had

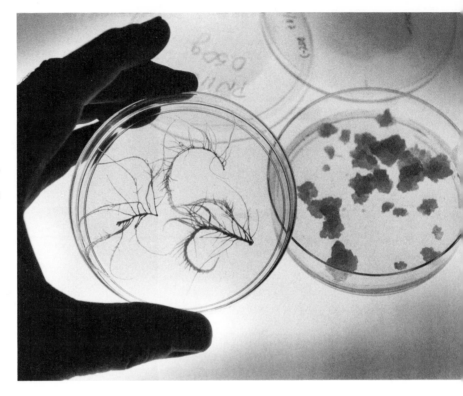

Soybean cells growing in the culture dish on the right form unorganized clumps because the cells' root-forming genes somehow get "turned off" in the laboratory. But cells in the dish at the left, to which geneticists have added another root-forming gene, grow roots. The gene was carried into the cells by *Agrobacterium tumefaciens,* a type of bacteria commonly found in soil. The research is part of an effort to produce improved soybeans.

Genetic Science

Continued

discovered two genes in the fruit fly *Drosophila melanogaster* that are very similar to oncogenes found in human and mouse tumors.

The researchers determined that the fly genes control important processes in development. One of the genes is known as *wingless* because in its absence, a fly cannot develop wings. The wingless gene, the investigators found, is nearly identical to a mouse cancer gene called *int-1.*

Another *Drosophila* gene identified by the researchers as similar to a known cancer gene is called *dorsal.* The dorsal gene plays a crucial role in a developing fly embryo, ensuring that different types of cells develop in their proper positions. The scientists discovered that the dorsal gene is almost the same as a human cancer gene called *c-rel,* which has been shown to cause cancerous changes in spleen cells.

The results of the *Drosophila* study support the theory that cancer genes are abnormal versions of genes that control cell growth and development. The identification of these genes in

fruit flies opens up new horizons for understanding what happens when a gene changes from a normal state to a cancer-causing state.

One reason that the two *Drosophila* genes resemble human and mouse genes is that fruit flies, mice, and human beings are all descended from simple organisms that evolved hundreds of millions of years ago. A number of genes from those primitive species are in the cells of most animals today. But over vast stretches of time, such genes have undergone slight alterations in many of the species that inherited them. That is why a mouse gene controlling a particular aspect of growth and development differs somewhat from a *Drosophila* gene that performs the same function.

Genetically altered bacterium tested. The first field test of a genetically engineered organism regulated by the Toxic Substances Control Act (TSCA) was approved in October 1987 by the U.S. Environmental Protection Agency (EPA). Most such organisms are expected to be covered by this act, passed

Genetic Science

Continued

by Congress in the early 1970's. An April 1987 test in California of a genetically altered strain of bacteria was approved under a different law, covering organisms that could be used as pesticides.

In its October action, the EPA gave permission to the Monsanto Company of St. Louis, Mo., to release a strain of bacteria containing two genes from another species of bacteria. The extra genes, which simply served as identifying markers, enabled the Monsanto researchers to keep track of the bacteria after they were released in November on a South Carolina test plot.

The purpose of the experiment, scheduled to run until mid-1989, is to learn how genetically engineered bacteria disperse in the environment. Many critics of genetic engineering warn that such organisms could spread over wide areas and produce unforeseen consequences. In February 1988, the Monsanto researchers issued a preliminary report on the South Carolina test that the company hoped would ease such fears. According to the re-

port, the altered bacteria decreased drastically in number after release and moved just a few inches from where they were released.

In a related matter, a study released in fall 1987 by the National Academy of Sciences in Washington, D.C., concluded that genetically engineered organisms pose no special hazards to human beings. The report argued against passing new laws to control genetic engineering research. Existing federal regulations are sufficient for protecting the environment, according to the academy.

DNA fingerprinting. An identification technique called *DNA fingerprinting*, developed by scientists in England, was becoming widely adopted in 1988. The procedure, which makes use of the fact that every person's DNA contains a unique molecular pattern, may be useful in criminal investigations as well as in studies of inherited disease and checks of animal pedigrees. See Close-Up. [David S. Haymer]

In WORLD BOOK, see CELL; GENETIC ENGINEERING; GENETICS.

Geology

The movement of hot rock deep within Earth may affect the motion of the continents and ocean basins and may even be responsible for past mass extinctions of species, according to research reported in September 1987. Geophysicists Vincent Courtillot and Jean Besse of the Laboratory of Paleomagnetism and Geodynamics in Paris brought together evidence from a number of geological studies and suggested that there is a connection between reversals of Earth's magnetic field, the apparent movement of Earth's rotational poles, the breakup of continents, and mass extinctions.

Their research supports the theory that at least some of the mass extinctions that have occurred in the past, including the mass extinction 65 million years ago in which the dinosaurs died out, were caused by periods of intense volcanic activity. Other scientists have argued that the dinosaurs and many other species died out because a huge asteroid collided with Earth.

Crustal movement. Courtillot and Besse began their research with a

study of *polar wander*—the apparent movement of Earth's rotational poles—over the past 350 million years. The rotational poles are the places where Earth's *spin axis*—the imaginary line about which Earth rotates—intersects the surface.

From studies of the magnetic fields of ancient rocks, scientists know that the points on Earth's surface marking the rotational poles have changed over time. The poles remain fixed while Earth moves beneath them because the angle of Earth's spin axis never changes. But for convenience, geologists describe Earth as "fixed" and the poles as "wandering."

Some polar wander is due to the movement of the tectonic plates that make up Earth's crust. Some wandering, however, is caused by the movement of the entire *lithosphere*—the upper mantle and crust, including the plates.

Geological studies had revealed two periods in the past 350 million years when there was little polar wander— that is, when the lithosphere was relatively stable, moving only slightly in relation to Earth's core and spin axis. These stable periods occurred from 270 million to 310 million years ago and from 110 million to 170 million years ago. Between 170 million and about 250 million years ago, the lithosphere moved at the rate of about 5 centimeters (2 inches) per year.

Magnetic reversals. Courtillot and Besse then examined the data on the frequency of reversals of Earth's magnetic field. Scientists have long known—also by studying the magnetism in ancient rocks—that Earth's magnetic field reverses: The north magnetic pole becomes the south magnetic pole. When this occurs, the needle of a compass swings around so that the north end points south. Eventually, the poles return to their normal orientation.

The period during which the magnetic field remains stable in its orientation is called a *chron*. Chrons usually last several hundred thousand years, though some chrons may last millions of years. These very long chrons are called *superchrons*. When the scientists compared the data on polar wander with that on magnetic reversals, they discovered an interesting relationship. They found that the superchrons occurred at about the same time as periods of little lithospheric motion. For example, from 310 million to 270 million years ago—a period that includes most of the first superchron—the lithosphere moved only about 1 centimeter (⅓ inch) per year.

The scientists noted that there was a mass extinction 250 million years ago, at the end of the superchron. Also about this time, Earth experienced a period of intense volcanic activity. About 50 million years later, lithosphere movement caused the huge land mass known as Pangaea to break apart, with the pieces eventually forming the present continents.

Courtillot and Besse found a similar set of events surrounding the second superchron, which lasted from 120 million to 80 million years ago, though the changes in lithosphere motion and magnetic reversals began about 50 million years before this. Some 170 million years ago, lithospheric motion dropped sharply, from about 5 centi-

meters to about 1 centimeter per year. Also about 170 million years ago, the number of magnetic reversals began to decrease, dwindling to zero about 120 million years ago. About 80 million years ago, at the end of the superchron, Earth began to experience another period of intense volcanic activity. Relatively soon afterward, about 65 million years ago, there was another mass extinction, in which the dinosaurs died out.

The scientists also noted that periods of frequent magnetic reversals were accompanied by periods of rapid lithospheric motion. For example, the number of magnetic reversals increased between 250 million and 170 million years ago. At this time, the lithosphere was sliding rapidly over the mantle. When the number of magnetic reversals declined, lithospheric movement dropped sharply.

Cold and hot currents. The French geophysicists theorized that all these events are related. Like many earth scientists, Courtillot and Besse believe that reversals in Earth's magnetic field result from changes in the circulation patterns of the liquid iron and nickel that make up Earth's outer core. They argue that these changes result from the movement of currents of cooler material in the outer core. According to the scientists, these currents are created when there are sharp temperature differences between the cooler mantle and the hot, underlying outer core. The mantle rock cools some of the molten material at the boundary between the two layers, causing currents of cooler molten material to sink deeper into the outer core. These currents create turbulence in the outer core, disrupting the circulation patterns there. As the patterns change, the magnetic field generated by the moving liquid rock reverses.

As the lower mantle is heated by the outer core, however, the temperature difference narrows and fewer currents are created. The outer core becomes less turbulent, and the number of magnetic reversals declines and finally ceases. During this period, the upper mantle is relatively cool, and so the lithosphere does not move rapidly.

Eventually, as the core continues to heat the base of the mantle, the rock

The L.A. Shakes

Rubble from a building destroyed by an earthquake that struck the Los Angeles area on Oct. 1, 1987, covers parked cars, *above.* The quake caused seven deaths and more than $358 million in damage. It occurred along a previously unidentified extension of the Whittier Fault, a break in Earth's crust about 12 kilometers (7½ miles) below the surface, *right.* This extension is a thrust fault, *below right,* created when pressure on a block of crust becomes so great that one part of the block is thrust horizontally over another part. This results in overlapping layers of rock, similar to the rock layers—only about 5 centimeters (2 inches) thick—indicated by arrows, *below.*

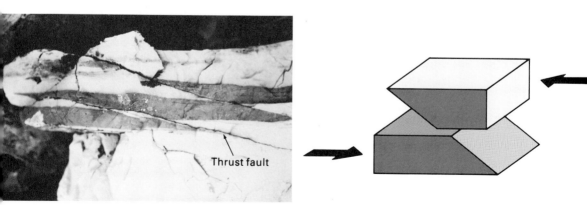

Thrust fault

there becomes so warm that currents of hot rock again begin to flow upward to the upper mantle. By warming and softening the upper mantle, these currents enable the overlying lithosphere to move more easily. As a result, the amount of polar wander increases. The hot currents in the mantle may also act like blowtorches on the base of the lithosphere, tearing continents and oceans apart and powering volcanoes.

As the hot currents rise through the mantle, cooler rock from the upper mantle sinks to the mantle-core boundary. According to Courtillot and Besse, this cooler rock begins the process all over again as the temperature difference between the outer core and the mantle increases. The temperature contrast again triggers turbulence in the outer core, increasing the number of magnetic reversals. During this part of the cycle, the upper mantle is still relatively hot because of the hot currents that rose from the lower mantle, and so the lithosphere moves fairly rapidly.

Volcanoes and extinctions. Courtillot and Besse suggest that large-scale volcanic activity following the two superchrons may have caused the mass extinctions 250 million and 65 million years ago. Since 1980, many paleontologists and geochemists have argued that the mass extinction 65 million years ago—and perhaps other extinctions as well—were the result of the collision of an asteroid with Earth. They theorize that the collision threw large amounts of dust into the atmosphere, creating a huge cloud that blocked sunlight from reaching Earth. In the cold and darkness that followed, many species of plants and animals died out. Advocates of the volcanism theory argue that intense volcanic activity could have caused the same conditions. Despite the controversy, many geologists welcomed Courtillot and Besse's theory because it provides a concise explanation for many geologic phenomena.

Sound maps of the Gulf of Mexico. Using a sophisticated device that converts sound waves to visual images, the United States Geological Survey (USGS) in early 1988 published the first atlas of the floor of the Gulf of Mexico. The maps of the gulf floor were created by a team of scientists led by marine geologist and geophysicist Bonnie McGregor of the USGS, using a sonar device called GLORIA. GLORIA stands for *Geological Long Range Inclined Asdic.* (*Asdic* is a British term for *sonar.*)

Like other sonar devices, GLORIA uses sound waves to identify underwater objects. The device consists of a sound transmitter and receivers, which a ship tows about 50 meters (165 feet) beneath the ocean surface. The transmitter sends out sound waves that scan a section of the sea floor about 18 meters (60 feet) wide. The return echoes bouncing off the sea floor are picked up by the receivers, which analyze the signals and produce visual images. GLORIA, which was developed in the late 1960's, has revolutionized seafloor mapping by enabling scientists to map large areas of otherwise inaccessible sea floor fairly quickly.

The most spectacular feature McGregor and her team observed in the western Gulf of Mexico was the Sigsbee Scarp, an underwater cliff off the coast of Texas. The scarp, which is 500 meters (1,650 feet) high, lies at the base of the continental slope, a gradually inclined region that connects the continental shelf with the gulf's *abyssal plain*—the flat plain that makes up most of the floor of the gulf. Ordinarily, the base of the continental slope merges gently and almost unnoticeably with the abyssal plain.

Seismic studies, analyzing shock waves sent through the rock, have revealed that the scarp consists mainly of rock salt. This rock salt is part of a massive deposit that extends inland to northern Texas and Louisiana and was laid down about 160 million years ago when the gulf was formed. Since then, the deposit has been covered with deep layers of sediment. The scarp exists because the sediments on the continental slope, which are more than 1 kilometer (½ mile) thick, are squeezing out the underlying rock salt like toothpaste from a tube. As a result, the scarp is slowly moving toward the abyssal plain.   [William W. Hay]

In the Special Reports section, see CHANGING VIEWS OF DINOSAURS; FINDING OUT HOW OLD THINGS ARE. In WORLD BOOK, see GEOLOGY.

Immunology

The development of possible vaccines against AIDS (acquired immune deficiency syndrome) continued in earnest in 1987 and 1988. As of mid-May 1988, some 62,200 people in the United States had contracted this immunity-destroying disorder, and 35,051 had died.

In October and November 1987, the United States Food and Drug Administration approved two experimental vaccines against the virus that causes AIDS—human immunodeficiency virus (HIV)—for human trials, and scientists were conducting animal tests with several other potential vaccines. Tests of still other vaccines got underway in other countries. But in early 1988, researchers reported that results so far were not encouraging and that an effective AIDS vaccine would probably not be a reality for years. In the Special Reports section, see THE SEARCH FOR AN AIDS VACCINE.

Targeting cancer cells. A natural *toxin* (poison) from bacteria might kill cancer cells without harming normal cells, according to a March 1988 report by

Ira Pastan, an immunologist at the National Cancer Institute (NCI) in Bethesda, Md. One major problem with anticancer drugs is that they harm normal cells as well as cancer cells.

Pastan said a toxin produced by *Pseudomonas* bacteria is highly effective at killing cancer cells. He explained that the toxin is much less harmful to normal cells because they have fewer *receptors* for the toxin than cancer cells do. Receptors are "docking points" on the surface of a cell that enable various kinds of molecules—in this case, molecules of the toxin—to attach themselves to the cell and thereby gain entrance to it.

The NCI researcher said he had isolated the *Pseudomonas* genes responsible for production of the toxin, so it should be possible to manufacture large quantities of the substance. Pastan said he hoped the toxin would become a valuable anticancer tool.

Preventing cancer's spread. One of the major challenges facing medicine today is the treatment of tumors that have spread from their primary site to

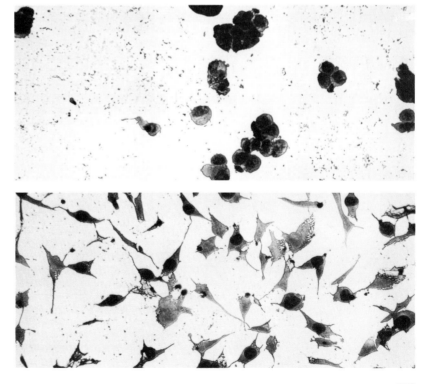

Human breast-cancer cells, *above right,* change shape, *below right,* after being treated with *autocrine motility factor* (AMF), a substance secreted by tumor cells. Researchers studying *metastasis*—the spread of a cancer to a new area of the body—reported in September 1987 that the new shape helps a cancer cell move. Finding a way to counteract AMF might help keep cancers from spreading.

Immunology

other parts of the body. These secondary tumors, called *metastases*, often cause the patient's death.

Scientists meeting at the National Institutes of Health in Bethesda in January 1988 reported that two experimental compounds have shown promise in limiting the spread of cancers. The compounds mimic natural substances in the body that block the penetration of malignant cells into organs.

One of those natural substances, laminin, is a protein component of the *basement membrane*, a layer of fibrous tissue between cells. George Martin, a researcher at the National Institute of Dental Research in Bethesda, reported that he had developed a synthetic compound similar to laminin that decreases the incidence of metastases in animals with *melanoma*, a deadly skin cancer that also affects human beings.

A related substance, fibronectin, aids in binding cells to one another. Kenneth Yamada, an NCI scientist, said a synthetic compound resembling fibronectin apparently keeps cancer cells from breaking away to form new tumors. Yamada injected the compound into eight mice with melanoma. All of the treated animals were alive 14 months later, while untreated mice with melanoma died within 6 weeks.

Both synthetic substances have drawbacks, however. The compounds remain active for only a short time, and they may have some adverse side effects.

Preventing hepatitis B. A plant extract may help prevent the hepatitis B virus from multiplying in the body, according to a report by a Philadelphia researcher in March 1988. Hepatitis B, a liver inflammation caused by a virus, can be prevented with vaccines. But for unvaccinated persons who pick up the virus, there has been no way to keep the disease from developing.

Immunologist Baruch S. Blumberg of Fox Chase Cancer Center in Philadelphia said an extract from tropical plants of the genus *Phyllanthus* seems to be effective in combating the virus. In the laboratory, this substance prevented the virus from producing an enzyme it needs to reproduce.

Blumberg also used the plant extract to treat woodchucks that had been infected with the hepatitis B virus. The extract reduced the amount of virus in 24 of 30 animals.

Malaria vaccine. An important advance against malaria, an infectious disease caused by a parasite, was announced in March 1988 by scientists in Bogotá, Colombia. The leader of the research team, immunologist Manuel E. Patarroyo of the National University of Colombia's Institute of Immunology, reported that an experimental vaccine proved effective in stopping malarial infections after the parasite had multiplied in red blood cells.

An estimated 200 million people around the world are infected with malaria, and 1 million to 2 million victims die each year. The disease is caused by *protozoans* (one-celled animals) called *Plasmodia* that are spread by mosquitoes.

When the parasites enter the body in a mosquito bite, they travel to the liver, where they multiply and change form. After a few days, the parasites burst out of the liver and infect red blood cells.

Most experimental vaccines combat the parasites early in the infection before they enter the liver. But if even one *Plasmodium* escapes destruction and reaches the liver, it can cause a full-blown case of malaria.

Patarroyo and his colleagues tested their vaccine, called SPf(66)30, on five volunteers, who were vaccinated with SPf(66)30 and then, after 80 days, injected with *Plasmodium*-infected red blood cells. Four unvaccinated volunteers in a control group were also injected with infected blood cells.

Among the vaccinated volunteers, four people developed, at most, mild symptoms of malaria that cleared up within three weeks. The fifth volunteer developed a severe malarial infection, as did the four controls who had not received the vaccine. All five malaria victims were treated with drugs.

The injection of human patients with a disease-causing microorganism poses ethical problems and is not permitted in the United States.

The researchers also tested a second vaccine. That preparation, however, provided less protection against malaria than SPf(66)30.   [Paul Katz]

In WORLD BOOK, see AIDS; CANCER; HEPATITIS; IMMUNITY; MALARIA.

Materials Science

A new field known as *high-temperature superconductivity* dominated materials science research in 1987 and 1988. Superconducting materials can conduct or carry an *electric current* (a flow of electrons) with no resistance so that no electrical energy is lost in the material.

Until 1986, most known superconductors were metals or *alloys* (metal mixtures) that become superconducting when cooled to temperatures near absolute zero ($-273.15°C$ or $-459.67°F$.), using liquid helium as the refrigerant. Liquid helium is costly and it is expensive to use, so metal and alloy superconductors are used in only a few devices.

A class of superconductors discovered in 1986, however, becomes superconducting at much higher temperatures. The new materials are *ceramics*, solids that are neither metals nor plastics. (Ceramics are the materials of pottery and dinner plates.)

Some of the new ceramic materials become superconducting at temperatures above the boiling point of liquid nitrogen, $-196°C$ or $-321°F$. Liquid nitrogen costs much less than liquid helium and is much less expensive to use. So the cost of reaching and maintaining the temperature at which superconductivity occurs is greatly reduced. The discovery of these new high-temperature metal oxide ceramic superconductors therefore has the potential to improve electrical technology. In the Special Reports section, see PLUGGING INTO SUPERCONDUCTORS.

Improving superconducting ceramics. First, however, researchers must increase the amount of current that the materials can carry in the superconducting state and solve certain manufacturing problems. The main production problem is the brittleness that is characteristic of ceramics. Many potential applications—such as electromagnets, electric motors, and electric generators—would require windings made of superconducting wire. Researchers are trying to make wire out of these brittle materials.

Four ceramic families. By June 1988, scientists had discovered four varieties of ceramic superconductors. The first,

"Forget gold. Strategic materials are where it's at."

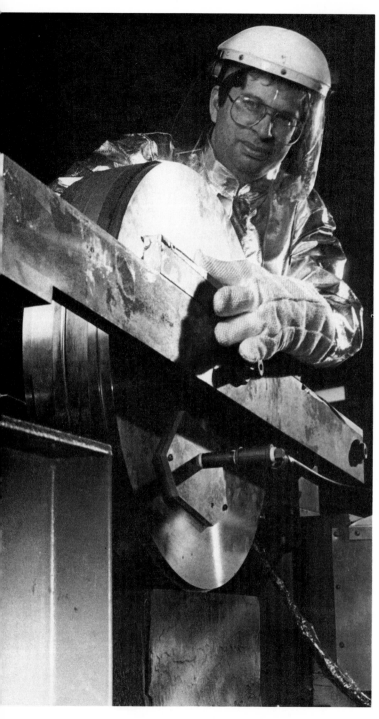

An ultrasound scanner mounted on a wheel sends high-frequency sound waves—beyond the range of human hearing—down into a slab of steel to detect hidden flaws in the metal. The device, developed by government and industry scientists, could save a steel mill up to $1 million a year in wasted metal.

announced in late 1986, is made up of the chemical elements barium, lanthanum, copper, and oxygen, and becomes superconducting at about −243°C (−405°F.).

The second variety originated with a material announced in January 1987 and later improved. The improved substance is made up of yttrium, barium, copper, and oxygen, and becomes superconducting at −180°C (−292°F.).

In January 1988, scientists in Japan reported on a third family of ceramic superconductors. These materials are made up of various mixtures of bismuth, strontium, calcium, copper, and oxygen. One member of this family becomes superconducting near −173°C (−279°F.).

And in February and March 1988, researchers in the United States announced yet another variety, composed of thallium, barium, calcium, copper, and oxygen. One such substance becomes superconducting at −148°C (−234°F.).

Easy to make. High-temperature superconductors are easy to manufacture by mixing and grinding certain chemical compounds that contain the necessary elements, then heating the mixture to produce a chemical reaction. Scientists in a number of laboratories have also grown single crystals of the yttrium-based materials by heating a mixture of the proper elements, then allowing the temperature to fall slowly.

Thin films. Many potential applications would require films made of the new superconductors to be deposited on layers of other materials. In one such application, the film would take the form of incredibly tiny, intricate electric circuits on computer chips. Such a film would be about 0.001 millimeter thick.

Some thin films of the yttrium-based material can carry currents that are high enough for most potential applications. Materials scientists are now trying to produce superconducting ceramics that could be used for large-scale applications such as electric power lines, yet would carry about as much current as the films.

[Clark W. White and Lynn A. Boatner]

In WORLD BOOK, see PHYSICS.

Medical Research

The first conclusive evidence that smoking increases the risk of heart disease in women was reported in November 1987 by a team of researchers from Harvard Medical School in Boston and Queensland Institute of Medical Research in Brisbane, Australia. Earlier studies linked smoking and heart disease in men.

The researchers tracked 119,404 female nurses between 1976 and 1982. At the beginning of the study, all the nurses were from 35 to 55 years old and none were known to have heart disease. About 30 per cent of the women smoked. The smokers were divided into six groups, depending on the number of cigarettes they smoked daily. For example, the lightest smokers smoked from 1 to 4 cigarettes per day. The heaviest smokers smoked 45 or more cigarettes per day.

By the end of the study, 65 of the women had suffered a fatal heart attack. Among these women, 60 were smokers. The greatest number of deaths—27—occurred among women who smoked 25 or more cigarettes per day. Another 239 of the women in the study suffered nonfatal heart attacks. Among these women, 198 were smokers, almost half of whom smoked at least 25 cigarettes per day.

The researchers calculated that the women who smoked more than 25 cigarettes per day were 5½ times more likely to suffer a fatal heart attack and nearly 6 times more likely to suffer a nonfatal heart attack than nonsmokers. When the data on fatal and nonfatal heart attacks were combined, the researchers found that the heaviest smokers were nearly 11 times more likely to suffer a heart attack than nonsmokers. Even the lightest smokers increased their chances of heart attack. They were nearly 2½ times as likely to be stricken as nonsmokers.

The researchers found, however, that former smokers were only slightly more likely to suffer a heart attack than those who had never smoked. They concluded that the effects of smoking are not permanent and that even the heaviest smokers can reduce their heart attack risk by quitting.

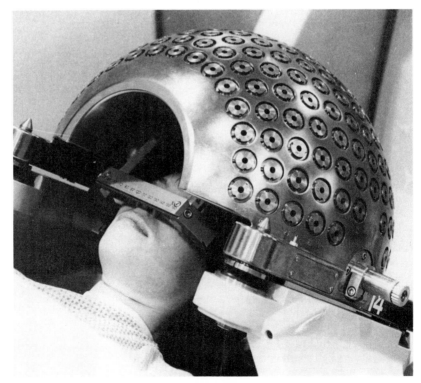

A helmet-shaped medical device called a gamma knife can destroy brain tumors and obstructions in blood vessels too deep-seated to be removed surgically. The device at Presbyterian-University Hospital in Pittsburgh, Pa., focuses more than 200 gamma rays on the problem area.

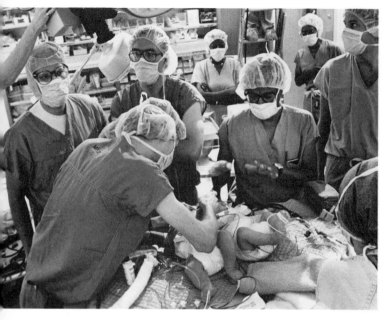

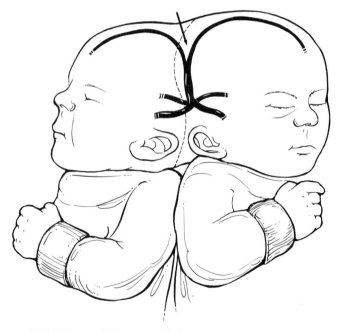

Brain Surgery for Siamese Twins
Anesthesiologists at Johns Hopkins Children's Center in Baltimore, *top,* prepare 7-month-old Siamese twins Patrick and Benjamin Binder of West Germany for surgery in September 1987. The twins were born joined at the back of the head and shared the main vein (indicated by arrow, *above*) that drains blood from the brain. In a 22-hour operation, a 70-member surgical team fashioned new veins from tissue from the babies' hearts. Surgeons later reconstructed the twins' skulls. The twins returned to West Germany in April 1988 with doctors still unsure of the extent of the brain damage they suffered.

Metabolism and weight gain. Some people are more likely to become overweight because their bodies need less energy for metabolism and normal daily activities than because they eat too much, according to a study published in February 1988. Weight experts have long argued about whether obesity is mainly the result of overeating or is largely due to low *metabolic rates.* (The metabolic rate is the rate at which the body converts food into energy. Food not burned as fuel is stored as fat.)

The study, conducted in Phoenix by researchers affiliated with the National Institutes of Health in Bethesda, Md., focused on three groups of American Indians living in the Southwestern United States. From 80 to 85 per cent of these Indians become obese by the time they reach their early 20's.

The researchers had several goals. First, they wanted to determine whether there is a link between metabolic rates and weight gain. They also wanted to learn whether there is a connection between *total daily energy expenditure* and weight gain. (Total daily energy expenditure includes metabolism as well as the calories burned for ordinary daily activities such as sleeping, eating, and watching television.)

To determine whether metabolism is related to weight gain, the researchers first measured the metabolic rates of 126 men and women. All the volunteers were weighed at the beginning of the study. After fasting overnight for 12 hours, they were asked to lie on their back and remain motionless but awake for 1 hour. During that period, each volunteer's head was covered by a hood fitted with devices to measure the amount of oxygen used and the amount of carbon dioxide produced—two major indicators of metabolic rate. People who have a high metabolism use more oxygen and produce more carbon dioxide than those who have a low metabolism.

These measurements enabled the researchers to calculate the number of calories the volunteers burned while at rest. The volunteers were classified as having a low resting metabolic rate if they burned fewer than 1,705 calories per day. They were placed in a middle category if they burned from 1,706 to

1,797 calories per day. And they were classified as having the highest metabolic rates if they used more than 1,798 calories per day.

One year after the test, all the volunteers were weighed again. The researchers also kept track of some of the volunteers for up to four years after the test. The researchers compared the volunteers' metabolic rates with their weight gains. They found that those with the lowest metabolic rates gained an average of 2.7 kilograms (6 pounds) per year. The volunteers in the middle metabolic group gained an average of 0.23 kilogram (½ pound) per year. The weight of those with the highest metabolic rates, however, remained essentially unchanged.

Testing energy expenditure. To determine whether weight gain was related to total energy expenditure, the researchers conducted another test with 95 men and women. Each volunteer spent 24 hours in a sealed chamber equipped with devices to measure the amount of oxygen inhaled and carbon dioxide exhaled. The volunteers were allowed to engage in normal daily activities but were not permitted to exercise vigorously. The researchers found that the volunteers burned from 1,930 to 2,625 calories per day.

Each participant was weighed before the test and again 21 months later. The researchers reported that those who burned the lowest number of calories during the test gained more weight than those who burned the greatest number of calories.

The researchers noted that the study did not determine whether the Indians who gained weight were also eating more. But they argued that the results of both experiments suggest that low metabolism and low energy expenditure accounted for most of the subjects' weight gain. Similarities in the metabolism of members of the same family also led the researchers to conclude that the tendency toward low energy expenditure is inherited, a finding that supports other studies showing that there is a link between obesity and heredity.

Obesity and activity level. Babies who are active, even those born to overweight mothers, are less likely to become overweight than babies who are passive, according to a study reported in February 1988 by a team of researchers at the Dunn Nutrition Unit in Cambridge, England, and the Massachusetts Institute of Technology in Cambridge, Mass. The researchers compared the weight, eating habits, and energy expenditure of 6 babies born to thin women and 12 babies born to obese women.

The researchers found that six of the babies became overweight during their first year. All were children of overweight mothers. None of the other babies of overweight mothers or the babies born to thin mothers became overweight.

The researchers determined that both the normal-weight and overweight babies had similar metabolic rates and consumed approximately the same number of calories. The overweight babies, however, burned about 20 per cent fewer calories per week than the normal-weight babies.

The researchers concluded that the overweight babies were fatter because they expended less energy and not because they ate more. And the scientists speculated that lower levels of activity accounted for the lower rate of energy used. They suggested that overweight mothers could help prevent their children from becoming overweight by keeping them active.

Blood pressure guidelines. New guidelines for treating patients with *hypertension* (high blood pressure) were issued in May 1988 by the National Heart, Lung, and Blood Institute in Bethesda. The guidelines were based on the latest scientific research on the causes and treatment of high blood pressure.

The recommendations defined high blood pressure as 140/90. (The first number—the *systolic* pressure—represents the pressure in the blood vessels as the heart muscle contracts. The second number—the *diastolic* pressure—represents the pressure in the blood vessels as the heart muscle relaxes.)

The guidelines suggested a step-by-step treatment plan that includes both drugs and changes in life style. They suggested that physicians avoid drug treatment for patients with diastolic pressures of 90 to 94. Instead, they recommended that doctors urge these

Aspirin: A Potent Weapon Against Heart Attack?

In December 1987, one of the largest medical studies in history was halted three years ahead of schedule—not because the volunteers were in danger but because the result of the study was so dramatic that the researchers saw no point in waiting to announce the good news. The result, announced in January 1988, was that taking one aspirin every other day seems to lower the risk of a first heart attack among men middle-aged and older by almost 50 per cent.

Earlier, smaller studies had shown that low doses of aspirin reduce the likelihood of a second heart attack. Previously, however, there was no evidence that taking aspirin regularly would prevent the first attack.

The study, called the Physicians' Health Study, was organized by a group of researchers led by epidemiologist Charles H. Hennekens of Harvard Medical School in Cambridge, Mass., and Brigham and Women's Hospital in Boston. The volunteers in the study, which began in 1982, were 22,071 healthy male physicians aged 40 to 84. Half the doctors took one 325-milligram aspirin tablet every other day. The other half took a *placebo* (inactive look-alike).

Taking one aspirin every other day seems to greatly lower the risk of a first heart attack among men who are middle-aged or older.

Every six months, the researchers counted the number of volunteers in each group who had suffered a heart attack or a stroke. They found that by late 1987—the fifth year of the study— 189 of the doctors taking the placebo but only 104 of those taking aspirin had suffered a heart attack. The researchers calculated that the risk of heart attack was 47 per cent lower in the aspirin-taking group. In addition, the researchers found that 18 of the heart attack victims in the placebo group died. In contrast, there were only 5 fatal heart attacks in the aspirin group.

Many heart attacks are triggered by the formation of blood clots in the narrow portions of the arteries that carry blood to the heart muscle. Aspirin apparently is effective in helping prevent heart attacks because it reduces the blood's ability to clot.

Aspirin's anticlotting action may be hazardous for some people, however. The researchers found that 80 of the volunteers who took aspirin suffered a stroke, compared with 70 men who took the placebo. The researchers concluded that these numbers were too close to indicate an increased likelihood of stroke among volunteers in the aspirin group.

But when the researchers looked at the types of stroke involved, the results were more worrisome. There are two main types of strokes—one caused by hemorrhage and the other by a blood clot. Hemorrhagic stroke, which is less common than strokes caused by blood clots, is caused by bleeding in the blood vessels of the brain. Ten volunteers in the aspirin group suffered a hemorrhagic stroke, compared with only two in the placebo group. In other words, the volunteers in the aspirin group were five times more likely to suffer a hemorrhagic stroke than those in the placebo group. The researchers emphasized, however, that these findings were based on only a few cases.

The researchers also pointed out that none of the volunteers died of another of aspirin's relatively common side effects—gastrointestinal bleeding.

In their report on the study, Hennekens and his colleagues warned physicians not to prescribe aspirin routinely to all their patients without weighing the possible benefit of preventing a heart attack against the risks of provoking hemorrhagic stroke or gastrointestinal bleeding. In addition, they called attention to a study of 5,139 male physicians in Great Britain, also reported in January, that seemed to challenge their findings. In this study, the rate of heart attacks among volunteers taking 500 milligrams of aspirin daily was not significantly lower than the rate among the volunteers who took only a placebo.   [Beverly Merz]

borderline patients to stop smoking, lose weight if necessary, consume less than six grams of salt and no more than two alcoholic drinks daily, and begin a regular aerobic exercise program. If these life-style changes fail to lower the patient's diastolic blood pressure, the report suggested that the physician prescribe drugs to lower blood pressure.

The guidelines also warned that certain types of drugs do not work well for some groups of patients. The report stressed that physicians should order several kinds of laboratory tests to determine which type of drug is best for a particular patient. There are four basic types of drugs, and each works in a different way. For example, diuretics lower blood pressure by reducing the volume of blood, and calcium antagonists lower blood pressure by reducing the intensity of contractions in blood vessels. For complex reasons, these two drugs are usually most effective for blacks and older people. The other two drugs also reduce contractions in blood vessels, but in different ways.

If one of the four suggested drugs fails to lower the patient's diastolic blood pressure to at least 90, the report advised increasing the dosage of the drug, substituting another drug, or adding a second, third, or even fourth drug.

Shock waves for gallstones. Shock-wave therapy, a technique commonly used to smash kidney stones into fragments that can be passed out of the body through the urinary system, may also be an effective means of eliminating certain types of gallstones, according to a study reported in February 1988 by a team of researchers at the University of Munich in West Germany. Shock-wave therapy, called *lithotripsy*, has eliminated the need for major surgery for many patients suffering from kidney stones. Currently, the most common treatment for gallstones is the surgical removal of the gall bladder. Patients may also be treated with drugs to dissolve the stones. Drug therapy, however, often takes two years.

In lithotripsy, the patient is partially submerged in a water bath. (The water is needed to transmit the shock waves.)

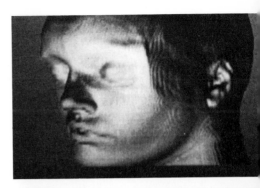

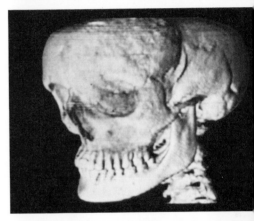

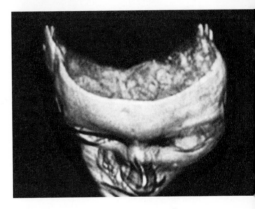

Three-dimensional images of the face of a woman with abnormal bone growth were created by a new computer system that combines two-dimensional "slices" from computerized tomography (CT) scans. The graphics system can rotate 3-D images of soft tissue in any direction to aid doctors in making a diagnosis or planning surgery. The graphics can provide a view of the outer surface of the skin, *top,* the underlying bone, *middle,* or a cross-sectional view of both bone and skin, *above.*

Cholesterol Levels and Recommended Treatment

Level of Cholesterol	Treatment
Desirable level	
Less than 180 milligrams per deciliter of blood (mg/dl) (ages 20-29) Less than 200 mg/dl (ages 30 and over)	None. Cholesterol level should be checked every five years.
Borderline High	
200-239 mg/dl	Reduce total fat intake to less than 30 per cent of daily calories and saturated fat intake to 10 per cent of calories. Begin aerobic exercise (after checking with doctor).
Borderline High with Risk Factors	
200-239 mg/dl plus two or more risk factors (being male, having high blood pressure, smoking cigarettes, having diabetes, being severely obese, having low levels of high density lipoproteins, having a family history of early coronary heart disease)	Restrict saturated fat to 7 per cent of daily calories. If six months of dieting alone fails to reduce cholesterol levels, combine dieting and treatment with cholesterol-lowering drugs.
High	
240 mg/dl or higher	Same as borderline high with risk factors.

Source: Adapted from the National Cholesterol Education Program.

Medical Research

Continued

The first detailed guidelines for identifying and treating people with high blood cholesterol levels were issued in October 1987 by a panel of health experts assembled by the United States government. The panel's standards for determining normal cholesterol levels were stricter than those previously used by many doctors.

A high-energy spark discharged by an underwater electrode produces the shock waves. The waves strike a reflector, which focuses them on a single point in the patient's body.

The West German researchers wanted to determine if lithotripsy could crush gallstones into fragments small enough to be dissolved in the gall bladder by drugs or to be eliminated through the bile duct, through which *bile* (a digestive liquid) flows from the liver and gall bladder to the small intestine. The researchers hoped that the use of lithotripsy could eliminate the need for gall bladder surgery.

They used the technique on 175 patients with gallstones. The patients chosen for the study had no more than three gallstones—with none larger than 30 millimeters (1 inch) in diameter and none containing calcium salts. These salts, which are found in many gallstones, cannot be dissolved by the drugs that are normally used to treat gallstones.

In preparation for the procedure, gallstone-dissolving drugs were given to the patients beginning 12 days before they underwent lithotripsy. The patients received general or local anesthesia and were placed in a water bath. Two ultrasound systems monitored the position of the gallstones from different angles to ensure that the gall bladder, which moves as a person breathes, remained visible. (In ultrasound, reflected sound waves produce images of objects and organs in the body.)

The length of the treatment ranged from 13 to 165 minutes, with an average of about 41 minutes. The treatment ended when large gallstones were no longer visible on the ultrasound monitors or when the patient had received 1,600 shock waves. (Animal studies had shown that a greater number of shock waves could damage the gall bladder.)

The researchers examined the patients with ultrasound every two to six months after the lithotripsy for two years. They found that stones and fragments had disappeared in 30 per cent of the patients after two months;

in 78 per cent after 12 months; and in 93 per cent after 24 months. The patients continued to take gallstone-dissolving drugs for three months after their gallstones disappeared.

The patients suffered few side effects. Some of the patients experienced mild pain as the fragments passed through the bile duct.

The researchers concluded that lithotripsy—in combination with drugs—appears to be a safe and effective treatment for eliminating certain types of gallstones. They noted, however, that the study did not last long enough to determine whether gallstones eliminated in this way will recur.

Drug treatment for breast cancer. All women with *invasive* breast cancer should have drug therapy after surgery, even if the cancer has not spread to the lymph nodes, according to a recommendation issued in May 1988 by the National Cancer Institute (NCI) in Bethesda. In invasive breast cancer, the cancer has spread beyond the original site to other breast tissue. Previously, the NCI had recommended drug therapy only for women whose cancer had spread to the lymph nodes. The drug therapy consists of *chemotherapy*, which kills cancer cells, and *hormonal therapy*, which prevents the cells from growing.

The recommendation was based on three new studies that provided strong evidence that women who were treated with drug therapy after surgery were less likely to develop breast cancer again. The studies showed that breast cancer recurred in up to one-third of women whose cancer was caught in its early stages but who did not receive drug treatment. In contrast, only 16 per cent of the women who received the most aggressive form of chemotherapy—treatment with three types of cancer-killing drugs—suffered a recurrence of their cancer. Hormonal therapy or chemotherapy with two anticancer drugs also prevented a return of the cancer but not as effectively as chemotherapy with the three anticancer drugs. [Beverly Merz]

In WORLD BOOK, see CANCER; HYPERTENSION; WEIGHT CONTROL.

Meteorology

A recurring pattern in the way lightning strikes the ground during thunderstorms was detected by meteorologists Richard T. Orville, Ronald W. Henderson, and Lance F. Bosart at the State University of New York in Albany according to a report published in February 1988. A lightning stroke may carry either positive or negative charges from a thunderstorm cloud to the ground. Negative charges are the most common. Only about 1 to 10 per cent of all lightning flashes have a positive charge, but they are more powerful and are of longer duration. As a result, they are more hazardous. Previous studies have shown that positive strokes are more likely to start fires.

In their study, the Albany researchers measured the location and type of charge of thousands of lightning strokes by using a newly installed network of special detectors. By plotting a map of all the strikes that occurred during one hour of a thunderstorm in northern Florida, these researchers were able to see where the two types of lightning bolts were located.

On the map, all the strikes were scattered around a line that ran from the southwest to the northeast—the direction that the wind traveled during the storm. Although negative strokes were found everywhere along this line, the stronger positive strokes were concentrated downwind.

The Albany meteorologists explained this distribution by noting that in a system of thunderstorms, negative charges tend to develop at the bottom of the clouds and positive charges at the top. The more frequent negative lightning bolts are discharged to the ground soon after the charge forms. Because the speed of winds in the region around a thunderstorm normally increases with increasing height, the faster winds in the higher atmosphere blow the positively charged top of the cloud downwind or ahead of the lower part of the storm. Over time, the cloud becomes tilted with the positive, or top, part of the cloud leading the storm system. The positive charge in the storm tracked by the researchers was blown downwind toward the

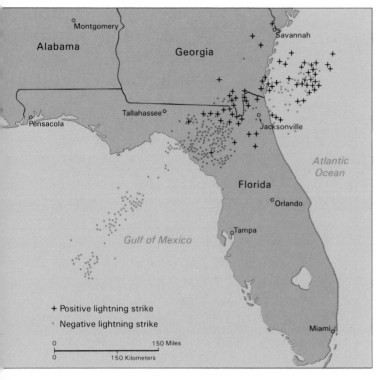

+ Positive lightning strike
· Negative lightning strike

0   150 Miles
0   150 Kilometers

Meteorology

Continued

By using a lightning detector network that recorded the location of positive and negative lightning strokes during a storm over northern Florida, meteorologists at the State University of New York at Albany in February 1988 published a map, *above,* showing that the rare and more dangerous positive lightning bolts occurred downwind as the storm traveled from the southwest to the northeast.

northeast, where the charge from several clouds accumulated to produce the positive lightning bolts.

Now that lightning detector networks cover most of the United States, further studies of this distribution pattern should lead to better predictions of lightning hazards from the more dangerous positive bolts. Lightning causes more deaths annually in the United States than any other weather-related phenomenon, and it is blamed for nearly $1 billion in property damage annually.

Doppler radar continued to grow in importance during the year as a tool for weather forecasters and research meteorologists. In November 1987, the National Weather Service (NWS) of the National Oceanic and Atmospheric Administration signed a contract with UNISYS, an electronics company based in New York City, for 115 Doppler weather radars. The new Doppler radars will be part of the Next Generation Weather Radar program, a 15-year effort by the NWS to develop a state-of-the-art weather ra-

dar system in the United States. The first Doppler radar in this system was scheduled to be installed in autumn 1988 at Kansas City, Mo.

Doppler radar is based on the *Doppler effect,* the apparent change in the frequency of light, sound, or radio waves coming from an object as it moves closer or farther away. Conventional radar can detect the size and location of a thunderstorm by bouncing radio signals off raindrops. Doppler radar can also determine the direction and speed of winds within the storm by detecting the shifts in the wavelengths of the reflected radio signals.

Doppler radar therefore allows meteorologists to observe the airflow within the storm. Some large Doppler radars are so sensitive that they can detect radio waves reflected by tiny insects and dust particles from the "clear air" where raindrops are not present. These echoes allow meteorologists to observe wind-flow patterns outside the rainstorm.

Forecasting severe weather. Research meteorologist James W. Wilson of the

Meteorology

National Center for Atmospheric Research in Boulder, Colo., conducted a seven-week research program from June to August 1987 to evaluate new techniques for providing more detailed and timely forecasting of thunderstorms in and around airports. Thunderstorms can produce many kinds of airflows that are hazardous to aircraft. One of these, called a *microburst*, is a concentrated core of cold air that descends rapidly from the base of a thunderstorm. When this core of air strikes the ground, strong *wind shears* (abrupt changes in wind speed and direction over short distances) are produced as the outflowing air pushes the ground air out of its way. Microbursts are the suspected cause of several accidents that occurred when aircraft encountered these wind shears during take-off or landing.

Wilson's research focused on observing the airflow around Denver's Stapleton International Airport with a large Doppler radar. The radar observations were combined with data collected by research aircraft, weather balloons, and other instruments to learn the details of atmospheric conditions just prior to the formation of thunderstorms around the airport.

Some scientists believe that 80 per cent or more of these hazardous storms form along invisible boundaries that separate slightly different wind currents. Although invisible to the eye, these boundaries can be observed in great detail with Doppler radar. Wilson's research may enable weather forecasters to identify and warn areas at a high risk of being struck by hazardous winds some 30 to 90 minutes in advance of the storm's development.

Climate change in Antarctica? A 10-year study of local climate conditions in Taylor Valley in Victoria Land, Antarctica, was reported in the fall of 1987 by research scientists George M. Simmons, Jr., of Virginia Polytechnic Institute and State University in Blacksburg; Christopher P. McKay of the National Aeronautics and Space Administration's Ames Research Center in Moffett Field, Calif.; and Robert Wharton, Jr., of the Desert Research Institute of the University of Nevada in Las Vegas. The researchers found evidence of profound climatic changes in the Taylor Valley region. During each Southern Hemisphere summer from 1977 to 1987, the scientists visited this region of Antarctica to observe any changes occurring in ice-covered lakes there and to retrieve data from equipment that monitored conditions in the area during the winter. Changes in ice thickness and in layers of sediments on lake bottoms provide clues about climate.

To see firsthand the events occurring in one lake—Lake Hoare—the team used scuba-diving equipment to work under the layer of ice—3 to 5 meters (10 to 16 feet) thick—that covers the lake. They measured ice thickness and lake water levels, observed the organisms living in the lake, and collected samples of those organisms. In the 10 years they have been monitoring Lake Hoare, there has been a 2-meter (6½-foot) thinning of the ice cover and a rise in the lake's water level. Scientists noted similar changes in other lakes in the valley.

The scientists also studied samples from sediment on the bottom of Lake Hoare and other lakes. There is a link between the build-up of sediments and the thickness of the ice cover. The thickness of the ice cover controls the amount of sunlight reaching the organisms living in the lakes, and this, in turn, determines how many organisms will thrive. The ice thickness also controls the rate at which sand and a type of soil called *loess* filter down through the ice. The number of organisms living in the lake and the amount of material filtering through the ice each year determine the thickness of the sediment layer deposited on the lake bottom for that year. Thus, changes in the thickness of the ice cover are recorded in the layers of sediment on the lake bottoms.

The layers of sediment at the bottom of Lake Hoare preserve at least 10,000 years of local climatic history. According to the sediment record, the 2-meter thinning observed over the 10-year period by Simmons and his colleagues typically occurs over a period of thousands of years. This indicates a recent, profound climatic change in the area.   [John T. Snow]

In WORLD BOOK, see METEOROLOGY; WEATHER.

New findings supporting the view that the use of cocaine may cause harmful, long-term changes in the brain were announced in November 1987 by neuroscientists at the National Institute of Mental Health in Bethesda, Md. The researchers—Farouk Karoum, Ralph Fawcett, and Richard J. Wyatt—discovered a deficiency of an important chemical in the brains of rats that had been given heavy doses of the drug.

The scientists dosed the rats with cocaine twice daily for periods up to three weeks. Afterward, they studied the rats' brains for the presence of *neurotransmitters*, chemicals that transmit impulses between brain cells. They found that *dopamine*, an important neurotransmitter, was greatly reduced in the animals' brains. The loss was particularly severe in an area called the *frontal cortex*, which—in the human brain—is involved in thinking, reasoning, and understanding. A serious dopamine deficiency was also evident in the *hypothalamus*, a brain region involved in regulating hormones that control growth and sexual maturation.

In another experiment, the researchers gave cocaine to rats for one week. They then let the animals live normally, with no further doses of cocaine, for six weeks before examining their brains. As before, there was a loss of dopamine in the brain tissues.

The scientists said cocaine may cause the same sorts of changes in the human brain. They warned that the drug, by suppressing the production of dopamine and other neurotransmitters, might lessen the ability to think and disrupt hormone balance. Moreover, they said, such changes may persist even if cocaine use is stopped.

Brain-implant surgery reevaluated. A new surgical technique for the treatment of Parkinson's disease has produced less-dramatic results than had been hoped for, a number of United States doctors reported in 1988. As a result, the procedure, which involves implanting cells from the adrenal glands into the brain, was being reevaluated at U.S. medical centers.

The technique was reported in April 1987 by surgeons in Mexico City, Mexico, who reported good results with several Parkinson's disease patients. Soon afterward, a number of physicians in the United States began doing the operation. The procedure supposedly increased the production of dopamine, which is deficient in the brains of Parkinson's victims.

The Mexican doctors said in 1988 that their patients continued to show improvement a year after surgery. American physicians who tried the procedure, however, said while it provided some relief from the disease, patients still required medication.

Meanwhile in 1988, the Mexico City doctors had begun treating Parkinson's sufferers with implants of brain cells from fetuses. They reported in January that the first two patients to receive the treatment—a 35-year-old woman and a 50-year-old man—experienced significant relief from their symptoms.

Many U.S. physicians tended to believe the claims of success with fetal tissue. Neuroscientists have speculated that fetal brain cells would be superior to other kinds of tissues in stimulating the production of dopamine and other brain chemicals. Research with fetal-brain implants in animals has yielded promising results.

The operations announced by the Mexican surgeons in 1988 marked the first time that tissue from the brain of one human being had been implanted in the brain of another human being. The landmark surgery set off a debate in the United States—where similar operations were being considered at several major medical centers—on the ethics of using aborted fetuses as a source of transplant tissue.

In March, the Administration of President Ronald Reagan ordered the National Institutes of Health (NIH) in Bethesda to hold off on treating Parkinson's patients with fetal cells until the ethical issues were resolved. A government committee will decide whether the NIH will be allowed to proceed with its research plans or to fund private fetal-cell research.

The importance of touching. Stimulation and physical contact in infancy may help preserve mental powers in old age. That finding, based on studies with rats, was reported in February 1988 by neuroscientist Michael J. Meaney of McGill University in Montreal, Canada, and his colleagues.

Scanning the Dyslexic Brain

Posple with dyslexia, a neurological disorber, eer many sdrow, letters, and numbers in reverse and or have great bifficulty with reabing and writing.

From 5 to 20 per cent of the United States population suffers from *dyslexia*, certain severe reading and writing disabilities. Dyslexia is often hereditary, though it can also be caused by a brain injury. Language is processed differently in the dyslexic brain than in the normal brain, causing dyslexics to see many words and letters in reverse. Printing in a book might look like the sentence above to a typical dyslexic. Neuroscientists are beginning to use brain scans to look for structural differences between the normal brain and the dyslexic brain.

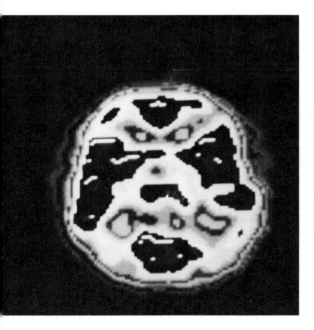 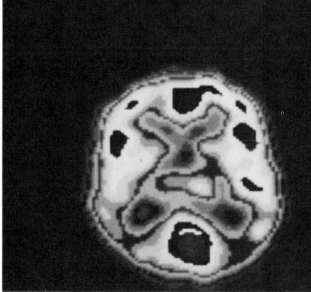

A technique called positron emission tomography (PET) scanning reveals differences in the brains of two volunteers as they read. The normal person's brain, *above left,* shows much more activity (dark patches) than the dyslexic person's brain, *above right,* in areas involved with language.

The researchers raised two groups of rats in the laboratory from infancy to the age of 2 years—old age for a rat. Both groups of animals received identical care, except that a researcher handled the members of one group for 15 minutes every day during the first 3 weeks of life. Rats in the other group were not handled.

After two years, the scientists studied the rats' brains under a microscope. They found that the rats that were not handled in infancy had lost more *neurons* (brain cells) than the handled rats had lost. Most of the losses occurred in a brain area called the *hippocampus*, a structure known to be involved in learning and memory. And, indeed, the rats that were handled in infancy had been much more able in old age to learn and remember tasks, such as finding their way through a maze, than the other rats.

Apparently, being handled early in life helped change the ability of the rats' brains to handle certain hormones released in the brain in response to stress. In the other group of rats, these hormones probably caused the loss of neurons in the hippocampus, impairing learning ability.

Further research of this kind may help improve our understanding of human aging.

Brain-destroying seeds. Many brain scientists suspect that several degenerative diseases of the nervous system may be caused by *toxins* (poisons) in the environment. That theory received a boost from research findings reported in July 1987 by neurotoxicologist Peter S. Spencer and his co-workers at the Albert Einstein College of Medicine in New York City.

The researchers studied a nervous-system disease that afflicts people in Guam and at least two other areas of the western Pacific Ocean. This disorder is called amyotrophic lateral sclerosis-Parkinsonism-dementia complex (ALS-PD) because it has the features of three other nervous-system diseases: *amyotrophic lateral sclerosis* (ALS, also known as Lou Gehrig's disease), which causes a loss of muscle coordination and is usually fatal; Parkinson's

Neuroscience

Continued

disease, a chronic condition of tremors and muscle weakness; and Alzheimer's disease, a type of *dementia* (a progressive loss of memory and reasoning ability).

The disease affecting the people of the western Pacific is neither inherited nor transmissible, and it is becoming increasingly rare. For those reasons, researchers have theorized that the disease is caused by an environmental factor that is peculiar to the life style of people in the affected areas—a factor that is also becoming less prevalent.

Spencer and his associates reported that they had found just such a factor in the seeds of the cycad, a large plant similar to the palm tree. The people of Guam ate large amounts of cycad seeds during the 1940's, when World War II created food shortages in the Pacific Islands. In addition, the seeds were used in folk medicine in all three areas where the disease has occurred. But the use of cycad seeds has become less common since the 1950's.

Cycad seeds contain a toxin known as BMAA. When the researchers fed this substance to monkeys, the animals developed neurological symptoms similar to those of the victims of the islanders' disease. The monkeys also suffered a loss of brain cells. These findings suggest that ALS, Parkinson's disease, and Alzheimer's disease might also be caused, at least in part, by environmental toxins.

Word processing. A new application of *positron emission tomography* (PET) to the study of how the brain processes language and speech was reported in February 1988 by neurologist Marcus Raichle and his co-workers at Washington University School of Medicine in St. Louis, Mo. The researchers found that such processing is more complex than anyone had suspected.

PET is a method for producing images of the brain's chemical activity. The technique uses a radioactive form of a substance, usually the sugar *glucose*, that the body normally uses to carry out biochemical activities. Injected into a blood vessel, the radioactive substance makes its way to the brain, where it is quickly absorbed and used by brain tissues. The radioactive glucose emits *positrons*—positively charged electrons. When the positrons

encounter electrons, the two kinds of particles destroy each other and produce tiny bursts of high-energy radiation called *gamma rays.*

A special computerized scanner detects the gamma radiation in various parts of the brain. Brain areas showing the greatest amount of gamma radiation are using the most glucose and therefore are doing the most work.

Raichle and his colleagues injected 17 volunteers with radioactive oxygen in water. The volunteers then took part in several tests. In one test they were asked to read or listen to single words. In another, they had to think of or say words associated with other words—for example, to say "eat" or "sweet" when they heard the word *cake.* During each test, a PET scanner recorded brain activity.

The researchers found that some areas of the brain were active during all the tasks but that certain of those areas were utilized only in specific kinds of language tasks, such as reading or speaking. Their findings showed that learning how the brain handles the full range of language use will be a challenging task.

High IQ, low energy. Another PET-scan study, also reported in February 1988, shed new light on links between the workings of the brain and intelligence. Psychologist Richard Haier of the University of California at Irvine said his findings indicate that the smarter one is, the less brain energy one uses in solving mental tasks requiring abstract reasoning.

Haier gave eight volunteers a nonverbal test requiring them to match various abstract designs. As each person was tested, a PET scanner monitored glucose usage in the volunteer's brain.

With all the volunteers, the PET scans showed increased activity in brain areas involved in abstract thinking. Unexpectedly, however, the brains of those who performed most poorly on the test were much more active than the brains of the higher scorers. This result seemed to show that people of higher intelligence are able to use their brain more efficiently than other people.   [George Adelman]

In WORLD BOOK, see BRAIN; NERVOUS SYSTEM.

Nobel Prizes

In October 1987, the Royal Academy of Sciences in Stockholm, Sweden, awarded Nobel Prizes in chemistry and physics to two scientists from the United States, one from France, one from Switzerland, and one from West Germany. Also in October, the Karolinska Institute in Stockholm awarded the Nobel Prize for physiology or medicine to a Japanese scientist. Each of the three prizes included a cash award of about $340,000, which was divided if the prize was shared.

Chemistry. The Nobel Prize for chemistry was shared by Donald J. Cram of the University of California at Los Angeles; Jean-Marie Lehn of the Louis Pasteur University in Strasbourg, France; and Charles J. Pedersen, who until his retirement in 1969 worked for the U.S. firm of E. I. du Pont de Nemours & Company. The three were honored for their research in *host-guest chemistry*, the means by which molecules selectively play "host" to other "guest" molecules, recognizing and binding with them like a key fitting into a lock.

Pedersen laid the foundations with his discovery of compounds called *crown ethers* that couple with electrically charged atoms called *ions*. Cram and Lehn, working independently, built on Pedersen's studies by producing artificial "host" molecules with cavities of the right size and shape to attract and hold specific "guest" molecules.

Host-guest chemistry has many possible applications. It may be used, for example, to isolate molecules of valuable or toxic substances from the earth.

Physics. The Nobel Prize for physics was awarded to Swiss physicist K. Alex Müller and West German crystallographer J. Georg Bednorz of the International Business Machines Corporation (IBM) Research Laboratory in Zurich, Switzerland, for their discovery of relatively high-temperature superconductivity. *Superconductivity* is the ability of some materials, when cooled to a point called the *critical* or *transition temperature*, to conduct electric current without resistance, thus wasting almost no energy.

Biologist Susumu Tonegawa, *right,* of M.I.T. in Cambridge, Mass., won the 1987 Nobel Prize in physiology or medicine for research on the genetics of the immune system. Crystallographer J. Georg Bednorz and physicist K. Alex Müller, *bottom right,* of the IBM Research Laboratory in Zurich, Switzerland, shared the prize in physics for discovering a new *superconductor,* a material that carries electric current without resistance.

Previously, scientists had produced superconductivity only in metals or alloys cooled to near absolute zero, or $-273.15°C$ ($-459.67°F$.). The cooling was done with liquid helium, which is expensive. Müller and Bednorz found a ceramic material made of the elements barium, lanthanum, copper, and oxygen that became superconducting at a critical temperature of about $-243°C$ ($-405°F$.), about 12 Celsius degrees (22 Fahrenheit degrees) higher than any superconductor then known.

The two scientists' findings, published in January 1986, inspired an explosion of research. Within months, other scientists had found ceramics that became superconducting at a level of cooling possible with liquid nitrogen, which is cheaper and easier to handle than liquid helium.

Researchers are working to make the brittle ceramic superconductors pliable enough to be shaped into wires and other electrical parts without breaking. If they succeed, the new materials could have important applications in faster computers, more efficient electrical generators and power lines, and high-speed maglev trains suspended off the track by superconducting electromagnets. In the Special Reports section, see PLUGGING INTO SUPERCONDUCTORS.

Physiology or medicine. The Nobel Prize for physiology or medicine went to Susumu Tonegawa, a Japanese-born molecular biologist at the Massachusetts Institute of Technology in Cambridge, for his research on the genetics of the immune system.

Tonegawa discovered how the body's immune cells, with a limited number of genes, can produce tailor-made antibodies to an almost limitless number of disease-producing agents. He showed that the immune cells rearrange pieces of their genes to make many different antibodies, each fitted to fight a specific infection. His work could help make more effective vaccines and find cures for such diseases as cancer and AIDS (acquired immune deficiency syndrome). [Sara Dreyfuss]

In WORLD BOOK, see NOBEL PRIZES.

Nutrition

Nutrition research in 1987 and 1988 focused on dietary changes designed to reduce the risk of heart disease and cancer.

Cholesterol and heart attacks. At the American Heart Association meeting in March 1988, scientists reported the first convincing evidence that cholesterol in the diet can increase the risk of a fatal heart attack. Cholesterol is a fatty substance found in many foods, such as butter, eggs, and meat—and also manufactured by the body's own cells.

Preventive medicine specialist Richard B. Shekelle of the University of Texas School of Public Health in Houston and cardiologist Jeremiah Stamler of Northwestern University's medical school in Chicago studied the diets, blood cholesterol levels, and number of heart attack deaths of male employees of Western Electric Company in Chicago over a 25-year period starting in 1957 and 1958. The researchers found that men who consumed more than 500 milligrams of cholesterol per day (about the amount contained in two eggs) had a 22 per cent higher risk of suffering a fatal heart attack than men who consumed 150 milligrams or less.

Meat fat consumption. There may be some confusion among consumers about how to lower their intake of meat fat, according to an October 1987 report by anthropologist William L. Rathje and dietitian E. E. Ho of the University of Arizona in Tucson. Using research methods developed for archaeology, Rathje and Ho recorded discarded food wrappers and food scraps they found in household garbage in Tucson from 1979 to 1985. Such items provide a good indication of general dietary patterns.

The researchers found no change in the amount of red-meat fat discarded from 1979 to 1982. In 1983, the rate of discarded fat nearly doubled and then stabilized at that level. The purchase of red meat with visible fat, such as chops, steaks, and roasts, also declined from 1982 to 1985. But the purchase of meat with hidden fat, such as ground beef, sausage, and luncheon

Fake Fats May Transform Our Diets

Low-calorie, cholesterol-free fat substitutes may become available in the next few years to diet-conscious consumers in the United States. These products, which will be sold under the brand names Simplesse and Olestra, are designed to replace conventional fats in many desserts, snack products, and other fattening foods. When made with the fake fats, such foods have much the same taste and texture as before but only a small fraction of the calories.

Simplesse, announced in January 1988 by the NutraSweet Company of Skokie, Ill., is made from proteins extracted from egg whites or milk. In a patented process, the proteins are gently heated and blended into spherical particles so tiny that more than 50 billion of them will fit into a teaspoon. The microscopic protein globules roll easily over one another, giving them a smooth and creamy texture. In the mouth, the protein blend feels like fat. "This creates the smoothness and richness we know as fat," said NutraSweet Chairman Robert Shapiro. "It's really an illusion of the taste buds."

That illusion, however, may not be totally convincing. Jeanne Voltz, a cookbook author who tasted ice cream made with Simplesse, remarked, "There was a taste that was missing and a slight granular quality."

Simplesse contains just $1\frac{1}{3}$ calories per gram, compared with 9 calories per gram for fats. Foods made with the fat substitute are thus substantially lower in calories than their traditional counterparts. Ice cream lovers will be happy to know that 120 milliliters (4 fluid ounces) of ice cream, normally 283 calories, will contain only 130 calories—a 54 per cent reduction—when the butterfat is replaced by Simplesse. Other foods offer even greater reductions in calories. For example, a 30-milliliter (1-ounce) dollop of sour cream, which ordinarily contains 26 calories, contains just 10 calories with Simplesse—a difference of 62 per cent—while a pat of margarine drops from 36 calories to 8 with Simplesse, a 78 per cent reduction.

Simplesse will be used mostly in dairy products, salad dressings, and mayonnaise. Foods that require cooking cannot be made with Simplesse because high heat causes the product to congeal, just as the white of an egg stiffens when the egg is boiled.

Olestra, developed by the Procter & Gamble Company of Cincinnati, Ohio, can be subjected to baking and frying and thus may be used in such products as French fries, crackers, and cookies. Olestra is a *sucrose polyester*, a compound formed by combining *sucrose* (table sugar) with long, chainlike molecules called fatty acids. Although it looks and tastes much like ordinary vegetable shortening, Olestra cannot be digested because its molecules are too large to be broken down by human digestive enzymes. Since Olestra is not absorbed by the body, it is calorie-free. A serving of French fries made with Olestra contains only the calories of the potatoes—approximately 130 calories, compared with about 220 for regular fries.

In addition to being lower in calories, foods made with Simplesse and Olestra are free of cholesterol, an important consideration for people concerned about the danger of heart disease. An adviser to the NutraSweet Company, nutritional biochemist Vernon Young of Massachusetts Institute of Technology in Cambridge, predicted that Simplesse would "enable consum-

Simplesse is made of proteins, obtained from milk or egg whites, that are processed into a blend of slippery microscopic globules with the "mouth feel" of fats. Simplesse is destroyed by heating, so it will be used only in foods such as ice cream and mayonnaise.

ers to more easily meet recommended fat-reduction goals" set forth by the American Heart Association, the American Medical Association, and other health organizations. And Procter & Gamble claims that Olestra actually lowers the amount of cholesterol in the blood.

Procter & Gamble's research suggests that as Olestra moves through the digestive tract, it binds to molecules of cholesterol from other foods, or cholesterol produced by the liver, and transports them out of the body, thereby lowering blood cholesterol levels. Physician Charles Glueck, director of the Cholesterol Center at the Jewish Hospital of Cincinnati, who has conducted extensive clinical trials of Olestra, said the product, "when given in addition to or instead of dietary fat, reduces serum [blood] cholesterol by as much as 20 per cent." Most important, he added, the reduction occurs in the type of cholesterol molecules that are known as *low-density lipoproteins*, which research indicates are the primary culprit in the development of heart disease.

That apparent benefit, however, raises the possibility that fat-soluble vitamins—vitamins A, D, E, and K—might also bind to Olestra and thus be excreted from the body. If so, using the fat substitute might lead to the development of vitamin deficiencies.

There are other concerns as well. Some researchers think that because Olestra passes through the intestines without being absorbed, it might have a laxative effect on some people, similar to mineral oil. Even more worrisome are Procter & Gamble's findings that Olestra causes tumors and liver changes in laboratory rats.

These health concerns are causing the U.S. Food and Drug Administration (FDA) to take a close look at Olestra before it approves the fat substitute for sale in the United States. The FDA has also withheld its approval from Simplesse. NutraSweet officials had originally assumed that because Simplesse is an all-natural product, they would not need FDA clearance to market it. The FDA, however, disagreed and is requiring the company to test Simplesse on animals. Thus, it may be months or even several years before products made with either of these fat substitutes are available to consumers. In the meantime, at least three other companies in the United States are developing fat substitutes of their own.

Nutrition experts question whether any of these products would actually help overweight Americans slim down. The knowledge that once-fattening foods now contain fewer calories might simply encourage many people to eat larger amounts of their favorite foods than they did before.   [Constance Kies]

meat, either held constant or increased during this period.

Nutrition education has stressed the desirability of discarding, rather than eating, the visible fat on meat. The researchers speculated that many individuals follow the recommendations about obvious fat but are unaware of the hidden fat in some processed meat products.

Cholesterol guidelines. In October 1987, a federal panel provided physicians, other health professionals, and educators with the first authoritative guidelines for identifying and treating adult patients with high blood cholesterol. The panel's report, issued by the National Cholesterol Education Program of the National Heart, Lung, and Blood Institute in Bethesda, Md., marked the first time that a national panel of experts had reached a consensus recommendation on cholesterol treatment.

According to the panel's guidelines, desirable blood cholesterol levels are those below 200 milligrams per deciliter of blood. Levels between 200 and 239 milligrams per deciliter are borderline. Cholesterol levels in excess of 240 are considered too high.

The panel called for all adults to be tested to determine their blood cholesterol levels and for those testing borderline or high to modify their diet. Such people should reduce their total fat intake to 30 per cent or less of the daily calorie intake, and no more than one-third of that should be in the form of *saturated fats*, the type found in animal and dairy products. Cholesterol intake should be restricted to 300 milligrams or less per day—a little more than the amount in one egg.

If these dietary changes fail to lower blood cholesterol to desirable levels within six months, the panel recommends stricter reduction of dietary fat. In addition, the person's physician should prescribe cholesterol-lowering drugs.

Dietary fiber intake of Americans may be much less than previously estimated, according to a report by nutritionist Elaine Lanza and her research associates at the National Cancer Institute in Bethesda, Md., in November 1987. Fiber, the part of plant foods that the body does not digest, is

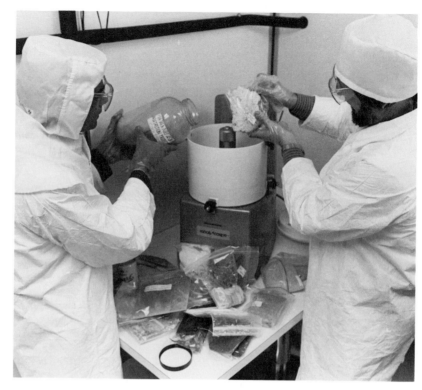

Nutritionists at the National Bureau of Standards in Gaithersburg, Md., pour into a blender the food and beverages that make up a typical daily diet in the United States. Part of the mixture will be analyzed for *trace elements*—minerals such as iron and zinc present in small amounts in the diet. The rest of it will be freeze-dried as a record of the typical 1980's American diet. This is part of an international effort to analyze and record the nutrients in typical diets of 12 nations.

Nutrition

Continued

thought to protect against diabetes, heart disease, obesity, colon cancer, and many intestinal disorders.

Lanza and her colleagues used data from the Second National Health and Nutrition Examination Survey, covering the years 1976 to 1980—a study by the federal government that gives an accurate sample of the entire U.S. population aged 6 months to 74 years, except for individuals living away from home in hospitals, prisons, or similar institutions. The average fiber intake of men was 12.9 grams (0.455 ounce) per day, and that of women was 9.4 grams (0.332 ounce) per day, far less than the 20 grams (0.7 ounce) per day recommended by nutritionists. White men and women had higher fiber intakes than did black men and women. Fiber intake also increased with advancing age.

Carotenoids against cancer. Yellow-orange pigments called *carotenoids*, found in such foods as carrots, squash, apricots, and spinach, may reduce cancer risk. The anticancer benefits of carotenoids were evaluated at a Boston

meeting of scientists in July 1987. According to biochemist Andrija Kornhauser of the U.S. Food and Drug Administration, people with a high intake of carotenoid-containing foods—dark green and yellow fruits and vegetables—have a lower incidence of cancer, particularly skin cancer, than those who eat small amounts of these foods. Animal studies have shown that carotenoids may also reduce the rate of growth of colon and lung cancers.

Nutritionists speculate that carotenoids may prevent cancer because they are *antioxidants*—that is, they prevent chemicals from reacting with oxygen. Research indicates that certain chemicals cause cancer only after combining with oxygen. Carotenoids may thus counteract the harmful, cancer-producing effects of smoking or other environmental factors. Few scientists recommend carotenoid supplements for possible cancer prevention, but there is general agreement that carotenoids are not harmful, even in relatively large doses.   [Constance Kies]

In WORLD BOOK, see NUTRITION.

Oceanography

Deep ocean waters can be swift and stormy, moving far less gently and steadily over the sea floor than was previously believed, according to a February 1988 report. Oceanographers Thomas F. Gross of the Skidaway Institute of Oceanography in Savannah, Ga.; Albert J. Williams III of Woods Hole Oceanographic Institution in Woods Hole, Mass.; and Arthur R. M. Nowell of the University of Washington in Seattle based their findings on data obtained from September 1985 to September 1986 with instruments secured to the sea floor at a depth of 4,880 meters (16,170 feet) in the northwest Atlantic Ocean off Nova Scotia, Canada. The instruments measured the speed and turbulence of water currents and the amount of sediments stirred up by those currents at five different levels on and above the seabed.

The measurements enabled the researchers to identify large *storms* (major disruptions of the normal current flow) on the seabed. A major disruption in June 1986 confirmed that a lo-cal storm could move large amounts of sediments and cause major alterations in the sea floor. Scientists have linked these storms to *eddies* (whirlpools) that swirl in the upper waters of the ocean and transfer part of their energy to the sea floor.

Understanding storm activity is important before the seabed can be used for purposes that require long-term stability. For example, the ocean floor has been proposed as a dump site for nuclear and toxic wastes. It will now be necessary to determine whether seabed storms could stir up and disperse waste-laden sediments. It is also important that military planners know whether seabed listening devices used to track submarines would be damaged by such storms.

Formation of the Himalaya. Sample cores of sea-floor sediments taken by scientists on board the research drill ship *JOIDES Resolution* have provided new evidence about the age and evolution of the world's highest mountain range, the Himalaya. Chief scientists James R. Cochran of Columbia Uni-

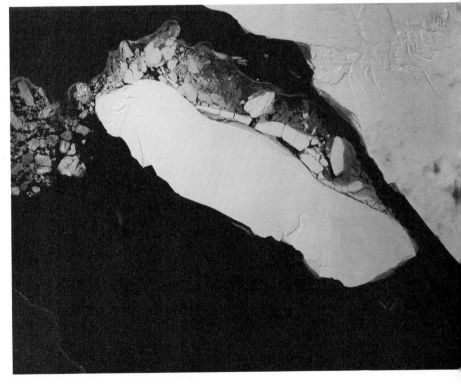

A giant iceberg 153 kilometers (95 miles) in length floats off the coast of Antarctica's Ross Ice Shelf in this satellite photograph taken in October 1987. The breakaway of this ice mass entirely eliminated the Bay of Whales. Oceanographers were concerned that the breakup of so much ice might be a sign of a climate change in Antarctica.

Oceanography

Continued

A new deep-sea research vehicle, developed by the University of California's Scripps Institution of Oceanography in San Diego, conducted its first scientific operations in August 1987. Named RUM III—as the third in a series of Remote Underwater Manipulators—the crewless vehicle is operated by remote control and can explore at depths of up to 6,000 meters (20,000 feet).

versity's Lamont-Doherty Geological Observatory in Palisades, N.Y., and Dorrick A. V. Stow of Nottingham University in England and their colleagues reported in December 1987 that based on the ages of fossils found in sediment cores, the Himalaya formed at least 20 million years ago, or about 10 million years earlier than geologists had previously suspected.

The sediments in which the fossils were found were originally part of the Himalaya, but as the mountains eroded, the sediments were washed into the Ganges and Brahmaputra rivers, which carried more than 3.3 billion metric tons (3 billion short tons) of rocks, gravel, and soils down to the Bay of Bengal. The sediments then spread along the sea floor, creating a region of deep sediments known as the *Bengal fan*, which covers 3 million square kilometers (1.1 million square miles) and stretches southward more than 2,500 kilometers (1,550 miles). During July and August 1987, the crew of the *Resolution* drilled a series of holes up to 1,000 meters (3,300 feet)

deep into the sea floor in this region.

Tiny fossils contained in cores taken from the edge of the Bengal fan indicated that the formation of the Himalaya may have taken place in several stages. In the first stage, about 20 million years ago, mountains formed but then eroded almost completely. The mountains then re-formed about 4 million years ago, setting in motion again the long cycle of mountain erosion and river runoff, to deposit sediments on the sea floor.

Deep rock. During November and December 1987, researchers on board the *Resolution* recovered more than 435 meters (1,426 feet) of rock core samples from the deepest layer of Earth's *crust*—the outermost layer of Earth's surface. Drilling in remote waters of the Indian Ocean, the crew retrieved a rock core from *magma* (molten rock) that formed more than 12 million years ago. As the molten rock cooled, it formed a coarse crystalline rock called *gabbro* that comprises the ocean crust's deepest layer.

Previously, marine geologists had

Oceanography

Continued

collected gabbro by dredging the sea floor, but this method jumbled and mixed together the samples they collected. By drilling into the gabbro, however, the geologists were able to collect a continuous section that provided a record of how the gabbro formed. Marine geologists will use these samples to determine how magma rises from deep within Earth's interior, how it cools, then hardens, and how the circulation of cold seawater changes the heated rocks inside Earth's crust.

Marine snow. Particles of plant debris and fecal matter from marine animals—called *marine snow* because, to an underwater observer, they resemble a snowstorm—may create nutrient-rich areas in ocean waters that are otherwise poor in nutrients. From 1987 to 1988, marine biologists Alice L. Alldredge of the University of California at Santa Barbara and Yehuda Cohen of Hebrew University in Jerusalem, Israel, analyzed snow particles collected from the Santa Barbara Channel.

Based on chemical studies, the researchers determined that a microscopic but nutrient-rich environment surrounds these particles. As the naturally sticky particles fall through the water, they grow—in much the same way a snowball grows as it rolls through real snow. The particles attract organisms such as amebas and protozoans, which feed on the rich nutrients surrounding the marine snow.

These particles, some of which grow to a size of several centimeters, may play an important role in the ecology of the oceans, according to the researchers. The nutrient-rich environment that surrounds the particles acts like an oasis where microscopic plants and animals can feed, even in waters where other nutrients—such as phosphate, ammonium, and nitrate—are scarce. Marine snow also provides nutrition for organisms at higher levels in the marine food chain, such as certain kinds of shellfish. Finally, marine snow helps remove pollutants from the oceans by attracting such heavy toxic metals as lead.   [Lauriston R. King]

In WORLD BOOK, see OCEAN.

Paleontology

Reports published in 1988 on rare fossilized reptile embryos—among the first ever found—have provided new details of the early life cycles of ancient reptiles. In February 1988, paleontologist P. Martin Sander of the Paleontological Institute and Museum of the University of Zurich in Switzerland reported the discovery in southern Switzerland of a tiny fossil embryo of a nothosaur, an extinct lizardlike reptile that lived about 225 million years ago, during the Triassic Period.

The nothosaur, which grew up to 30 centimeters (12 inches) in length, was an aquatic animal with paddlelike limbs that lived in the shallow seas that covered much of Europe at that time. The embryonic nothosaur is the smallest fossil reptile ever found.

More dinosaur eggs. A study of 26 dinosaur embryos found in their shells was reported in March 1988 by paleontologist John R. Horner of the Museum of the Rockies in Bozeman, Mont., and anatomist David B. Weishampel of Johns Hopkins University in Baltimore. The eggs containing the embryos, which are about 75 million years old, were found in the mid-1980's in Montana in fossilized nests. The nests were regularly spaced mounds of earth that had been lined with vegetation. Horner and Weishampel studied the embryos using a computerized tomography (CT) scanner, an X-ray device usually employed to provide cross-sectional images of the inside of the body. The scientists also partially removed the shell from one of the embryos.

The embryos belonged to two types of dinosaurs. The first is a previously unknown species of dinosaur the scientists named *orodromeus* (mountain runner). This dinosaur was a type of hypsilophodont—a small, agile dinosaur that walked upright on two legs. An examination of the embryos revealed that their limb joints were fully developed, suggesting that these dinosaurs matured rapidly and were able to scamper about in search of food shortly after hatching.

Horner and Weishampel also found fossilized embryos of *maiasaura*, a

297

A scientist holds a 30-million-year-old wing bone from the largest known flying sea bird. The bird, whose discovery in Charleston, S.C., was reported in November 1987, weighed nearly 40 kilograms (90 pounds) and had a wingspan of about 5.5 meters (18 feet). The bird apparently used its huge wings to glide long distances over the ocean.

duck-billed dinosaur. Horner and another colleague found the first known fossils of this dinosaur in 1978. The limb joints of the maiasaura embryos were not fully developed. According to the scientists, this finding supports a theory proposed earlier by Horner—based on maiasaura's growth rate and nesting habits—that this dinosaur spent a good deal of its early life in the nest, where it was fed by its parents.

Slowly changing trilobites. A detailed study of ancient fossil trilobites reported in November 1987 has provided new support for the classical view of evolution as a process that occurs slowly and steadily over time. Trilobites, now extinct, were small shelled animals distantly related to modern horseshoe crabs.

The idea that evolutionary changes occur in spurts, not steadily, was suggested in the early 1970's by paleontologists Stephen J. Gould of Harvard University in Cambridge, Mass., and Niles Eldredge of the American Museum of Natural History in New York City. They theorized that new species arise suddenly within short periods of time that are followed by immensely longer spans when little or no evolutionary change takes place.

The new findings, reported by paleontologist Peter R. Sheldon of Trinity College in Dublin, Ireland, were based on a study of 15,000 fossil trilobites found in rocks from Wales in Great Britain. The rocks spanned a 3-million-year period, from 465 million to 468 million years ago. Sheldon observed that the number of "ribs" on the tails of eight types of trilobites increased over time and that in general the increase was gradual.

Oldest fish. The discovery in southern Bolivia of the remains of the oldest known fossil fish was reported in January 1988 by an international team of paleontologists headed by Philippe Janvier of the French National Research Center in Paris. The fossils were found in slabs of rock dating from 470 million years ago, when much of what is now Bolivia was covered by shallow seas. The fossil fish were related to modern lampreys. The fish were about 46 centimeters (18 inches) long and 15 centimeters (6 inches) wide.

Paleontology

Continued

A Pygmy Terror
A fossilized dinosaur skull, *right,* mislabeled when it was found in Montana in the early 1940's, was identified in April 1988 as that of a pygmy tyrannosaur, a previously unknown type of meat-eating tyrannosaur. The pygmy tyrannosaur, which was named *nanotyrannus,* was 5 meters (17 feet) long and weighed about 450 kilograms (1,000 pounds). The drawing, *above,* shows the nanotyrannus with some present-day meat-eaters—a Siberian tiger, a polar bear, and a man—and with a normal-sized tyrannosaurus rex.

Paleontology

Continued

The discovery of a 40-million-year-old frog encased in amber was reported in September 1987. The frog, found in a mine in the Dominican Republic, is the only known frog specimen preserved in this way. The frog, along with other animals from the same area also found entombed in amber, has provided evidence that a diverse group of animals occupied the Caribbean islands far earlier than scientists had believed.

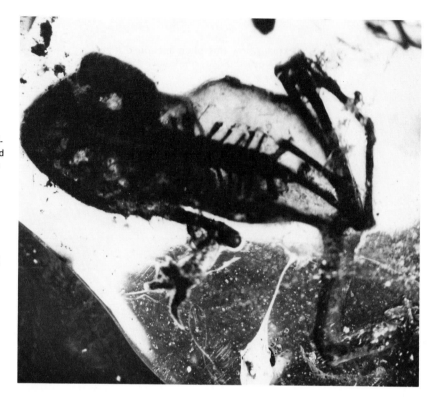

Flap over archaeopteryx. New evidence confirming the authenticity of a fossil representing what may be the oldest bird was published in August 1987 by the British Museum in London, which owns the fossil. In 1985, astronomers Sir Fred Hoyle and N. Chandra Wickramasinghe of University College in Cardiff, Wales, charged that the 140-million-year-old fossil of a creature called archaeopteryx was a forgery. They claimed that the feather impressions on the fossil were added in the mid-1800's, when the fossil was found, by pressing modern feathers into a mixture of ground-up limestone and organic glue laid over the genuine fossil of a featherless dinosaur.

In response, the museum in 1986 published a detailed study of the fossil that rebutted the scientists' charges. The latest evidence, published in 1987, consists of photographs of archaeopteryx taken under ultraviolet light. When exposed to this kind of light, organic materials, such as bones, *fluoresce* (give off light). Museum researchers found, however, that the feather impressions on the fossil did not fluoresce, proving that they could not have been made using organic glue, as Hoyle and Wickramasinghe charged.

Early bird. The discovery of a previously unknown fossil bird slightly younger than archaeopteryx was reported in February 1988 by a team of scientists headed by paleontologist J. S. Sanz of the Autonomous University in Madrid, Spain. The fossil was found in Spain in rocks about 125 million years old.

The fossil bird, which was 9 centimeters (3½ inches) long and had feathers and clawed feet, appears to have been a transitional species between archaeopteryxlike ancestors and later birds. The bird also had bone features necessary for flight, suggesting that birds capable of sustained flight appeared shortly after archaeopteryx.   [Carlton E. Brett]

In the Special Reports section, see CHANGING VIEWS OF DINOSAURS. In WORLD BOOK, see DINOSAUR; TRILOBITE.

Physics, Fluids and Solids

Physicists in 1987 and 1988 continued their attempts to adapt a theory that describes *superconductivity* in metals to explain how this phenomenon occurs in *ceramics*. Superconductivity is the ability of a material to conduct or carry *electric current* (a flow of electrons) without resistance. A superconducting material loses its resistance when chilled to a particular *critical temperature* near *absolute zero* ($-273.15°C$ or $-459.67°F$.). A ceramic is a solid material that is neither a metal nor a plastic; dinnerware, for example, is made of ceramics.

Until 1986, most known superconductors were metals or *alloys* (metal mixtures). Scientists found new ceramic superconductors in 1986, 1987, and 1988. See MATERIALS SCIENCE.

These new materials are also called *high-temperature superconductors* because their critical temperatures are much higher than those of other superconductors. The highest such temperature reported by June 1988 was about $-148°C$ ($-234°F$.), for a ceramic made up of the chemical elements thallium, calcium, barium, copper, and oxygen. The highest critical temperature for a metal alloy superconductor is $-250°C$ ($-418°F$.).

Commercial potential. The cost of reaching and maintaining the critical temperatures of the metal superconductors is so high that these materials are used in only a few devices, such as giant particle accelerators. The critical temperatures of the high-temperature superconductors are much less expensive to attain and hold, however, so applications of these materials could bring about astonishing new products. In the Special Reports section, see PLUGGING INTO SUPERCONDUCTORS.

Before the new materials can be used in practical devices, however, scientists and engineers must solve a number of technical problems. A thorough understanding of how superconductivity occurs in these materials might well make many of these problems easier to solve and enable researchers to create superconductors with even higher critical temperatures.

The current explanation. In 1957, United States physicists John Bardeen, Leon N. Cooper, and J. Robert Schrieffer developed the so-called BCS theory (named after their last initials) to explain superconductivity in metals and alloys. The three scientists shared the 1972 Nobel Prize in physics for their work.

The BCS theory describes superconductivity as a phenomenon involving an unusual interaction between electrons. At temperatures above its critical temperature, a superconductor resists electric current just as does an ordinary conductor, such as a copper wire—by absorbing energy from the flowing electrons. These electrons transfer energy by colliding with atoms in the crystal structure of the material.

By contrast, electrons flow unhindered through a superconductor that has been chilled to its critical temperature or below. According to the BCS theory, these electrons pass through the superconductor as so-called *Cooper pairs*. A Cooper pair is a set of two electrons that, as a unit, cannot transfer energy to a superconductor's crystal structure. No energy transfer can occur because the tendency of one electron in a Cooper pair to contribute energy to the crystal structure is balanced exactly by the tendency of this electron's "partner" to absorb energy from that structure.

But all electrons are negatively charged, and objects that have the same charge repel one another, so Bardeen, Cooper, and Schrieffer had to explain how two objects that naturally repel each other could form a "partnership." The three physicists explained Cooper-pair formation in terms of the positive electric charge carried by the atoms in the crystal structure, and the vibration of these atoms.

The main cause of this vibration is the atoms' own *heat energy*, or energy of motion. The hotter the material, the more the atoms vibrate, and so the more frequently the electrons that make up an electric current collide with the atoms. As a superconductor is chilled, the atoms in the crystal structure vibrate less, so the flowing electrons collide with the atoms less frequently. In other words, the resistance decreases.

At the critical temperature, the flowing electrons take control of atomic vibration in a way that makes the

Beams of ultrasound suspend foam balls in midair in a "container without walls." Such containers could be used in the manufacture of pure glass switches for computers that operate by light pulses. Making glass in containers with walls disrupts the molecular structure of the glass.

material's electrical resistance vanish. Objects with opposite electric charges attract each other, so when a negatively charged electron flows past a positively charged atom, the electron attracts the atom, momentarily deforming the crystal structure. This atom, in turn, attracts another electron. The net result of the two attractions is an attractive force between the two electrons that form a Cooper pair.

This process affects all the electrons that make up the current, so the current flows unhindered through the superconductor. If the superconductor is raised above its critical temperature, however, the increased heat energy of the atoms causes enough vibration in the atoms to break up the Cooper pairs. As a result, the material ceases to superconduct.

Problems with BCS. Scientists believe that Cooper pairs also form in ceramic superconductors. They suspect, however, that attractive forces stronger than those involved in metallic superconductors keep the Cooper pairs together in ceramics.

Physicist Philip W. Anderson of Princeton University in Princeton, N.J., suggested in early 1987 that Cooper pairs in ceramics are held together by certain electrons. These electrons are not part of the current. Rather, they are associated with the bonding between atoms in the crystal. In fact, these so-called *valence electrons* hold the atoms together in chemical bonds.

Some valence electrons are free to jump between the two atoms they are holding together. Because electrons are negatively charged, this jumping affects the charge of the two atoms involved in a jump. The atom from which a valence electron jumps gains positive charge, while the atom to which the electron jumps gains negative charge.

According to Anderson, a flowing electron in an electric current can influence the jumping of a valence electron. And a jumping valence electron, in turn, can influence another electron in the current. In this way, valence electrons make flowing electrons form Cooper pairs.

Details of this proposal are extremely complicated. The key to understanding it is that both the BCS theory for metals and Anderson's proposal for ceramics involve the formation of Cooper pairs caused by the movement of electric charge under the influence of flowing electrons. In the BCS theory for metals, the charges are positive charges on atoms in the crystal structure, while in Anderson's proposal, they are negative charges on valence electrons.

Lasers trap atoms. Two groups of researchers reported in December 1987 that they had used pressure exerted by laser beams to create an unusual kind of crystal. Scientists have known since the late 1800's that light can exert pressure on matter. For example, light from the sun is partly responsible for the deflection of the gas particles streaming out of the nucleus of a comet, so that a comet's tail is always turned away from the sun.

Scientists at the Max Planck Institute of Quantum Optics in Garching, West Germany, and at the Time and Frequency Division of the National Bureau of Standards in Boulder, Colo.,

used the pressure of laser light to slow down, and magnets and electric charges to confine, atoms in a vacuum chamber. Because their energy of motion had almost ceased, the atoms' temperature was close to absolute zero.

The scientists observed that a small group of electrically charged atoms confined in this way form an ordered structure resembling a normal crystal. The distance between the atoms in this structure, however, is much larger than that in normal crystals. Atoms in normal crystals are about 0.1 to 1 nanometer apart, while the distance between atoms in the structure created by the lasers is about 20,000 nanometers. (One nanometer equals one-billionth of a meter.)

Also, the bonds between the atoms are much weaker than those in a normal crystal. The structure survives because its temperature is so low. If it were much higher, the atoms' energy of motion would shake the weak structure apart.   [Alexander Hellemans]

In WORLD BOOK, see CRYSTAL; PHYSICS.

Physics,
Subatomic

Researchers in several nations in 1987 and 1988 continued their efforts to "weigh" *neutrinos*, subatomic particles that are closely related to electrons. Neutrinos differ from electrons in electric charge and in their *mass*. (Mass is the amount of matter in an object, and is responsible for the object's weight.) Electrons have a negative electric charge, while neutrinos have no charge.

Electric charge enables electrons to interact readily with one another and with other subatomic particles. In fact, interactions involving electrons are responsible for all chemical reactions. Neutrinos, on the other hand, interact very feebly with other forms of matter.

These qualities make the odds against detecting a neutrino as high as 1 million trillion to 1. As a result, most experiments on neutrinos settle for indirect evidence of these particles, studying more easily observed particles produced along with the neutrino.

There are three kinds of neutrinos—*electron*, *mu*, and *tau* neutrinos. The electron neutrino is essentially an

electrically neutral electron, but it is already known to be at least 10,000 times lighter than its electrically charged cousin, and could be many times lighter still. Mu and tau electrons might turn out to be heavier, but no one is sure whether any kind of neutrino has any mass at all.

Scientists in several fields would like to know whether neutrinos have mass and, if so, how much. Astronomers, for example, want to know whether neutrinos are massive enough to make up a mysterious halo of so-called *dark matter* that surrounds every galaxy.

Researchers involved in subatomic physics usually express mass in energy units called *electron volts* (eV). (One electron volt is the amount of energy an electron gains when it moves across an electric potential of 1 volt.) This use of energy units is convenient because, in subatomic physics, transformations between mass and various forms of energy, such as energy of motion, are commonplace.

The most sensitive experiments on neutrino mass study the *beta decay* of the tritium isotope, a form of hydrogen. Beta decay involves the nucleus of the tritium isotope. This nucleus is made up of one positively charged proton and two neutrons, which have no charge.

In beta decay, one of the neutrons transforms itself into a proton. In the process, the neutron emits an electron and an electron neutrino, both of which fly away from the isotope. This emission releases about 18,000 eV of energy, nearly all of which is divided up between the emitted electron and neutrino. An electron near the nucleus can absorb the remainder. How big a share of energy each particle gets is determined by pure chance, and varies from one decay to the next.

The key to this experiment is to determine the smallest amount of energy the neutrino can receive. This amount must be its mass. Because only the electron is observable, however, the experimenter must measure the maximum energy of the electron, then subtract this from the energy available for the electron and the neutrino.

The experiment is difficult because both the total energy and the energy available for the electron are at least 1,000 times larger than the expected mass of the neutrino. This means that the experimenters must measure the energy of a moving electron to a precision of less than 0.1 per cent. The experiment also takes patience, because only about 1 electron in 1 million gets close enough to the maximum energy to help with the estimate. In addition, the total energy available for sharing is hard to determine, because the electron or electrons orbiting the nucleus sometimes claim a share of about 30 to 40 eV.

In 1980, a team of 11 Soviet scientists at the Institute for Theoretical and Experimental Physics in Moscow announced that they had overcome the experimental difficulties, and were confident that the neutrino mass was not zero. By 1987, they had narrowed the range of the mass estimate to between 17 and 40 eV. A 1986 measurement by six Swiss researchers at the University of Zurich indicated, how-

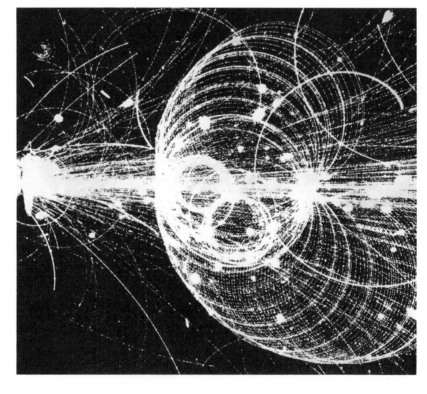

Hundreds of subatomic particles emerge when a sulfur nucleus collides with a gold nucleus during experiments conducted in September and October 1987 at the European Laboratory for Particle Physics (CERN) near Geneva, Switzerland. Scientists studied the collisions, representing the highest energies ever produced in a laboratory, for evidence of a *quark-gluon plasma,* a state of matter thought to have existed at the dawn of time.

ever, that the neutrino had a mass of 18 eV at most, and that it might have no mass at all. Two other measurements taken in 1987 favored the upper limit of 18 eV, but were not sensitive enough to settle the issue. A team of 20 researchers at Japan's Tokyo Institute for Nuclear Studies made one of the measurements, and 9 scientists from Princeton University in Princeton, N.J., the University of California at San Diego, and Los Alamos National Laboratory in Los Alamos, N. Mex., made the second measurement.

The difference between the Soviets' results and the other teams' data may be a matter of chemistry. The tritium in the Russian experiment was part of a rather complicated molecule, which could alter the share of energy taken by orbiting electrons. The Zurich and Tokyo groups used simpler molecules, while the Princeton-California-Los Alamos team chose the simplest arrangement of all, tritium isotopes that were not bound in molecules.

Rare decay observed. Physicists from the University of California at Irvine in August 1987 announced the discovery of a rare radioactive process called *double beta decay*. In this process, a nucleus simultaneously converts two neutrons to protons and emits two electrons and two neutrinos. Physicists had been searching for evidence of double beta decay for more than 50 years, and the leader of the Irvine team, Michael Moe, had devoted more than 14 years to the effort.

The Irvine team detected the telltale two-electron emission in a 14-gram (0.5-ounce) sample of the chemical element selenium 82. The nucleus of this element has 34 protons. Every few days, one nucleus in the selenium converted itself into a nucleus of krypton 82, which has 36 protons.

Quark-gluon plasma. Efforts to produce an exotic new state of matter, the so-called *quark-gluon plasma* (QGP), made considerable progress in 1987. Quarks are the building blocks from which subatomic particles such as protons and neutrons are made. Gluons are the "glue" that holds quarks together. This glue is so strong that quarks and gluons have never been observed by themselves.

Particle theory suggests that if enough energy is packed into a region the size of a small nucleus, quarks and gluons then become free to wander through this region for a brief instant. Such tight packing may occur when middle-sized or large nuclei collide in a *particle accelerator* (atom smasher) at speeds close to the speed of light—299,792 kilometers (186,282 miles) per second. No particle accelerator was designed to accelerate large nuclei to such speeds, but several accelerators have recently been modified to enable them to do so.

The most ambitious effort to date took place in 1987 at the Super Proton Synchrotron (SPS) at the European Laboratory for Particle Physics (CERN) near Geneva, Switzerland. In early 1987, this circular machine accelerated oxygen nuclei to 99.999 per cent of the speed of light, and slammed them into stationary lead nuclei. Each oxygen nucleus carried more than 3 trillion electron volts (TeV) of energy.

In a collision at this speed, hundreds of new particles are created by conversion of energy to mass. Most of these particles represent a few common types, and travel in basically the same direction as the original nucleus. If a QGP forms, however, it spews energy in all directions, much of it in the form of so-called *strange* and *charmed* particles that are rare in ordinary collisions. Thus the telltale signs of QGP are an increase in the spread of the particles and a jump in the number of rare particles produced.

Although the bulk of the particles created at CERN were characteristic of ordinary collisions, there were hints of the beginning of QGP formation. In late 1987, the researchers repeated the experiment with a beam of sulfur nuclei, which are twice as heavy as oxygen nuclei—and therefore more likely to generate a QGP. In mid-1988, scientists were still analyzing the results of the sulfur experiments.

Collisions at SLC. In March 1988, the Stanford Linear Accelerator Center (SLAC) in Palo Alto, Calif., began to generate data from particle collisions at the Stanford Linear Collider (SLC). This machine is the first to produce head-on collisions between electrons and *positrons* (positively charged elec-

"Particles, particles, particles."

trons) in two beams that pass through each other only once.

SLAC's linear accelerator, which is about 3.2 kilometers (2 miles) long, speeds electron and positron beams simultaneously to an energy of 50 billion eV. At the exit end of the linear accelerator, magnets first steer electrons and positrons in opposite directions, then turn them back for a head-on rush toward the final collision.

All other colliding-beam machines circulate their beams in opposite directions around "race tracks," so each beam gets many chances to collide with the other.

To generate a useful number of collisions, the SLC creates 180 bunches of each type of particle per second. Each bunch must contain 10 billion particles and be focused to a spot a few micrometers in diameter. (One micrometer equals about $\frac{1}{25,000}$ of an inch.)

To steer and focus the beams requires huge magnets constructed and aligned to microscopic precision. By mid-April 1988, the SLC generated beams that had the necessary numbers

of particles, and had focused the beams close to the required diameter. The beams must be run on a steady, 24-hour-per-day schedule required to generate useful numbers of collisions.

Super Collider. The United States Department of Energy (DOE) in January 1988 narrowed to seven the list of qualified sites for what would be the largest accelerator of all, the Superconducting Super Collider (SSC). The SSC is to be an 85-kilometer (53-mile) oval track for two proton beams with a combined energy of 40 trillion eV.

Originally, 25 states offered 43 sites for what would be the largest and—with a price tag of about $5.3 billion—the most expensive scientific instrument ever built. The seven "finalist" sites are in Arizona, Colorado, Illinois, Michigan, North Carolina, Tennessee, and Texas. The DOE planned to announce the final choice in mid-1988. Construction funding, however, was far from assured. [Robert H. March]

In WORLD BOOK, see NEUTRINO; PARTICLE ACCELERATOR; PARTICLE PHYSICS; QUARK.

Psychology

Images produced by a technique called *positron emission tomography* or PET scanning reveal that the brains of people who scored well on an intelligence test, *right,* used less energy than the brains of people who did poorly, *left,* a University of California at Irvine psychologist reported in February 1988. Radioactive glucose injected into the volunteers produces what appear here as dark areas on PET scan images revealing where the brain is using glucose for energy.

Psychologists in 1987 and 1988 delved deeper into the workings of the human brain with the ultimate goal of understanding the biological basis of such things as intelligence and personality. Brain researchers, using an imaging technique called *positron emission tomography* or PET scanning, made the paradoxical finding that people who do well on intelligence tests expend less mental energy taking the tests than do people who perform poorly.

Scientists use PET scans, which reveal the biochemical activity of body tissue, primarily to study brain function. The scans enable researchers to monitor the areas of the brain that are absorbing *glucose,* a form of sugar that the brain uses as fuel. The patient or volunteer is injected with radioactively labeled glucose, which emits gamma rays, a form of radiation. The PET scanner records the radiation patterns as color images. The parts of the brain that show up highly colored on the scan are the areas that absorbed the most glucose and, therefore, expended the most energy.

Working smarter, not harder. Psychologist Richard J. Haier of the University of California at Irvine presented his PET scan findings in February 1988 in Boston at the annual meeting of the American Association for the Advancement of Science. After injecting eight volunteers with radioactive glucose, Haier made PET scans of the subjects as they took a mental test. The resulting scans showed that the level of brain activity was lowest in people who scored well on the test.

"Although one might assume that a good performer's brain would work harder than that of a subject who did poorly, our data suggest that the opposite is true," said Haier. He theorized that people who do well on mental tests may expend less energy because they have more efficient *neural circuitry*—that is, better connections between their brain cells.

Recognizing a lying smile. There may be a reliable way to detect lying smiles, according to psychologists Paul Ekman and Wallace V. Friesen, both of the University of California at San Fran-

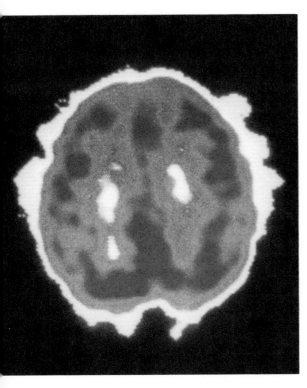

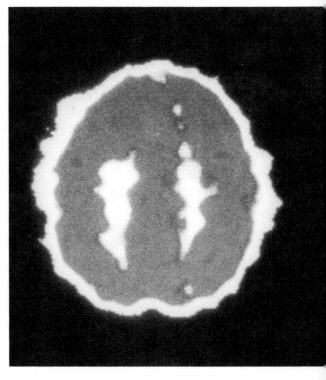

Psychology

Continued

cisco, and Maureen O'Sullivan of the University of San Francisco. They reported on their study in the March 1988 *Journal of Personality and Social Psychology*. Ekman has studied facial expressions and emotions for nearly 20 years. The psychologists found that there are subtle physical differences between smiles reflecting genuine enjoyment and smiles trying to conceal unpleasant reactions.

The researchers had 31 student nurses watch a pleasant nature film and then an unpleasant film showing amputations and burns. The nurses were interviewed and secretly videotaped during and immediately after watching each film. The investigators had instructed the nurses to describe their feelings about the pleasant film frankly but to conceal their distress about the unpleasant film. They were to try convincing the interviewer that they were watching another enjoyable film. The researchers explained that nurses would encounter many unpleasant situations in their profession and would need to mask their anxiety and disgust and to appear confident and optimistic.

People trained to recognize emotions based on the movement of facial muscles then examined the tapes of the nurses without knowing which film the nurses had been watching during the taping. The trained observers found two types of smiles: one when the nurses were truthfully describing an enjoyable experience and a different smile when they were deceptively describing an unpleasant experience as pleasant.

The truthful smile included activity of the muscles that circle the eyes and the muscle that pulls the corners of the mouth upward. The deceptive smile mimicked the genuine smile in pulling the corners of the mouth upward but also involved muscle movements that raised the upper lip and pulled down the corners of the mouth—movements associated with emotional distress. Despite the nurses' efforts to mask their feelings, observers were able to find subtle facial clues to the nurses' true reactions.

The psychologists concluded that smiles should not be considered a single category of behavior. Further research may determine how different smiles may provide different social signals, have different functions in social interaction, and relate to different aspects of our inner experiences.

Army studies the unconventional. The United States Army, seeking ways to enhance the performance of its soldiers, has investigated the possibility of using some unconventional psychological techniques, such as sleep-learning. In 1984, the U.S. Army Research Institute for the Behavioral and Social Sciences asked the National Research Council (NRC), the research arm of the National Academy of Sciences in Washington, D.C., to form a committee to study the potential value of certain of these techniques. The NRC report, released in December 1987, concluded that some of these psychological methods of enhancing performance may be useful and deserve further study, while others have little or no scientific validity.

Among the techniques reviewed were:

■ Sleep-learning. This is instruction given to a sleeping person, usually by playing a tape recording while the person slumbers, on the theory that the sleeper's unconscious mind can absorb the information. Experiments since then have shown that during light sleep it is possible to reinforce what people already know and to prepare them for material they plan to learn. Psychologist John A. Swets, chairman of the NRC committee, explained that "without effort or intention or even awareness," sleeping people can absorb certain kinds of information, such as vocabulary.

■ Mental practice. This involves watching champion athletes perform and mentally repeating or rehearsing their moves as the task is performed. The committee concluded that this technique "is effective in enhancing the performance of motor skills." This type of mental practice is especially effective in helping people improve skills that require a systematic approach, such as learning to throw darts or fire a rifle.

■ Biofeedback. The committee disputed claims that a technique called *biofeedback* can reduce emotional or mental stress and thus enhance per-

Psychology

Continued

formance. Biofeedback involves the use of various measuring devices, such as electroencephalographs and thermometers, that enable people to monitor and eventually consciously control their internal body functions such as blood pressure, brain waves, heartbeat, and circulation. Biofeedback can help reduce muscle tension, according to the NRC report, but it does not seem to relieve stress, nor does the relaxed state it produces necessarily improve physical or mental performance. Studies of athletes and musicians, for example, do not show that they become more skillful by learning to control muscle tension.

■ Brain hemispheric synchronization. Training the brain's left and right halves, called *hemispheres*, to work together or targeting specific hemispheres of the brain for different messages has been said to facilitate sleep, concentration, learning, and even recovery from surgery. Scientific studies suggest that the left hemisphere of the brain largely controls the ability to use language, mathematics, and logic. The right hemisphere is the major center for musical and artistic ability and the expression of emotion. But both hemispheres must work together. The NRC committee found no evidence that people can make use of the fact that the brain's hemispheres have different functions. The panel also concluded that brain power does not increase by simultaneously trying to give each hemisphere a separate task to perform.

■ Parapsychology. The committee studied research reports on such phenomena as *extrasensory perception* (gaining information without using the known sense organs), including mind reading, seeing into the future, and *psychokinesis* (the ability to use mental powers to move physical objects). The committee found "no scientific justification from research conducted over a period of 130 years for the existence" of these parapsychological phenomena and concluded that "there is no reason for direct involvement by the Army at this time." [Robert J. Trotter]

In WORLD BOOK, see PSYCHOLOGY.

Public Health

The first-ever nationwide mailing about a public health crisis was sent in May and June 1988, when the United States government mailed a pamphlet about AIDS (acquired immune deficiency syndrome) to 107 million households. The eight-page pamphlet reached nearly every residential address in the United States.

AIDS is a fatal disease that attacks the body's immune system, leaving it unable to fight off infections. By mid-May 1988, about 62,200 Americans had been diagnosed with AIDS since the disease was identified in 1981, and more than half—35,051—had died.

The 1988 public health booklet described in simple language how the disease is transmitted through sexual contact, needles or syringes shared by drug abusers, or infected blood. It also explained how the use of plastic sheaths called *condoms* can protect against sexually transmitted AIDS. In the Special Reports section, see THE SEARCH FOR AN AIDS VACCINE.

Nicotine called addictive. Surgeon General of the United States C. Everett Koop released a report on May 16, 1988, warning that the nicotine in tobacco is as addictive as heroin or cocaine. The report called for a ban on vending-machine sales of cigarettes and for tougher laws prohibiting the sale of tobacco products to minors. The surgeon general also recommended raising taxes on cigarettes and requiring a special license for the sale of tobacco products.

Cigarette smoking among adults fell to the lowest level ever recorded in the United States, the U.S. Public Health Service (PHS) reported in September 1987. The PHS found that 26.5 per cent of adult Americans smoked cigarettes in 1986. In 1949, the peak year for smoking according to a nationwide survey, an estimated 44 per cent of Americans used cigarettes.

The 1986 information on smoking came from the Adult Use of Tobacco Survey, a nationwide telephone survey of more than 13,000 people aged 17 or older. The Office on Smoking and Health of the PHS carried out the survey to determine knowledge, attitudes,

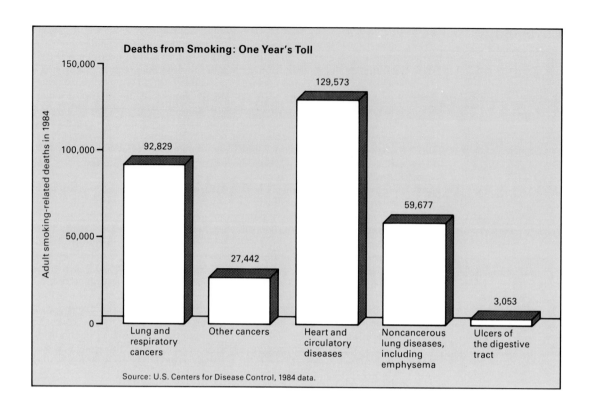

Deaths from Smoking: One Year's Toll

Adult smoking-related deaths in 1984

- Lung and respiratory cancers: 92,829
- Other cancers: 27,442
- Heart and circulatory diseases: 129,573
- Noncancerous lung diseases, including emphysema: 59,677
- Ulcers of the digestive tract: 3,053

Source: U.S. Centers for Disease Control, 1984 data.

Public Health

Continued

Smoking-related diseases caused an estimated 312,574 adult deaths in the United States in 1984, according to a study reported in October 1987 by the U.S. Centers for Disease Control. This makes smoking the nation's chief avoidable cause of death.

and practices regarding the use of tobacco. Cigarette smokers were defined as people who had smoked at least 100 cigarettes in their lifetime and were currently smoking cigarettes.

Smoking rates differed between males and females, with 29.5 per cent of all men reporting that they were current smokers, compared with 23.8 per cent of all women. Smoking rates varied even more dramatically according to age and race. For example, 24.4 per cent of all men in the 17- to 24-year-old age group smoked, compared with 37.1 per cent of those aged 35 to 44. Still more dramatic was the variation by age among black men. Of those in the 17- to 24-year-old age group, 14.3 per cent smoked, and for black men aged 25 to 34 years, the rate more than tripled to 45.9 per cent.

The 1979 Surgeon General's Report on Health Promotion and Disease Prevention had identified cigarette smoking as "the single most important preventable cause of death." The surgeon general, the top public health official in the United States, blamed smoking

for the premature death of approximately 320,000 Americans.

Although numerous surveys have shown a decline in smoking rates in the United States since the 1960's, the 1986 Adult Use of Tobacco Survey indicated that an estimated 46.8 million American adults continue to smoke cigarettes. Public health experts called for greater cooperation among public agencies, private organizations, health care providers, and others to encourage people to quit smoking—or never to start.

Aspirin cuts heart attack risk? Taking one aspirin tablet every other day may be an effective way to reduce the risk of heart attack, according to the preliminary results of a study reported in January 1988. The study involved more than 22,000 healthy male physicians 40 to 84 years of age. Half of the participants took an ordinary aspirin tablet every other day, and the other half took a *placebo* (a look-alike pill with no active ingredients). The participants were not told whether they had been given aspirin or the placebo.

Public Health

Continued

In December 1987, a preliminary analysis found a 47 per cent reduction in the risk of heart attack in the group of physicians who were taking aspirin every other day. The lifesaving effects of aspirin were so dramatic that the study was halted immediately and the results quickly made public. See MEDICAL RESEARCH (Close-Up).

Workplace murder. Violent death has become an important problem in the workplace, according to two studies reported in late 1987. In the past, public health experts have underestimated the extent of this problem.

Epidemiologist Jess F. Kraus of the University of California at Los Angeles reported in October 1987 that the risk of work-related homicide was 1.5 per 100,000 for all workers in California and more than four times greater for men than for women—2.2 versus 0.5 per 100,000 workers, respectively. By occupation, homicide rates were highest for police officers, followed by taxi drivers, private security guards, and owners or managers of eating or drinking places, convenience stores, liquor stores, and similar establishments. Shooting caused more than three-fourths of all work-related homicides, though a higher proportion of female than male workers were killed by cutting or stabbing.

In a study of on-the-job fatalities among women in Texas, epidemiologist Harold Davis and his colleagues at the federal Centers for Disease Control in Atlanta, Ga., reported in December 1987 that homicides accounted for 53 per cent of workplace deaths. In contrast, motor-vehicle related injuries were responsible for 26 per cent of job-related deaths among women. Homicide rates were especially high for women working in gasoline service stations; food, bakery, and dairy stores; and eating and drinking places. The occupations with the highest homicide rates included grocery clerks, food-counter and fountain workers, and store managers. Firearms were involved in 70 per cent of these homicides.   [Richard A. Goodman]

In WORLD BOOK, see PUBLIC HEALTH.

Science Education

A public perception that science education offers a means of easing economic problems in the United States resulted in increased attention and support for science teaching during 1987 and 1988. Many Americans believed that if U.S. students received better science education, the United States would be better able to compete in world markets.

Stiffer standards for teachers remained high on the agenda for action. The Holmes Group, a consortium of education deans from 40 leading universities, continued in 1987 and 1988 to plan programs for member colleges. In its 1986 report *Tomorrow's Teachers*, the Holmes Group proposed that prospective teachers earn a bachelor's degree in the subject they plan to teach, rather than in education as is usual.

New certification programs began to provide special recognition to teachers who reflect the highest ideals of their profession. The National Board for Professional Teaching Standards, proposed and funded by the Carnegie Corporation of New York, began its work in May 1987. The board will issue national credentials to teachers who meet high standards of subject knowledge and teaching ability.

In January 1988, the National Science Teachers Association (NSTA), the world's largest organization dedicated to improving science teaching, completed the first year of its national teacher-certification program. The association certified 75 teachers as having met its strict standards for training and experience. Teachers may receive NSTA certification to teach science at the elementary, middle or junior high school, or high school level. In addition, high-school teachers may be certified in biology, chemistry, physics, physical science, earth and space science, or general science.

Science/Technology/Society (S/T/S). The S/T/S movement gained momentum throughout the United States in 1987. The S/T/S approach calls for teachers to use students' own experiences with technology and actual community or global problems as a basis for teaching science. For example, a

Science
Education
Continued

student's interest in television might lead to a study of electromagnetism, or the problem of drug abuse might lead to a study of the chemical process of addiction.

A new organization—the National Association for Science/Technology/Society—was created in late 1987. The association, headquartered at Pennsylvania State University in University Park, planned to develop new directions, goals, materials, and approaches for science education, stressing the links between science and society.

Funding to support improvements in science education increased. The federal Department of Education boosted funds to the states for higher education by 50 per cent in 1987, compared with 1986 appropriations, under Title II of the Education for Economic Security Act of 1984. The Department of Education also funded a new National Center for Improving Science Education, which opened in Washington, D.C., in November 1987. The center's mission is to compile the findings and recommendations of various study groups that have reported on science education, and—based on the groups' recommendations—to promote reforms in science teaching.

The National Science Foundation (NSF), an independent federal agency that supports scientific research and teaching, increased its science education budget by 40 per cent in the 1988 fiscal year. Nearly $140 million was made available in 1988 for a variety of science education programs at the NSF. The appropriation was $24.2-million more than the NSF had originally requested.

Serving the underserved. Major efforts began in 1987 and 1988 to provide better science education for what are called underserved groups in U.S. society, including girls and women, members of minority groups, and disabled persons. In early 1988, U.S. Secretary of Education William J. Bennett announced the availability of $4 million in funds to address these problems.   [Robert E. Yager]

In WORLD BOOK, see EDUCATION; SCIENCE PROJECTS.

Science
Student
Awards

Winners in the 47th annual Westinghouse Science Talent Search were announced on Feb. 29, 1988, and winners of the 39th annual International Science and Engineering Fair, in May. Science Service, a nonprofit educational organization in Washington, D.C., administered both competitions.

Science Talent Search winners. The 40 finalists were chosen from 1,339 seniors from high schools throughout the United States. The top 10 finalists received scholarships totaling $110,000 provided by the Westinghouse Electric Corporation.

First place and a $20,000 scholarship went to 16-year-old Chetan Nayak, a student at Stuyvesant High School in New York City. Nayak won for applying *quantum theory*, the idea that energy travels in tiny bundles called *quanta*, to the *unified field theory*, which deals with the interaction of electromagnetic and gravitational forces.

Second place and a $15,000 scholarship went to Janet Tseng, 17, a classmate of Nayak's at Stuyvesant High. It was the first time that the first and second prizes had gone to students at the same school. Tseng's winning project was a study of a parasitic intestinal infection called *Cryptosporidium*, which afflicts many victims of AIDS (acquired immune deficiency syndrome).

Third place and a $15,000 scholarship went to Benjamin S. Abella, 17, of the University of Chicago Laboratory Schools High School, for a genetic study of *Rhodobacter capsulata*, one of the nitrogen-fixing bacteria that take nitrogen from the air and convert it into nitrogen compounds that can be used by other living things.

The other top 10 winners, in order, were Vijay S. Pande, 17, of Langley High School in McLean, Va.; Brian D. Conrad, 17, of Centereach High School in Centereach, N.Y.; Weiva Yu Sieh, 17, of Bronx High School of Science in New York City; Stacey E. Beaulieu, 17, of Palm Beach Gardens High School in Palm Beach Gardens, Fla.; Kurt M. Cuffey, 18, of State College Area Senior High School in State College, Pa.; Brian C. Hooker, 17, of Benjamin E. Mays High School in At-

Science Student Awards

Continued

First- and second-place winners in the 47th annual Westinghouse Science Talent Search in February 1988 were classmates Chetan Nayak, center, and Janet Tseng, left, of Stuyvesant High School in New York City. Third place went to Benjamin S. Abella, right, of the University of Chicago Laboratory Schools High School.

lanta, Ga.; and Meredith A. Albrecht, 17, of Evanston Township High School in Evanston, Ill.

Science fair winners. The 39th annual International Science and Engineering Fair took place May 8-14, 1988, in Knoxville, Tenn. The 721 contestants were chosen from finalists at local science fairs in the United States and other countries.

First through Fourth Award winners were selected in each of 13 categories. The First Award winners of $500 were Luke S. Sheffer, 15, of North Junior High School in Colorado Springs, Colo., in behavioral and social sciences; Paul B. Han, 16, of Alhambra High School in Alhambra, Calif., in biochemistry; Jean S. Wang, 15, of Eleanor Roosevelt High School in Greenbelt, Md., in botany; Bill Rubin, 18, of Arundel Senior High School in Gambrills, Md., in chemistry; and Nabeel Shirazi, 17, of Beavercreek High School in Ohio in computer science.

Also, Siobhan Lanigan-O'Keeffe, 18, of Navan Community College in Navan, Ireland, in earth and space science;

Scott M. Wright, 18, of Tuscarawas Valley High School in Zoarville, Ohio, in engineering; Gina L. Rose, 16, of North Penn High School in Lansdale, Pa., in environmental sciences; Brian Conrad, who won fifth place in the earlier Westinghouse talent search, in mathematics; Wade S. Geary, 18, of Davis High School in Kaysville, Utah, in medicine and health; Jeffrey H. Richmond, 17, of South Side High School in Rockville Centre, N.Y., in microbiology; Steven Y. Litvin, 17, of Wilson Senior High School in Reading, Pa., in physics; and Margaret L. Montgomery, 18, of Long Beach High School in Long Beach, Miss., in the field of zoology.

Physics Olympiad. The 18th annual International Physics Olympiad took place July 2-13, 1987, in Jena, East Germany. A total of 3 gold, 10 silver, and 14 bronze medals were awarded. Three of the five U.S. team members—Bryan Beatty of Knoxville, Eli Glezer of San Diego, and Normand Modine of Oak Ridge, Tenn.—won bronze medals.   [Sara Dreyfuss]

Space Technology

The United States space program struggled during late 1987 and early 1988 to regain the momentum lost when the space shuttle *Challenger* exploded in January 1986, killing all seven crew members. In early 1988, President Ronald Reagan signed a new national space policy that set a long-term course for the U.S. space program. And progress in redesigning the space shuttle's flawed solid rocket boosters, the cause of the *Challenger* accident, enabled the National Aeronautics and Space Administration (NASA) to set late summer 1988 as the tentative target date for launch of the first shuttle since the *Challenger* disaster.

Space shuttle. Progress continued on shuttle repairs and plans. On Aug. 1, 1987, Rockwell International Corporation was awarded a $1.3-billion NASA contract to build a new space-shuttle orbiter that would replace the *Challenger*. The new spacecraft's first flight is scheduled for 1992.

The shuttle program achieved a major milestone on Aug. 30, 1987, when Morton Thiokol Incorporated, the company that makes the shuttle's solid rocket boosters, successfully test-fired a redesigned booster. The new booster incorporated all of the major modifications called for after an investigation of the *Challenger* accident. The inquiry disclosed that faulty seals in booster joints caused the tragedy, but it found many other design problems in the booster that also needed correction.

A significant setback to the redesign efforts occurred on Dec. 23, 1987, however, when a motor part in the solid rocket booster malfunctioned during a test at a Morton Thiokol facility near Brigham City, Utah. The component failure was unrelated to the booster joint problem, and had the event occurred in flight, there would have been no danger to the shuttle. But the problem raised new questions about the redesign efforts because the component that failed was supposed to be superior to the element it replaced.

Ride Report. In a reassessment of the U.S. space program after the *Challenger* accident, top NASA officials realized that the agency lacked long-

A redesigned shuttle booster rocket is successfully test-fired at a desert facility near Brigham City, Utah, in August 1987. The redesigned booster incorporated all the major modifications called for by an inquiry into the cause of the January 1986 *Challenger* disaster. The test showed no leaking of hot gases from the joints that connect the booster's main segments—the type of leak that caused the *Challenger* explosion.

term space exploration goals. NASA designated astronaut Sally K. Ride, a physicist and the first U.S. woman to fly in space, to head a task force to study the problem. The resulting Ride Report, issued on Aug. 17, 1987, called for an aggressive program to develop new space technology, complete the U.S. space station in the mid-1900's, and then establish a manned base on the moon.

The Ride Report said that a manned outpost on the planet Mars should be the ultimate goal of the U.S. program. The report said that a base established on the moon would provide the experience for a Mars mission.

Space station. The building of the U.S. space station officially got underway on Dec. 1, 1987, with the award of more than $5 billion in contracts to four aerospace companies. McDonnell Douglas Corporation was awarded $1.9 billion to build the structural backbone of the station and other key components. Boeing Company was awarded more than $750 million to build the station's living and working areas. Rocketdyne Division of Rockwell International was awarded more than $1.6 billion to develop the station's solar-powered electrical system. General Electric Company was awarded about $800 million to build an unmanned, free-flying platform that will carry scientific instruments.

The space station would be the first permanent manned outpost in space for the United States. Support for the station in the U.S. Congress weakened, however, and during early 1988, some observers expressed doubt that Congress would approve adequate funding for the project, which is expected to cost at least $14 billion.

National space policy. On Feb. 11, 1988, President Reagan released details of his new space policy, setting as a formal national goal the expansion of U.S. manned space flight beyond Earth orbit. As a result, NASA was given the go-ahead to study manned missions to the moon and Mars.

The new policy also seeks to shift much of the national space effort to private enterprise. Toward that end, the President approved a plan for the government to lease space on a privately developed orbiting research lab-oratory. The commercially developed space facility could be operational by about 1993, pending approval by Congress. The research laboratory would be unmanned, performing automated experiments to develop new materials and drugs under the conditions of weightlessness in space.

The Soviet space program. The Soviet Union's space program continued its aggressive launch schedule in 1987, with a total of 95 launches that carried 116 satellites into orbit. In early 1988, the Soviets launched rockets at a blistering pace. During March alone, Russia sent 12 new satellites into orbit, compared with none for the United States during the same period. The Soviets, however, suffered at least four major satellite launch failures between June 1987 and June 1988.

In addition to launching new unmanned space missions nearly every week during 1987 and early 1988, the Soviet space program also continued its strong emphasis on manned flight. *Mir* space station cosmonauts Yuri Romanenko and Alexander Laveikin performed two spacewalks on June 12 and June 16, 1987, to install a large new solar array on the space station for converting sunlight to electricity. The new array increased electrical power on the station by more than 30 per cent. The cosmonauts also conducted observations of objects in deep space using telescopes ferried to the station by the *Kvant* (*Quantum*) astrophysics module.

By midsummer, Soviet physicians grew concerned about an irregular heartbeat that Laveikin had developed. Although his condition was not considered an emergency, Soviet space officials decided to replace Laveikin with a crew member of another mission scheduled to visit the station.

That crew was launched up to *Mir* on July 22 in the *Soyuz TM-3* spacecraft. The *Soyuz TM-3* crew exchanged one member for Laveikin and returned to Earth on July 30. On December 21, the Soviets launched a complete replacement crew to the station, and on December 29, Romanenko and two other cosmonauts returned to Earth. The end of Romanenko's flight set a 326-day manned-flight record. Other cosmo-

Space Technology

Continued

Soviet cosmonaut Yuri Romanenko beams with contentment on his return to Earth in December 1987 after a record 326 days in space aboard the space station *Mir*.

nauts will attempt to break his record by staying in the station through the end of 1988. Medical data from the flight concerning the effect on the body of long-term weightlessness will be important to the Soviet development of a manned flight to Mars. A round-trip Mars flight will require about two years of weightlessness.

Unmanned Soviet space operations scored many successes and a few failures during 1987 and 1988. One major Soviet unmanned success involved the July 25, 1987, launch of the *Cosmos 1,870*, a scientific Earth-survey platform, into a polar orbit. This massive spacecraft—the largest of its kind ever launched, about the size of a school bus—carries a radar that can observe Earth and ocean phenomena during day or night.

A Soviet mission that malfunctioned but ended successfully was the *Cosmos 1,887* biological satellite. On October 12, the spacecraft landed in eastern Siberia, about 3,200 kilometers (2,000 miles) off target, but it was recovered a day later. The spacecraft carried two monkeys, some rats, fish, and insects, which spent about 12 days in space to provide research data on the effects of weightlessness.

Europe and Asia. The 13-nation European Space Agency achieved an important success on Sept. 15, 1987, when an Ariane rocket launched two communications satellites—one European and the other Australian—into *geosynchronous* orbit. (Geosynchronous satellites orbit 35,900 kilometers [22,300 miles] above Earth at exactly the same speed as Earth's rotation. Thus, they appear to be fixed in position and are in range of certain Earth stations at all times.)

On March 11, 1988, an Ariane rocket placed two other communications satellites—one French and one American—into geosynchronous orbit.

Japan launched two communications satellites—one in August 1987 and another in February 1988. China launched two low-altitude satellites in late 1987, and a communications satellite in early 1988. [Craig P. Covault]

In WORLD BOOK, see SPACE TRAVEL.

Zoology

For lions, variety may be more than just the spice of life—it may be the key to successful breeding, according to a report in September 1987 by scientists at the National Zoological Park in Washington, D.C. The scientists discovered a link between lions' genetic variability and their possession of traits important for reproduction.

Zoo zoologist David E. Wildt led a team of scientists that studied two groups of lions in the east African country of Tanzania and one group from the Gir Forest in India. One of the African groups lives in a vast, ancient volcanic crater. All 100 animals in that group are descended from about 10 lions that survived an epidemic in 1962. The Indian lions, which are also related to one another, are the descendants of about 20 common ancestors that lived in the early 1900's.

The scientists took blood samples from male lions in each group. They analyzed the components in the animals' blood and evaluated the genetic differences between individuals in each group. They found that the lions living in the crater were more genetically alike than the other African lions and that the lions in India were almost exactly alike.

The scientists also collected semen from the lions and measured the level of *testosterone*, a sex hormone, in their blood. The tests revealed that the Indian lions and the lions in the crater had fewer and less active sperm than the other African lions. These two groups of lions also had lower levels of testosterone.

These abnormalities seem to affect the lions' ability to reproduce. In India, one male lion in a zoo has fathered no cubs, and three other males have sired either just one or no liveborn cubs. The researchers concluded that the lack of variety in their genetic makeup may also make the lions more liable to be wiped out by disease.

Quaking katydid. Some katydids use quivers as well as calls to attract mates, biologists working in Panama reported in October 1987. The "katy did" call for which this variety of grasshopper is

Biologists from the University of Georgia attach a depth-recording device to the back of a leatherback turtle as part of an ongoing study of these deep-diving animals. The data show that the turtles routinely dive to more than 300 meters (1,000 feet), and in one dive a turtle plunged more than 1,190 meters (3,900 feet), the deepest dive ever recorded for an air-breathing animal.

317

Zoology

Continued

A California condor chick, the first ever conceived and hatched in captivity, is carefully helped out of its shell by zoologists at San Diego Wild Animal Park, *above*. Five days later, the chick, named Molloko by zoo personnel, gets a meal from "mother"—a hand puppet resembling an adult condor, *above right*.

named is a mixed blessing. A male katydid "sings" by rubbing the bases of its front wings together. The sound attracts mates, but it also lets potential predators know where the insect is.

Bats are a major predator of katydids. So where bats are plentiful, katydids have evolved a different mating strategy, according to biologists Jacqueline J. Belwood of the University of Florida and Glenn K. Morris of the University of Toronto in Canada.

Belwood and Morris compared the songs of katydid species living in forests with songs of katydids living in cleared areas, where there are fewer bats. They found that the forest-dwelling insects produce a different call. Instead of chirping often in a wide range of sound frequencies, these males use a purer, higher-pitched call and spend more time sitting quietly. This strategy makes it more difficult for bats to find them.

The researchers demonstrated the protective value of this less frequent and higher-pitched call. They put katydids from both forests and clearings

into a large cage with bats. Males from the forests that called less than once a minute survived an average of 34 minutes before being tracked down and eaten by a bat. The noisier insects from the clearings, which tended to call about once a second, were caught in an average of 26 seconds.

But the protective call of the forest katydid also makes it harder for potential mates to find him. To help females track them down, males also bounce up and down vigorously on the twigs or plant stems where they are perched. This bouncing produces vibrations that a female can recognize from several yards away. The vibrations are not detected by bats.

Loudmouth males. In contrast to the quiet katydids, male deer, or stags, that make lots of noise have the most success in mating, a British zoologist reported in December 1987. Karen McComb of the Large Animal Research Group in Cambridge, England, concluded from her studies of red deer that the male's calls seem to attract females and make them ready to mate sooner. This was the first time that the noises made by male mammals were shown to affect the female reproductive cycle.

During the fall, male red deer round up groups of females. They ward off other stags from their harem by "roaring"—making low-pitched calls by exhaling. They make the same noises when chasing female deer.

McComb studied red deer on a farm in New Zealand. Several weeks before the deer were ready to mate, she divided the females into three groups of about 50 deer each. She exposed one group to recorded roars played over loudspeakers. The second group was kept with a sterile male that roared and pursued the females despite being unable to mate with them. The third group had no contact with males and heard no male roars.

After two weeks, females from all three groups were allowed to mate with fertile males. Females that were exposed to recorded roars or kept with the roaring but sterile male were ready to mate an average of six days earlier than females from the third group.

Those six days could be crucial, McComb said, because males lack the stamina to maintain their harems for very long. The sooner a female is ready to mate, the more likely she is to become pregnant and to have healthy offspring that survive.

Egg swap. A novel variation on *brood parasitism*, a form of behavior in which an animal tricks other animals into rearing its young, was reported in January 1988 by biologists at Yale University in New Haven, Conn. Brood parasitism has been noted most often among birds that lay their eggs in other birds' nests, such as the cowbird and the cuckoo. But the Yale scientists, Charles E. Brown and Mary Bomberger, discovered that at least one kind of bird—the cliff swallow—lays its eggs in its own nest and then moves one or more eggs to other nests.

Brown and Bomberger studied a community of cliff swallows in Nebraska. As part of their research, the scientists marked 204 eggs in 50 swallow nests in one nesting area. Later, they checked the nests and found that 3 of them—6 per cent—contained marked eggs from other nests.

The researchers also observed 4,821 nests in a larger area and noted apparent egg transfers in 306 of them. Although this study was less precise than the experiment with the marked eggs, the result was again about 6 per cent.

Brown and Bomberger speculated that the cliff swallows may move their eggs to improve the likelihood that the eggs will hatch. The birds seem to know which of their neighbors are most adept at incubating eggs, and they choose those birds as "foster parents" for their offspring. Only about 10 per cent of the transferred eggs failed to hatch, compared with a 25 per cent failure rate in the swallow community as a whole.

Egg moving may also be the birds' strategy for not "putting all their eggs in one basket," the scientists said. The swallows' nests are often destroyed by rockslides. By distributing eggs to other nests, a parent may increase the chances that some eggs will not be destroyed. Moreover, by tricking other birds into caring for its young, a female swallow may save energy that over a lifetime enables that swallow to lay more eggs than its less sneaky neighbors.

Sponge-munching turtles. Sponges, which contain poisonous chemicals and a skeleton of glassy needles, are among the sea's most unpalatable creatures—but not for the hawksbill turtle. Zoologist Anne Meylan of the American Museum of Natural History in New York City reported in January 1988 that the diet of this endangered sea turtle consists mainly of sponges.

Meylan examined the intestinal contents of 61 dead hawksbill turtles collected in various parts of the Caribbean Sea. All but one turtle had eaten sponges, and 51 had apparently fed on sponges almost exclusively.

Meylan found that the turtles tend to be very selective in the kinds of sponges they eat; 10 species of sponges account for almost 80 per cent of the turtles' diet. Some of these sponge species are poisonous to fish and to people but evidently do not harm the turtles. Nor do the turtles seem to be affected by the glassy needles that make up the sponges' internal skeleton, even though the turtles have apparently not evolved any specialized

Three baby broad-snouted caymans, close cousins of alligators, were among 18 hatched in July 1987 at the Bronx Zoo in New York City. The hatching of the endangered animals marked the first time that a second generation of rare *crocodilians* (crocodiles and their relatives) had been bred in captivity.

Zoology

Continued

means of digesting this sharp material.

Meylan also studied a number of hawksbill turtles from Texas, Mexico, South Africa, and the Pacific Coast of Panama and found that they, too, fed almost exclusively on sponges. But the turtle's diet has nothing to do with its status as an endangered species; hawksbill turtles have been widely hunted for their shells.

Good neighbors. Just as shoppers share information about the best bargains, some sea birds tell one another where the best fish are. That finding was reported in September 1987 by Erick Greene, a biologist at Princeton University in New Jersey. Greene studied the hunting habits of ospreys, large hawks that live in coastal colonies and hunt in groups.

Greene observed osprey colonies in Nova Scotia, Canada, for four hours each day from early May until mid-September. He watched from a cliff where he could see the ospreys' nests and their fishing areas.

The biologist noted that four fish—flounder, pollack, alewife, and smelt—

accounted for more than 90 per cent of the osprey diet. All of these fish except flounder travel in schools, so finding one fish usually indicates that more are nearby. Thus, Greene observed, when an osprey returned with a pollack, alewife, or smelt, other birds in the colony tended to go fishing. But if the fish brought in was a flounder, the other birds did not react.

Greene's most remarkable finding, though, was that birds returning with fish other than flounder sometimes did a "dance" in the air to let their neighbors know about their find. As they approached the colony, they called out to the other birds and flew back and forth. Immediately, all the male osprey took off toward the "dancer" and began hunting the school from which the first fish had been caught. By sharing information at the colony site, Greene said, the birds were able to reduce the amount of time spent searching for fish.   [Elizabeth J. Pennisi and
Thomas R. Tobin]

In WORLD BOOK, see ANIMAL; ZOOLOGY.

Science You Can Use

In areas selected for their current interest, *Science Year* presents information that the reader as a consumer can use in making decisions—from buying products to caring for personal health and well-being.

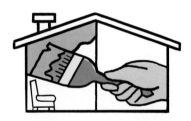

How Cellular Phones Work

A construction superintendent uses a cellular telephone to convert his car into a mobile phone booth. Mobile phones are handy tools for workers whose jobs call for a great deal of local travel by automobile.

Cellular mobile phones are being installed in more automobiles every day. What started out as a luxury item is promoted in advertising as a necessity for people whose business depends upon being able to reach other people via telephone. In addition, what began as a permanently installed car phone is now small enough to be carried in a briefcase.

Portable phones are made possible by cellular radio, a new technology whose growth has been astounding even in this high-tech age. In October 1987, just four years after the first commercial cellular system went into operation, the millionth customer signed up for cellular service. By the end of 1987, there were 312 systems operating in 205 cities.

How cellular mobile telephones work is a fascinating technological story. A cellular mobile telephone sends messages on radio waves. Citizens band (CB) radios also transmit on radio frequencies, but they produce scratchy, static-filled sounds, and the number of users who can be on the system at the same time is severely limited. A cellular mobile phone, on the other hand, sounds at least as clear as a regular wired phone, and a cellular system can handle more than 300 calls at the same time. The key to its clarity and capacity lies in a clever combination of radio, telephone, and computer technologies.

A cellular system has three main parts, all equipped with computers—a central switching office, a network of low-powered radio antennas, and the customers' telephones. The switching office controls the cellular network itself as callers move around within the system, and connects the cellular system to the regular telephone network. This connection is made with radio links, by ordinary telephone wires, or through *fiber-optic cables*. These cables contain hair-thin strands of glass through which information flows as pulses of light.

The next major part of a cellular system is its radio antennas. An antenna may be mounted on its own radio tower or on a hilltop, a water tower, or the roof of a building.

The *cells* in a cellular system are areas from which radio signals can be beamed to or from an antenna. Each antenna serves one cell. The radio signal broadcast by a typical antenna spreads out in all directions and extends into adjacent cells. If a cellular system's radio signals could be seen, they would look like overlapping circles. Engineers envision the cells as six-sided areas that look like a honeycomb. Radio links, telephone wires, or fiber-optic cables connect the antennas to the switching station.

Cellular systems come in many sizes. A major metropolitan system may have 40 cells, while a system in a smaller city could have only 1.

There are three types of cellular telephones: *car phones*, *transportable phones*, and *portable phones*. Car phones are permanently mounted and operate off the car's battery. Most car phones have a built-in speaker, so that the caller can drive and talk without having to hold the telephone receiver, thus leaving both hands free for driving. Some speakers clip onto car visors.

How a Cellular System Works

A cellular system is a "honeycomb" of invisible cells, each created by and served by an antenna that relays radio messages to and from mobile telephones. Messages travel between antennas and the central switching network over wires or optical fibers. A switching office routes messages so rapidly that callers can converse without interruption—even when driving from one cell into another.

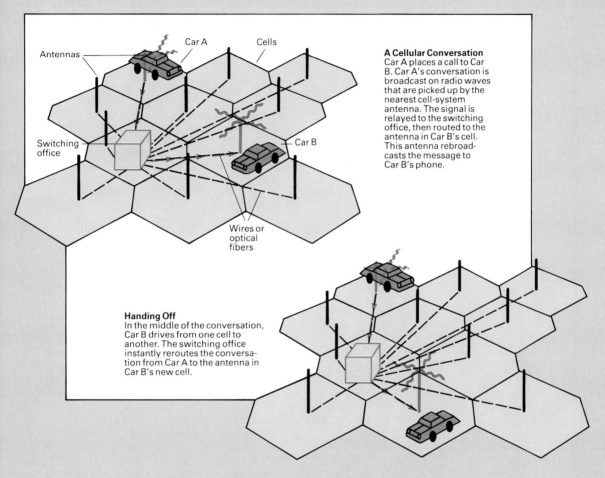

Antennas

Car A

Cells

Switching office

Car B

Wires or optical fibers

A Cellular Conversation
Car A places a call to Car B. Car A's conversation is broadcast on radio waves that are picked up by the nearest cell-system antenna. The signal is relayed to the switching office, then routed to the antenna in Car B's cell. This antenna rebroadcasts the message to Car B's phone.

Handing Off
In the middle of the conversation, Car B drives from one cell to another. The switching office instantly reroutes the conversation from Car A to the antenna in Car B's new cell.

A car phone costs approximately $700.

The transportable phone is a battery-operated phone that the user can carry around in a case. A user can make or receive a call on a transportable phone from anywhere in a cell—a sidewalk, for example, a booth in his or her favorite restaurant, or even a beach. A transportable weighs about 4.5 kilograms (10 pounds) and costs about $1,000. Transportables have as much power as car phones and many of the same features.

Portable phones have less power and operate for less time on one battery charge, but they are becoming popular because they are light and small. A portable model fits easily into a briefcase. One portable weighs 790 grams (28 ounces) and measures about 19 centimeters (7½ inches) long by 4 centimeters (1½ inches) wide. Portable phones cost about $1,500.

Calls can go from a cellular phone to a house or office phone or between two cellular phones. Suppose John, who is driving through cell A in the middle of town, wishes to talk on his car phone with Mary, who is driving a car in cell Z a few miles away. Mary has been expecting calls, so she has turned her car phone on.

When John dials Mary, his car phone broadcasts a signal containing Mary's telephone number. Nearby antennas, including the antenna in cell A, pick up John's signal, measure its strength, and transmit the measurements and the signal to the switching station.

The station's computer reacts to John's signal in an instant. It uses the information from John's phone to locate John and to assign the antenna in cell A to him. It also instructs its own antenna to broadcast a "ring" signal to Mary's phone.

Mary's phone responds by broadcasting a signal that is picked up by nearby antennas, including the antenna in cell Z. These antennas measure the strength of the signal and transmit the measurements and the signal to the switching station.

The station uses this information to locate Mary and to assign the antenna in cell Z to her. It also assigns radio frequencies to both phones and tunes the phones to transmit and receive on these frequencies.

Mary picks up her receiver, and John and Mary begin their conversation. When John speaks, his car phone broadcasts his words over the radio frequency assigned to his phone. The antenna in cell A picks up John's broadcast and sends it to the switching station. The switching station then transmits the message to cell Z's antenna, which broadcasts a radio message that Mary's car phone picks up. When Mary speaks, the flow of information is exactly reversed.

At regular intervals throughout the conversation, both phones broadcast signals that enable the switching station to track both cars. So if Mary drives from cell Z into neighboring cell Y during the conversation, the switching station will make a *handoff* to keep the conversation going. The switching station will stop transmitting to the antenna in cell Z and begin transmitting to cell Y's antenna.

The two antennas will follow suit, with cell Z's antenna ending its broadcast and the antenna in cell Y picking up the message precisely where cell Z left off. This switching process will oc-

cur so rapidly that Mary will not be aware of it.

The use of cells enables a system to transmit many calls on one frequency at the same time. This is an essential capability because the Federal Communications Commission (FCC)—the government agency that regulates communications in the United States—has assigned a limited number of frequencies to cellular radio.

An antenna's radio signal is strong enough to be picked up by cars in its own cell, but is barely audible in adjacent cells and cannot be heard at all beyond the adjacent cells. This means that a system can use the same frequency in two different cells at the same time, provided these cells are separated by a third cell that does *not* use this frequency.

Despite their convenience, cellular systems still have a few drawbacks. One is the price of calls. A cellular customer pays as much as 40 cents per minute, a much higher rate than most long-distance rates over a regular telephone system.

A second drawback is gaps in coverage. In many places, one or two small unserviced rural areas are sandwiched between large urban areas where cellular radio is available.

The cellular industry has a bright future, because advances in antenna design and computer technology promise to solve such problems as shortage of frequencies that plague the industry in crowded areas. For example, researchers are working to *digitize* cellular systems, enabling systems to transmit each message as a series of pulses representing 0's and 1's—the *bits*, or binary digits, of computer language. Electronic devices in a digital system would manipulate these bits in ways that would enable the system to crowd even more calls onto a single frequency and to provide even more advanced services.

A second major development on the horizon is cellular transmission by satellite, enabling messages to reach the most remote places on Earth. Someday, two people a continent apart, and perhaps far from civilization, may talk with each other over pocket radios. The cellular radio revolution would be complete.   [Arthur R. Brodsky]

Defending Yourself Against Salmonella

It happens at summer picnics, on airplane flights, at neighborhood dinner parties, and even in the finest of restaurants—people become sick from the food they eat. The problem is nothing new. But what *is* new is the overwhelming number of cases of food poisoning recently attributed to one particular bacteria—*salmonella*. Consumers were shocked to learn in the summer of 1987 that *salmonellosis* (salmonella poisoning) is much more common than had been imagined. Medical experts said that 90 per cent of the cases go unreported because its victims mistake it for a bout with something they call "intestinal flu."

The Centers for Disease Control (CDC) in Atlanta, Ga., estimates that each year as many as 4 million people in the United States get sick with salmonellosis. Its symptoms range from mild diarrhea to severe abdominal cramps and fever. Symptoms typically begin within 7 to 48 hours after eating tainted food. Most cases are mild, but some can be fatal. Daniel C. Rodrigue, a CDC specialist in epidemic diseases, estimates that 1,000 to 4,000 people die of salmonellosis each year in the United States. The very young and the very old are most susceptible to this illness because their body's disease-fighting immune system cannot fight off the infection. In addition, illnesses that weaken the immune system, such as cancer or AIDS (acquired immune deficiency syndrome), make people more susceptible to salmonellosis.

Animal-protein foods such as poultry, red meat, milk, and eggs are the main carriers of salmonella. The Department of Agriculture's Food Safety and Inspection Service estimates that salmonella contaminates 35 per cent of the chicken, 12 per cent of the pork, and 3 to 5 per cent of the beef sold to consumers.

In the summer of 1987, the National Academy of Sciences (NAS) reported that nearly 4 out of every 10 broiler chickens sold in U.S. supermarkets are

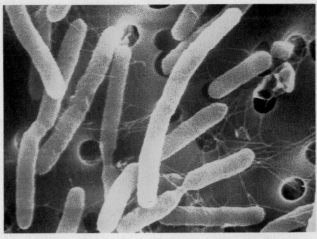

Salmonella bacteria (shown greatly magnified, with color added) cause a form of food poisoning called *salmonellosis,* which strikes up to 4 million people in the United States each year.

contaminated with the bacteria. The report emphasized that the method of inspecting poultry—used since 1957—is a critical part of the problem. Federal law requires government inspectors to observe all 4 billion broiler chickens that make their way to the market place each year. Inspectors have from one to three seconds to examine each chicken carcass visually for bruises and other signs of disease. No one can see salmonella bacteria with the naked eye, however. They are so small that millions of them would fit on the head of a pin. As a result, the inspectors cannot protect the public from the danger of salmonellosis.

News of the NAS report traveled swiftly. The day after the NAS issued its findings, most major newspapers carried the story about germ-laden chickens and the outdated inspection procedure.

Federal and state laws governing plant cleanliness do not fully address the salmonella problem. Contamination occurs in even the most pristine plants, because the salmonella bacteria come from the birds themselves. These bacteria, common inhabitants of the intestinal tracts of both animals and human beings, contaminate the

Curbing Salmonella at Home

Cook poultry to an internal temperature of 82° to 85°C (180° to 185°F.) to destroy salmonella. If you do not have a meat thermometer, cook the meat until it is no longer pink. When you pierce the meat with a fork, the meat juices should run clear.

Use a separate cutting board for raw meat to prevent the spread of salmonella from the juices of raw meat to other foods. After cutting raw meat, wash the board with hot, soapy water to kill salmonella. Also wash anything else, including your hands, touched by raw meat.

When grilling outdoors, do not use the same plate to carry cooked meat as was used to carry out the raw meat. The first plate contains juices that may be contaminated with salmonella.

Refrigerate leftovers immediately to prevent salmonella from multiplying, because salmonella thrive at temperatures between 4° and 60°C (40° and 140°F.). Make sure that your refrigerator's internal temperature is below 4°C. Transfer food to small containers for quick cooling, because large containers of food take longer to cool.

Take the same precautions at picnics that you take at home. The temperature of ice water is 0°C (32°F.), so an ice chest makes an excellent refrigerator even after most of the ice has melted.

DON'T

DO

meat of poultry when the intestines are removed. The microorganisms then can cling to human skin and the skins of any fruits and vegetables that come in contact with the contaminated meat or juices.

Then in April 1988, researchers led by Michael E. St. Louis, also a CDC specialist in epidemic diseases, reported that grade A eggs—or foods containing them—caused 27 of 65 salmonellosis outbreaks in the Northeastern United States between January 1985 and May 1987. Experts had known previously that dirty or cracked eggs contaminated by chicken droppings could cause the disease. Experts had not thought, however, that grade A eggs caused salmonellosis because these eggs are inspected for cracks and disinfected before shipment. More research is needed to determine how grade A eggs become contaminated.

Given the right conditions, any of the 2,000 strains of salmonella can grow and multiply rapidly. When food is kept at temperatures between 4° and 60°C (40° and 140°F.), salmonella bacteria thrive. This is why experts warn that food should be served hot, then stored at cold temperatures, and should not be left out at room temperature for more than an hour or two.

Unfortunately for consumers, there is no easy formula for predicting how rapidly salmonella will reproduce. Salmonella expert Jean-Yves D'Aoust of Canada's Department of Health and Welfare points out that the bacteria prefer certain foods over others and that animal-protein foods provide the best conditions for rapid bacterial reproduction. Temperature, moisture, and many other factors also influence their growth rate.

Another unpredictable—and frightening—aspect of salmonella concerns the relationship between the amount of bacteria that a food contains and the risk of catching salmonellosis. For years, researchers believed that it took millions of salmonella bacteria to make a person sick. According to D'Aoust, however, studies of salmonellosis outbreaks over the past several years indicate that small numbers of bacteria—sometimes as few as 1 to 15 cells—may make some people sick.

What can be done about salmonella poisoning? The food industry is working on methods to limit salmonella contamination and to improve the poultry inspection procedure. Changes may take a great deal of time, however, perhaps several years. In the meantime, the consumer will have to fight salmonella in the kitchen.

A few basic food-handling practices can help consumers limit the chances of infection:

■ Keep meat and meat-containing dishes out of the temperature danger zone of 4° to 60°C. The less hospitable you make conditions for bacteria, the less chance they will have to grow and cause infection.

■ Be sure to cook poultry thoroughly, because cooking destroys salmonella. The meat's internal temperature should reach 82° to 85°C (180° to 185°F.). To measure this temperature with a meat thermometer, stick the tip of the thermometer into the thickest part of the thigh or breast away from the bone. If you do not have a meat thermometer, cook the poultry until the meat is no longer pink. When you poke the meat with a fork, the juices should run clear.

■ Cook eggs thoroughly. Boiling kills the bacteria in 7 minutes, poaching in 5 minutes, and frying in 6 minutes—3 minutes for each side.

■ Use a separate cutting board for meat, and wash cutting boards, knives, counter tops, and your hands—anything that raw chicken or other meat has touched—with hot soapy water to kill bacteria. Better yet, if you have any doubt about the cleanliness of a cutting board or counter top, clean the surface with a weak solution of bleach.

■ As cooked chicken or hamburgers come off the oven or grill, put them onto a clean plate, not the plate you used to carry the raw meat. Juices on this plate may harbor bacteria.

■ When the meal is over, refrigerate leftover meat immediately. Divide large casserole dishes, pots of soup, or large dishes of food into small containers for quick cooling. And before eating leftovers, heat them thoroughly.

Following all these steps may take a few extra minutes in the kitchen. Considering the dangers of salmonella bacteria, however, that would be time well spent.   [Maureen Callahan]

Sorting out Per Cents from Percentage Points

We hear about numbers expressed as per cents and percentages every day, and we remember our mathematics teacher telling us that "per cent means hundredths." But after that, things can get a little vague. Many numbers given in percentages—such as the growth rate of the economy, the inflation rate, and the unemployment rate—are obviously important, but somehow mysterious. This is partly because the people who bombard us with statistics involving percentages often make the mistake of confusing differences between percentages with growth rates. This mistake can have a shocking effect, especially when it involves our personal finances.

For example, suppose the city council announced last year that property taxes would rise from 8 per cent to 10 per cent, a difference of 2 percentage points. Last year my tax bill was $1,800. If I had expected this year's tax to be 2 per cent higher, or $1,836, I would have been in for a shock. This year's tax was $2,250, a whopping 25 per cent more than last year's bill.

Did the city figure my bill incorrectly? Did the city council lie about the increase? Exactly what happened?

The council did not lie, and the bill was correct. I confused a *difference* with a *growth rate*.

Notice what seems to be a trivial distinction in terms: The difference was expressed as *percentage points*, but the growth rate was *per cent*. This distinction is far from trivial, however, when it comes to money. In fact, it is crucial. Unfortunately, some speakers and writers fail to make this distinction.

A difference between percentages is exactly what it sounds like—one percentage minus another. A growth rate, on the other hand, tells how much a changing quantity, such as the amount of a tax, has risen relative to its old level. Perhaps I did not read the newspaper account of the tax increase carefully enough. If I had, I would have been able to calculate the growth rate in the following way: Subtract the old percentage level from the new percentage level, then divide by the old level. In the case of the property tax, I subtract 8 from 10 and divide the answer—2—by 8. I compute a growth rate of 0.25, or 25 per cent.

If percentages are so confusing, why do we use them in the first place? Because percentages are an excellent means of comparing quantities that are expressed in relative terms, when the relationship between the quantities is not easy to see.

The field of sports provides plenty of examples of such quantities. For example, suppose my softball team has won 15 of its 20 games, while my cousin's team has won 18 out of 25. My cousin's team has more victories, but which team has the better overall record? When we convert the quantities to percentages, the relationship becomes clear. In each case, we divide the number of games won by the number played, and then we multiply the result by 100. The result tells me that my team is doing slightly better than my cousin's. My team has won 75 per cent of its games, while my cousin's team has won only 72 per cent.

Another common mistake involving percentages is a failure to change denominators. Every percentage figure begins with a division of one number by another, and the number by which we divide is called the denominator. We can accidentally use the wrong denominator in certain circumstances.

For example, this denominator "trap" is easy to fall into in problems involving the *unemployment rate*, a percentage calculated by the United States Department of Labor. The unemployment rate is the number of people who are unemployed and looking for work divided by the number of people in the *work force*—the number of unemployed people looking for work plus the number of employed.

I could fall into the trap of failing to change denominators while reading a newspaper article that says: In mid-1986, the unemployment rate was 7 per cent; in mid-1987, 6 per cent. The difference was 1 percentage point.

Does this mean that an extra 1 per cent of the work force found jobs be-

tween mid-1986 and mid-1987? The article states that in mid-1986 the work force was 118 million. If I multiply this by 1 per cent I get an answer of 1.18 million for the number of people who found jobs between mid-1986 and mid-1987. But then I read that the number of employed actually rose from 110 million to 113 million during that period, an increase of 3 million. How do all these bits and pieces of information fit together?

The answer to this puzzle is that the work force, the denominator used to calculate unemployment rates, shifted during the year. More people entered the work force than left it, so the work force—and the denominator—rose from 118 million to 120 million. In mid-1986, the number of unemployed was 8.3 million, so the unemployment rate was 8.3 million divided by 118 million, or 7 per cent. In mid-1987, 7.2 million workers were unemployed so the rate was 7.2 million divided by the new denominator, 120 million, or 6 per cent.

Avoid the denominator "trap": Be on the lookout for a shifting denominator. [Donald W. Swanton]

Decoding
Bar Codes

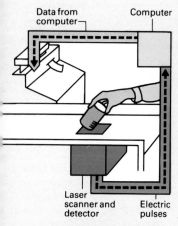

Data from computer

Computer

Laser scanner and detector

Electric pulses

How a Scanner Reads a Bar Code
When an item, such as a soup can, passes over a scanner window in the checkout counter, a laser beam "reads" the code by bouncing off the lines and spaces. The reflected light strikes a detector, which translates the reflections into electric pulses. These pulses feed information to a computer, which subtracts the soup from the inventory records and determines the price that appears on the cash register.

Pick up virtually any item in a supermarket or any other retail store and you are likely to find a pattern of thin black lines on the package. This is a bar code, and bar codes are used almost everywhere today. They are used so widely because they enable people to keep track of inventories and to record transactions at lightning speed.

At the supermarket checkout counter, for example, a clerk no longer has to punch prices and other product information into a cash register. Instead, the clerk merely passes each item over a small window in the counter. Below the window, a device called an *optical scanner* uses laser beams to "read" the information in the bar code.

Each bar code is a self-contained message with information encoded in the widths of the dark bars and the light spaces between the bars. The bars and spaces can represent letters of the alphabet, numbers, and certain special symbols such as an asterisk. Light patterns reflected off the bar code are picked up by light-sensitive devices in the scanner. The light patterns are converted to electric signals and sent to a computer.

The computer uses the information in various ways. In the supermarket, the computer sends the description and price of an item that has been scanned to the cash register, which displays this information for the customer and prints it on the sales receipt. The computer also subtracts the item from the store's inventory records. And in some stores, the computer even alerts the store manager when the supply of the item falls below a certain level.

Libraries use bar codes at checkout desks. When an individual checks a book out, the librarian records the transaction by scanning the bar code on the individual's library card and the code on the book. Manufacturing plants use a similar technique for checking tools out of toolrooms. In warehouses, bar codes provide a fast,

accurate method of tracking and controlling the movement of goods and materials from the time they are received until they are shipped.

Many large manufacturing plants also use bar codes to reduce the amount of manual record-keeping required to calculate their employees' paychecks. Workers at these plants wear badges containing bar-coded employee identification numbers. When an employee enters or leaves the plant, a scanner reads the badge and sends the identification number and the time to the company computer.

Bar codes first appeared in the 1960's, when the railroad industry used a bar code to monitor the use and location of the more than 2 million freight cars in the United States and Canada. Although more than 95 per cent of the freight cars had bar-code labels attached to them by 1974, the industry abandoned the system in the late 1970's because of the difficulty of maintaining the labels and automatic scanners in the rough environment of railroad yards. Since then, more than 50 bar codes have been developed for various other industries.

Four bar-code systems—Universal Product Code (UPC), Codabar, Interleaved 2 of 5, and Code 39—are in wide use in retail stores and industry. The UPC was developed by the grocery industry and scanner manufacturers and was adopted by that industry in 1973. Then the retail industry made the UPC its standard for identifying apparel, drugs, and other nonfood items.

More than 90 per cent of the items in supermarkets have UPC bar codes printed on them. A computer in a typical supermarket may have information on 20,000 items. A computer in a large department store has many times that number.

All bar codes have a digital, or numbered, format. The bars and spaces in a UPC symbol, for example, represent 12 digits. The function of each digit

Code border

Code border

0 | 4 8 0 0 1 | 2 6 5 1 6 | 5

Number System Character: "0" means that this is a nationally branded grocery item that was not packaged at the store.

Manufacturer Identification Number: "48001" means that this is a product of Best Foods.

Code border

Item Code Number: "26516" designates a 0.95-liter (32-fluid-ounce) jar of Hellmann's mayonnaise.

Check Digit: This number enables the scanning machine to verify the code by using a certain mathematical formula.

depends upon its location. The first digit, called the *number system character*, indicates a type of product. For example, 3 indicates a drug or some other health-related product; and 5, a refund coupon. The next five digits are the *manufacturer identification number*, which indicates what company produced the item. Next is the five-digit *item code number* assigned by the manufacturer to identify the specific item. Following these 11 digits is a single *check digit*, which enables the scanner to verify the accuracy of the code it has scanned.

Two bars and two spaces make up each digit. The widths of the individual bars and spaces vary and are measured in units called *data elements*. A bar or space can be 1, 2, 3, or 4 data elements wide, but the two bars and two spaces must occupy a total of 7 data elements.

The data elements, in turn, represent 0's and 1's, the binary numbers that make up the "alphabet" of computer language. A space element represents a 0; a bar element, a 1.

The UPC uses a "trick" to enable a scanner to read the pattern of bars and spaces in either direction. The symbols representing the first six digits always have an odd number of bar elements, while the last six digits have an even number of bar elements. So by counting the number of bar elements in the first six digits, the scanner can determine the direction in which it is reading.

What happens if the scanner fails to read the UPC code? Anything that complicated would be extremely difficult for a human being to learn to read. So, to make life easier at the checkout counter, the number system character, the manufacturer and item numbers, and the check digit are printed along with the bars as part of the UPC symbol. If the scanner does not read the UPC, the checkout clerk punches these numbers into the cash register, which sends the appropriate signals to the computer.

Codabar, Interleaved 2 of 5, and Code 39 use only two widths, rather than four, for bars and spaces. Be-

What the Bars on Grocery Labels Mean
The Universal Product Code is the bar code used in grocery stores. The lines and spaces of the bar code represent numbers that identify the product and its manufacturer, plus a digit that enables the scanning machine to check the code. In addition, three code borders "tell" the scanner when it is at the beginning, middle, and end of a code. The numbers represented by the code are also printed so the clerk can punch them into the cash register if the scanner does not work.

Cracking the USPS Code

The United States Postal Service (USPS) is making increased use of automation to sort and route mail. As a result, many envelopes that arrive at homes and offices have a bar code printed on them. The ZIP code for Stony Brook, N.Y., for example, looks like this:

|ₙₙₙₙ‖ₙₙₙₙ‖‖‖ₙₙₙₙ‖ₙₙₙ‖ₙₙₙₙₙₙ‖ₙₙₙₙ‖ₙₙₗ‖ₙ‖ₙₙ|

Use the following seven steps to "crack" the bar code for Stony Brook:

1. Disregard the long bar at each end of the code. These bars tell the scanning machine, "Message coming" and "Message complete."

2. The remaining bars represent 0's and 1's, the *binary digits* that make up computer language. Change the short bars to 0's and the long bars to 1's. You should get this number:

000110001110001101000100110010

3. Divide this number into six groups of five digits each by "counting off" as follows:

00011   00011   10001   10100   01001   10010

4. Now list all the numbers you can think of that are made up of three 0's and two 1's. There are only 10 such numbers, and you may write them in any order. Try to do this step without looking at the list below:

10001   10100   01001   01100   00110   10010   11000   01010   00101   00011

5. Arrange these numbers in order of size, from the smallest to the largest. You should end up with this list:

00011   00101   00110   01001   01010   01100   10001   10010   10100   11000

6. Next, assign the *decimal digits* (0 through 9) to these numbers. Assign "1" to the smallest number, "2" to the second-smallest, and so on, until you get to the largest number, to which you assign "0." You should produce the following list:

00011 = 1   00101 = 2   00110 = 3   01001 = 4   01010 = 5
01100 = 6   10001 = 7   10010 = 8   10100 = 9   11000 = 0

7. Finally, use this list to convert the six groups of five binary digits from step 3 to six decimal digits, as follows:

00011   00011   10001   10100   01001   10010
  1   1   7   9   4   8

The first five decimal digits—11794—are the ZIP code for Stony Brook. The sixth digit—8—is a numeral used by the scanner's computer to make certain that the scanner has read the ZIP code correctly. The computer manipulates the sixth digit according to the same mathematical formula that the computer in the bar code printer uses to calculate it. According to this formula, the printer's computer adds the five digits of the ZIP code, then inserts whatever sixth digit is necessary to make the sum of all six digits end in 0. In this case,
1 + 1 + 7 + 9 + 4 = 22, so the sixth digit 8 was inserted to make the sum of all six digits—30—end in 0.

cause the codes have fewer widths for scanners to recognize and computers to interpret, they do not require such sophisticated reading equipment. However, one of them—Codabar—is quite complex, the result of a trade-off that also makes it extremely reliable. The use of special characters and the insertion of a wide space between characters decreases the likelihood of a reading error, but also complicates the production of printed codes for individual items.

Codabar was developed in 1972 for the retail industry, but department stores found it too complex and never accepted it. Libraries, delivery services, and organizations in the medical industry use it extensively, however, because of its reliability. The American Blood Commission, for example, marks bags of donated blood in Codabar. This code uses 20 characters, each represented by four bars and the three spaces between them.

The Interleaved 2 of 5 code lacks Codabar's extra reliability, but it is simpler than both Codabar and the UPC. In fact, Interleaved 2 of 5 would make an excellent code for the grocery industry. But by the time the code was invented in the early 1970's, the UPC was firmly established in that industry for items sold to consumers.

The grocery industry adopted Interleaved 2 of 5 for shipping containers, however. The code has also been widely accepted to keep track of goods in warehouses and to inventory parts in manufacturing plants.

In the Interleaved 2 of 5 code, each number from 0 through 9 is represented by a combination of either two wide bars and three narrow bars or two wide spaces and three narrow spaces. The bars and spaces representing two-digit numbers are interleaved with each other. For example, in the symbol for the number 57, the 5 is represented by bars and the 7 by spaces between the bars.

Code 39, developed in 1975, uses five bars and their four intervening spaces to represent 10 numbers from 0 through 9, the 26 letters of the alphabet, and 8 special characters. Because it can represent letters as well as numbers, many government agencies and industrial organizations use Code 39 as their standard. The Department of Defense, for example, uses Code 39 to keep track of parts, record shipping and receiving operations, and manage inventories. The Automotive Industry Action Group, a trade association of the major North American automobile manufacturers and suppliers, uses Code 39 to keep track of auto parts.

Hospitals and clinics are adopting the Health Industry Bar Code (HIBC), which employs Code 39's system of symbols. In some hospitals, for example, each patient wears a wristband that is bar-coded with a patient identification number. When a patient receives a prescription drug, a nurse uses a scanner to check the bar code on the wristband with the bar code on the prescription label.

The U.S. Postal Service has begun to use its own bar code on envelopes and post cards in order to sort and route mail automatically. The bar code represents the ZIP code of the letter's destination. The code is extremely simple, consisting of short bars, which are read as 0's, and tall bars, read as 1's.

After a letter is mailed, it goes to a local distribution center. There, the letter travels on a conveyor belt past a clerk who reads the ZIP code that was put on the envelope by the sender. The clerk types the ZIP code on a machine that prints the corresponding bar code on the envelope. Thereafter, automatic equipment can route the letter to the recipient's local post office. If the nine-digit ZIP code is used, the mail can even be routed automatically to the local letter carrier.

Versatile, lightning-fast bar-code systems seem destined to become an even larger part of the technological scene. They have already entered the vast home electronics market, for example. The giant Japanese firm Sony Corporation sells a videocassette recorder (VCR) that has its own scanner. The TV viewer can scan bar codes printed in cable-television guide booklets to set the VCR to record certain motion pictures and special television programs.

Because they enable us to transmit repeatedly used numbers and words instantly and conveniently, bar codes promise to play an ever-greater role in our lives. [Marian Visich, Jr.]

What Makes
Paint Stick

One of the most famous paintings of Western civilization, *The Last Supper* by Italian genius Leonardo da Vinci, began to flake away soon after he completed the work in about 1497. This wall painting was a triumph of art, but a failure of surface chemistry.

Today, anybody who merely wants to cover an interior or exterior wall with paint can easily outclass Leonardo when it comes to making paint stick. Modern chemistry has developed paints that look good, do an excellent job of protecting the surfaces they cover, and are extremely durable.

But with so many paints available today, how do we know which paint is best for a given job? The best advice is to discuss the job with a reliable paint dealer. A little knowledge of paint chemistry and surface preparation can help you talk the dealer's language.

Paints are made up of three kinds of materials—pigments, binders, and liquids. *Pigments* are solid particles that give paints their color. *Binders*, which include plastics and resins, make paints dry to a filmy consistency, hold the pigments to the surface, and protect the surface. *Liquids* give paints their fluid form, making them easy to apply. The liquid is also known as the *base*, and there are two main types of base—oil and water.

To protect and beautify a surface effectively, a paint must have certain properties. It must be easy to apply smoothly and evenly. It must stick to the surface, forming a single, unbroken film of uniform thickness.

For safety's sake, the paint should not be highly poisonous or flammable. For convenience, it should dry quickly, be easy to clean up, and last a long time in storage.

Once the paint is dry, it should resist chemicals, water, and sunlight. Interior paints must resist cleaning solvents, while exterior paints have to contend with weather.

In addition, the paint should be simple to touch up, easy to wipe clean, and strong and flexible enough to resist dents and scratches. The color should resist fading.

No paint excels in all these ways, however. So you must find a paint that has the best balance of properties for the job you want it to do.

Paints bind to surfaces in two basic ways—mechanically and chemically. In *mechanical binding*, the paint locks itself to the surface by filling in tiny holes and uneven areas in the surface. In *chemical binding*, atoms in the paint form bonds with surface atoms so that the paint and the surface become one continuous material. Thus, chemical binding forms a smoother surface than does mechanical binding.

Two critical properties of paints—strength and stability—depend on what happens to the molecules that make up the binders. When oil-based paints dry, molecules of their binders join to form surface films that are tougher and more stable than are those of water-based paints. The way in which the long, chainlike molecules of the binders join is called *cross-linking*. When the paint dries, chemical bonds form between the chains, resulting in netlike structures that are extremely tough. This makes oil-based paint best for most outdoor surfaces.

Oil-based paints are brittle when they dry, however, and they crack easily. Other disadvantages of oil-based paints include the need to use thinning and cleaning solvents such as turpentine that may have strong-smelling, flammable, even toxic fumes.

Oil-based paints also tend to deteriorate quickly in storage. The binders in the unused paint, over time, may begin to cross-link in the can, forming a thick "skin" and eventually drying up altogether. To combat these problems, paint chemists have developed additives that limit cross-linking, reduce the amount of solvent required, and cut the rate of drying in the can.

Most water-based paints form a hard surface by *solvent evaporation*. The wa-

Results of Painting Surfaces Improperly

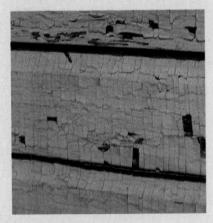

Alligatoring can occur when many layers of paint accumulate on a surface.

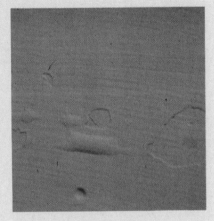

Blistering often results from applying an oil-based paint to a moist surface.

Cracking is caused by moisture, inferior paint, or the uneven application of paint.

Peeling is due to painting a surface that is dirty, too moist, or too glossy.

ter dries and the binders stick to one another mechanically. The resulting films on surfaces are not as strong as those of oil-based paints.

Water-based paints are chemically stable, however, and their fumes are not poisonous or flammable. In addition, spills and paint-coated brushes are easy to clean up. This makes them good for interior walls.

Older water-based paints, such as whitewashes and lacquers, did not hold up well over time and were difficult to apply. Newer latex paints go a long way toward solving these prob-

lems. Their binders are plastics whose molecules overlap one another as they dry, forming tough, netlike structures. The addition of *surfactants*—soaplike molecules that reduce the surface tension of the paint—makes latex paint spread more evenly.

One problem with latex paints is that microorganisms reproduce easily in them before the paint is used, making the paint turn sour. Paint chemists have minimized souring by adding antibacterial and antifungal chemicals to the paints.

Another problem with latex paints is

Preparing Surfaces and Choosing the Right Paint

Exterior Surfaces

Type of Surface	Preparation	Paint
New Wood	Use primer to seal. Putty or caulk nailheads, cracks, and areas around windows. Use knot sealer to prevent resin in knots from staining paint.	Latex, oil-based, or *alkyd*-based paint. (An alkyd is an artificial chemical base.) Stain; varnish.
Previously painted wood	Remove chipped, blistered, or powdered paint by scraping. Remove unusually stubborn old paint by such means as a chemical stripper. Replace loose or shrunken putty and caulk. Prime bare areas.	Latex, oil-based, or alkyd-based paint.
Wood deck or stairs	Prime with paintable water-repellent preservative.	Porch and deck enamel.
Aluminum gutters	Remove dirt and cracking and flaking paint. Prime bare areas with primer manufactured for aluminum or galvanized steel.	Metal enamel or any paint suitable for exterior wood.
Wrought iron fencing	Remove rust and dirt as well as cracked and peeling paint. Coat bare areas with a metal primer.	Metal enamel or any paint suitable for exterior wood.
Cement block	Fill large holes with cement grout. For a top coat of masonry paint, prime with masonry surface conditioner. For other top coats, prime with alkali-resistant paint. (An alkali is a substance such as lime that can destroy paint films.)	Exterior latex paint.
Concrete patios	For a top coating of masonry paint, prime with masonry surface conditioner. For other top coats, prime with alkali-resistant paint.	Alkyd masonry paint or any paint suitable for exterior wood.

Interior Surfaces

Type of Surface	Preparation	Paint
Woodwork	For a top coat of paint on new wood, first cover with a primer. For paint on previously painted wood, remove any peeling and cracked paint, then sand. For a top coat of stain on open-grained woods such as oak, undercoat with paste wood filler. Close-grain woods such as maple do not need a filler.	Latex, or alkyd-based flat, semigloss, or high-gloss paint. Stain; varnish; or polyurethane varnish.
Refinishing wooden floors	Sand off old finish. For a top coat of floor enamel, apply wood filler, then prime with same paint as top coat. For a top coat of sealer, varnish, or lacquer, undercoat with wood filler to fill the pores of the wood, providing a smooth finish.	Floor enamel; floor sealer; varnish; clear floor lacquer; polyurethane varnish.
Previously painted plaster and drywall	Scrub off grease and dirt.	Latex or alkyd-based semigloss or gloss enamel paint for heavy-use areas such as kitchens and bathrooms. Latex or alkyd-based flat paint or semigloss enamel paint for moderate-use areas such as halls and children's rooms. Latex or alkyd-based flat paint for light-use areas such as living rooms and bedrooms.
New plaster	Wait three or four weeks after plaster is applied before priming.	
New drywall	Sand joint compound lightly to provide an even finish, then cover with latex prime coat.	

Source: The National Paint and Coatings Association.

the difficulty in getting a glossy finish. Gloss depends upon smoothness. The smoother the film, the glossier the finish. And smoothness depends on how the paint sticks to the surface.

Because water-based paints tend to bind more mechanically than chemically, they do not form as smooth a film as do chemical bonds and so it is difficult to get a glossy surface with a latex paint. Acrylic binders in modern water-based paints, however, form such strong chemical bonds with surface atoms that they dry to a gloss approaching that of oil-based paints.

The surface plays as important a role in the sticking process as the paint. The best paint in the world cannot do the job unless the surface is prepared to accept it.

The surface must be very clean. Even greasy fingerprints can prevent a paint from sticking well.

The surface must be smooth. Paint can hide slight imperfections, but not bumps or pits. The surface should not be glossy, however. Paint needs some roughness to latch onto, particularly if the paint relies heavily on mechanical binding. A *primer* (undercoat) can roughen a surface and improve mechanical binding.

The surface and the paint must suit each other chemically. A surface that absorbs liquids extremely well, for example, must be sealed with a primer or a thin liquid called a *sealer* to prevent the paint from soaking in too far. A sealer dries to form a film that paints cannot soak through.

A surface, such as a plastic, that can be damaged by a paint's chemical solvents also must be protected with a primer. If the paint relies on the formation of chemical bonds for adhesion, the surface must contain the types of atoms that can form those bonds. If the surface does not contain such atoms, you must put them on the surface by coating it with a primer. Metal surfaces, for example, do not form strong chemical bonds with many exterior paints, so they require a coat of a special primer made for metals.

If you are using an oil-based paint, the surface must be dry, because oil and water do not mix. Water is an enemy of oil-based paint and can cause blistering and bleeding.

To prepare a surface properly, follow these six steps:

1. Examine the surface closely and diagnose any problems. If there are several layers of old paint, the new paint's resistance to temperature changes will be reduced, so you should remove the old paint. If a panel of wood has rotted, replace it.

2. If old paint is blistered or peeling, remove it by scraping, by heating and scraping, or by applying a chemical paint remover. If paint is severely blistered, you may have a moisture problem. Water vapor may be leaking through the wall. The only way to solve this problem is to install a moisture barrier—usually a sheet of thin plastic—in the wall.

3. Clean the surface thoroughly. Follow rinsing instructions on the cleanser label to remove harmful residues.

4. Fill small cracks and holes with a caulking compound, joint compound, plaster, putty, or plastic wood. Then sand the excess filler, bumps, and other irregularities. When you are finished with your repair work, the surface should feel smooth to the touch, but not slick.

5. Clean the surface again to remove all dust generated by the repair work.

6. Add a coat of primer or sealer, if appropriate.

The same chemicals that provide a paint with desirable qualities such as a smooth, durable surface and fast drying may also be dangerous, so a few simple precautions are necessary:

■ Work with adequate ventilation.

■ Avoid open flames such as burning cigarettes and gas pilot lights when using turpentine and other flammable solvents for oil-based paints.

■ Close the containers of flammable liquids tightly and, when finished, store them carefully.

■ Dispose of solvent-soaked rags as you finish with them. Heaps of such rags are a fire hazard because they can burst into flame spontaneously.

■ Wear gloves and other protective clothing to protect your skin.

■ Read all product labels and follow manufacturers' instructions.

Now you should be ready to talk with your dealer about what kind of paint to use. Then—move over, Leonardo.   [Peter J. Andrews]

People in Science

Imagination and vision are two qualities that all great scientists bring to their research. This section profiles two of today's top scientists—a physicist and a biologist—and tells how vision and imagination led one to revolutionary concepts about the cosmos and the other to new ways of explaining certain human behaviors.

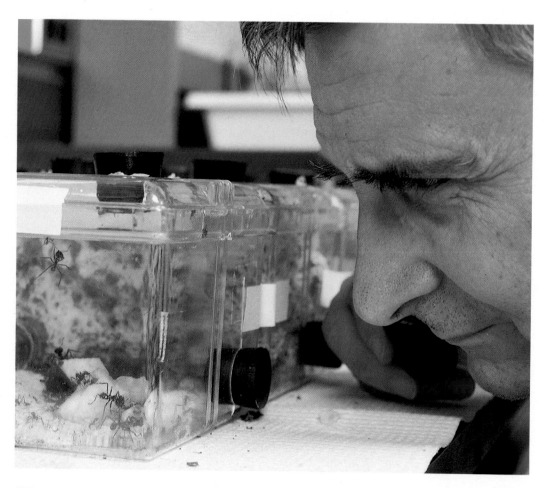

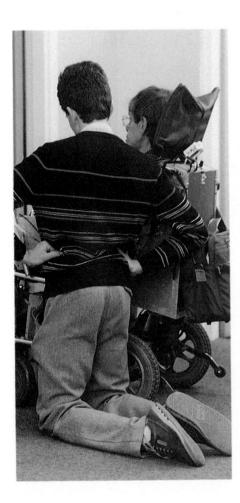

This theoretical physicist moved to the forefront of his field while an incurable disease was gradually crippling his body.

Stephen W. Hawking

BY DON N. PAGE

English physicist Stephen W. Hawking is widely regarded as being one of the world's most brilliant living scientists. He has blazed new trails in the wilderness of theoretical physics with pioneering concepts about bizarre regions of space called *black holes*. He has helped extend the frontier of our understanding of the universe back to the very moment of its creation—and beyond. He is a leading expert on gravity and has moved toward a goal that evaded the German-born genius Albert Einstein (1879-1955)—a mathematical description of the entire universe and the forces that have governed it since the beginning of time. Hawking now holds the post of Lucasian Professor of Mathematics at Cambridge University in England, a position once held by Sir Isaac Newton (1642-1727).

Splendid as these achievements are, the setting in which they were accomplished gives them even more luster. Since the early 1960's, when he was in his early 20's, Stephen Hawking has had a disease that has gradually disabled him so that he can no longer walk, write, or even speak. He suffers from amyotrophic lateral sclerosis (ALS)—also called Lou Gehrig's disease after the American baseball star who died of it. ALS is a gradually crippling, incurable disease of the nervous system.

Hawking communicates mainly by squeezing a handheld switch to display words on the monitor of a computer mounted on his wheelchair. The computer also has a voice synthesizer, so Hawking can make himself heard.

Stephen William Hawking was born in Oxford, England, on Jan. 8, 1942, and grew up in London and nearby St. Albans. His father, a physician who conducted research on tropical diseases, encouraged him to become a scientist. Hawking preferred mathematics to biological research, but his father argued that it would be too hard to get a job in math. So Stephen chose to study the closely related subject of physics when he entered Oxford University in 1959.

Hawking was less than a hard-working student. At Oxford, it was not socially acceptable to work too hard, so Hawking studied only about an hour a day. This lack of effort led to a mediocre performance on his final exam in 1962. Unlike their counterparts in the United States, university students in Great Britain take three years of course work to receive a bachelor's degree. At the end of the third year, they take a final exam on all their courses. Each student who passes receives an ordinary degree or a degree with one of three or four classes of honors, the highest of which is *first-class honors*.

Hawking's performance on his final exam nearly cost him the first-class honors he needed to receive a scholarship to do graduate work at Cambridge University. Fortunately, there was an oral exam for borderline cases, and Hawking answered the questions so well that the examiners realized he was smarter than most of them. So they gave him first-class honors.

Hawking began his graduate studies at Cambridge in 1962, specializing in *cosmology*, the study of the origin and evolution of the universe. But then he noticed some difficulty with his muscular coordination. Even during his last year at Oxford, he had tended to stumble and to slur his words. Physicians diagnosed his illness as ALS in January 1963.

ALS is a gradual deterioration of the nerves of the brain and spinal cord. These nerves govern almost all *voluntary movements* of the muscles (movements we can control at will), such as those involved in walking and speaking. As the nerves deteriorate, less and less of each muscle receives commands from the brain, so the victim cannot move the muscles. As a result, the unused parts of the muscles rapidly waste away.

ALS does not devastate the entire body, however. The disease does not hinder eye movements, though they are voluntary, nor does it affect the nerves of the sense organs. Thus, an ALS victim can see, hear, feel, taste, and smell normally. Furthermore, ALS does not damage nerves that control involuntary muscle movements such as the beating of the heart. The disease gradually hampers breathing and swallowing, however, functions that involve both voluntary and involuntary movements.

Soon, Hawking could not speak without slurring his words. Doctors predicted that he would die within a couple of years, as is typi-

The author:
Don N. Page is professor of physics at Pennsylvania State University in University Park, and is a professional associate and a close friend of Stephen Hawking. From 1976 to 1979, while studying as a postdoctoral researcher with Hawking at Cambridge University in England, Page lived in the Hawking household. He has returned each summer to work with Hawking.

Hawking, who has a neurological disease, begins his day with a trip in his motorized wheelchair to his office at Cambridge University. His route takes him over the River Cam, lined with green fields, *above,* and along a busy street, *left,* where he stops to converse with a student.

cal of ALS patients. This news depressed Hawking deeply. He would need three years to obtain a Ph.D. degree, so he saw little reason to continue his studies. Even before the bad news from his doctor, Hawking had been having trouble finding a good topic for his Ph.D. *thesis* (a long research paper written by a candidate for a degree). He had wanted to write his thesis about the expansion of the universe. Scientists believe that the universe began 10 billion to 20 billion years ago with an explosion called the *big bang*, when an incredibly powerful fireball burst into existence. They also believe that the universe has been expanding ever since. But to make headway in understanding this expansion required more advanced mathematics than Hawking had learned at Oxford. As a result of all this, Hawking accomplished very little research during his first two years as a graduate student.

The situation eventually brightened, however. The progress of the disease slowed, and Hawking realized he would live longer than he had thought. He also acquired another purpose in life. On Jan. 1, 1963, Hawking had met Jane Wilde. Over the next two years, when Wilde was a language student at Westfield College in London, their friendship blossomed into a much deeper relationship. Eventually, they decided to marry. This decision forced Hawking to rethink his future. He realized he would have to work hard on his Ph.D. thesis and get a job. Hawking now recognizes his engagement as the main turning point in his career.

Jane and Stephen were married in July 1965. Jane was still an undergraduate student, and during her final year of language studies, she commuted between Cambridge and London, a distance of about 80 kilometers (50 miles).

Hawking reached another turning point in 1965, when he read a scholarly article on black holes by English mathematician Roger Penrose, a research associate at Birkbeck College in London. A black hole is a region of space in which the gravity is incredibly strong. Nothing that falls into a black hole can escape from it, not even light. Penrose wrote about black holes that form when stars burn themselves out and collapse under the force of their own weight. To form a black hole, a star must have at least three times the *mass* of the sun. (Mass is the quantity of matter an object contains and determines its weight.) Cosmologists say that such a star will form a black hole measuring at least 15 kilometers (9 miles) in diameter.

Penrose showed mathematically that there would be something

Hawking "talks" by means of an ingenious computer system that puts words and numbers onto a screen attached to his wheelchair and also onto a computer he uses as a word processor. Hawking constructs a sentence for a colleague, *right,* by squeezing a switch to select words from a list on the computer screen, *below.*

Next Page of Words

naked	need	new	nor
name	negative	Newcastle	normal
napkin	neglect	newspaper	normally
nation	neglible	newton	north
national	neighbour	Newton's	nose
natural	neither	next	nostril
nature	nerve	nhs	not
near	nervous	nice	notably
nearer	network	night	notation
nearest	neurone	no	note
nearly	neutrino	nobel	nothing
necessaril	neutron	noise	notice
necessary	never	non	now
neck	neverthelenone	nu

TALKING   70/69/360

It doesn't matter what the exact numbers are. The point is there are ▮

called a *singularity* inside a black hole. A singularity is even more amazing than a black hole. Anything falling into a singularity would be utterly destroyed, usually by being squeezed out of existence. But Penrose said something even more astounding than this—something that we can hardly imagine: that time itself would come to an end for whatever fell into a singularity. Penrose based his mathematics on Einstein's general theory of relativity, published in 1916 and still regarded as the best description of gravity.

Inspired by Penrose's article, Hawking adapted Penrose's mathematics to his thesis. Hawking produced *theorems* (mathematically proven statements) showing that a singularity existed when time began with the big bang.

Hawking's first theorems about singularities made up the final chapter of his thesis, "Properties of Expanding Universes," for which Hawking received his Ph.D. in 1966. That same year, he and Penrose shared the Adams Prize—Cambridge University's highest award in mathematics and physics—for work on singularities.

Because his work was so outstanding, Hawking quickly advanced up the academic ladder. Since 1965, he has been a fellow of Gonville and Caius College, one of the 31 colleges that make up Cambridge University, conducting theoretical research and supervising students. In 1968, he became a member of the graduate staff of Cambridge's Institute of Theoretical Astronomy. In 1972, his title changed to research assistant, and in 1975, he became a *reader* (associate professor).

In 1977, Cambridge University bestowed a high honor on Hawking by creating a special professorship for him. At the age of 35, Hawking became Professor of Gravitational Physics. In England, scholars rarely become professors at such an early age. In fact, there are so few professorships in England that most British scholars never reach that position.

An even more prestigious title awaited Hawking. In 1979, he became Lucasian Professor of Mathematics, the most illustrious position at the university. In addition to Newton, individuals who held this position have included English mathematician and computer pioneer Charles Babbage (1791-1871) and British theoretical physicist Paul A. M. Dirac (1902-1984), who discovered the fundamental equation governing the electron.

As Hawking moved up academically, he continued to produce remarkable theorems about gravity. The details of these theorems are so difficult that even physics professors have trouble grasping some of them. The outlines of Hawking's ideas, however, are fairly easy to comprehend. And because they involve strange objects, bizarre phenomena, and astonishingly large and small numbers, they are fascinating to think about.

One of Hawking's first important contributions concerned the size of black holes. A black hole tends to grow because whatever falls into it makes its gravitational attraction even stronger. Hawking showed precisely what it is about a black hole that usually grows—the area of its surface. Some black holes, such as those at the centers of some galaxies, may become huge—tens of billions of kilometers across—even larger than the diameter of Pluto's orbit around the sun.

Other black holes, however, are tiny. These black holes formed, not from the collapse of stars, but from the collapse of very dense matter less than one second after the big bang. In 1971, Hawking showed mathematically that such black holes could still be small today. Amazingly, a small black hole could have more mass than the Great Wall of China yet be smaller than an atomic nucleus, which is a few one-trillionths of a millimeter across. Hawking realized a miniature black hole would obey the laws of *quantum mechanics*, a theory that describes the world of atoms and subatomic particles. He became convinced that an astonishing aspect of quantum mechanics would cause black holes to lose energy and mass. According to quantum mechanics, the "empty" space at the surface of a black hole would emit pairs of subatomic particles that would have different kinds of energy. One particle would have what physicists call *positive energy*—what we know as ordinary energy. Strangely, the other particle would have *negative energy*, which can cancel out positive energy.

The particle with negative energy would fall into the black hole, decreasing the energy of the black hole. This peculiar process would decrease the mass of the black hole because energy is equivalent to mass, according to Einstein's famous equation $E = mc^2$. (E represents energy; m, mass; and c, the speed of light.) Meanwhile, the particle with positive energy would escape from the region just outside the black hole. To an observer at a distance from the black hole—an astronaut in a spacecraft orbiting it, for example—the particle with positive energy would appear to come from within the black hole.

In 1973, Hawking began to calculate how rapidly a black hole would lose energy and mass in this way. The problem was extremely difficult. And by this time, disease had confined Hawking to a wheelchair and made it virtually impossible for him to write down the complex mathematical equations. He had to do all his calculations mentally—a task that physicist Werner Israel of the University of Alberta in Canada compared with Mozart's composing an entire symphony in his head. Hawking stripped the problem down to its essential features; nevertheless, it still required a great deal of mental mathematics.

Hawking determined that a black hole could lose all its energy and mass by means of the negative energy phenomenon, eventually disappearing in a mighty explosion. In the last second of its existence, it would emit 100 billion trillion watts of power—enough to meet the needs of the United States for 10,000 years.

Hawking makes several trips each year to visit colleagues and give lectures at various places throughout the world. In March 1988, he attended a reception, *above left,* at Rockefeller University in New York City to promote his recently published book, *A Brief History of Time.* While on campus, *above,* he enjoyed a ride in the sunshine, accompanied by Nicola N. Khuri, a physicist at the university.

Other scientists were skeptical about Hawking's idea. When Hawking presented the theory at a scientific conference at the Rutherford Laboratory near Oxford in February 1974, the conference moderator declared that the idea was "rubbish" and quickly cut off the discussion scheduled to follow. And hours later, the moderator was still telling people at the conference what a ridiculous idea it was.

After Hawking published his calculations in 1975, however, physicists accepted that a black hole could indeed vanish explosively. In recognition of the importance of Hawking's work, the particles of positive energy escaping from the region of a black hole came to be known as *Hawking radiation.* Scientists now consider the conception of Hawking radiation to be a major triumph of theoretical physics, because it provided the first detailed description of connections between three key areas of physics: gravity, quantum mechanics, and *thermodynamics*, which deals with the relationships between heat and other forms of energy.

Hawking is now trying to describe these connections in even more detail. Beginning in 1975, he developed a mathematical technique involving quantum mechanics to describe the conditions that existed when the universe and time came into being with the big bang. Eventually, he realized that it was not necessary for there to have been a singularity at the beginning of the big bang.

In 1983, Hawking and physicist James Hartle of the University of California at Santa Barbara worked out the mathematics of this idea. Hawking and Hartle then began to calculate the history of an

Hawking takes time out from a work session at home for a fatherly chat with Timmy, youngest of his three children.

imaginary model of the universe that began with the conditions described by their mathematics.

So far, the complex calculations have shown that the model universe would evolve into a universe much like our own. Creatures living in that universe could move back and forth freely in space, but could move only forward in time—as we can. That universe would be nearly the same in all directions—as ours is, with nearly equal numbers of galaxies in all directions. And that universe would have started out very small, but could have grown very large—as ours has.

Hawking and Hartle seem to be on the right track, but their work has a basic limitation. It cannot describe the actual universe thoroughly because it relies on two concepts that have not yet been combined successfully at the deepest level of understanding. The first concept, Einstein's general theory of relativity, explains gravity, which is one of the four fundamental forces of nature. The second concept, the theory of quantum mechanics, has been successfully applied to only the other three forces—the electromagnetic force, responsible for electricity and magnetism; the strong force, which holds the atomic nucleus together; and the weak force, which governs certain kinds of radioactive decay.

No one—not even Einstein—has been able to resolve the difficulties of combining the general theory of relativity and quantum mechanics. But the technique developed by Hawking has given scientists a glimpse of what an all-encompassing theory may be like.

Hawking maintains a daily routine that includes such ordinary activities as catching up on the news at the breakfast table, *above left,* and chatting in the living room, *above,* with his wife, Jane (center), and a family friend.

For his scientific achievements, Hawking has won a large number of honors, including the Pius XI Gold Medal of the Pontifical Academy of Science, the Dannie Heineman Prize of the American Institute of Physics and the American Physical Society, and the Wolf Foundation Prize in Physics.

How has Hawking accomplished so much despite his disability? He does not consider the disability to be a significant disadvantage in theoretical physics, because it has not impaired his ability to think. In fact, he believes it may have helped, because he has not had to teach regular courses or do much administrative work.

Hawking's main problems are his lack of mobility and the difficulty of communicating ideas to other people. In order to move around his home and office, and get between the two, he uses an electric wheelchair that his weakened but still functioning arm and hand muscles can control with a joystick. He pilots his wheelchair at a good clip, and he can maneuver it through narrow passageways. Hawking loves to demonstrate how well he can control the chair. When Great Britain's Prince Charles met Hawking in 1978, he was fascinated by Hawking's wheelchair. Hawking proudly showed how he could spin around in it—and ran over the prince's toes in the process.

Hawking travels by air several times a year to scientific conferences throughout the world. He drives his wheelchair up to the door of the aircraft, and then his associates carry him on board and place him in his seat. Hawking usually travels with three nurses, who

Attended by a nurse, Hawking travels to his next meeting on the University of Cambridge campus. But the greater journey takes place in his mind, where he travels via mathematics and imagination to the moment when time and space began.

take turns caring for him around the clock, and a technical assistant who helps him give his lectures and operate his computer. Hawking has flown to the United States several dozen times and to the Soviet Union seven times. In the spring of 1985, he went on a lecture tour around the world, stopping in China to give several lectures and drive his wheelchair on the Great Wall. And in March 1988, he traveled to New York City to introduce *A Brief History of Time: From the Big Bang to Black Holes*, a book that he wrote to outline some of his ideas for readers who do not have a scientific background.

Reading poses special problems for Hawking. He may ask an associate to hold open an article or a short section of a book for him. For longer material, he has photocopied pages set out side by side on a table so that he can move around in his wheelchair and read them. Lengthy articles that Hawking might wish to read over a period of many days go into a mechanical page-turner that he can control by a joystick.

Getting information to others is Hawking's major communications problem. After the first few years of ALS, Hawking could no longer write easily or clearly, so he communicated mostly by speaking. He dictated his scientific papers to a secretary, and a coauthor or colleague occasionally worked out equations that were too long for Hawking to do in his head.

Until 1978, Hawking lectured by making a special effort to speak loudly and clearly, often with the aid of a microphone. During a lecture, an associate projected notes and diagrams onto a screen in the front of the room so that everyone could grasp the main points of Hawking's lecture even without understanding everything he said. But over the years, Hawking's voice became weaker, and he began to notice that hardly anyone was laughing at the one-line jokes he sprinkled throughout his lectures. He realized that only his family and closest associates could understand what he was saying. So in 1978, Hawking began to have a colleague deliver his lectures, with the colleague sometimes acting as a translator right on the lecture platform.

Hawking lost his speech altogether in the summer of 1985, because of a complication of ALS. While visiting a laboratory near Geneva, Switzerland, he developed pneumonia due to the build-up of food in his lungs. The muscles that control swallowing had become so weak that some food was going down his windpipe to his lungs, rather than down his esophagus to his stomach. After several weeks of respiratory therapy, he was still too weak to breathe on his own. So surgeons opened a hole through his neck into his windpipe. Hawking eventually became strong enough to breathe through this hole without a respirator. When he breathes, however, air no longer goes past his vocal cords, so he cannot speak at all.

The first months after the surgery were very discouraging, because Hawking's last fairly effective means of communication was gone. At first, all he could do was signal "yes" or "no" with his eyebrows. This made it very difficult to communicate anything complicated. For the first time since the early stages of his illness, Hawking appeared to lose the will to live.

New methods of communication soon were developed for Hawking, however. For a while, he spelled out words with his eyes. While a colleague watched, he looked at different parts of a chart to choose between different groups of letters. Then the colleague presented a chart of the chosen group so that Hawking could select the letter he wanted. This technique was better than the eyebrow method but was still extremely slow. Then in May 1986, David Mason, an engineer and the husband of one of Hawking's nurses, helped Hawking design the computer system for his wheelchair. This system enables Hawking to select or spell out about 10 words per minute, and even "speaks" for him. It also enables him to write papers directly into a word processor.

When Hawking turns the computer on, the letters of the alphabet appear on the computer screen, which Hawking and four or five other people can read at one time. A *cursor* (electronic pointer) then begins to move past the letters. When the cursor gets to the first letter of the word Hawking wants, he squeezes the switch he holds in his hand. The screen then shows a list of words beginning with that letter, and the cursor begins to move past the words. If Hawking sees the word he wants, he presses the switch again, and that word is added to whatever he is writing.

On the other hand, if the computer does not have the word Hawking wants—such as *supergravity* or *sag gosht* (one of his favorite Indian foods)—he can go back to the alphabet, choose the sequence of letters that spell out the word, and even add that word to the computer's 2,500-word vocabulary.

To "speak" by means of the speech synthesizer, Hawking waits for the cursor to reach a special place on the screen, then squeezes the switch to turn on the speech synthesizer. This device pronounces most words fairly well and even provides inflection, lowering its pitch at the end of a statement and raising its pitch at the end of a question. The synthesizer was made in California, however, and during his lectures, Hawking sometimes pauses to apologize for the machine's American accent.

Hawking is so weak that a nurse must be nearby around the clock to clear out his lungs when too much fluid accumulates in them, and to check that his breathing and other bodily functions are working. Twice a week, a physiotherapist stretches and exercises his hand, arm, and leg muscles.

Hawking usually leaves for his office at 10 A.M. or later, but his mental work often begins shortly after he wakes up at 7 A.M. He takes about half an hour to travel in his wheelchair to the Department of Applied Mathematics and Theoretical Physics near the center of Cambridge. His scenic route takes him over green fields behind the Cambridge colleges, across the small River Cam, which flows gently through town, past King's College with its magnificent Gothic chapel completed in 1515 during the reign of King Henry VIII, through a large gate with two massive wooden doors, and across a busy street.

Hawking arrives at his office in time for the coffee hour at 11 A.M., when faculty members, new Ph.D.'s, graduate students, and visitors gather in a large room for refreshments. This and the tea hour at 4 P.M. are times for talking about physics and comparing calculations, as well as for discussing politics and personal activities. The scientists sit around low tables, drink their tea or coffee, and write equations on white plastic tabletops that are easy to wash off afterward.

Around noon, Hawking goes back to his office to write on his computer, read papers written by other scientists, or read and answer mail. Shortly after 1 P.M., Hawking, his nurse, and sometimes students or other scientists head for lunch at a cafeteria in the Graduate Centre, about a block from his office. The Graduate Centre is in a pleasant setting, overlooking the River Cam where a grain mill once stood.

Once or twice a week in the afternoon, a scientist—usually from another university—presents a talk at the math and physics department. Hawking tends to become sleepy in the afternoon, so he insists on open windows to let in fresh air during these talks. With this precaution, he usually remains quite attentive—at least for an interesting talk—and may ask several questions of the speaker. If the discussion threatens to go beyond 4 P.M., however, Hawking will remind those present that it is tea time. After tea, Hawking may work with his secretary until about 5:30 P.M., and then he, his students, and his colleagues begin a long period of uninterrupted discussion about cosmology.

One evening a week, Hawking dines at Gonville and Caius College. There, he can engage in learned conversation about a wide range of subjects with scholars from many fields, not just science. On other evenings, Hawking has dinner with his family. He, Jane, and their three children have a wide variety of interests, so there is plenty to talk about at home. Jane tutors students in French and Spanish, languages in which she specialized to obtain her Ph.D. She also sings in a choral group, and she and Stephen are involved in a nuclear disarmament organization.

Their son Robert, who was born in 1967, is studying science at Cambridge University and is involved in church activities. Daughter Lucy, born in 1970, is a high school student, and she acts in local drama groups. And Timothy, who was born in 1979, studies the piano and the cello in addition to his usual schoolwork.

Hawking gets a great deal of work done while following a busy schedule because he has learned to concentrate on physics even while he is in the midst of something else. He has made his great advances because he has learned to focus on what is really important, to strip away nonessential details and go right to the heart of a problem.

Hawking's advances have made him one of the greatest theoretical physicists alive. His ideas, if correct, will have fulfilled his daring ambition to discover how the universe began. Hawking still has another great problem to investigate, however, for as he admits, "I still don't know *why* it began."

For further reading:

Davies, Paul. *The Edge of Infinity.* Simon & Schuster, 1981.
Hawking, Stephen W. *A Brief History of Time: From the Big Bang to Black Holes.* Bantam, 1988.
Islam, Jamal N. *The Ultimate Fate of the Universe.* Cambridge Univ. Press, 1983.
Pagels, Heinz R. *Perfect Symmetry: The Search for the Beginning of Time.* Simon & Schuster, 1985.
Trefil, James S. *Space, Time, Infinity: The Smithsonian Views the Universe.* Pantheon, 1985.
Weinberg, Steven. *The First Three Minutes: A Modern View of the Origin of the Universe.* Basic Books, 1982.

This Harvard University biologist and expert on ants says biological laws are the basis of social behavior among human beings as well as ants.

Edward O. Wilson

BY PETER R. LIMBURG

A giant ant from Borneo—plated in gold and palladium—sits on the desk of biologist Edward O. Wilson in his book-lined office at Harvard University's Museum of Comparative Zoology in Cambridge, Mass. More than 2.5 centimeters (1 inch) long with wicked-looking jaws, the Borneo ant is a monster compared with other ants. It was a gift from friends to celebrate the publication in 1975 of Wilson's revolutionary and controversial book on social behavior, *Sociobiology: The New Synthesis*, a study of the biological basis for the social behavior of ants, human beings, and other animals.

The gift was especially appropriate because ants have been at the center of Wilson's life and scientific career. He first became interested in ants at the age of 10, and today he keeps about 20 ant colonies in his office. His first success as a scientist came with path-breaking discoveries about how ants communicate chemically, and his observations of the social behavior of ants led to his later contributions in the field of sociobiology.

But Wilson is more than just one of the world's leading authorities on ants. This mild-mannered gentleman is also a behavioral scientist, a *taxonomist* (a scientist who classifies organisms), a population biologist, an ecologist, a geneticist, a conservationist, and a philoso-

Wilson's interest in insects developed at an early age, and he often collected butterflies in the fields of his native South.

The author:
Peter R. Limburg is a free-lance writer.

pher. While most scientists spend their careers becoming more and more expert in an ever-narrowing specialty, Wilson's search for knowledge has led him in the opposite direction. He has steadily expanded his range of expertise.

Edward Osborne Wilson, Jr., was born on June 10, 1929, in Birmingham, Ala. He was an only child, and his parents were divorced when he was 7 years old. He was raised by a stepmother and his father, who had a job with the federal government that required him to move frequently from one city to another. Between the first grade and his senior year in high school, Wilson attended 16 different schools throughout the South. Always a newcomer, and younger than most of his classmates, Wilson found it difficult to make friends. To fill the gap in his social life, he developed an impassioned interest in nature. The woods and fields were seldom more than a short bicycle ride away from his home. And at every school he made at least one close friend who shared his love of nature.

Insects became Wilson's main interest, in part because of a freak fishing accident at the age of 7 that cost him the sight of his right eye. He had hooked a fish and had given a mighty heave on the line; the fish flew out of the water, and its spiny fin jabbed his right eye. As a result, Wilson found that his limited vision was a handicap for observing birds and other animals. But the eyesight in his remaining left eye was excellent for examining insects.

When Wilson was 9, he and his family moved to Washington, D.C. There, Wilson visited the Smithsonian Institution and the National Zoological Park almost every day. With a young friend, Ellis G. MacLeod, he collected butterflies in Washington's Rock Creek Park. Once, the two boys found a huge colony of yellow ants, which captured their imagination. Both of them resolved to become *entomologists* (scientists who study insects), and in a rare fulfillment of boyhood dreams, both of them actually did. MacLeod went on to become a professor of entomology at the University of Illinois in Urbana-Champaign.

Wilson's academic preparation for his scientific career came at the University of Alabama, where he majored in biology, earning his B.S. degree in 1949 and his M.S. degree in 1950. Wilson began work on his Ph.D. degree in entomology at the University of Tennessee in 1950. But he switched to Harvard later that year at the urging of a friend on the Harvard faculty, who pointed out that among other benefits, the university's collection of ants is the largest in the world.

At Harvard, Wilson became an ambitious young *myrmecologist* (a scientist who specializes in the study of ants). In 1953, while still a graduate student, Wilson was elected to Harvard's prestigious Society of Fellows, which carried with it a grant for three years of unrestricted study anywhere in the world. That summer, he went to Cuba and Mexico to study tropical ants, which have the greatest

Wilson narrowed his early interest in insects to the study of ants. He is still fascinated by them and studies the miniature world of ant colonies in his office at Harvard University in Cambridge, Mass.

diversity among the 10,000 or so species of ants known to science. Back at Harvard that fall, he attended a lecture by the world-famous *ethologist* (animal-behavior specialist) Konrad Lorenz. It gave Wilson's career a new direction. As Lorenz described how the behavior of birds and fish was guided by cues of sight and sound, Wilson suddenly realized that the unique social behavior of ants must be governed primarily by chemical cues of scent and taste. He decided to explore this largely unknown field of animal behavior.

Five years after conceiving this research project, Wilson discovered that insects use hormonelike chemical substances—now known as *pheromones*—to communicate with one another. For years, entomologists had suspected that scent played a major role in insect communication. For example, they knew that ants mark a scent trail between their nests and a source of food so that other ants from the nest can locate the food source. Studies had shown that ants can distinguish between their own nest mates and other ants of the same species that belong to a different nest. But no one knew just how the insects produced their scent signals.

Working with a captive colony of fire ants one day in 1959, Wilson observed that after an ant found food, it crouched close to the ground as it returned to the nest. Every few steps, its tail turned down until its sting touched the ground, and an invisible droplet of some chemical substance was deposited on the ground. The other ants followed this trail of droplets to the food.

Wilson speculated that the droplets came from glands at the rear of the ant's abdomen. He removed the two main glands that make up the ant's poison apparatus at the base of the sting. The dissection was difficult because these glands are tiny specks, barely visible without a microscope. Wilson washed the glands, crushed them, and marked scent trails with them along a table. He expected that, at most, some of the ants might follow the trails. But when he marked a trail with one of the crushed glands, known as Dufour's gland, an astonishing thing happened. Dozens of ants immediately poured out of the nest, ran to the end of the trail, and milled around looking for the food that wasn't there.

That night, too excited to sleep, Wilson thought out an explanation for how the social behavior of ants is governed by a small number of message-carrying chemicals. He speculated that some chemicals communicate the location of food and that others warn of danger. He theorized that each substance might be produced by a different gland and stored in special reservoirs in the insect's body until the insect needed to use it.

Wilson was right. Continuing his research, he found pheromones in the jaw glands of fire ants and harvester ants that are used to warn of danger, such as raids by other ants. Later, he discovered substances that tell ants when one of their nest mates is dead. When ants smell the odor from the substances, they carry the body off to a refuse pile. Wilson painted ant-sized wooden dummies with these substances, and the ants dutifully carried them off to the "graveyard." In a final test, he painted live ants with the death-smell chemicals. Their nest mates grabbed them and carried them, alive and kicking furiously, off to the refuse pile. They were not allowed back in the nest until they had cleaned off all traces of the death odor.

Some ants even use pheromones in a kind of psychological warfare. For example, in 1971, Wilson and a colleague found that when ants known as slave makers raid the nests of other species, they spray the victims with a substance that causes fear. The terrified victims flee their nest in panic and never return. The slave makers then carry the victims' *larvae* and *pupae* (the immature stages of an ant) back to their own nest and raise them as workers.

Ants can communicate by nonchemical means, such as making various noises or by creating vibrations. Wilson and other scientists, however, found that most of an ant's 10 to 20 communication signals are chemicals.

Wilson's research in chemical communication lasted many years, but during that period, he also began and completed a number of other projects. He received his Ph.D. degree from Harvard in late

1955. Earlier that year he married a young Boston woman named Irene Kelley. In 1956, when he was 26, Harvard appointed him assistant professor of biology. In 1958, he became an associate professor of zoology, with full tenure. He was appointed full professor of zoology in 1964. In 1976, he was appointed Frank B. Baird, Jr., Professor of Science, and since 1973, he also has been curator of entomology at Harvard's Museum of Comparative Zoology.

Another of Wilson's research interests was in the field of *biogeography*, the study of the geographical distribution of plants and animals. In the 1960's, Wilson began working with ecologist Robert H. MacArthur, then of the University of Pennsylvania in Philadelphia. Using data Wilson gathered in the 1950's on ants of the South Pacific islands, along with other researchers' findings on island birds, they determined definite patterns in the number of species on the islands and where those species were to be found. In essence, they discovered how to calculate mathematically the relationship between the size of an island and the number of species that can live there. The larger the island, the more species it can support. This sounds elementary, but Wilson and MacArthur developed mathematical equations that could predict precisely the relationship between the number of species and the size of the habitat.

Their theory of biogeography has importance far beyond the population of island species. Each time a natural area is reduced in size—when part of a forest is cut down for lumber or to clear land for farming, for example, or when part of a wetland is replaced by a shopping center—the number of species that can live in the remaining natural area declines. Some species become extinct. Wilson and MacArthur's mathematical formulas, refined by later researchers, have become invaluable to administrators and planners of national parks and nature reserves. For example, Wilson and MacArthur showed that a group of interconnected large reserves can protect many more species than scattered, small reserves. This knowledge has helped those who plan and develop parks and nature reserves to save as many species as possible.

Wilson's findings and his years of research on ants in tropical rain forests have made him an eloquent advocate of conservation, especially on behalf of efforts to save the world's rain forests from destruction. Tropical rain forests are being cleared in developing countries to make way for urban and agricultural development. In 1986, he was a principal speaker at a conference held in Washington, D.C., and sponsored by the National Academy of Sciences and the Smithsonian Institution, which called attention to the extinction of plant and animal life as a result of this destruction.

But Wilson is best known for his contributions to the field of sociobiology. His interest in this area grew over many years as a result of his studies of *social insects*—insects that live in organized communities and depend on one another for survival. Two events, nearly

A 10-month field trip to New Guinea, *right,* and other areas of the South Pacific in 1955 helped Wilson establish a reputation as one of the world's foremost authorities on tropical ants.

10 years apart, helped guide him in this direction. One occurred in 1955, when he became the research supervisor of a graduate student named Stuart Altmann, who was studying the sociobiology of monkeys. A summer in the field with Altmann made Wilson think that there could be some underlying biological principle explaining the social behavior of both monkeys and ants.

Then, in 1964, Wilson happened to read a provocative article by a young British entomologist, William D. Hamilton. Hamilton's article suggested a solution for a problem that had long bothered biologists who study the evolution of species: the phenomenon of *altruism* among insects. In human terms, altruism is unselfish, even self-sacrificing, behavior for the good of others. As applied to social insects, it refers chiefly to the self-sacrifice of the worker ants, which cannot reproduce themselves but which do the food gathering and other labor to keep the colony alive. It also refers to the self-sacrificing behavior of ant and termite soldiers, which routinely give their lives in defense of the colony—or of honey bee workers, which die in the act of stinging an intruder. Of course, the self-sacrificing behavior of insects is instinctive and is not the result of a conscious decision as is human altruism.

Ants, bees, wasps, and termites live in highly organized groups, or *colonies*. In these colonies, the members have a division of labor by *castes* (classes). Most members of a colony belong to the worker

Wilson and a colleague study ants on a strip of tree bark in a tropical rain forest in Costa Rica during a trip in 1987. Field trips are still a vital part of Wilson's ant research.

caste. Workers are sexually undeveloped females, so they cannot reproduce. They build and repair the nest, gather and share food, and feed and care for the queen caste.

Among ants and termites, there is also a soldier caste, according to Wilson, though some scientists do not classify soldiers as a separate caste. Soldiers are sterile females like the workers, but they are larger with huge heads and sharp, powerful *mandibles* (jaws). Their mandibles are shaped for fighting but not for work, so the soldiers cannot share in nest-building or food-gathering. Their only job is to defend the nest.

Reproduction is the sole job of the queens and males. Males are little more than "flying sperm dispensers," as Wilson puts it. Their sole purpose in life is to fertilize the queen's eggs, and their lives are short, only a few weeks or months. Male honey bees die in the act of mating; males of other species die a few days later. Queens live the longest, from 10 to 20 years. The queens are specialized egg-laying machines, with grotesquely swollen abdomens that look like tiny sausages. Their egg-laying capacity is enormous. A queen of a South American army ant species, for example, can lay from 100,000 to 300,000 eggs in less than a week.

A remarkable phenomenon among ants, bees, and wasps is that the queen determines whether her offspring will be male or female.

A queen makes only one mating flight. During that flight, she collects a lifetime supply of sperm from a number of males and stores it in a special receptacle within her body. At egg-laying times, she can either fertilize the eggs by squeezing some of the stored sperm onto the eggs as they pass through her egg-laying passage or she can withhold the sperm. Fertilized eggs develop into female workers and soldiers or, in special cases, young queens that will found colonies of their own. Unfertilized eggs develop into males.

Insect altruism seems to pose a problem for the theory of natural selection proposed by British naturalist Charles R. Darwin in 1859. According to Darwin, the survival of a species depends on the survival of the individual organisms that compose the species. The individuals best fitted to survive live to reproduce themselves, while those least fitted perish in the struggle for scarce resources or because they are more vulnerable to predators. Thus, the traits that ensure survival are transmitted individually from one generation to the next. How, then, could evolution have selected the worker castes of ants and other social insects? They cannot even reproduce themselves, and yet they are vital to the survival of their species.

At a seminar with a selected group of graduate students, Wilson leads a freewheeling discussion on sociobiology, the theory that some social behaviors in animals are genetically programmed. This theory, which includes human beings, generated a great deal of controversy when he first proposed it in 1975.

Darwin, who was himself perplexed by the problem, tried to explain it by saying that in the case of social insects the forces of natural selection applied to the entire colony or *family* of insects rather than to individual insects. Hamilton took Darwin's thought a step further by suggesting that insect altruism was a way of guaranteeing the survival of the insect's *genes* (hereditary material). With some simple mathematical equations, Hamilton proved that female workers have more genes in common with the sisters they care for and help feed than they have with the mother queen that lays the colony's eggs. Because males come from unfertilized eggs, they pass on *all* of their genes to their daughters, but females inherit only *half* of their mother's genes. Hamilton used a mathematical formula to show that this means that sisters share three-quarters of the same genes. Thus, by caring for their young sisters, these sterile females do more to perpetuate their own genes than they could if they mated and had their own offspring. Their own offspring would have half of their genes and half of the father's genes.

In his classic work, *Sociobiology: The New Synthesis*, Wilson drew on Hamilton's discovery and declared that, in effect, an organism does

Wilson listens attentively as a student responds to a question during a seminar. Students find that Wilson gives their ideas the same consideration that he would accord his colleagues' views.

not live for itself. Its primary function is to reproduce genes, and the individual organism simply serves as the temporary carrier of those genes. In this view, an organism is only the genetic material's way of making more genetic material. The organism's brain is engineered to perpetuate this genetic material by helping the organism survive long enough to reproduce. In his book, Wilson applied this theory to a variety of animals ranging from slime-mold amebas to African wild dogs, fish, birds, crocodiles, dolphins, elephants, monkeys, apes, and human beings.

The major themes of this book were the evolution of cooperative behavior, altruism, and the variety of ways in which animals communicate—by visual or chemical signals, sound, and touch. But Wilson also explored such topics as the function of play, learning, and the beginnings of culture.

In the final chapter of *Sociobiology*, Wilson attempted to trace the genetic evolution of human behavior and to assess the extent to which our actions and responses are guided by patterns encoded in our genes. Among the qualities that distinguish human beings from other animals, Wilson said, are speech and what he calls *soft-core altruism*—"I'll help you today if you'll help me tomorrow."

Wilson leads a busy academic life of research and teaching. In his private library at Harvard, Wilson pores over the details of his schedule with a secretary.

For research on the social behavior of ants, Wilson keeps a large collection of ant colonies at Harvard. Plastic trays containing different ant species line a table in Wilson's office, *above.* In a room adjacent to his office, *left,* additional trays hold thousands of ants representing a wide variety of species.

Years of study have not lessened Wilson's enthusiasm for his subject.
He remains a scientist who "celebrates ants."

When *Sociobiology* was published in 1975, it touched off a controversy. Many other natural and social scientists—among them some of Wilson's friends and colleagues at Harvard—disputed Wilson's thesis that biological laws govern human social behavior. Some critics accused Wilson—falsely, in his opinion—of constructing a theory that justified inequalities and exploitation in society on the basis that such abuses were biologically determined. Wilson pointed out that he had plainly warned against such misinterpretation.

Some extremely vocal student activists demonstrated against Wilson and heckled him when he spoke to audiences, characterizing his views as racist. The worst incident of harassment came in February 1978 when Wilson was about to present a paper at the annual meeting of the American Association for the Advancement of Science in Washington, D.C. Just as he began to speak, several demonstrators charged onto the stage and poured water over his head.

This giant ant from Borneo—a gift from friends to celebrate the publication of Wilson's book *Sociobiology: The New Synthesis*—sits on Wilson's office desk, carrying the brave standard of his research goals.

Wilson refused to be silenced, however, and in 1978, he published *On Human Nature* to explain his scientific theories to the general public. The book was widely acclaimed and won Wilson the Pulitzer Prize for general nonfiction in 1979. The theme of the book was the influence of genetically determined patterns on human behavior, particularly their influence on altruism, sexuality, aggression, and religion. Wilson argued that these patterns have developed as survival mechanisms over more than 1 million years and still guide human behavior today.

Some of the behavior patterns Wilson used as examples of his theory are an inborn fear of the dark, of snakes and spiders, and of heights. Other patterns include basic facial expressions that people of all races and cultures understand without explanation; a preference for meat in the diet; a taboo against incest; a powerful, permanently active sex drive; a peculiarly human kind of altruism displayed in acts of self-sacrifice; and a tendency to divide other human beings into "them" and "us"—that is, foe or friend.

Drawing on the work of anthropologists, Wilson traced the emergence of human society from the earliest bands of hunter-gatherers. These early human beings had learned to band together for defense against bigger, more powerful meat-eaters, such as lions and hyenas, and for greater success in hunting and foraging. For most of the last 2 million years, human beings lived in small roving bands, usually made up of about 25 people and never much larger than 100. These bands were like big families and had their own territories, which they defended. They saw other people as competitors for food, water, and shelter.

Wilson claims that one of the most significant events in human development took place about 250,000 years ago, when, he says, the human brain stopped growing at a uniform rate. At that point, he argues, cultural evolution began to take the upper hand over biological evolution. Wilson believes, however, that the behavioral instincts that early human beings had developed before brain growth halted are still part of our genetic makeup. Many of these instincts, such as dislike of strangers and readiness to fight them, serve us badly in a densely populated, industrialized world. We gain nothing, however, Wilson notes, by pretending that these destructive and dangerous drives do not exist. Instead, he says, we can control them only if we are aware of them.

Wilson also made new observations about altruism. Human altruism differs from the totally unselfish *hard-core altruism* found in ants, bees, and termites. Our soft-core altruism, he says, is based on self-interest, enlightened or otherwise. Hard-core altruism expects nothing in return for self-sacrifice. Soft-core altruism expects to get something in return for altruistic behavior, either directly for the individual or indirectly for the social group (enlightened self-interest). Despite the selfish basis of this kind of altruism, Wilson calls it the key to human society because it makes human cooperation possible outside of the family or tribe. This ability to cooperate, he claims, is the basis of civilization. Hard-core altruism, on the other hand, would be the enemy of civilization, Wilson believes, because it would limit cooperation to one's own family or tribe. All other people would be regarded as enemies.

Despite the controversy that greeted it, sociobiology appears to have weathered the storm of criticism. While it is still not universally accepted as a new science, the heated exchanges that marked the early debates have ended, replaced by rational discussion.

Surveying his long scientific career, Wilson says that at the age of 59, his principal contributions to science are probably behind him. But his years of productive research have given him a number of insights into the qualities needed for a fruitful scientific career, insights that might prove helpful to young scientists. Wilson lists these qualities in this order: the capacity for sustained hard work; a deep and lasting interest in the subject matter; the ability to survive defeat and discouragement; moderate intelligence (genius is not necessary); the ability to choose a subject and a problem that will lead to discoveries; and the ability to distinguish between sound and unsound ideas to avoid wasting time on unproductive projects.

The best source of inspiration for a biologist, Wilson says, is to "fall in love with a group of organisms" and see what scientific questions they can answer. "That's the kind of biologist I am," he concludes. "I celebrate ants."

For further reading:

Caplan, Arthur L., ed. *The Sociobiology Debate*. Harper & Row, 1978.

Wilson, Edward O. "In the Queendom of the Ants." In *Leaders in the Study of Animal Behavior*, edited by Donald A. Dewsbury. Bucknell University Press, 1985.

Wilson, Edward O. *On Human Nature*. Harvard University Press, 1978. *Sociobiology: The New Synthesis*. Harvard University Press, 1975. *The Insect Societies*. Harvard University Press, 1971.

To commemorate the 20th anniversary of the first moon
landing in 1969, this special supplement section reviews
major achievements of the United States manned space
and interplanetary exploration programs since the space
age began with the launch of a Soviet satellite in 1957.

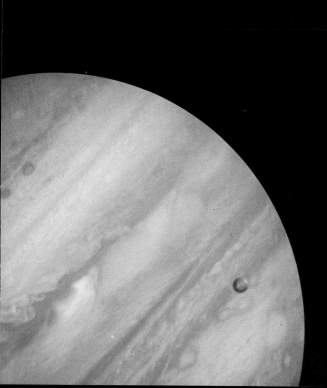

First Steps in Space

Sputnik

The space age began on Oct. 4, 1957, when the Soviet Union launched *Sputnik 1,* the first artificial satellite to orbit Earth. *Sputnik 2* carried a dog named Laika into space in November 1957.

Explorer

The first U.S. satellite, a bullet-shaped craft called *Explorer 1,* was launched into Earth orbit on Jan. 31, 1958. There have been more than 60 research satellites in the Explorer series. Some probed Earth's upper atmosphere; others studied radiation from intergalactic space.

Vostok

Vostok 1, launched on April 12, 1961, carried Soviet cosmonaut Yuri Gagarin, the first human being to fly in space. Later spacecraft in the Vostok series were used for both manned and unmanned flights.

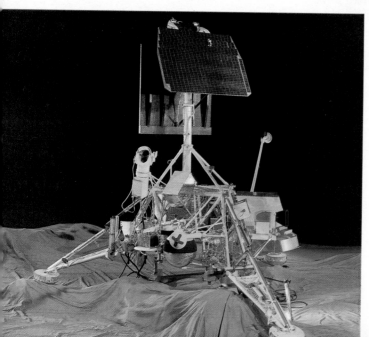

Surveyor

The lunar probe, *Surveyor I,* on May 30, 1966, became the first U.S. craft to make a soft landing on the moon. There were seven probes in the Surveyor series, all designed to perfect the technology needed for landing people on the moon.

The Mercury Space Capsule

Project Mercury was organized in 1958 to investigate the effects of space flight on the human body. The bell-shaped Mercury capsule had a bottom diameter of 1.9 meters (6.2 feet) and a top diameter of 81.3 centimeters (2.7 feet). Only one astronaut could fit into its cramped interior. The first flights were unmanned tests or tests with monkeys. Then, in May 1961, Alan B. Shepard, Jr., *inset,* made a 490-kilometer (302-mile) suborbital flight to become the first U.S. astronaut in space. In February 1962, John H. Glenn, Jr., *above,* made the first U.S. manned orbit of Earth in a capsule called *Friendship 7.*

Flight and Launch Date	Crew	Accomplishment
MR-3 (*Freedom 7*) May 5, 1961	Alan B. Shepard, Jr.	First United States astronaut in space.
MR-4 (*Liberty Bell 7*) July 21, 1961	Virgil I. Grissom	Completed second suborbital flight in space.
MA-6 (*Friendship 7*) Feb. 20, 1962	John H. Glenn, Jr.	First U.S. astronaut to orbit Earth.
MA-7 (*Aurora 7*) May 24, 1962	M. Scott Carpenter	Duplicated Glenn's three orbits of Earth.
MA-8 (*Sigma 7*) Oct. 3, 1962	Walter M. Schirra, Jr.	During six orbits, helped develop techniques for longer space flights.
MA-9 (*Faith 7*) May 15, 1963	L. Gordon Cooper	Spent more than a day in space, the longest Mercury flight.

Project Gemini

The Gemini Spacecraft
Gemini, a Latin word meaning *twins,* was the name of the second stage in the development of the U.S. manned space program. The Gemini spacecraft, 5.7 meters (18.7 feet) long with a maximum diameter of about 3 meters (10 feet), could accommodate two astronauts strapped in side by side. The Gemini program allowed engineers and astronauts to develop the technology and skills necessary for Project Apollo, the moon-landing program. There were 10 manned missions in the Gemini program. *Gemini 1* and *2* were unmanned tests.

Flight and Launch Date	Crew	Accomplishment
Gemini 3 March 23, 1965	Virgil I. Grissom and John W. Young	Performed first manual maneuvers of a U.S. spacecraft.
Gemini 4 June 3, 1965	James A. McDivitt and Edward H. White II	White became the first U.S. astronaut to walk in space.
Gemini 5 Aug. 21, 1965	L. Gordon Cooper and Charles Conrad, Jr.	Circled Earth for eight days, setting a record for the longest stay in space.
Gemini 6 Dec. 15, 1965	Walter M. Schirra, Jr., and Thomas P. Stafford	With *Gemini 7*, performed the first *rendezvous* (meeting) of two vehicles in space.
Gemini 7 Dec. 4, 1965	Frank Borman and James A. Lovell, Jr.	Confirmed by a 14-day flight that no lasting harm results merely from being weightless.
Gemini 8 March 16, 1966	Neil A. Armstrong and David R. Scott	Completed the world's first docking in space with an unmanned Agena target vehicle.
Gemini 9 June 3, 1966	Stafford and Eugene A. Cernan	Performed maneuvers with a target vehicle. Cernan made a two-hour space walk.
Gemini 10 July 18, 1966	Young and Michael Collins	Docked with a target vehicle and rendezvoused with another target vehicle.
Gemini 11 Sept. 12, 1966	Conrad and Richard F. Gordon, Jr.	Accomplished the world's first docking maneuver during a craft's first orbit.
Gemini 12 Nov. 11, 1966	Lovell and Edwin E. Aldrin, Jr.	Aldrin completed about 20 tasks while standing or walking outside the spacecraft for 5½ hours.

Project Apollo

Flight and Launch Date	Crew	Accomplishment
Apollo 7 Oct. 11, 1968	Walter M. Schirra, Jr., Donn Eisele, and Walter Cunningham	Orbited Earth for 11 days.
Apollo 8 Dec. 21, 1968	Frank Borman, James A. Lovell, Jr., and William Anders	Orbited the moon 10 times. Verified the suitability of proposed landing sites.
Apollo 9 March 3, 1969	James A. McDivitt, David R. Scott, Russell L. Schweickart	Completed the first manned, orbital flight test of the lunar module (LM).
Apollo 10 May 18, 1969	Thomas P. Stafford, Jr., John W. Young, Eugene A. Cernan	Practiced docking with the LM in preparation for the lunar landing.
Apollo 11 July 16, 1969	Neil A. Armstrong, Michael Collins, and Edwin E. Aldrin, Jr.	Armstrong became the first person to set foot on the moon, on July 20, 1969. Armstrong and Aldrin explored the moon's dry Sea of Tranquility.
Apollo 12 Nov. 14, 1969	Charles Conrad, Jr., Richard F. Gordon, Jr., and Alan L. Bean	Explored the dry Ocean of Storms on the moon. Set up scientific instruments to return data to Earth about moon geology.
Apollo 13 April 11, 1970	Lovell, John L. Swigert, Jr., Fred W. Haise, Jr.	An explosion in the service module cut off oxygen supplies and forced the crew to cut short their mission. They used the LM rockets to head the command module toward Earth.
Apollo 14 Jan. 31, 1971	Alan B. Shepard, Jr., Stuart A. Roosa, and Edgar D. Mitchell	Explored the Fra Mauro region of the moon, using a cartlike device to collect rock samples.
Apollo 15 July 26, 1971	Scott, Alfred M. Worden, Jr., and James B. Irwin	Scott and Irwin made the first motor trip on the moon in the lunar roving vehicle.
Apollo 16 April 16, 1972	Young, Thomas K. Mattingly II, and Charles M. Duke, Jr.	Explored other, more extensive regions of the moon and made new findings about the moon's geology.
Apollo 17 Dec. 7, 1972	Cernan, Ronald E. Evans, and Harrison H. Schmitt, Jr.	The last and longest of the Apollo missions, ending December 19. Cernan and Schmitt traveled farther in the lunar roving vehicle and collected more rock samples than any previous mission.

The Apollo Spacecraft

The Apollo spacecraft, designed to carry people to the moon, consisted of two basic parts—the command module, which could hold three astronauts, and the service module, which contained air and water supplies as well as a propulsion system. The Apollo spacecraft also carried a lunar module (LM) for transporting astronauts to and from the surface of the moon. There were many unmanned test flights of the Apollo craft. The first manned flight was designated *Apollo 7.* On four manned flights before the *Apollo 11* moon landing, astronauts carried out a variety of test activities, including spacewalks. One tragedy marred the Apollo program: On Jan. 27, 1967, astronauts Virgil Grissom, Edward White II, and Roger Chaffee were killed by a fire during a ground-test of the spacecraft.

The Moon
Landings

The Historic Flight of *Apollo 11*
"The *Eagle* has landed," radioed *Apollo 11* astronaut Neil A. Armstrong as the lunar landing module, *right,* safely touched down on July 20, 1969. Armstrong stepped out to become the first man on the moon. He later photographed Edwin E. Aldrin, Jr., *above,* the second man on the moon, viewing an American flag set amid the astronauts' bootprints in the lunar soil.

Exploring the Moon
Each of the six moon landings that followed *Apollo 11* expanded our knowledge about the moon. The lunar roving vehicle, *above,* first used by *Apollo 15* astronauts in July 1971, allowed astronauts to travel farther from the landing site. Geologist/astronaut Harrison H. Schmitt, Jr., *right,* collected a wide variety of moon-rocks to bring back to Earth during the *Apollo 17* mission, which ended the Apollo program in December 1972.

Pioneer Probes

Flight	Launch Date	Accomplishment
Pioneer 1	Oct. 11, 1958	Failed to reach moon, but returned scientific data for 43 hours.
Pioneer 2	Nov. 8, 1958	Third rocket stage failed. Spacecraft reached a distance of 1,550 kilometers (963 miles) from Earth.
Pioneer 3	Dec. 6, 1958	Discovered a second radiation belt surrounding Earth but failed to reach moon.
Pioneer 4	March 3, 1959	Passed within 60,000 kilometers (37,000 miles) of the moon.
Pioneer 5	March 11, 1960	Returned first data from space on solar flares.
Pioneer 6	Dec. 16, 1965	Gathered scientific data on the nature of space between Earth and the planet Venus, such as cosmic rays and the solar wind.
Pioneer 7	Aug. 17, 1966	Recorded data on the sun and on the effects of Earth's magnetic field at widely separate points in interplanetary space.
Pioneer 8	Dec. 13, 1967	Continued program of gathering data on the influence of the sun on interplanetary space.
Pioneer 9	Nov. 8, 1968	Collected data on the electromagnetic and ionized-gas properties of interplanetary space.
Pioneer 10	March 3, 1972	Explored the asteroid belt and the planet Jupiter. On June 13, 1983, became the first spacecraft to travel out of the solar system into interstellar space.
Pioneer 11	April 6, 1973	Investigated interplanetary space, the asteroid belt, Jupiter, and Saturn.

The Pioneer Program
The early missions in this series of 11 lunar, solar, and interplanetary probes—in the late 1950's—represented the first U.S. spacecraft to be propelled beyond Earth orbit. *Pioneer 1,* a probe that failed to reach the moon, was the first craft launched by the National Aeronautics and Space Administration. *Pioneer 10* was the first space-craft to leave our solar system on a journey to-ward other stars.

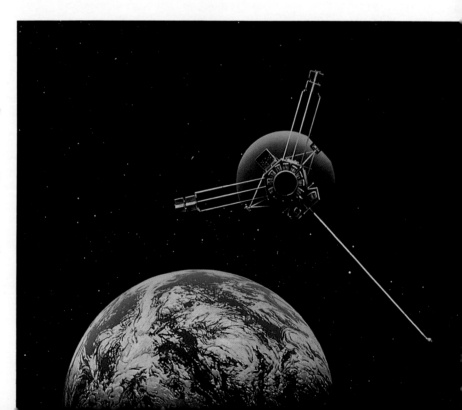

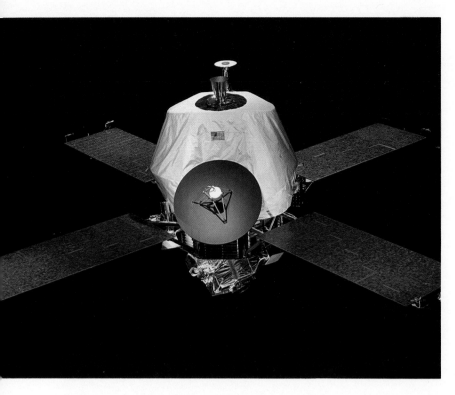

Mariner Probes

Mariner Interplanetary Missions

There were 10 missions in the Mariner program, all probes to the planets Mars, Venus, and Mercury. Three Mariner spacecraft failed to accomplish their missions. Most, however, were spectacularly successful, and *Mariner 9* was the first craft to orbit Mars.

Flight	Launch Date	Accomplishment
Mariner 1	July 22, 1962	Rocket veered off course after liftoff and was destroyed.
Mariner 2	Aug. 27, 1962	Made first successful probe of another planet as it passed within 34,839 kilometers (21,648 miles) of Venus. Found surface temperatures of Venus were about 427°C (800°F.). Did not detect a magnetic field around the planet.
Mariner 3	Nov. 5, 1964	Communications with the spacecraft were lost.
Mariner 4	Nov. 28, 1964	Came within 9,846 kilometers (6,118 miles) of the planet Mars and took 22 photographs of the Martian surface.
Mariner 5	June 14, 1967	Came within 3,946 kilometers (2,452 miles) of the planet Venus and gathered data on the Venusian atmosphere.
Mariner 6	Feb. 25, 1969	Passed within 3,200 kilometers (2,000 miles) of Mars and investigated the Martian atmosphere.
Mariner 7	March 27, 1969	This third fly-by mission to Mars passed within 3,518 kilometers (2,186 miles) of the planet and took a sequence of 93 pictures.
Mariner 8	May 8, 1971	Mission failed due to rocket malfunction.
Mariner 9	May 30, 1971	Became the first space probe to orbit Mars on Nov. 13, 1971. Transmitted back to Earth 6,876 photographs used to map the Martian surface.
Mariner 10	Nov. 3, 1973	Flew by both Venus and Mercury; returned the first close-up pictures of the surface of Mercury and data on Mercury's atmosphere.

Mars/Venus
Missions

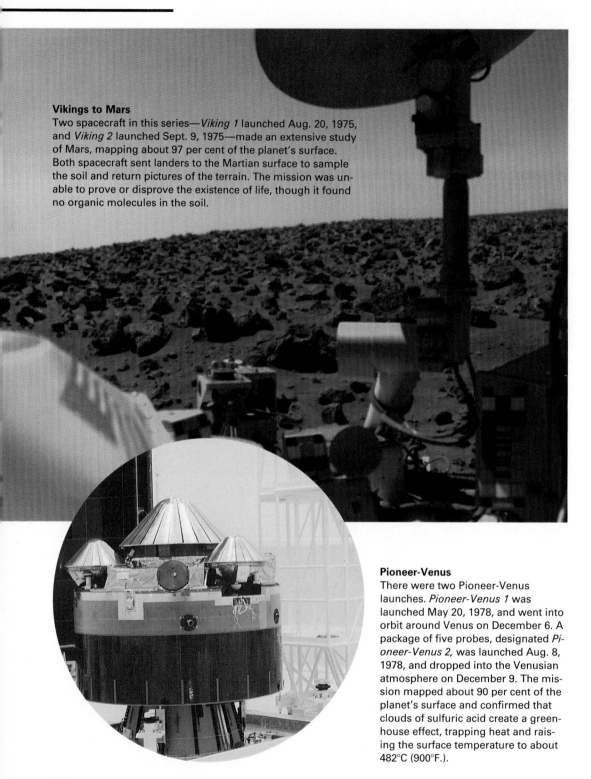

Vikings to Mars
Two spacecraft in this series—*Viking 1* launched Aug. 20, 1975, and *Viking 2* launched Sept. 9, 1975—made an extensive study of Mars, mapping about 97 per cent of the planet's surface. Both spacecraft sent landers to the Martian surface to sample the soil and return pictures of the terrain. The mission was unable to prove or disprove the existence of life, though it found no organic molecules in the soil.

Pioneer-Venus
There were two Pioneer-Venus launches. *Pioneer-Venus 1* was launched May 20, 1978, and went into orbit around Venus on December 6. A package of five probes, designated *Pioneer-Venus 2,* was launched Aug. 8, 1978, and dropped into the Venusian atmosphere on December 9. The mission mapped about 90 per cent of the planet's surface and confirmed that clouds of sulfuric acid create a greenhouse effect, trapping heat and raising the surface temperature to about 482°C (900°F.).

Voyager Probes

To the Outer Solar System

There were two spacecraft in the Voyager series—*Voyager 1* launched Sept. 5, 1977, and *Voyager 2* launched Aug. 20, 1977. The mission of the Voyagers was to explore the giant planets Jupiter and Saturn. But *Voyager 2* continued on to Uranus and Neptune. *Voyager 1* was set on a path that will take it out of our solar system.

Exploring Uranus

Voyager 2 in 1986 made its fly-by of Uranus, about 3 billion kilometers (1.9 billion miles) from Earth. Its instruments discovered 10 small moons, bringing the known total to 15, and 2 more rings, bringing the total to 11. *Voyager 2* then headed out toward Neptune.

The Rings of Saturn

Stunning views of Saturn and its massive ring system were provided by both *Voyager 1* in November 1980 and *Voyager 2* in August 1981. *Voyager 1* was then hurled toward interstellar space.

Jupiter's Atmosphere

Both Voyagers reached Jupiter in 1979 and returned a wealth of data about the planet's dense, thick atmosphere, including a detailed study of the swirling winds called the Great Red Spot.

The Space Shuttle

A Reusable Spacecraft

A new era in space began in 1981, when the United States launched the first reusable space shuttle, officially called the Space Transport System (STS). The shuttle takes off like a rocket and lands like an airplane, *below*. It consists of three stages—reusable solid rocket boosters, which detach and parachute to the ocean; an external fuel tank, which detaches and breaks up in Earth's atmosphere; and an orbiter, which carries up to seven people. Inside the pressurized cabin, astronauts such as Sally K. Ride, *far left,* work in shirtsleeves rather than space suits. By the mid-1980's, five orbiters had been built, including the prototype *Enterprise,* which never flew in space. The shuttle completed 24 missions, but exploded on the 25th mission, killing all seven people aboard.

Flight and Launch Date	Accomplishment
STS-1 (*Columbia*) April 12, 1981	The first rocket launch and airplanelike landing of a spacecraft with wings and landing gear.
STS-2 (*Columbia*) Nov. 12, 1981	Tested the shuttle's remote manipulator arm, used for tasks such as launching and retrieving satellites.
STS-3 (*Columbia*) March 22, 1982	Conducted space science, medical, and materials-processing experiments as well as tests of orbiter function.
STS-4 (*Columbia*) June 27, 1982	The last of the test flights for *Columbia.* The Space Transportation System was certified operational.

Flight and Launch Date	Accomplishment
STS-5 (*Columbia*) Nov. 11, 1982	First launch of satellites from *Columbia*'s cargo bay.
STS-6 (*Challenger*) April 4, 1983	First space walks by U.S. astronauts since 1974 as they worked in the shuttle's open cargo bay. Launched a satellite.
STS-7 (*Challenger*) June 18, 1983	Sally K. Ride became first U.S. woman in space. Remote manipulator arm used to release and retrieve a scientific satellite.
STS-8 (*Challenger*) Aug. 30, 1983	Guion S. Bluford, Jr., became the first black U.S. astronaut in space; the first night launching and landing of the space shuttle.
STS-9 (*Columbia*) Nov. 28, 1983	Carried European-built Spacelab in the cargo bay; experiments included mixing metals and forming of crystals under the conditions of weightlessness in space.
STS-10 (*Challenger*) Feb. 3, 1984	Astronauts used jet-powered manned maneuvering units to walk in space without lifelines. Two satellites launched, failed to reach proper orbits.
STS-11 (*Challenger*) April 6, 1984	The *Solar Maximum Mission Observatory,* a satellite launched in 1980, was retrieved and repaired in the cargo bay.
STS-12 (*Discovery*) Aug. 30, 1984	First flight of the orbiter *Discovery.* Tested equipment for purifying hormone; three communications satellites deployed.
STS-13 (*Challenger*) Oct. 5, 1984	Kathryn D. Sullivan made first space walk by a U.S. woman. Marc Garneau was the first Canadian in space. Climate research satellite launched; large camera and radar system took detailed photographs of Earth's surface.
STS-14 (*Discovery*) Nov. 8, 1984	Launched two satellites and retrieved and brought to Earth for repair two others that had failed to reach proper orbit.
STS-15 (*Discovery*) Jan. 24, 1985	Secret military mission; an information blackout imposed by the U.S. Department of Defense.
STS-16 (*Discovery*) April 12, 1985	U.S. Senator E. Jacob Garn (R., Utah) became the first member of Congress to fly in space. Canadian communications satellite launched; launch failure of a military communications satellite.
STS-17 (*Challenger*) April 29, 1985	Spacelab mission; experiments involved 2 monkeys and 24 rats. Launched one satellite.
STS-18 (*Discovery*) June 17, 1985	Launched three communications satellites and six smaller satellites. Launched and retrieved *Spartan,* a platform that carried instruments for observing Xrays from the center of the Milky Way galaxy.
STS-19 (*Challenger*) July 29, 1985	Spacelab mission. Carried infrared, solar, and X-ray telescopes in the cargo bay to make observations of the sun, stars, and galaxies. Achieved a lower orbit than planned due to the shut-off of a main engine.
STS-20 (*Discovery*) Aug. 27, 1985	Launched three satellites and captured a crippled satellite using the remote manipulator arm; repaired the satellite in the cargo bay.
STS-21 (*Atlantis*) Oct. 3, 1985	First flight of the orbiter *Atlantis,* reportedly carrying a payload for the U.S. Department of Defense.
STS-22 (*Challenger*) Oct. 30, 1985	Joint Spacelab mission with West Germany; two West German and one Dutch scientist conducted about 80 experiments in Spacelab.
STS-23 (*Atlantis*) Nov. 26, 1985	During space walks, astronauts demonstrated techniques for assembling large structures in space, such as might be used for building a permanent space station. The crew launched three communications satellites. Rodolfo Neri Vela became the first Mexican to ride in a shuttle.
STS-24 (*Columbia*) Jan. 12, 1986	Launched the most powerful communications satellite to date but failed in another part of its mission—to photograph Halley's Comet.
STS-25 (*Challenger*) Jan. 28, 1986	Spacecraft exploded 73 seconds after liftoff, killing all seven crew members: Francis R. Scobee, mission commander; Michael J. Smith, pilot; Judith A. Resnik, Ellison S. Onizuka, and Ronald E. McNair, mission specialists; Gregory B. Jarvis, payload specialist; and Christa McAuliffe, schoolteacher-observer.

Space Stations

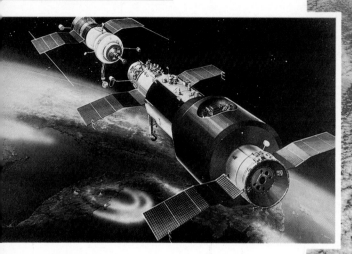

Salyut
The Soviet Union has excelled in the development of space stations. In seven versions of its Salyut, cosmonauts ferried up in Soyuz spacecraft made record-breaking stays. The longest, 237 days, ended on Oct. 2, 1984.

Skylab
The first U.S. space station, *Skylab,* was launched into Earth orbit on May 14, 1973. Three crews visited *Skylab* using Apollo spacecraft as ferries. The first crew repaired the space station, which had been damaged during launch. The other crews carried out astronomical observations and medical, materials, and biological experiments. *Skylab* fell from orbit and broke up in Earth's atmosphere in 1979.

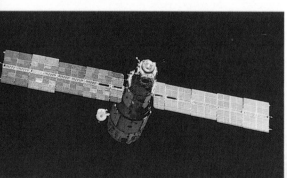

Mir
A new Soviet space station, *Mir,* was launched into orbit in February 1986. This model was designed for longer stays than those in the Salyuts. One cosmonaut ended a 326-day mission in *Mir* on Dec. 29, 1987.

Permanent U.S. Space Station
The next stage of the U.S. manned space program calls for a permanent space station to be assembled in orbit. During the 1990's, crews will be carried to the station by the shuttle.

384

Index

This index covers the contents of the 1989, 1988, and 1987 editions of SCIENCE YEAR, The World Book Science Annual.

Each index entry gives the edition year and a page number—for example, 89–143. The first number, 89, indicates the edition year, and the second number, 143, is the page number on which the desired information begins.

There are two types of entries in the index.

In the first type, the index entry (in **boldface**) is followed immediately by numbers:

Energy, 89–258, 88–260, 87–258

This means that SCIENCE YEAR has an article titled Energy, and that in the 1989 edition the article begins on page 258. In the 1988 edition, the article begins on page 260, and in the 1987 edition it is on page 258.

In the second type of entry, the boldface title is followed by a clue word instead of by numbers:

Doppler effect: dating methods, Special Report, 89–207; galactic astronomy, 88–232

This means that there is no SCIENCE YEAR article titled Doppler effect, but that information about this topic can be found in a Special Report in the 1989 edition on page 207. There is also information on this topic in the Galactic Astronomy article of the 1988 edition on page 232.

When the clue word is "il.," the reference is to an illustration only:

Stegosaurus: il., 89–67

This means there is an illustration of this animal in the 1989 SCIENCE YEAR, on page 67.

The various "See" and "See also" cross-references in the index direct the reader to other entries within the index:

Horticulture. See **Agriculture; Botany;** and **Plant.**

This means that for the location of information on horticulture—look under the boldface index entries

Agriculture, Botany, and **Plant.**

Index

A

A-68 protein: neuroscience, 88-290
Abell 370: astronomy, 89-225
Abella, Benjamin S.: student science awards, 89-312
Absolute dating: dating methods, Special Report, 89-199
Absolute zero: physics, 88-299; states of matter, Special Report, 88-188; superconductivity, Special Report, 89-106
Absorption lines: astronomy, 89-228; il., 89-204
Accutane: drugs, 89-252
Acetylcholine: addiction, Special Report, 88-123
Acetylsalicylic acid: plant defenses, Special Report, 89-130
Acid rain: environment, 89-263, 88-264, 87-262; meteorology, 87-281
Acne: Consumer Science, 88-334; drugs, 89-252
Acquired immune deficiency syndrome. See AIDS.
Acromesomelic dysplasia: anthropology, 89-218
Activase: drugs, 89-251
Addiction: public health, 89-309; Special Report, 88-117
Additives: Ames, Bruce N., 88-33
Adrenal-gland tissue implant: neuroscience, 88-288
Adriamycin: biological rhythms, Special Report, 88-38
Advanced Tactical Fighter (ATF): aircraft design, Special Report, 88-178
Aerial photography: remote sensing devices, Special Report, 87-171
Aeronautical engineering: aircraft design, Special Report, 88-171
Agriculture, 89-212, 88-212, 87-212; Anasazi, Special Report, 89-32; archaeology, 88-218, 87-220; Biosphere II, Special Report, 89-144; camel, Special Report, 88-58; environment, 88-266. See also **Botany; Climate.**
AIDS: computer drug design, Special Report, 89-141; drugs, 88-251; immunology, 89-273, 88-274; medical research, 88-276; Pasteur Institute, Special Report, 89-179; public health, 89-309, 88-308; Special Report, 89-155, 87-112
Air pollution. See Pollution.
Air-traffic transponder: electronics, 88-259
Airborne Antarctic Ozone Experiment: ozone hole, Special Report, 89-81
Aircraft design: Special Report, 88-171
Albertosaurus: il., 89-46
Alcohol addiction: addiction, Special Report, 88-118
Algae: environment, 89-263, 87-261; il., 87-238; Great Barrier Reef, Special Report, 89-16
Alkaloid: plant defenses, Special Report, 89-121

Allele: white-tailed deer, Special Report, 89-98
Alligator: Everglades, Special Report, 88-16
Allosaurus: dinosaur, Special Report, 89-44; il., 89-74
Alpha keto isocaproate: agriculture, 89-214
Alpha particle: indoor air pollution, Special Report, 88-145
ALS. See Amyotrophic lateral sclerosis.
ALU (arithmetic-logic unit): computer chips, Special Report, 88-206
Aluminum-air batteries: energy, 88-260
Alzheimer's disease: genetic science, 88-267; neuroscience, 89-289, 88-289
Ames, Bruce N.: People in Science, 88-339
Ames test: Ames, Bruce, 88-343
Amino acids: computer drug design, Special Report, 89-136; chemistry, 88-241; genetic science, 89-264; molecular biology, 87-284
Amish: genetic science, 88-266
Amphetamine: addiction, Special Report, 88-120
Amphibian: zoology, 88-320
Amplification: cancer genes, Special Report, 88-165
Amyloid protein: genetic science, 88-268
Amyotrophic lateral sclerosis (ALS): Hawking, Stephen W., 89-341; neuroscience, 89-288
Anasazi Indians: archaeology, 88-220; Special Report, 89-26, 87-178
Andromeda nebula: dating methods, Special Report, 89-207
Animal: Biosphere II, Special Report, 89-144; Madagascar, Special Report, 87-87; monarch butterfly, Special Report, 89-14; ozone hole, Special Report, 89-88; white-tailed deer, Special Report, 89-91; Wilson, Edward, 89-357. See also **Zoology.**
Anorexia nervosa: eating disorders, Special Report, 87-59
Ant: Wilson, Edward, 89-357
Antarctic Ice Sheet: glacier, Special Report, 88-70
Antarctica: environment, 89-261; meteorology, 89-285; oceanography, 88-294; ozone hole, Special Report, 89-78
Anthropology, 89-215, 88-215, 87-216; books, 88-235
Antibiotic: chemistry, 89-240; drugs, 88-252, 87-251; Pasteur Institute, Special Report, 89-176
Antibody: AIDS, Special Report, 89-157, 87-114; computer drug design, Special Report, 89-139
Anticollision system: electronics, 88-259
Antigen: AIDS, Special Report, 89-157, 87-114
Antihistamine: Pasteur Institute, Special Report, 89-177
Anti-idiotype: AIDS, Special Report, 89-163

Antimatter: physics, 88-302; states of matter, Special Report, 88-193
Antioxidant: nutrition, 89-294
Antiparticle: states of matter, Special Report, 88-193
Antitoxin: Pasteur Institute, Special Report, 89-173
Anxiety: drugs, 88-253
Apatosaurus: dinosaur, Special Report, 89-44
Ape: anthropology, 88-217
Aphid: plant defenses, Special Report, 89-121
Aphrodite Terra: astronomy, 89-234
Apollo, Project: il., 89-375
Apparent brightness: dating methods, Special Report, 89-207; galaxies, Special Report, 87-47
Appendix: botany, 89-237
Appetite: chemistry, 88-240
Apple Computer: computer hardware, 89-243, 88-244; computer software, 89-245
Arc: astronomy, 89-225, 88-225
ARC (AIDS-related conditions): AIDS, Special Report, 87-123
Archaeology, New World, 89-219, 88-218, 87-219; Anasazi, Special Report, 89-26; Aztecs, Special Report, 87-30; remote sensing devices, Special Report, 87-169
Archaeology, Old World, 89-221, 88-221, 87-222; books, 89-235, 87-235; Paleolithic art, Special Report, 88-42
Archaeopteryx: dinosaur, Special Report, 89-57; paleontology, 89-300, 88-296
Arctic: ozone hole, Special Report, 89-85
Ariel (moon): Uranus, Special Report, 88-111
Arsphenamine: computer drug design, Special Report, 89-135
Art: Dinosaur artist, Special Report, 89-62. See also **Prehistoric art.**
Arthritis: computer drug design, Special Report, 89-141
ARV (AIDS-associated retrovirus): AIDS, Special Report, 87-117
Asbestos: environment, 89-263; indoor air pollution, Special Report, 88-149
Asexual reproduction: Great Barrier Reef, Special Report, 89-15
Aspirin: medical research, Close-Up, 89-280; public health, 89-310
Assassin bug: plant defenses, Special Report, 89-129
Asteroid: dinosaur, Special Report, 89-59; geology, 89-272; paleontology, 88-298
Astronomy: books, 89-235, 88-235
Astronomy, Extragalactic, 89-225, 88-225, 87-225; dating methods, Special Report, 89-205; galaxies, Special Report, 87-45; Hawking, Stephen W., 89-341; physics, 88-302; shadow matter, Special Report, 87-184
Astronomy, Galactic, 89-230, 88-229, 87-228. See also **Galaxy; Star.**
Astronomy, Solar System, 89-232, 88-232, 87-231; Mars, Special

Report, 87-127; Uranus, Special Report, 88-101

Atlit-Yam: archaeology, 89-221

Atmosphere: Biosphere II, Special Report, 89-144; Close-Up, 88-265; oceanography, 88-295; ozone hole, Special Report, 89-78. See also **Pollution.**

Atom: computer drug design, Special Report, 89-134; laser, Special Report, 87-145; physics, 89-302, 88-304; states of matter, Special Report, 88-184; superconductivity, Special Report, 89-106

Atom smasher. See Particle accelerator.

Atomic clock: dating methods, Special Report, 89-200

Australopithecus: anthropology, 88-215

Autism: immunology, 88-275

Autocrine motility factor (AMF), il., 89-273

Autologous blood donation: medicine, 88-282

Automobile: energy, 89-258

AVG: botany, 89-238

Aviation: aircraft design, Special Report, 88-171

Axon: addiction, Special Report, 88-120; molecular biology, 88-287

Azidothymidine (AZT): drugs, 88-251

Aztecs: Special Report, 87-28

B

B₁₂, Vitamin: nutrition, 88-293

B cell: AIDS, Special Report, 87-114; immunology, 88-275

Bacillus. See Bacteria.

Bacteria: agriculture, 89-213, 88-212, 87-213; Biosphere II, Special Report, 89-147; computer drug design, Special Report, 89-139; dentistry, 88-251; genetic science, 89-268; Pasteur Institute, Special Report, 89-173. See also **Salmonella.**

Bactrian camel: camel, Special Report, 88-60

Bar code: Consumer Science, 89-330

Barbiturate: addiction, Special Report, 88-119

Base: cancer genes, Special Report, 88-159; molecular biology, 88-285

Basement membrane: immunology, 89-274

Bath (England): Roman Bath, Special Report, 88-83

Battery: energy, 88-260

BCS theory: physics, 89-301; superconductivity, Special Report, 89-113

Bednorz, J. Georg: Nobel Prizes, 89-290

Bee: agriculture, 89-212; Close-Up, 87-214; Wilson, Edward, 89-362

Beetle: World Book Supplement, 88-381

Bell X-1 (airplane): aircraft design, Special Report, 88-175

Bends. See Decompression sickness.

Bengal fan: oceanography, 89-296

Beta decay: physics, 89-303, 88-304

Beta format. See Video systems.

Big bang theory: galaxies, Special Report, 87-56; Hawking, Stephen W., 89-345; states of matter, Special Report, 88-192

Big bluestem grass: ecology, 87-253

Binary code: computer chips, Special Report, 88-200

Binary star: galactic astronomy, 89-231, 88-229, 87-230

Binding site: computer drug design, Special Report, 89-134

Binnig, Gerd: Nobel Prizes, 88-290

Biochemical genetics: Ames, Bruce N., 88-341

Biochip: computer chips, Special Report, 88-209

Biodegradation: agriculture, 88-214

Bioenergy: ecology, 88-255

Bioerosion: Great Barrier Reef, Special Report, 89-21

Biofeedback: psychology, 89-308

Biogeography: Wilson, Edward, 89-361

Biological rhythms: Special Report, 88-27

Biology: Biosphere II, Special Report, 89-143; books, 89-235, 88-235, 87-236; Pasteur Institute, Special Report, 89-181; Wilson, Edward, 89-357; World Book Supplement, 88-366. See also **Animal; Botany; Cell; Ecology; Molecular biology; Plant; Zoology.**

Biosphere II: Special Report, 89-143

Biphasic schedule: biological rhythms, Special Report, 88-32

Bird: Close-Up, 87-319; dinosaur, Special Report, 89-57; ecology, 89-253, 87-255; environment, 88-264; Everglades, Special Report, 88-16; paleontology, 89-300; plant defenses, Special Report, 89-129; zoology, 89-319, 87-315

Birth defects: drugs, 89-252

Black Death: archaeology, 89-224

Black hole: galaxies, Special Report, 87-46; Hawking, Stephen W., 89-341

Black smoker: deep-sea drilling, Special Report, 88-139

Blindness: neuroscience, 88-290

Blood: AIDS, Special Report, 87-114; camel, Special Report, 88-66; chemistry, 87-241; medical research, 88-276, 87-274

Blood-brain barrier: neuroscience, 88-288

Blood clotting: chemistry, 89-242; nutrition, 88-292

Blood transfusion: medicine, 88-282

Blood vessels: chemistry, 89-242

BMAA: neuroscience, 89-289

Boat: archaeology, 89-222

Body temperature: biological rhythms, Special Report, 88-32

Bone, Fossil: dinosaur, Special Report, 89-44; dinosaur artist, Special Report, 89-62

Bone marrow: drugs, 88-252; medicine, 88-280

Books of Science, 89-235, 88-235, 86-233

Borer: Great Barrier Reef, Special Report, 89-21

Botany, 89-237, 88-238, 87-238. See also **Agriculture; Plant.**

Brain: addiction, Special Report, 88-117; anthropology, 88-218; drugs, 87-252; ils., 89-277, 278; medicine, 88-281, 87-275; psychology, 89-307; Special Report, 87-157; Wilson, Edward, 89-369. See also **Neuroscience; Psychology.**

Brain tissue transplant: medical research, 88-276; neuroscience, 89-286, 88-288

Brattain, Walter H.: deaths, 89-248

Breast cancer: il., 89-273; medical research, 89-283

Breeding: white-tailed deer, Special Report, 89-92; zoology, 89-317

Bromine: ozone hole, Special Report, 89-84

Brood parasitism: zoology, 89-319, 88-317

Brown dwarf star: astronomy, 89-232

Browse (food): white-tailed deer, Special Report, 89-95

Bubonic plague: archaeology, 89-224

Bugleweed: plant defenses, Special Report, 89-123

Bulimia: eating disorders, Special Report, 87-59

Burial site: archaeology, 89-219

Burkitt's lymphoma: cancer genes, Special Report, 88-163

Business Class: computer software, 89-245

Buspirone: drugs, 88-253

Butterfly: monarch butterfly, Special Report, 87-14; plant defenses, Special Report, 89-128

Byte: computer chips, Special Report, 88-201

C

Cabbage butterfly: plant defenses, Special Report, 89-128

CAD/CAM system: computer graphics, Special Report, 87-102

Caesarean section: medicine, 88-280

Calcium: dentistry, 88-250; nutrition, 88-292, 87-288

Calculator: computer chips, Special Report, 88-200

Callisto (moon): astronomy, 89-234

Camel: Special Report, 88-58

Camera. See Photography: Video systems.

Camphor weed: plant defenses, Special Report, 89-129

Cancer: AIDS, Special Report, 89-156; Ames, Bruce N., 88-339; cancer genes, Special Report, 88-157; chemistry, 89-241; computer drug design, Special Report, 89-141; environment, 89-262; immunology, 89-273, 88-274, 87-271; indoor air pollution, Special Report, 88-143; medical research, 89-276, 87-274; medicine, 87-278; molecular biology, 87-283; nutrition, 89-294; public health, 87-307

Index

Cram, Donald J.: Nobel Prizes, 89-290

Credit card: Close-Up, 88-258

Cretaceous Period: dinosaur, Special Report, 89-46; paleontology, 88-298

Cretaceous-Tertiary (K-T) boundary: paleontology, 88-298

Critical temperature: energy, 88-260; Nobel Prizes, 89-290; physics, 89-301, 88-299; superconductivity, Special Report, 89-106

Cro-Magnon Man: Paleolithic art, Special Report, 88-42

Crown-of-thorns starfish: Great Barrier Reef, Special Report, 89-12

Crust, Earth: oceanography, 89-296

Crystal: agriculture, 88-212; chemistry, 88-244, 87-242; Close-Up, 88-243; computer drug design, Special Report, 89-135; glacier, Special Report, 88-73; physics, 89-302

Crystal lattice: states of matter, Special Report, 88-184; superconductivity, Special Report, 89-107

Cud: camel, Special Report, 88-62; white-tailed deer, Special Report, 89-97

Cyandide: plant defenses, Special Report, 89-121

Cycad: neuroscience, 89-289

Cystic fibrosis: genetics, 87-266

D

D, Vitamin: nutrition, 88-292

Dairy industry: agriculture, 88-212

Dark Ages: archaeology, 88-224

Dark matter: astronomy, 89-227, 87-227; galaxies, Special Report, 87-57; physics, 89-303

Darwin, Charles: Wilson, Edward, 89-364. See also **Evolution**.

Darwin's finch: ecology, 89-253

Data processing. See **Computer**.

Dating methods: Anasazi, Special Report, 89-28; anthropology, 89-215; astronomy, 89-230; Paleolithic art, Special Report, 88-47; Special Report, 89-197

Deaths of scientists, 89-248, 88-248, 87-248

Decompression sickness: tunneling, Special Report, 89-186

Deep-sea drilling: seismic tomography, Special Report, 87-207; Special Report, 88-128

Deep Tunnel: tunneling, Special Report, 89-189

Deer: white-tailed deer, Special Report, 89-91; zoology, 89-318

Defenses, Plant: Special Report, 89-119

Deinonychus: dinosaur, Special Report, 89-46; dinosaur artist, Special Report, 89-63

Dentistry, 89-250, 88-250, 87-250; Consumer Science, 88-331

Deoxyribonucleic acid. See **DNA**.

Depressant: addiction, Special Report, 88-119

Depression: biological rhythms, Special Report, 88-37; psychology, 88-305

Desert: Biosphere II, Special Report, 89-143

Developmental biology: Pasteur Institute, Special Report, 89-181

Diet: Ames, Bruce N., 88-347; Biosphere II, Special Report, 89-152; chemistry, 88-240; dentistry, 88-251; medical research, 89-279, 88-279; white-tailed deer, Special Report, 89-99. See also **Nutrition**.

Dietary supplements: nutrition, 88-292

Differentiation: cancer genes, Special Report, 88-162; Uranus, Special Report, 88-114

Digestive system: white-tailed deer, Special Report, 89-96

Digital audiotape (DAT) decks: electronics, 88-257

Digital code: computer chips, Special Report, 88-200; Consumer Science, 89-324

Dinosaur: dinosaur artist, Special Report, 89-62; paleontology, 89-297, 88-297, 87-296; Special Report, 89-42

Diphtheria: Pasteur Institute, Special Report, 89-173

Disease: AIDS, Special Report, 89-155, 87-113; genetic science, 89-265; Pasteur Institute, Special Report, 89-168. See also **Immunology; Medicine; Public health;** names of specific diseases.

Disk-operating system (DOS): computer software, 89-246

Diuretic: medical research, 89-281

DNA (deoxyribonucleic acid): AIDS, Special Report, 89-157, 87-119; Ames, Bruce N., 88-339; anthropology, 88-217; cancer genes, Special Report, 88-158; genetic science, 89-265; molecular biology, 88-285

DNA fingerprinting: Close-Up, 89-266; genetic science, 89-269

Domatia: il., 237

Dome: glacier, Special Report, 88-70

Dopamine: addiction, Special Report, 88-121; drugs, 87-252; medical research, 88-276; neuroscience, 89-286, 88-289

Doppler effect: astronomy, 89-225, 230, 88-232; dating methods, Special Report, 89-207

Doppler radar: meteorology, 89-284, 88-285

Double beta decay: physics, 89-305

Downie, Allan W.: deaths, 89-248

Drag: aircraft design, Special Report, 88-175

Draper, Charles S.: deaths, 89-248

Dreaming: psychology, 87-305

Drill-and-blast method: tunneling, Special Report, 89-186

Drilling. See **Deep-sea drilling; Tunneling**

Dromedary: camel, Special Report, 88-60

Drosophila: genetic science, 89-268

Drought: agriculture, 89-212; environment, 89-261

Drugs, 89-251, 88-251, 87-251; addiction, Special Report, 88-117; AIDS, Special Report, 89-167, 87-125; computer drug design, Special Report, 89-133; eating disorders, Special Report, 87-68; medical research, 89-281; plant defenses, Special Report, 89-120. See also **Immunology**.

Dryptosaurus: il., 89-62

Dufour's gland: Wilson, Edward, 89-360

Dugong: Great Barrier Reef, Special Report, 89-20

Dwarfism: anthropology, 89-218

Dyslexia: il., 89-287

E

Earth core: geology, 88-270

Earth sciences: books, 88-235, 87-236; dating methods, Special Report, 89-197; seismic tomography, Special Report, 87-197. See also **Geology; Oceanography; Paleontology**.

Earthquake: geology, 88-269, 87-269; il., 89-271; seismic tomography, Special Report, 87-198

Eating disorders: Special Report, 87-58

Eco RI: molecular biology, 88-285

Ecology, 89-253, 88-253, 87-253; Biosphere II, Special Report, 89-143; books, 88-235; Everglades, Special Report, 88-11; Great Barrier Reef, Special Report, 89-12; Madagascar, Special Report, 87-96. See also **Environment; Pesticide**.

Ecosystem: Biosphere II, Special Report, 89-144; ecology, 88-253

Edge community: white-tailed deer, Special Report, 89-95

Egg, Fossil: dinosaur, Special Report, 89-55; paleontology, 89-297

Eggs: Consumer Science, 89-325

Egypt, Ancient: archaeology, 89-222

Einstein, Albert: Close-Up, 88-236; Hawking, Stephen W., 89-341; shadow matter, Special Report, 87-184

El Mirador: archaeology, 89-221

El Niño: ecology, 89-253; meteorology, 88-284, 87-280

Electric current. See **Electricity**.

Electricity: energy, 89-258, 88-260; computer chips, Special Report, 88-203; lightning, Special Report, 87-72; physics, 89-298; states of matter, Special Report, 88-188. See also **Electronics; Superconductivity**.

Electromagnet: physics, 88-301; superconductivity, Special Report, 89-108

Electromagnetic force: Hawking, Stephen W., 89-350

Electromagnetic spectrum: astronomy, 88-232; remote sensing devices, Special Report, 87-172

Electron: Consumer Science, 87-330; laser, Special Report, 87-145;

Index

Index

Index

Plasma (physics): Max Planck Society, 87-363; states of matter, Special Report, 88-190
Plasmodia: immunology, 89-274
Plate tectonics theory: astronomy, 89-234; deep-sea drilling, Special Report, 88-130; geology, 89-269, 88-269, 87-266; Mars, Special Report, 87-141; oceanography, 87-291
Plateosaurus: dinosaur, Special Report, 89-45
Plume: oceanography, 88-294
Pluto: astronomy, il., 89-233
Pneumonia: AIDS, Special Report, 89-156
Point mutation: cancer genes, Special Report, 88-162
Poison. See **Pesticide; Toxin.**
Polanyi, John C.: Nobel Prizes, 88-290
Polar vortex: ozone hole, Special Report, 89-81
Polar wander: geology, 89-269
Pollen studies: Anasazi, Special Report, 89-33
Pollution: agriculture, 88-214; environment, 88-262, 87-260; Everglades, Special Report, 88-21; Great Barrier Reef, Special Report, 89-23; indoor air pollution, Special Report, 88-143; meteorology, 88-282, 87-281; oceanography, 88-295; ozone hole, Special Report, 89-83; zoology, 88-317. See also **Ecology; Environment.**
Polymer: astronomy, 89-232; chemistry, 87-243
Polyp: Great Barrier Reef, Special Report, 89-15
Population, Animal: Wilson, Edward, 89-361; white-tailed deer, Special Report, 89-92
Population, Human: ecology, 88-256
Portable phone: Consumer Science, 89-322
Positive charge. See **Electricity.**
Positive energy: Hawking, Stephen W., 89-348
Positive ion: states of matter, Special Report, 88-190
Positron: neuroscience, 89-289; physics, 89-305, 88-302, 87-302
Positron emission tomography (PET): drugs, 87-252; neuroscience, 89-289; psychology, 89-307
Potassium: eating disorders, Special Report, 87-64
Potassium-argon dating: dating methods, Special Report, 89-201
Potato: plant defenses, Special Report, 89-121
Pottery: Anasazi, Special Report, 89-28
Poultry: Consumer Science, 89-325
Prairie dog: zoology, 87-317
Praying mantis: zoology, 87-316
Precambrian: dating methods, Special Report, 89-199
Predator: ecology, 87-255
Pregnancy: Consumer Science, 87-334; medicine, 88-280
Prehistoric art: archaeology, 88-218; Paleolithic art, Special Report, 88-42

Prehistoric people: anthropology, 89-215, 88-215; archaeology, 89-220; Paleolithic art, Special Report, 88-42
Price tag, Electronic: il., 89-257
Principia (Newton): Close-Up, 88-236
Program. See **Computer software.**
Protein: AIDS, Special Report, 87-118; Ames, Bruce N., 88-341; cancer genes, Special Report, 88-159; computer drug design, Special Report, 89-134; molecular biology, 87-282; neuroscience, 88-289, 87-284
Protein folding: computer drug design, Special Report, 89-138
Protein sequencing: computer drug design, Special Report, 89-138
Proteinase inhibitor: plant defenses, Special Report, 89-123
Protoavis: dinosaur, Special Report, 89-58; paleontology, 88-296
Protoceratops: il., 89-74
Protooncogenes: cancer genes, Special Report, 88-158
Protoplast: agriculture, 88-213; botany, 87-238
Protostar: astronomy, 88-231
Pseudomonas: agriculture, 88-212; drugs, 88-252; immunology, 89-273
Psychoactive drug: addiction, Special Report, 88-118
Psychokinesis: psychology, 89-309
Psychology, 89-307, 88-305, 87-303; Special Report, 87-61
Public health, 89-309, 88-308, 87-306; indoor air pollution, Special Report, 88-143
Pueblo: Anasazi, Special Report, 89-26
Pueblo Indians: Anasazi, Special Report, 89-26; archaeology, 88-220
Pulsar: astronomy, 89-230
Pygmy: anthropology, 88-218
Pyramid: archaeology, 89-223

Q

Quahog: archaeology, 89-219
Quantum mechanics: Hawking, Stephen W., 89-348; shadow matter, Special Report, 87-188
Quark: physics, 89-305, 88-303, 87-300; shadow matter, Special Report, 87-188; states of matter, Special Report, 88-192
Quark-gluon plasma (QGP): physics, 89-305
Quasar: astronomy, 89-227, 88-226, 87-225; ils., 89-204, 88-227
Queen (insect): Wilson, Edward, 89-363
Quetzalcóatl: Aztecs, Special Report, 87-31

R

Rabi, Isidor Isaac: deaths, 89-249
Rabies: Pasteur Institute, Special Report, 89-172
Radar: aircraft design, Special Report, 88-178; geology, 88-272

Radiation: dating methods, Special Report, 89-200; indoor air pollution, Special Report, 88-145; nutrition, Close-Up, 87-289
Radio waves: astronomy, 88-232
Radioactivity. See **Radiation.**
Radiocarbon dating: Anasazi, Special Report, 89-28; dating methods, Special Report, 89-200
Radium: Special Report, 88-145
Radon: environment, 89-262, 88-264; indoor air pollution, Special Report, 88-143
Radon daughter: indoor air pollution, Special Report, 88-145
Ragwort: ecology, 89-254
Railroad: tunneling, Special Report, 89-186
Rain forest: Biosphere II, Special Report, 89-143; ecology, 88-254
RAM (random-access memory) chip: computer chips, Special Report, 88-206; computer hardware, 87-244
Rare earth: superconductivity, Special Report, 89-113
Reactor. See **Nuclear reactor.**
Reading Prong: indoor air pollution, Special Report, 88-147
Receptor: addiction, Special Report, 88-120; AIDS, Special Report, 89-157, 87-119; drugs, 87-252; immunology, 89-273
Recognition site: chemistry, 87-243; molecular biology, 88-285
Red giant star: astronomy, 88-230; dating methods, Special Report, 89-208
Red limit: astronomy, 89-228
Red shift: astronomy, 89-225, 87-226; dating methods, Special Report, 89-207; galaxies, Special Report, 87-51
Reduced instruction set computing (RISC): computer hardware, 89-244
Reef. See **Coral reef.**
Regulatory gene: Pasteur Institute, Special Report, 89-176
Relative dating: dating methods, Special Report, 89-199
Relativity, Theory of: Hawking, Stephen W., 89-347; shadow matter, Special Report, 87-184
Remote sensing devices: Special Report, 87-169
Renin: computer drug design, Special Report, 89-141
Reptile: dinosaur, Special Report, 89-45; paleontology, 89-297
Resin: plant defenses, Special Report, 89-120
Resistance, Electrical: physics, 88-298; superconductivity, Special Report, 89-106
Restriction enzyme: genetics, 89-266; molecular biology, 88-285
Retin-A: drugs, 89-253
Retinoblastoma: cancer genes, Special Report, 88-166
Retrovirus: AIDS, Special Report, 89-157, 87-119
Reverse transcriptase: AIDS, Special Report, 89-157, 87-121
Rhinovirus: computer drug design, Special Report, 89-140;

Index

immunology, 87-270; medical research, 87-272

Rhizobacteria: agriculture, 89-213

Rhodopsin: chemistry, 89-240

Ribonucleic acid. See **RNA.**

Rice: agriculture, 88-213

Ride Report: space technology, 89-314

Ridge, Ocean: astronomy, 89-234; seismic tomography, Special Report, 87-203

Ring of Fire: deep-sea drilling, Special Report, 88-131

RNA (ribonucleic acid): AIDS, Special Report, 89-157, 87-119; astronomy, 88-234; genetic science, 89-264, 87-265. See also **Cell; DNA; Virus.**

Roads: Anasazi, Special Report, 89-36

Robotics: electronics, 87-257

Rock: oceanography, 89-296; seismic tomography, Special Report, 87-198; tunneling, Special Report, 89-182. See also **Geology.**

Rohrer, Heinrich: Nobel Prizes, 88-290

ROM (read-only memory) chip: computer chips, Special Report, 88-206

Roman Bath: Special Report, 88-83

Root: botany, 89-237, 88-239

Rotational poles: geology, 89-269, 88-272

Rubidium dating: dating methods, Special Report, 89-205

Rubisco: botany, 88-239

Rumen: white-tailed deer, Special Report, 89-96

Ruska, Ernst: deaths, 89-249; Nobel Prizes, 88-290

S

Sahara rivers: geology, 88-272

Salicylic acid: botany, 89-237

Saliva: dentistry, 89-250, 88-251

Salmonella: Anasazi, Special Report, 89-39; Consumer Science, 89-325

Salmonellosis. See **Salmonella.**

Salvarsan: computer drug design, Special Report, 89-135

Salyut space station: il., 89-384

San Andreas Fault: geology, 88-269

Sanduleak -69, 202: astronomy, Close-Up, 89-226

Satellite, Communications. See **Communications satellite.**

Saturated fat: nutrition, 89-293

Saturn: il., 89-381

Savanna: Biosphere II, Special Report, 89-143

Scanning tunneling microscope (STM): chemistry, 88-242; il., 89-242

Scent: Wilson, Edward, 89-359

Schiff base salts: chemistry, 89-240

Schizophrenia: neuroscience, 88-288

Scholastic Aptitude Test: psychology, 87-303

Science: World Book Supplement, 87-372

Science, History of: books, 89-235

Science education, 89-311, 88-310, 87-308; science high schools, 88-351

Science Student Awards: 89-313, 88-312, 87-309

Science/Technology/Society (S/T/S): science education, 89-311

Scramjet: aircraft design, Special Report, 88-183

Sea-floor spreading: deep-sea drilling, Special Report, 88-131

Seal (animal): zoology, 88-317

Seasonal affective disorder (SAD): biological rhythms: Special Report, 88-37

Seat-belt laws: public health, 88-309

Security system: Consumer Science, 88-328

Sedimentary rock: dating methods, Special Report, 89-198

Seikan Tunnel: tunneling, Special Report, 89-182

Seismic tomography: geology, 88-270; Special Report, 87-197

Seismic waves: seismic tomography, Special Report, 87-198

Seismology. See **Earthquake; Geology.**

Semiconductor: computer chips, Special Report, 88-203; electronics, 88-256, 87-256

Sensor: Consumer Science, 88-328

Serotonin: addiction, Special Report, 88-121; eating disorders, Special Report, 87-68

Sex determination: genetic science, 89-267; Wilson, Edward, 89-363

Sexual reproduction: Great Barrier Reef, Special Report, 89-15

Shadow matter: Special Report, 87-183

Shape memory effect: Close-Up, 88-243

Shepherd moon: Uranus, Special Report, 88-107

Shiftwork: biological rhythms, Special Report, 88-35

Shock-wave therapy: medical research, 89-281

Shotcrete: deep tunneling, Special Report, 89-191

Siamese twins: il., 89-278

Sigsbee Scarp: geology, 89-272

Silicon: chemistry, 88-244; computer chips, Special Report, 88-199

Silurian: dating methods, Special Report, 89-199

Simplesse: nutrition, 89-292

Singularity: Hawking, Stephen W., 89-347

61 Cygni: dating methods, Special Report, 89-205

Skin: Consumer Science, 88-334; drugs, 89-191

Skin cancer: AIDS, Special Report, 89-156; immunology, 89-274; nutrition, 89-294; ozone hole, Special Report, 89-78

Skull X ray: medicine, 88-281

Skylab space station: il., 89-384

SLAC Linear Collider: physics, 88-304

Slave maker (ant): Wilson, Edward, 89-360

Sleep: biological rhythms, Special Report, 88-32

Sleep-learning: psychology, 89-308

Slotta, Karl H.: deaths, 89-249

Slurry shield: tunneling, Special Report, 89-189

Smallpox: computer drug design, Special Report, 89-135

Smart card: Close-Up, 88-258

Smile: psychology, 89-307

Smoking: addiction, Special Report, 88-125; dentistry, 89-250; environment, 89-262; medical research, 89-277; public health, 89-309, 88-309

Social insect: Wilson, Edward, 89-361

Sociobiology: Wilson, Edward, 89-357

Software. See **Computer software.**

Solar energy: energy, 89-258

Solar nebula: astronomy, 89-233; astronomy, Close-Up, 89-227

Soldier caste: Wilson, Edward, 89-362

Solids. See **Physics, Fluids and Solids.**

Somatotropin: agriculture, 88-212

Sonar: deep-sea drilling, Special Report, 88-135; geology, 89-272, 87-268; neuroscience, 88-290

South Pole: ozone hole, Special Report, 89-81

Soybean: il., 89-268

Space shuttle: Close-Up, 87-312; deaths, 87-249; il., 89-382; space technology, 89-314, 88-313, 87-311

Space station: il., 89-384; space technology, 89-315

Space technology, 89-314, 88-313, 87-311; Biosphere II, Special Report, 89-153; books, 89-236; chemistry, 89-243; Mars, Special Report, 87-129; Uranus, Special Report, 88-101; World Book Supplement, 89-372

Spacelab: space, 87-311

Space-time: shadow matter, Special Report, 87-184

Spectrometer. See **Spectroscopy.**

Spectroscopy: astronomy, 89-225; dating methods, Special Report, 89-207; galaxies, Special Report, 87-53; ozone hole, Special Report, 89-80; Uranus, Special Report, 88-104

Spectrum: dating methods, Special Report, 89-207

Speech synthesizer: Hawking, Stephen W., 89-353

SPf(66)30 (vaccine): immunology, 89-274

Spin axis: geology, 88-272

Split-brain experiments: brain, Special Report, 87-159

Sponge: zoology, 89-319

Sputnik (satellite): il., 89-372

Squall line: meteorology, 88-285

Squid: paleontology, 87-294

Standard candle method: galaxies, Special Report, 87-47

Standard Model: physics, 87-300

Stanford Linear Collider (SLC): physics, 89-305

Star: astronomy, 88-225, 231, 87-228; dating methods, Special Report, 89-205; Hawking, Stephen W., 89-346; shadow matter, Special Report, 87-195. See also **Galaxy.**

Starfish: Great Barrier Reef, Special Report, 89-12
States of matter: Special Report, 88-184
Stealth airplane: aircraft design, Special Report, 88-178
Stegosaurus: il., 89-67
Steptoe, Patrick C.: deaths, 89-249
Steroid drugs: computer drug design, Special Report, 89-141; drugs, 89-252
Stimulant: addiction, Special Report, 88-119
Stomach: white-tailed deer, Special Report, 89-96
Stomata: botany, 89-238, 87-238
Stone Age: anthropology, 89-218
Stonehenge: remote sensing devices, Special Report, 87-171
Storm: oceanography, 89-295
Strange particles: physics, 89-305
Strategic Defense Initiative (SDI): computer hardware, 87-245; laser, Special Report, 87-152
Stratosphere: Close-Up, 88-265; ozone hole, Special Report, 89-79
Stratum: dating methods, Special Report, 89-198
Stroke: medical research, Close-Up, 89-280; medicine, 87-275; neuroscience, 87-286; nutrition, 88-292
Strömgren, Bengt: deaths, 89-249
Strong force: Hawking, Stephen W., 89-350; physics, 87-300; shadow matter, Special Report, 87-188
Structural gene: Pasteur Institute, Special Report, 89-176
Subduction: deep-sea drilling, Special Report, 88-131; seismic tomography, Special Report, 87-204
Sugar: dentistry, 88-250
Sulfur dioxide: energy, 87-259; environment, 87-262
Sumer: archaeology, 88-222
Sun: astronomy, 88-234; ozone hole, Special Report, 89-78; states of matter, Special Report, 88-190
Sunraycer: energy, 89-258
Sunspots: astronomy, 88-234
Super Proton Synchrotron (SPS): physics, 89-305
Superchron: geology, 89-270
Supercluster: astronomy, 89-228
Superconducting Super Collider (SSC): physics, 89-306, 88-301; superconductivity, Special Report, 89-116
Superconductivity: computer chips, Special Report, 88-209; energy, 88-260; materials science, 89-275; Nobel Prizes, 89-290; physics, 89-301, 88-298, 303; Special Report, 89-106; states of matter, Special Report, 88-188
Supercritical wing: aircraft design, Special Report, 88-176
Superfluidity: states of matter, Special Report, 88-188
Supergravity theories: shadow matter, Special Report, 87-190
Supernova: astronomy, 89-226, 230; 88-225; Close-Up, 88-228; dating

methods, Special Report, 89-209; il., 88-231; physics, 88-302
Surveyor **(satellite):** il., 89-372
Synapse: addiction, Special Report, 88-120

T

T-lymphocyte: drugs, 88-252
Tannin: plant defenses, Special Report, 89-123
Tartar: Consumer Science, 88-331
Tasaday: Close-Up, 88-217
Tau neutrino: physics, 89-303
Taung skulls: il., 89-215
Teaching, Science. See **Science education.**
Technology: books, 88-237, 87-237
Tectonics. See **Plate tectonics theory.**
Teeth. See **Dentistry.**
Teeth, Fossil: anthropology, 87-217; dinosaur, Special Report, 89-44
Telephone: Consumer Science, 89-322
Telescope: dating methods, Special Report, 89-207
Television. See **Video systems.**
Temperature: agriculture, 88-212; energy, 88-260; physics, 88-299; states of matter, Special Report, 88-187. See also **Climate.**
Temple of Sulis-Minerva: Roman Bath, Special Report, 88-89
Tenrec: il., 87-90
Terminus: glacier, Special Report, 88-71
Termite: Biosphere II, Special Report, 89-150; environment, 88-266; Wilson, Edward, 89-362
Terrane: geology, 87-266
Testosterone: zoology, 89-317
Tetracycline: dentistry, 89-250
Tetrahydrocannabinol (THC): drugs, 88-253
Tevatron collider: physics, 88-304, 87-300
Thames, River: tunneling, Special Report, 89-184
Tharsis: Mars, Special Report, 87-137
Thermal barrier: aircraft design, Special Report, 88-181
Thermodynamics: Hawking, Stephen W., 89-349
Thermoluminescence: anthropology, 89-215
13-cis-retinoic acid: Consumer Science, 88-335
Thistle: plant defenses, Special Report, 89-120
Thorium: dating methods, Special Report, 89-200; indoor air pollution, Special Report, 88-145
3-D video: electronics, 89-257
Thruster: deep-sea drilling, Special Report, 88-137
Thunderstorm: lightning, Special Report, 87-71; meteorology, 89-283, 285, 88-282
Tilapia: Biosphere II, Special Report, 89-152
Tissue plasminogen activator (t-PA): drugs, 89-251

Titania (moon): Uranus, Special Report, 88-109
Titanic: oceanography, Close-Up, 87-293
Tobacco: addiction, Special Report, 88-125; public health, 87-306
Tobacco hornworm: plant defenses, Special Report, 89-128
Tobacco plant: plant defenses, Special Report, 89-121
Tobacco smoke. See **Smoking.**
Tokamak Fusion Test Reactor (TFTR): energy, 88-260
Token: archaeology, 88-223
Tomato: plant defenses, Special Report, 89-122
Tomb. See **Burial site.**
Tonegawa, Susumu: Nobel Prizes, 89-291
Tonguestone: dating methods, Special Report, 89-198
Tool, Prehistoric: archaeology, 88-218, 87-222; il., 88-44
Toothbrush: Consumer Science, 88-331
Toothpaste: Consumer Science, 88-332
Touching: neuroscience, 89-286
Toxic fumes: indoor air pollution, Special Report, 88-151
Toxin: Ames, Bruce N., 88-346; immunology, 89-273; neuroscience, 89-288; plant defenses, Special Report, 89-120
tPA: drugs, 89-251
Tranquilizer: addiction, Special Report, 88-119; drugs, 88-253
Transfer RNA: genetic science, 89-265
Transistor: computer chips, Special Report, 88-203; superconductivity, Special Report, 89-111
Transition temperature. See **Critical temperature.**
Transplantation surgery: il., 87-270; neuroscience, 88-288
Transportable phone: Consumer Science, 89-322
Transportation: superconductivity, Special Report, 89-116
Tree islands: Everglades, Special Report, 88-13
Tree-ring dating: Anasazi, Special Report, 89-28
Trema: botany, 89-238
Tretinoin: drugs, 89-253
Triassic Period: dating methods, Special Report, 89-199; dinosaur, Special Report, 89-45; paleontology, 88-296
Triceratops: dinosaur, Special Report, 89-44; il., 89-69
Trichome: plant defenses, Special Report, 89-120
Trilobite: paleontology, 89-298
TRISTAN accelerator: physics, 88-304
Tritium: physics, 89-304
Tropics: Biosphere II, Special Report, 89-147
Troposphere: ozone hole, Special Report, 89-79
Tseng, Janet: student science awards, 89-312

Index

Acknowledgments

The publishers of *Science Year* gratefully acknowledge the courtesy of the following artists, photographers, publishers, institutions, agencies, and corporations for the illustrations in this volume. Credits should read from top to bottom, left to right on their respective pages. All entries marked with an asterisk (*) denote illustrations created exclusively for *Science Year.* All maps, charts, and diagrams were prepared by the *Science Year* staff unless otherwise noted.

Cover © Carl R. Sams II

4	© Jane Burton, Bruce Coleman Inc.; Richard Hook*
5	James Kamp, Black Star; NASA
8	*Claws & Teeth Against Horns & Beaks,* a painting by Mark Hallett, © Mark Hallett. All rights reserved. The Robbins Company; Joe Rogers*
9	James Kilkelly, DOT; Tom Herzberg*; Peter Menzel
10	© Lynn Funkhouse from Peter Arnold
14	© Fritz Prenzel, Bruce Coleman Ltd.; Four Seasons Hotels and Resorts
16	© Ron and Valerie Taylor
17	© Jane Burton, Bruce Coleman Inc.; © C. C. Lockwood, Earth Scenes; Terry Done, Australian Institute of Marine Science
19	© Carl Roessler, FPG; © Ron and Valerie Taylor, Bruce Coleman Inc.; Ron and Valerie Taylor
20	© E. Parer-Cook, Australasian Nature Transparencies; © Neville Coleman
21	© Ron and Valerie Taylor
22	Peter Harrison, James Cook University of North Queensland; P. Moran, Australian Institute of Marine Science
23	M. Cuthill, Australian Institute of Marine Science; Bruce Chalker, Australian Institute of Marine Science
24	Richard Hook*
27	© David Falconer, West Stock
29	© Paul Logsdon
30	Richard Hook*
34	American Museum of Natural History; © Terrence Moore; American Museum of Natural History
36	© Don Normark, West Stock; Richard Hook*
38	Richard Hook*; American Museum of Natural History
43	James Amos, © National Geographic Society
45	Peabody Museum of Natural History, Yale University
46	Field Museum of Natural History; David Hiser, Photographers Aspen
48	Peabody Museum of Natural History, Yale University; Dinosaur State Park
50	© Michael Abbey, Science Source from Photo Researchers; Armand de Ricqlès, University of Paris; Armand de Ricqlès, University of Paris
51	Museum of the Rockies
52	Martin Lockley
54	Museum of the Rockies
56	Museum für Naturkunde, Humboldt-Universität at Berlin; Sankar Chatterjee from National Geographic News Service
57	Nancy Lee Walter*
64	The Illustrated London News Picture Library; British Museum; © Alan Clifton, Aspect Picture Library
66	Smithsonian Institution
76	Roberta Polfus*
77	NASA
79–83	Roberta Polfus*
84	Mark Muller, National Science Foundation; NASA; Mark Muller, National Science Foundation
85	Mark Muller, National Science Foundation
86	Wolfgang Kaehler; Roberta Polfus*
87	Kent Hanson, DOT
88	Ann Hawthorne, National Science Foundation; Noel R. Kemp, Photo Researchers; Wolfgang Kaehler; Wolfgang Kaehler
90	© Carl R. Sams II
93	Bledsoe Collection, Arizona Historical Society; J. H. Witham and J. M. Jones, Illinois Natural History Survey
94	Art—Joe Rogers*
96	Gary W. Griffen, Animals Animals; Mark A. LaBarbera
97	© Leonard Lee Rue III
98	U.S. Forest Service
99	© C. C. Lockwood, Animals Animals; © Carl R. Sams II; © Carl R. Sams II
100	© Harry Engels, Photo Researchers; David Kenyon, Michigan Department of Natural Resources
101	David Kenyon, Michigan Department of Natural Resources
102	Mark A. LaBarbera; Wisconsin State Journal
104	Sara Woodward*; AT&T Bell Laboratories
105	Dan McCoy, Rainbow; Kaku Kurita, Gamma/Liaison; Dan McCoy, Rainbow
109	Sara Woodward*
110	Sara Woodward*; Rosemarie Fox Hicks*
112	Sara Woodward*; AT&T Bell Laboratories
115	James Kilkelly, DOT; James Kilkelly, DOT: Sara Woodward*; James Kilkelly, DOT
116	Greg Sharko, reprinted from *Popular Science* with permission. © 1988 Times Mirror Magazines, Inc.
117	Thomas J. Watson Research Center, IBM Corporation
118	© Michael Fogden, Bruce Coleman Inc.
122	Tom Herzberg*
123–124	© Thomas Eisner
125	© Adrienne T. Gibson, Earth Scenes; © Thomas Eisner; © Thomas Eisner; © Thomas Eisner
126	© Patti Murray, Earth Scenes; Isao Kubo, University of California at Berkeley
128	Tom Herzberg*
129–131	© Thomas Eisner
132	Polygen Corporation
135	© Julie Houck, Uniphoto
136	Trudy Rogers*
137	Genentech, Inc.
138	Axel T. Brunger, Yale University
140	James M. Hogle, Scripps Clinic
142	Richart T. Grimes
145	Carl Shaneff
146	Peter Menzel, Space Biospheres Ventures
147	Space Biospheres Ventures
149–150	Peter Menzel
151	Space Biospheres Ventures; Peter Menzel
154	Cary Henrie*
158	Lennart Nilsson, © Boehringer Ingelheim International GmbH
159–163	Cary Henrie*
164	Cary Henrie*; James Kamp, Black Star
168	Pasteur Institute
171	Culver; Pictorial Parade
172–178	Pasteur Institute
179	Gamma/Liaison
180	Pasteur Institute
183	The Robbins Company
185	Culver
188	Brian Delf*; The Metropolitan Sanitary District of Greater Chicago
190	Pan-Asia Newspaper Alliance
191	Pan-Asia Newspaper Alliance; Japan Railway Construction Corporation
192	Eurotunnel; © Denis Waugh
193	Brian Delf*
196	Joe Rogers*
201	Kevin Schafer, Tom Stack & Assoc.; Christian Autotte, Earth Images; John Cancalosi, Tom Stack & Assoc.; Joe Rogers*
202	Kim Heacox, Earth Images; Joe Rogers*
203	Joe Rogers*
204	Joe Rogers*; © Royal Observatory, Edinburgh (Original negative by U. K. Schmidt Telescope Unit)
206	Joe Rogers*
210	General Motors Corporation; U.S. Department of Agriculture; Walker Montgomery, *Research Reporter,* University of Georgia